79

D0811833

Small Earthquake in Chile

Small Earthquake in Chile

Allende's South America

ALISTAIR HORNE

The Viking Press   New York

ACKNOWLEDGMENTS

Agencia Literaria, Barcelona. For extracts from poems by Pablo Neruda in the original Spanish.

Delacorte Press and Jonathan Cape Ltd.: From *The Selected Poems of Pablo Neruda* edited by Nathaniel Tarn. Copyright © 1970 by Anthony Kerrigan, W. S. Merwin, Alistair Reid, and Nathaniel Tarn. Copyright © 1972 by Dell Publishing Co., Inc. A Seymour Lawrence Book/Delacorte Press. Used by permission.

Grossman Publishers: From *Twenty Love Poems and a Song of Despair* by Pablo Neruda, translated by W. S. Merwin. English translation Copyright © 1969 by W. S. Merwin. All rights reserved. Reprinted by permission of Grossman Publishers

Pantheon Books/a Division of Random House, Inc., and N.L.B., London: From *The Chilean Revolution: Conversations with Allende,* by Regis Debray. Copyright © 1971 by N.L.B., © 1971 by Random House, Inc., © 1971 by Salvador Allende.

Triquarterly, Evanston, Illinois, and *London Magazine:* From Carlos German Belli's poem *Segregation No. 1,* translated by Maureen Ahern Maurer.

Contents

List of Plates

7

To compañero Bill—

—the greatest of fellow-travellers—

—and compañera Nena

Foreword

It is a land of violence. Thunder and avalanches in the mountains, huge floods and storms on the plains. Volcanoes exploding. The earth shaking and splitting. The woods full of savage beasts and poisonous insects and deadly snakes. Knives are whipped out at a word. Whole families are murdered without any reason. Riots are sudden and bloody and often meaningless. . . . Such an energy in destruction. Such an apathy when something has to be mended or built. So much humour in despair. So much weary fatalism toward poverty and disease.

Christopher Isherwood: The Condor and the Cows

IN his autobiography Claud Cockburn describes a competition among the sub-editors of *The Times* for the most boring headline. The winning entry, by a comfortable margin, was:

SMALL EARTHQUAKE IN CHILE
Not many dead

This cynical apophthegm rather aptly summarizes traditional Anglo-Saxon attitudes to Latin America, not only then but now. Both American and British editors look hunted, or yawn cavernously whenever South America is mentioned, and those of the so-called 'serious' press admit that they have a hard enough time justifying the expenses of 'Our Own Correspondent', who covers this whole vast continent of two hundred million people single-handed – as often as not from the Hurlingham Club in Buenos Aires. Today the French and West German press provide wide coverage on events in South America, whereas only a very major Andean catastrophe with many thousands killed can briefly distract the British press from its wholehearted dedication to soccer, erotica, and the price of New Zealand butter. The public of the U.S.A. – allowing for the vastly greater immediacy of South America – is, if anything, worse served.

South Americans are, of course, themselves partly to blame. Chileans, for instance, have a favourite saying (or they used to): *En Chile no pasa nada* (In Chile nothing happens). But in the autumn of 1970 a small earthquake took place in Chile that emitted shock waves of quite unprecedented news-value. For the first time anywhere in the world, a Marxist President was elected in a free poll – though on a split vote with only a precarious 1.4 per cent majority. At least to North American eyes, it looked as if the Kremlin had suddenly planted a hob-nailed boot firmly on the American main-land; and, worst of all, by apparent invitation from the most enlightened electorate of them all. What did it mean? To probe the whys and wherefores of Dr Allende's *Unidad Popular* triumph, and to rewrite each other's interviews with the enigmatic doctor, journalists, historians and crystal-gazers from all over the globe converged on Santiago.

I was one. After years of absorption in European war and revolt, my eyes had – I suppose – become deflected to South America through my interest in Che Guevara. Now, all at once Dr Allende's small earthquake provided both an urgency and an opportunity. A visit to London by a lifelong friend, Bill Buckley, resulted in an off-the-cuff invitation to ac-company him on a flying, typical Buckley, trip. In two weeks he was planning to visit Colombia, Peru and – principally – Chile, wearing two hats; officially, as a member of the President's Advisory commission on information, to visit U.S.I.S. installations, and – privately – as the Knight Errant of American Conservatism, to write some articles for his column syndicated in 350 newspapers across the U.S.A. Apart from the wildly unpredictable delights of going with so stimulating and unconventional a travelling companion, I calculated that in those first two weeks I would have the benefits of seeing Allende and revolutionary South America through U.S. eyes; then, by myself and at a more leisurely pace, I could make my own assessments and talk to people whose ideologies might cause them to keep at a distance such an outspoken conservative as Bill. On the way back I would make a brief detour via Bolivia, in whose currently explosive condition, with most of the U.S.I.S. offices overrun or smashed up, the U.S. State Department was clearly not anxious to risk a visit by detonator Buckley.

So it would be Colombia, Peru, Chile and Bolivia; the four principal Andean countries, all of them experiencing profound political changes in their own separate ways, and collectively all being fundamentally affected by events in Chile. In Peru a radically left-wing military junta had seized power in October 1968; in Bolivia the death in April 1969 of their strong man Barrientos had precipitated a period of more than usual turbulence, culminating in the emergence in October 1970 of an extreme left-wing government under General Torres; in Chile there was now Allende; and only Colombia – ruled by a conventional Conservative–Liberal coalition – appeared to be the odd man out. But in Colombia, too, apparently there were strong revolutionary undercurrents at work.

I wanted to see, and write about, each of these countries in its own right; but above all, and inevitably, it would be in the context of the Chilean experience that I would be contemplating them. For what has happened in Chile, dramatically, is perhaps but one manifestation of what, in different forms, is happening all over Latin America; and the immediacy of its lessons will not, should not, be long confined to that continent. (For instance, the smugger elements of Fleet Street could do well to study the speed and success with which, in Chile, the Marxists have managed to erode the freedom of a once outstandingly free press – and without recourse to *any illegality*.) I should, no doubt, also have gone on to Argentina, to Uruguay to study the ways of the Tupamaros, to Rio to learn about the 'Squadron of Death' and brutal police repression of revolutionary cells; from Chile to Tierra del Fuego to interview the Yahgan Indians, or to Easter Island to converse with the monoliths. No doubt. But there is a limit to what the mind can absorb, let alone the pocket afford. A friendly journalist who interviewed me before I left Chile wrote: 'He has been everywhere and nowhere.' I was conscious of the paradox, as well as my own shortcomings. Lord Bryce, one of the more perceptive tourists to South America at the beginning of the century, commented

13

that of the visitors of his day 'few of those who have read have travelled and few of those who have travelled have read'. I had read voraciously, both before and afterwards; yet, at the end of it all, I am horribly aware of having neither seen enough nor read enough to understand completely the complexities of even one South American country, let alone four.

So this book is, consciously, an incomplete and impressionistic account, based on diaries which I kept as I went along (which, to my amazement, came to total nearly fifty thousand words) and supplemented by splashes of background information. Here and there events have been telescoped, and names altered, for obvious reasons.[1] Christopher Isherwood, who followed something of the same trail (though when the going was much tougher) nearly a generation ago, charmingly exculpated himself by declaring that a diarist 'ought to make a fool of himself, sometimes'. Certainly I expect to do so here, and am happy to apologize in advance. One of the easiest ways anyone writing about South America can make a fool of himself is by getting caught out by the march of time. In few parts of the world do events and personalities change so rapidly. For instance, in the forty-three-page index to John Gunther's vast compendium of knowledge, *Inside South America*, published in 1967, the names of men who were to become presidents of no less than six South American countries, just three years later, are not even mentioned. So I have tried to limit myself to things seen or heard, and nothing (or little) more. It is certainly too early for a historian to express any kind of view; on the other hand, little has happened in the intervening months that was not initiated during Allende's first ninety days while I was in Chile.

Another easy way to become a fool, in South American

---

[1] On the subject of names, South Americans identify each other on the somewhat complicated Spanish system: Christian name, then patronym and mother's name last of all. So if it appears that I am being familiar and calling a president by his second Christian name, I am not; for instance, by Anglo-American practice, the proper surname of Dr Alfredo Vásquez Carrizosa, foreign minister of Colombia, is Vásquez.

eyes, is to talk loosely about 'Americans' when you really mean a *Norte Americano*, a *Yanqui* or a *gringo*, – but worse still is the offence of generalizing about 'South Americans' as a kind of single amorphous entity. 'Why,' they complain, 'do Europeans expect to be treated as Frenchmen and Germans and Englishmen, and yet they lump us altogether into one ethnographic hold-all.' To commit the first sin, inadvertently, is all too possible – and, once again, I seek pardon in advance; if I deviate into this heresy, it is because I am also trying to make myself comprehensible to those late arrivals in the north who have come to call themselves 'Americans' too. But the second heresy is unpardonable. Immediately one leaves any country of South America to enter another, one is struck by the extraordinary *separateness* of each. To go from Chile to Bolivia, for example, is almost like switching planets, not just countries. More than any set of European countries, the nations of South America have tended to develop and exist oblivious of events beyond their immediate frontiers. Colombians are unaware of what goes on in Peru; Peruvians (at least until Allende) cared little about what Chile was up to; Chile glared icily across the Andes at Argentina; and nobody knew anything at all about Bolivia. When affluent Colombians, Peruvians and Chileans thought of 'abroad', it was Paris or London, not Rio and Buenos Aires. It is an attitude that has its origins in the centralization of the Spanish Empire, under which the Latin American colonies were ruled directly from Spain and forced to transact commerce with her, rather than with each other. The sense of mutual isolation has been increased by the fact that, since independence, most countries have been at odds – or worse – with their neighbour at some time or other; and, of course, nothing could be more conducive to autarchy than the impossible natural barriers of mountain, jungle and desert – or even just the incredible distances. (Santiago is 2,800 miles due south of Bogotá – or London to Teheran – and still there is a lot of South America left over at each end.) The common language too can be deceptive; a native of Bogotá might well have as much difficulty following a spirited *tête-à-tête* between two *Chilenas* as a Cornishman two Australians.

15

As Bill Buckley wrote in one of his columns:

the diplomatic imperative is on the one hand to recognize the individuality of Latin American countries while coping with the great historical tug which, expressing itself in Cuba and Chile, inescapably affects the destiny of, for instance, Colombia.

The common denominators that link South American countries are more pronounced than ever before. They go deeper than just the improvement of communications brought about by the jet and the transistor. So many of the really fundamental problems are shared. One may list a few. First and foremost, there is the nightmare, all-devouring monster called the *explosión demográfica*, universal to almost every country except possibly Bolivia and Paraguay, which makes the continental population growth rate, quite dramatically, the highest in the world. In seven years, from 1961 to 1968, the estimated population of Latin America as a whole rose from 211 million to 261 million. From this stem many of the other universal problems. There is the perennial gulf between the haves and the have-nots, widened in many countries over recent years, often simply because even the most booming, successful economy cannot keep pace with the burdens imposed by a spiralling birthrate; and, associated with this, there is the staggering growth of urban populations as the *campesinos* drift away from an unproductive agronomy. There is underdevelopment both in industry and agriculture, certainly in all the Andean bloc, and coupled with the latter the burning, universal issue of land reform. There is endemic inflation, either rampant or precariously controlled. And, as – with all its wealth and wisdom – it seems unable to solve (or, sometimes, even to understand) the basic South American dilemmas, there is a universal resentment and revulsion towards the colossus of the North that has recently become more imposing than ever before. A light-hearted Santiago *chiste* speaks volumes:

Q. What does a *Chileno* do when he finds his wife in bed with another man?
A. He goes out with a slingshot and breaks every window in the *Yanqui* Embassy.

16

And if U.S. Marines invade the privacy of the Dominican Republic, it is Chile that feels outraged.

Discontent with the apparent inability of governments to provide panaceas for the shared social ailments, dissatisfaction with the slow rate of reform, has brought about another common denominator throughout the continent; a resurgence of revolutionary undercurrents. Revolt has always been a by-word of South American life, but this is something new. The revolutionary instinct throughout Latin America has become – for the first time – polarized, and polarized on the Left. It is also polarized on the youth. Perhaps in no other part of the world has the rising generation in recent years become so committed to the revolutionary Left. In Bolivia, it is the university students who have assumed the mantle of Che; in Chile, they who have founded the extremist MIR; and in Uruguay it is the young sons of well-to-do families who have invented and run the Tupamaros. The contest in South America is no longer waged primarily between the knights of the C.I.A. and the M.V.D., between the Church and the secularists, or between oligarchs and Communists; it is no longer a matter of *Blanco v. Colorado*, Liberal *v.* Conservative, *Aprista v. Odrista*. Things have moved on. The struggle between the Right and the Left continues, of course, but what matters more now is the line-up of the rival factions of Marxists, and the schism between the conservative church and the revolutionary *tercer mundo* priests. It is the dialectic of which Castro and Allende represent the two opposite, visible poles. It is not in South-east Asia, the Middle East or Africa that *the* ideological battle of the seventies seems like to be waged, but in South America. Here, one feels, may well be the battleground where the orthodoxy of Soviet communism will triumph definitively over Maoism, or vice versa.

This, outstandingly, is what makes Allende so significant and all Andean America so fascinating – and so dangerous – as well as being a reason why Anglo-Saxon editors should smother their yawns and try to show an interest in the goings-on of what John Donne once called the 'unripe side of earth'.

'To begin to understand South America, you *have* to be a romantic,' a *Chilena* warned me. It is hard to know which is more difficult for a *gringo*; to be a romantic, in the true

17

Latin sense, or to resist being one. In Andean South America, you can barely pass a day without encountering something that provokes either distress or despair. Everywhere there are the insoluble miseries, the inequalities and unfairness of life that grind in upon the eye and the conscience. For all the fabulous wealth of natural wonders, any visit to South America would be intolerable to a half-sensitive person but for one thing: the wonderful warmth of the people. Whether in Chile, Colombia, Peru or poor poverty-stricken Bolivia, I have seldom encountered anywhere else in the world such universal friendliness, helpfulness and sheer boundless hospitality. It ranged from young way-outers of the MIR to middle-class farmers who were about to lose everything in Chile, to diplomats and oligarchs and government officials in all four countries. With such a burden of gratitude it would be invidious to single out here any to whom I owe particular appreciation, but if in the pages that follow I am able to express a fraction of the warmth I felt for the countries and people visited, I hope they will accept that in lieu of specific thanks.

I am also indebted to officers of the U.S. State Department and U.S.I.S. who showed me outstanding courtesy when travelling with William F. Buckley jr. in his official capacity; to the Latin American Centre at St Antony's College, Oxford; Chatham House, Canning House, the Chilean Embassy in London, and Christopher Roper of *Latin America* for various facilities and assistance received. My gratitude – and admiration – is due to Mrs Angus Nicol who once again typed and helped research the manuscript, and without whose self-sacrifices it could never have been completed in time.

Special permission to reprint material previously published in articles has been kindly granted me by Forum World Features, *Encounter*, the *Spectator*, the *Village Voice* (U.S.A.). I am grateful to Brian Crozier for permitting me to draw from his article written for Forum World Features, 'The Santiago Model'. My thanks are also due to Peter Smith of Reuters for invaluable help in assembling the illustrations.

I

Favourite Son Turns Cannibal

New York City, January 1971.

I am on my way to Greenwich, Connecticut, to lunch with a prominent Chilean self-exile, a recent refugee from Dr Allende's new Chile. The cab jolts horribly as it falls into a vast pot-hole in the middle of Park Avenue. Its driver is hunched morosely over the wheel; his buddy was bumped off a few nights ago in one of the senseless taxi hold-ups which are no longer news in New York City. We trundle past the rows of dismal 'Singles' bars where, in that peculiar brand of dedicated hopelessness, New Yorkers will shortly be repairing to grapple with their self-inflicted sexual wounds – or perhaps to shed the emasculating, lonely load of world power. The once 'alabaster city' has a shabbiness about it, a premature senility that causes one to wonder whether its inhabitants have simply lost interest in it and are longing for the under-taker to move in. On the train, the window by my seat is badly cracked and repaired with sticky tape, already yellow with age. The upholstery is jaded and torn; there is no longer the good-natured chaff one used to remember between con-ductor and passengers – who sit gloomily as if ashamed to be seen in such reduced circumstances. What has happened to the good old N.Y.N.H., with its miles of stainless steel coaches throbbing expectantly beneath the road level at Grand Central, its punctuality, its ebullient bar-car attendants; the combination of sheer horse-power and brisk efficiency that used to lend an air of excitement to any journey, that *did* seem to be a symbol of (North) America? What, indeed, has happened to America?

19

The train bursts out from the lower world into Harlem, but one thinks one is still in hell. For all the past attempts at slum clearance, the awful purplish brick tenements look much the same as they did when I first saw them as a child in 1940. This morning's *New York Times* has a brief item about Apollo 14, shortly to blast off. It is as hard as ever to believe that the astounding technocrats at Houston and the clear-eyed all-Americans in their shiny silver spacesuits belong to the same world as this Plutonian Harlem, the ten-year-old junkies and the 'Singles' and the cab-driver killers and all the other grim realities of the North American *condition humaine*. Now, evidently, the U.S. public is losing interest in space – and not just because of the cost of the whole business. Is it because the nation no longer has its eyes on the stars as, metaphorically, it used to, and which was always its most marvellous attribute? Certainly in her current state of de-moralization, in her apparent inability to get things right either at home or abroad, the United States seems to have lost that buoyant self-confidence, that old star-bound sense of mission that she could alter the world for better. Her enemies may well rejoice at this; I certainly don't. Having loved this great big crazy country so much, and from an early age, I can only feel an aching sadness; for the shock of revisiting New York in 1971 is like re-encountering an old passion now riddled with cirrhosis but still not able to keep her hands off the gin bottle.

So the thoughts run round my mind as the train makes its dispirited way towards Greenwich. One does not need to reach the Andes to realize that the U.S. image throughout Latin America is at an all-time low. And why? Because it has been deserted by that mystical attribute of *machismo* which so impresses Latin Americans and which is – after all – little more than the science of success and self-confidence. Fidel is *macho*, but Uncle Sam is not. 'Why have all the Andean Countries suddenly gone Left? Because *we're losing*. They see we're losing in Vietnam' a hawkish columnist remarked to me the other night during one of those endless, sterile, played-out arguments on Vietnam, that make one almost yearn for the glum solace of the 'Singles'. But the sense of 'we're losing' goes deeper, far deeper than Vietnam . . .

We finally pull into Greenwich. A thin, icy wind blows down a deserted platform. No sign of Chavela. My heart begins to sink. I have only three hours for lunch, before having to get back to New York, and I know enough about Chilean punctuality and Chavela's own special brand of hospitality to make me fear the worst. After twenty minutes or so, a car sweeps up in a flurry of snow. Out gets a large, vigorous and handsome lady with a thatch of straight, white hair, greeting me with great warmth, effusive with apology. In the back are a shivering son-in-law and grandchild; still dressed in tropical clothing, they too are 'exiles' who have just arrived from the Chilean midsummer that very day.

In her late sixties, Chavela Edwards is the widow of the head of the Edwards empire, one of the oldest, wealthiest and most powerful of all the Chilean oligarchies. Of English origin several generations back, there was hardly any aspect of Chilean life in which the Edwardses did not occupy a position of eminence: banking, shipping, aviation, insurance and breweries, and – above all – the press. They owned a sumptuous house in Santiago, several large and efficiently run farms, a ski lodge up in the mountains and a university. Within the tightly welded family monopoly, the most important component was Chile's leading newspaper, *El Mercurio*. Enormously influential and highly conservative, *El Mercurio* during the past election had fought tooth and nail against Allende – who had pledged that – should he be elected – he would 'get' *El Mercurio*.

In England, in October, I had briefly met Chavela's son, Agustín ('Doonie') Edwards, the present head of the family, and then President of *El Mercurio*. Doonie told a harrowing tale. Following the elections of September 1970, and even before the Chilean Congress had given its official ratification to Allende's victory, he had been forced to flee with his wife and six children at a moment's notice. He had received a number of menacing threats from the extremist MIR, (*Movimiento de Izquierda Revolucionaria*, the Chilean equivalent of the Tupamaros.) and semi-official warnings that he and his family might be seriously in danger if they remained in Chile. At a moment's notice they had taken off from an unscheduled airfield, literally – claimed Doonie – under fire from the

21

MIR. In its significance for Chile, it was an extraordinary state of affairs; as if, in England, Lords Thomson and Camrose had together fled to Bermuda on the advent of Mr Wilson. Had Doonie over-reacted? Until similar circumstances actually confront oneself and one's own family, it is not an easy judgement to pass.

Chavela insists on taking me to lunch at the house where she is living temporarily – 'just outside of Greenwich'. Doonie would be there. But first we must buy some provisions. My heart sinks further. Couldn't I *please* stand her lunch somewhere in Greenwich? No, out of the question. At the supermarket, the amazed housewives of Greenwich are asked collectively: 'Now what can I give this nice Englishman for lunch?' At last, a huge basket is filled. Then: 'but who can cook?' It is obviously not a necessity that has ever faced Chavela with her platoons of domestics in Chile. Through chattering teeth, the son-in-law admits that he can make a *tortilla*. The basket is emptied and refilled with eggs. A whole hour has gone by. At last we reach a large, comfortable, typical New York banker's house with 'A Edwards' on the mail-box. Doonie is all right. Now working for Pepsi-Cola, he is not over-anxious to talk about Chile. 'They' were already beginning to seize Edwards property in Chile. Things were getting worse and worse. 'You must go and see the people on *Mercurio*, and my mother will give you any other introductions you need.' We part.

In a two-roomed shack across the road, where Chavela is lodged, the frozen son-in-law is at work on his *tortilla*. I sit down on a box (there is no other furniture) to question Chavela about Chile. But the grandson has delightedly discovered a remote-control gadget for the T.V. – a fascinating new toy – and every few minutes our conversation is drowned by sudden blasts of pop. Then, a yell from the kitchen: 'There's nothing to turn the *tortilla* with.' Resourcefully Chavela produces a shoe-horn from under the bed. I find myself wondering whether the Russian grand-duchesses had managed as well after the 1917 Revolution. When at last the long awaited omelette is ready, I have barely half-an-hour to make it to the station. Slithering at high speed back along the icy road, Chavela furiously scribbles down names;

not, it turns out, those of Chilean politicians or journalists or captains of industry whom I should see, but her secretary, chauffeur, butler, cook and lady's maid – who would, of course, 'look after' me in Santiago. I picture the reception I might have if I rolled up to interview members of the Allende government in an Edwards Cadillac, and head back to New York, a little frustrated.

The hours before leaving for Bogotá are crammed with interviews and briefings by Latin American pundits from Washington, such as the special envoy from Dr Kissinger's office for whom I have had to truncate my visit to the hospitable Chavela. Some of it is 'off-the-record' for my travelling companion only; the rest is more interesting for what it reveals of official U.S. attitudes to South America than for the actual background information, masterfully presented as it is. The trauma induced by Allende's election, and by the general leftwards trend in the Andes as a whole, is unmistakable. And, as so often with reverses to U.S. policy, there is a manifest sense of personal rebuff. After so many recent slaps in the face abroad, the reactions of U.S. officialdom to each new setback seems increasingly to be one of jaded *déjà-vu*, rather than surprise or outrage. But Allende's Marxist triumph shocks because it has come about in the most unexpected context of all. Even the U.S. ambassador, Ed Korry – a former bureau chief of United Press, as well-informed as any ex-journalist should be – whom we were shortly to meet in Santiago, had predicted an electoral victory for Alessandri's conservative National Party.

The history of U.S. policy towards Latin America as a whole seems to be one constant swing of the pendulum between excesses: between studied indifference, ignorance and downright neglect and a kind of slushy romanticism of rediscovery; between paternalistic imperialism and reformist altruism backed with quite incredible generosity. In return, the U.S. – like any rich relation – has received little real gratitude for its best efforts. As John Mander recently remarked in *Static Society*: 'Seven fat years, and the people will thank God; seven lean years, and they will blame the United States.' Today, after some bad experiences, any new U.S. initiative tends to be written off as a machination by the

23

supposedly ubiquitous and all-powerful C.I.A. The U.S. was the first to recognize the new nations of Latin America after the Wars of Independence against Spain (1825), but her subsequent grabbing of vast hunks of Mexico suggested that this was not without an element of self-interest. Then, (from 1848 onwards) half a century of no interest, while the States consolidated its 'Manifest Destiny' westwards, was followed by forty years of imperialist involvement in the Caribbean, of which the annexation of the Panama Canal zone and the Spanish-American War of 1898, relieving Spain of her last remaining footholds, were focal points. In 1933 came the second Roosevelt and the 'Good Neighbour' policy. Although it often expressed itself in Carmen Miranda-style propaganda, with such films as Walt Disney's *Three Caballeros* – well-intentioned but wounding to Latin American *amour-propre* – the Good Neighbour era undoubtedly did much to improve the U.S. image down south. But, as was revealed by Washington's alarm at Brazil's apparent vulnerability to Axis designs, at Argentinian pro-Fascist sympathies and Nazi penetration of Chile, this too was strongly tinged with self-interest.

After 1945, when any strategic threat to South America had been removed and the reconstruction of Europe dominated U.S. thoughts, the 'good neighbours' were once more allowed to return to their stagnant backwater. Eisenhower carried forward the neglect of the Truman era; the good Dulles could barely keep awake when they played 'South of the Border'. Some strange inconsistencies of policy were allowed to occur. One of the highest U.S. decorations was awarded to Perez Jimenez, the unpalatable dictator of Venezuela; a few years later he was being extradited from Miami to face criminal charges at home. Military coups in quick succession in Argentina and Peru brought withdrawal of U.S. recognition from the latter, but not the former; yet the generals subsequently restored constitutional rule in Peru, but not in Argentina. Meanwhile, the petering out of the Korean War and the end of U.S. stockpiling brought a serious collapse of South American export earnings.

Warning of the mounting wave of resentment against the U.S. came during Vice-President Nixon's visit of 1958 when he was mobbed and spat upon. But it took the high-tension jolt of Castro really to shift U.S. policy towards Latin America as a whole. Although as a senator the newly elected President Kennedy had shown no particular interest in Latin America, when he spoke of it as the 'most important area in the world' for the U.S. he aroused a great wave of expectation. And he backed up his words by launching the Alliance for Progress, an imaginative scheme of economic aid on an unparalleled scale. Born at the Punta del Este conference of August 1961, the *Alianza* planned the expenditure of at least $100 billion over the next ten years, of which $80 billion would come from Latin American exchequers and the major part of the remaining $20 billion from the United States. For sheer size the programme dwarfed even the Marshall Plan, which totalled some $17 billion, but it was also a totally new form of aid, dependent on a charter of sweeping social reform. Only those governments which fulfilled the conditions laid down by the *Alianza* charter would qualify for the dollar funds. It was to aim for an annual overall per capita increase in income of 2.5 per cent.

In effect the U.S.A. was underwriting a social revolution in Latin America. Immediately it earned the hatred of the oligarchs, and later the mistrust of the apostles of reform in Latin America, as it came to seem to them that the *Alianza* was not going to live up to its ideals and was doing little more than bolstering up the old oligarchies. For, although the U.S. poured in over a billion dollars a year, building thousands of new schools and homes, irrigating millions of acres of new land and creating potable water systems across the continent, the *Alianza* turned out at best to be a part failure. Soon after Kennedy's death, it seemed to run out of steam. In Washington, despite hopes of 'Latinizing' the administration of the *Alianza*, U.S. bureaucracy bogged it down so that it became just another aid programme, linked to governments and technicians. In Latin America, hopes pinned upon finding a middle class eager for reform proved illusory. It is a shortcoming common to most of its nations, where there has never been anything to compare with the British industrial bourgeoisie of the Victorian era, which came to impose its own manners and morals on the nation as a whole. Instead – as Claudio Veliz, a distinguished Chilean writer points out – the emerging middle-classes in Latin America traditionally sought to become absorbed within the oligarchies; therefore they became firm supporters of the Establishment, not involving themselves with the implementation of significant agrarian or fiscal reforms. Managerial ability was also found lacking, and, above all, the united political leadership of the Spaaks, Schumans and Monnets, which had helped bring the Marshall Plan to fruition in Europe of the late 1940s, was just non-existent. One after another, the U.S. wooed nations and statesmen who seemed to promise to conform to the Kennedy ideals of social reform. One after another each was found to be wanting. Only one, the Chile of Eduardo Frei, at last gave grounds for hope; 'the last best hope', one U.S. author called it in the title of a book.

But the myth of Kennedy transcended the fate of the *Alianza*. To South Americans, he was something unique; Catholic, youthful and *macho*, he managed to capture that spirit of innate romanticism in a way which no pragmatic, materialist leader from North America has ever achieved. Kennedy's impact on Latin America was – and is – incalculable, and universal; in 1961 a popularity poll carried out at Bogotá's National University gave Kennedy a 71 per cent rating, compared with 28 per cent for Castro. In South America, I was to meet many people of all walks of life who regarded Kennedy, rightly or wrongly, as 'the only American statesman who thoroughly understood' the continent. He understood the frustrations of underdevelopment, the longing for change and the sensitivities of easily injured pride. And he was assassinated. They have never forgotten, or forgiven, that.

After Kennedy, at least in Latin American eyes, U.S. policy returned to its more familiar rhythm. Johnson tried to keep up the Kennedy momentum, but the priorities of Vietnam were too obsessing. Local economies continued to be shackled to the export of commodities or raw materials, rather than the encouraging of more profitable industrial products, and in not altering this status quo the 'partnership' of the *Alianza* began to seem to both nationalists and left-wingers little different from the U.S. imperialism of fifty years before. Also Johnson lacked the lyrical appeal of a

26

Kennedy. In 1964, he met the Panamanian riots with heavy-handedness, and the following year the U.S. Marines went ashore in the Dominican Republic in the good old style of Teddy Roosevelt. Nothing unites the individualist nations of Latin America more than an overt intervention by the northern colossus – and Johnson's adventure brought forth a continental howl; followed by a marked deterioration in the U.S. image. Meanwhile, from Washington's point of view, separately the Latin Americans were succumbing to government after government antipathetic to the *Alianza* principles of 'reform through representative democracy'. Argentina and Brazil were taken over by right-wing military regimes; while in Peru and then Bolivia, left-wing, nationalist military elements seized power and promptly set about expropriating U.S. companies.

Only in traditionally democratic but economically stagnant Chile did there seem to be a consistent ray of hope. After his election in 1964, Eduardo Frei and his left-of-centre Christian Democrats showed they meant business on reform. Inflation was cut, the rich made to pay their taxes, farmlands reallocated to the landless, slum rehousing projects and major educational improvement schemes launched. A compromise scheme providing for the progressive 'Chileanization' of the copper companies, Chile's biggest source of revenue, was agreed amicably by the United States. From its established scepticism about Latin American prospects in general, the U.S. reacted ecstatically towards Frei's Chile. Writers dug up and dusted off Bolívar's remark of long ago: 'If any American republic is to have a long life, I am inclined to believe it will be Chile. There, the spirit of liberty has never been extinguished; the vices of Europe and Asia arrived too late. . . .' And they gave wide circulation to de Gaulle's apostrophizing Chile (on his 1964 visit) as 'the pilot country of Latin America'. Chile was suddenly discovered to be 'the most important country in South America, and Eduardo Frei is its most important man . . . because of its effort to steer a decent middle way' (John Gunther).

Leonard Gross, who encapsulates much of the liberal adoration of Frei in the U.S., went so far as to claim (in 1967) that if Frei had lost to Allende in 1964 it would have meant:

first, the vindication of Nikita Khrushchev's theory of peaceful revolution; second, the intrusion of Marxism into the hemisphere, not on an isolated island, but in a respected mainland country; third, an end to U.S. influence in Chile, and a loss of influence throughout the hemisphere; fourth, the loss of a billion-dollar U.S. assistance investment. . . .

He added ominously that 'if Frei and Chile fail, the future for democracy in Latin America will seem grim'. To back up the reigning favourite, the U.S. poured in over $1.3 billion during the 1960s; over the past twenty years Chile received altogether from the U.S. more money per capita than any other country; private investment there totals somewhere over $850 million. 'Chileanization' of the copper mines was greeted as showing 'that confiscation of foreign owned industries through the crude device of expropriation is *passé*'.

Now, in U.S. eyes, Frei and Chile have failed. The shock, wrote Bill Buckley, was 'as though the child on whom we devoted the most attention and care had decided, upon finishing graduate school, to embrace cannibalism'.

To compound the shock, it is plain that there is added gloom in Washington at the unexpected speed with which Allende, after just two months in power, is already setting about the 'Marxification' of Chilean institutions. The press is being muzzled – they say – the army neutralized, the judiciary undermined, the remaining copper assets are certain to be completely taken over. We shall see. And what will Mr Nixon do? He will be 'cool and correct', will play wait-and-see, and adopt a 'low profile' position. It is an apt expression, reminding one of the man in the top hat bobbing behind children's coconut shies in days past. Keeping his head down seems about the best that any U.S. president could do, under the circumstances.

It is a cold Saturday afternoon, 16 January, when we take off for Bogotá. Travelling with W.F.B. jr is never a simple, uneventful affair. The first thing that happens, the tickets are left behind at the check-in counter. Each accuses the other of negligence. The rest of the plane is subjected to another ten minutes of soothing music while an emissary of the airlines makes the hundred-mile dash across the airport. Unruffled, Bill gets down to his usual airborne work routine. Out come the tape-recorder, typewriter and multiple dispatch cases that I am to lug halfway across South America. Dictating letters, writing a couple of columns, and possibly part of a new book, he can somehow still keep up a lively conversation. Did I know what coffee from Venezuela came to be called during the war? 'Stalingrad coffee, because it can't be taken!' I am not sure how amused the Venezuelan air stewardess is. Sooner or later a lurch of the plane causes an eruption of a Buckley dispatch case, filling the first class compartment with paper. Helping to gather it up, the pretty stewardess is promptly charmed into acting as a temporary unpaid secretary, licking up envelopes, and so on.

There is a brief pause to allow us to take in the horrors of Miami airport: the endless concourses seemingly leading nowhere, the stuffed baby crocodiles marked 'Souvenir from Havana' but with a stamp on their bellies saying 'Made in Colombia.' Bill is attacked, mercilessly, by fans. 'Pleased to meet you, Mr Buckley; I watched your programme last week and just wanted to shake your hand.' I am amazed by the universal urge of (North) Americans to make themselves known to public figures. Imagine an England in which everyone who spotted David Frost or Enoch Powell at a bus-stop wanted to shake hands with him! What a nightmare! Bill says it's normal; that's the only way to get to be President. One sweetly smiling lady announces that she has 'so enjoyed your debate at Oxford against Kissinger'. With cool affability Bill put her straight; it was Cambridge, and Galbraith. I hiss that this is no way to reach the White House. Later, the sweet smile turns on me: 'And I hear you're a great *medical* historian.' She is going to Bogotá for a Kodak conference. (Or was it Caracas, and Xerox?) As we leave Miami, Bill tells me about the hijacker who held up the pilot and ordered 'Take me to Miami!' Amazed, the pilot replied: 'But we're scheduled for Miami.' 'Yeah,' replied the hijacker, 'that's what they told me on the last two flights, and each time we landed in Havana!' At that precise moment, Bill, who never moves without a compass and an altimeter, notes that we are flying due south. 'My God, Al, we're heading straight for Cuba!' In

29

the distance we can already see a grey shape beneath the clouds. Abruptly the plane makes a ninety-degree turn, followed by two more before it continues its course. It is a bare fifteen minutes from take-off; just a passing reminder of what the presence of the alien, hostile island in the Caribbean means, daily, to the North American consciousness.

2

Land of Violence

Bogotá

Dino Pionzio meets us at Bogotá airport. A voluble ex-Neapolitan with a mephistophelean beard, Dino is a close friend of Bill's from Yale days, now political counsellor in the U.S. Embassy. Talking like a machine-gun, while all the time miraculously managing to keep a Vesuvian pipe going, he treats us to a remarkable rundown on all South America as we wait for our luggage to appear. When it does, my holdall looks suspiciously flaccid, and I discover that I am light of my shaving case and a new pair of shoes bought in New York. Dino suggests amiably that the theft was much more likely to have occurred at J.F.K., the Bogotanos being generally less light-fingered than his own countrymen, susceptible only to the more spectacular forms of crime. Nevertheless, for the next few days I keep hoping to spot a diminutive Colombian sporting a pair of outsize suedes like Charlie Chaplin.

In Colombia the great Andean cordillera splits into three, making it a nightmare for road builders and a paradise for bandits. Bogotá sits in a kind of upland arena that was once a lake bottom, 8,700 feet high, in the middle of one of the ranges. Colombians hasten to tell you how untypical Bogotá is, a little country of its own in a vast mass nearly five times the size of Britain, and certainly one feels remote from the scorching Caribbean littoral and Amazonian plains. I wake up with a vague sensation of tenseness and lurking irritability, recognizing symptoms experienced a year earlier at Mexico City's 7,500 feet. We are staying in the Tequendama, a Hilton-style pile part-owned (strangely enough) by the Colombian Army. Its base, a townlet of boutiques selling colombiana and emeralds, is where Britain's soccer pin-up, Bobby Moore, was once involved in what Mr Macmillan might have designated a 'little local difficulty'. But the jewel shop concerned has vanished; and so has the mysterious señorita and all the other principals involved in that episode. Outside my window the Cerros, jagged outposts of the Andes, rise up almost from the immediate foreground, an improbable tint of viridian green capped with a dazzling white. Set against it, just across the road, ant-like figures are finishing a not distasteful flamingo-pink skyscraper. The strong, tropical colouring, intensified by the thin air, is completed by a passionate sky. Great violet clouds swoop below the low peaks with disconcerting suddenness, full of menace but seeming never quite to bring rain. So very different from the pallid English skies that Romain Gary's 'Lady L.' thought 'went well with good manners and well-brought-up children', it is a factor that at once imposes on one's awareness with its latent ferocity.

In front of the Tequendama is a charming small colonial church, San Diego, that seems to belong more to an up-country village than a sophisticated city. Beyond it is the bull-ring, where Palomo Linares is billed to appear next Sunday.[1] I wondered what it would be like to face a murderous bull at this altitude, when reflexes tend to be slower and your heart pounds with any mild exertion. But tauromachy is evidently not the only spectacle witnessed in the Santa Maria ring. In the 1950s the crowd booed the flamboyant daughter of the then dictator, General Rojas Pinilla, after the first bull had been dedicated to her; the following Sunday, Rojas packed the Plaza with his supporters, and spectators who declined to cheer him at a given signal were knifed or cudgelled or thrown down over the barriers. Eight were killed and a hundred more injured. On my return to Colombia I was also to see the ring used for some unscheduled roughstuff.

[1] Colombia, Ecuador, Venezuela and Peru, with the oldest Spanish inheritances, are the only South American countries still to maintain the Plaza de Toros. Cock-fighting also thrives in many parts of Colombia; in Bogotá alone there are five *galleras*.

We are taken to admire the Plaza Bolívar, the centre of the old city, a vast paved square with a cathedral of rather austere late baroque style on one side, a statue to the *Libertador* in the centre, and numerous plaques to various martyrs who died during the ferocious *guerra a muerte* against Spain. In one corner is a low, typical colonial house, white-washed, with a patio surrounded by pendent wooden balconies, unmistakably and gloriously Spanish; it is a Bolívar museum and is full of encomia phrased in the most exquisitely flowery Spanish. The mantle of the *Libertador* hangs heavy over Colombia. He created it, gave it its independence, then fled into an exile of disillusion as his creatures turned against him and his grandiose schemes of a united continent; a sequence setting a baneful pattern that has plagued the South American nations ever since. Apart from the area immediately round the Plaza and a sprinkling of exquisite colonial churches, Bogotá is a modern city. The reason for this, chiefly, is a terrible bout of civic madness in 1948 – called the *Bogotazo* – which spread rapidly across the whole country, and during which much of Bogotá was burned down.

An American (Yanqui) once described Colombia as a mixture of 'Socrates and Jack the Ripper'. Colombians are proud to regard Bogotá as *the* intellectual and cultural capital of South America. They stress that its acclaimed founder, Jimenez de Quesada, was not a conquistador but a scholar and lawyer. There are supposedly more bookshops per square inch than anywhere else, and a more academically correct Spanish is spoken than in most parts of Spain. Even hotel porters use such delightful archaic courtesies as '*a sus ordenes, su Merced*'. Colombians are less proud of the other label, but will reluctantly admit there is a streak of violence – outstanding even by any other Latin South American standard – which runs through their history, and has deeply influenced it. Until quite recently, Bogotá was a deserted city after dark; nobody dared venture out. 'Never argue with a taxi driver,' cautions Dino, and then tells, among other horrendous tales, of a female compatriot who was recently belaboured with an iron bar and had both arms broken, after she had rashly remonstrated with a bus-driver for scraping her car. Many householders carry guns, or even have their own 'vigilantes'. Does this instinct for violence stem from some peculiar racial admixture of Moro-Spanish, Indian and Negro? From climatic conditions, or altitude? Is it a coincidence that Mexico City, which shares very similar altitude/climatic factors with Bogotá, also just beats it for the world's highest murder rate? Or was the instinct for violence instilled in Colombian society from very earliest days, from the *guerra a muerte*, when the *Libertador* himself showed the way with the unnecessary killing of eight hundred prisoners-of-war in one massacre.

At the end of the last century, Colombian Liberals and Conservatives fought out one of the most disastrous of the continent's civil wars. In his fascinating novel, *Nostromo*, written at the turn of the century, Joseph Conrad clearly had it in mind when he described:

stories of political outrage; friends, relatives, ruined, imprisoned, killed in the battles of senseless civil wars, barbarously executed in ferocious proscriptions, as though the government of the country had been a struggle of lust between bands of absurd devils let loose upon the land with sabres and uniforms and grandiloquent phrases. . . .

At least a hundred thousand Colombians perished in this Thousand Days War. But it was nothing compared to *La Violencia* that started as recently as 9 April 1948, with the assassination of Jorge Eliecer Gaitán, and which could have been equally well characterized by the passage from Conrad. Gaitán was a left-wing Liberal of unique personal magnetism and rhetorical power, greatly beloved by Colombia's legions of under-privileged. His enemies regarded him as a dangerous demagogue, and undoubtedly if he had survived he would have headed a radical, populist faction leading to the almost certain disruption of the long-established, precarious balance of Liberals and Conservatives. Possibly, he might have become another Castro. As it was, he was shot down in the street by an unknown gunman, who was immediately lynched. Enraged mobs then proceeded to burn down a large part of Bogotá, killing any political opponents they could lay their hands on, under the horrified eyes of the delegates to the

Ninth Inter-American Conference, including the U.S. secretary of state, General Marshall.[1] The *Bogotazo* spread across the whole country, degenerating into local feuds in which village massacred village, family slaughtered family – and was then revenged. 'We are riding a wildly spinning wheel where today's victims become tomorrow's executioners, and these, in turn, the future victims. Each victim feeds on the idea of retaliation, so that there will be enough hatred in Colombia for the next 150 years,' predicted one Colombian newspaper.

Accounts of the atrocities committed during *La Violencia* turn the stomach. Luckier victims escaped with nose, lips or ears cut off. Crucifixions were commonplace, while the more refined tortures had their own special names. There was the *corte de corbata*, whereby the throat would be delicately slit and the tongue extruded to hang down like a tie or *corbata;* the *corte de mica, corte de franela;* bocachiquiar, which consisted of making hundreds of small punctures from which the victim slowly bled to death; *picar para tamal* or 'cutting up the body of the living victim into small pieces, bit by bit'. Nobody was safe; pregnant women had their foetuses ripped out and replaced by roosters, infants were pitchforked, and children – sometimes as young as eight years old – were raped en masse. 'I find in our ethical situation,' wrote a distinguished Colombian, Luís Lopez de Mesa, 'an element and a refinement of horror unknown in the world, because the cruelty was applied, not to adversaries or possible rivals, but to brothers, equal in condition. . . .'

The forces of law and order were themselves often involved; one wretch had his tongue removed by the police, with the explanation, 'We're cutting it out so you won't ever again shout *vivas* to the Liberal Party.' Often motives were even less specific; in one incident bandits burned the hacienda of a wealthy Conservative landowner, killed his foreman and two sons and raped his daughter, and when he dazedly asked why, the answer was simply *'porque usted es rico y blanco.'*

There were no battle fronts in this terrible civil war, and

[1] Another to witness this devastating explosion of the proletariat was a young student agitator from Cuba, Fidel Castro.

Colombia's impossible geography rendered the divided police and army powerless to stop the killing. By the standards of today's South America, the actual political differences between the warring parties were slender enough. The Conservatives (Bolívar's party) stood, roughly, for central government, the ascendancy of the Church, and private property; the Liberals for federalism and secularization – but they did not go as far as anything so revolutionary as, for instance, land reform. The political folly of the *Violencia* is admirably characterized in that superb fantasy, *Cien Años de Soledad*[1] whose revolutionary hero, Colonel Aureliano Buendiá, 'organized thirty-two armed uprisings and he lost them all. He had seventeen male children by seventeen different women and they were exterminated one after the other on a single night. . . .' A Liberal, Aureliano becomes totally corrupted by the war, shoots his best friend in the name of the cause, and ends by forgetting the principles at issue: 'From now on we'll fight only for power.'

Sickened by this murderous anarchy, in 1953 Colombians welcomed a *coup d'état* by an army general, Gustavo Rojas Pinilla. 'As the nation cannot be without a government, and someone must govern,' declared Rojas with beguiling modesty, 'I assume the power.' At once Rojas declared an amnesty for any armed freebooters who surrendered, bringing a temporary pause to the *Violencia*. By its end, up to 300,000 Colombians were estimated to have been killed. In one small community alone, 503 out of 509 families were found to have lost some close relative. But, apart from being

[1] *One Hundred Years of Solitude* (in its English translation) by Gabriel García Márquez was published in 1967 and has already run to over twenty editions, or half a million copies. Colombia's leading fiction writer, García Márquez is a man of the Left — like almost all of Latin America's internationally known writers over the past ten years (with the outstanding exception of Argentina's Borges). The first Colombian novel truly to achieve international recognition, *Cien Años* is a unique classic wherein Latin Americans of almost any country admit to recognizing themselves. It is woven around two main events; an endless, senseless civil war (modelled on *La Violencia*), and the arrival and departure of a *Yanqui* banana enterprise (based on a débâcle of the United Fruit Company in 1928) which, bursting in upon its 'solitude', deprives an isolated community of its Arcadian innocence. More will be said about it later.

the man-on-horseback who happened to be around at the critical moment, Rojas quickly proved he had little aptitude for governing. Trying to emulate Perón, he ran the country into debt on showy programmes of social welfare (which in fact aided few) and on the customary extravagance that so often proves irresistible to Latin American generals when brought to power – the unrestrained purchase of prestige arms. Inflation took over, and by 1957 Colombia was gripped by a severe foreign exchange crisis.[1] That May, Rojas was ousted and exiled by a five-man military junta. But, in his unpopularity, he had achieved the seemingly impossible: reconciled the Liberals and Conservatives. Meeting discreetly in Spain, moderate leaders of the two warring factions hammered out an extraordinary truce. For a period of sixteen years, starting from 1958, the country would be ruled by a *Frente Nacional*, whereby there were to be elections every four years but the two main parties would share power (exclusively) at all levels by means of a parity system, and alternate for the Presidency. It is a little like Wimbledon; the toss was won by Liberal Lleras Camargo; followed by President Valencia, a lovable and hedonistic figure who caused a minor outrage at a reception for de Gaulle by crying out 'Long Live Spain!' The current service is in the Conservative court, since Misael Pastrana Borrero took it over from Liberal Lleras Restrepo in 1970. It is also the last service, because the sixteen year truce comes to an end in 1974. In so far as it brought a degree of peace and honest government to Colombia the *Frente Nacional* has been a success. But the patronyms of its leaders – Valencia, Restrepo, Lleras – are oligarchic ones familiar to Colombian history, and through dividing the political spoils between them the Liberals and Conservatives virtually disenfranchised the country's rapidly growing have-nots. Nor did they produce solutions for Colombia's basic problems, deferring to some future date the social revolution that the assassinated Gaitán had seemed to promise.

[1] During his subsequent trial, it was alleged that Rojas had wasted *five billion dollars* of national funds, and salted away ten million abroad on his own account.

La Violencia and the Wimbledon-style truce that followed it are uniquely Colombian phenomena, but their consequences assume patterns common, and vitally relevant, to other Latin American countries. First and foremost, there are the left-wing guerrillas. With growing discontent at the *Frente*'s torpidity in social reform, in the early 1960s the expiring *Violencia* was resurrected, and polarized in a different form. Much as Karl Marx himself tried to cast the Paris Commune of 1871 as a fundamentally proletarian revolution, so Marxists now claim the Colombian *Violencia* historically to have been a class struggle. In fact, it was not – any more than the Commune was – in so far as poor peasants murdered poor peasants with equal impartiality. Then, however, came Castro's triumph in Cuba, and later more substantial inspiration in the form of weapons, specialists at guerrilla warfare, and indoctrination material. Aided by the prevailing state of anarchy, several of the bigger armed bands during the *Violencia* had already set themselves up in Andean fastnesses as 'independent republics'. The most remarkable of these was called Marquetalia, which – with no roads connecting it to the rest of the country – covered some two thousand square miles south of Bogotá and lasted nearly fifteen years. It was originally founded, back in 1949, as 'Gaitania' by a peasant leader, 'Charro Negro', who was also a member of the Central Committee of the Communist Party. When he was killed in 1960, its name was changed and control passed to another member of the Central Committee, a legendary *pistolero* known as 'Tiro Fijo', or 'Dead Shot' – alias Manuel Marulanda. Gradually, because of Tiro Fijo's importance in its hierarchy, the PCC (Communist Party of Colombia) became committed to the defence of Marquetalia; finding itself, almost by accident, with a full-scale guerrilla movement on its hands.

But Rojas's timely amnesty of 1953 struck a heavy blow at the guerrilla movement, with its members laying down their arms by the thousand. (Indeed, had it not come at this time, Marquetalia might well have developed along the lines of Cuba's Sierra Maestra, the base from which Castro was able to launch his campaign to sweep out the Batista regime.) Then, in 1965, a rival set-up appeared on the scene, Castro-orientated and calling itself the *Ejército de Liberación Nacional* (National Liberation Army) (ELN). Attracting predominantly students, the most portentous feature of the ELN was its recruitment of a young priest of great personal appeal called Camilo Torres. It is worth digressing briefly on Torres, not only because of what his defection meant in Colombia, where the Church has the strongest influence on the continent, but because he represents a new phenomenon of great consequence in today's Latin American scene as a whole. Torres was born in 1929 of respectable upper class parents; his namesake and kinsman was one of Colombia's leading martyrs of the Wars of Independence. Part of his training he spent working with Abbé Pierre, the apostle of the down-and-outs of Paris. Increasingly frustrated by the failure of the ultra-conservative Colombian church to side with the forces of reform, by 1965 Torres was on the verge of breaking with it. He began his political career by founding a United Front, embracing factions of the extreme left as well as – initially – a significant body of 'progressive' Christian Democrats. Squaring his conscience, Torres made a declaration of impressive clarity that could well become a standard creed for Latin American priests caught up in similar conflict of the spirit:

As a Colombian, as a sociologist, as a Christian, as a priest, I am a revolutionary. I consider that the Communist Party has genuinely revolutionary elements, and thus . . . I cannot be anti-Communist . . . because, although they may not know it, many of them are true Christians. The Communists should be well aware that I will not join their party. . . . However, I am ready to fight with them for common aims; against the oligarchy and the domination of the United States, to seize power for the people. . . . The basic thing in Catholicism is loving one's neighbour. For this love to be true, it has to be effective. . . . We must therefore take power from the privileged minorities in order to give it to the poor majority. This is what a revolution is all about, if done properly. The Revolution can be peaceful if the minorities do not offer violent resistance. . . . Revolution is not only allowed to Christians but is obligatory for those who see in it the only effective and large-scale way of carrying out works of love for everybody.

Alarmed by Torres's extremism and the threat of Communist domination of his United Front, the Christian Democrats began to pull out. Swiftly the United Front disintegrated, and in disillusion Torres (now out of the Church) joined the ELN. From the mountains, he issued an explanatory proclamation in January 1966:

When the people called for a leader and found him in Jorge Eliecer Gaitán, the oligarchy killed him. The people will believe them no more. The people do not believe in elections. The people know that legal resources are exhausted. The people know that armed force is the only way. The people are desperate. . . . I have joined the National Liberation Army because I found there the same ideals as in the United Front.

A month later, Torres was killed in an ambush. The rumour ran round Bogotá that he had been shot by his own people, to provide both the Colombian Church and youth with an irresistible new martyr. Certainly, in the words of one of his sympathizers Richard Gott, 'as with Che Guevara, Camilo Torres in death was a more potent symbol than he had been when alive, especially outside his own country'. So be it.

In order not to be outflanked by this more vigorous rival, the ELN, the Soviet-line Communist Party promptly responded by according Tiro Fijo's peasants 'official' guerrilla status, and redesignating Marquetalia imposingly as the Rebel Armed Forces of Colombia (FARC). At the same time the Communists attempted frantically – but in vain – to dominate the whole Colombian guerrilla movement. An almost identical struggle was to develop with Che in Bolivia in 1967. Next, the Maoists made their bid with the creation, in January 1968, of a Popular Liberation Army, the *Ejército Popular de Liberación* (EPL) – just thoroughly to confuse things. Although the EPL was, apparently, the child less of Peking than of indigenous Maoists, it nevertheless established a precedent as the first Chinese-orientated guerrilla body in all Latin America, with Colombia the first to have three distinct – and mutually opposed – Marxist guerrilla movements; a precedent of quite outstanding significance in today's ideological war, and not just limited to continental boundaries.

Predictably, the PCC slated the 'Pekinese' EPL as 'small groups of "ultra-revolutionaries" embodying the most negative petty-bourgeois trends', and accused it of 'forcibly pushing the people into battles the meaning of which they do not understand, and are not yet prepared to wage'. The antagonism between the three rival sets of *guerrilleros* undoubtedly worked to the government's advantage. By 1968 it could claim that, whereas two years previously guerrillas had been operating in eight out of twenty-two departments, they were now all but liquidated; the most active group, the ELN, was said to have been reduced from five hundred men (in 1965) to seven.

Responsible for the military mopping-up operation had been a colonel called Alvaro Valencia Tovar, who had commanded the Colombian army's crack Fifth Brigade, based on Bucaramanga, and regarded by U.S. experts as perhaps the continent's most effective anti-guerrilla unit. Now a general, in charge of the Military Academy, Valencia Tovar was to be our first visit in Bogotá. Accompanied by Dino, and the chief U.S.I.S. officer, we are invited to his house, a pleasant one-storey villa surrounded by garden such as you might find in any North American suburb. The general is dressed in a civilian grey suit. On his desk he proudly displays a metal plaque with an oriental inscription on one side, and 'Captain Alvaro Valencia Tovar' on the other; a memento from the Korean War, to which Colombia was the only Latin American country to send a fighting unit. Aged forty-six, he is rather short, quiet-spoken with blue eyes, pink cheeks and fair hair, and could easily pass for a Dutchman; in fact, it would be hard to think of anyone conforming less to one's image of a South American general. But Valencia Tovar is evidently no ordinary general. Recently he published a novel, called *Uisheda*, which received acclaim as far off as the *New York Times*. The theme of *Uisheda* is that there is no point countering guerrillas with mere violence, that the only solution lies in producing more food, social reform, more jobs, – possibly an obvious concept, but not for a top professional soldier and rebel-killer in

41

Latin America – and where in the British or U.S. armies would you expect to find a budding novelist among the senior brass? The general's English is flawless, and lucid – although the U.S.I.O., one of those Americans who never uses one word when five will do, keeps interpolating his remarks in the most irritating way.

Militarily, claims the general, the insurgency situation is well in hand. The Maoist EPL is isolated and starving up in the mountains of Antioquia near the Panama isthmus. A group of the ELN that was allegedly planning the kidnap of a U.S. diplomat was rounded up just the previous week; otherwise for some time they have given the appearance of being in a state of disintegration. Over the past two years, Tiro Fijo's FARC, whom the general rates as the most efficient of the three bodies, have given up fighting the army altogether. But it is not because they have been physically defeated. Unfortunately, one can not claim that. The reasons are more disquieting. 'One has reason to believe,' says the general, 'that the FARC have had orders from Moscow to disengage from the country, give up guerrilla activity altogether, and concentrate on establishing revolutionary, but non-violent, nuclei in the cities.' It seems that they are having some success and that they are actually in control of several cities – notably in the south. 'Has the FARC perhaps been encouraged by the success of the Tupamaros' concentration on urban "terrorism" in the cities of Uruguay?' I ask. 'I don't think it's really that – yet,' replies the general. He thinks it is much more in line with the overall Soviet doctrine for South America; the steady peaceful penetration of political and social institutions with a view to appearing as a 'respectable' alternative government. 'This is, after all, what has brought them into a position of power in Chile now, and that must be very encouraging to the official Communist Parties all over the continent.' In tandem with this strategic withdrawal of the FARC, and equally disquieting, is the immense expansion of Soviet diplomatic and cultural activity since relations were resumed in 1968. The Russians are extremely busy in the universities, and over a hundred young Colombians are currently studying on scholarships in the Soviet Union. The next most disturbing factor, comments

Dino – and the general agrees – is the support that the Marxist revolutionaries are finding within the Church. Since the 'martyrdom' of Camilo Torres, a 'Golconda Group' of dissident priests has been founded in his memory under aegis of a Father García, and already several more priests have apparently exchanged their habits for machine-guns. If the Golconda strain were really to take root among the devout Colombians, this could well satisfy the 'fish in the sea' hypothesis expounded by Mao for the success of guerrilla movements.[1]

The root of the problem lies much deeper. 'Guerrillas can only succeed in an area of misery,' says Valencia Tovar, coming back to the theme of his *Uisheda*, 'and we can only counter them by reducing that misery.' It is all very well for the army to engage itself deeply – as indeed it does – in all manner of 'civic service' in the guerrilla territories: building roads, running schools, providing medical assistance. But basically everything is negated by Colombia's nightmare 'demographic explosion': the highest population growth rate in all South America and one of the highest in the world, 3.2 per cent per annum; 9.5 million Colombians in 1945, 21 million now, and rising at a rate of over half-a-million a year it will reach 34 million by 1995.

Dino and the general jointly sketch in the brutal facts of life stemming from these statistics. For the past two or three years, the Colombian economy has indeed been booming as never before. Inflation has been held steadier than in any other South American country; over the past twenty years the rate of industrial growth has been exceeded only by oil-based Venezuela; while in 1969 alone the G.N.P. rose by 6.5 per cent, a coefficient of expansion that would turn any British government green with envy. But all this is regularly

---

[1] Because of their constant state of dynamic turmoil, it is difficult ever to be certain about trends among Latin American guerrilla groups, but later developments suggest that Valencia Tovar may have been over-sanguine in his assessment. The very day after our meeting, the Bogotá papers reported the discovery by the army of a recently abandoned camp of the ELN where some thirty men were said to have encamped for three weeks.

reduced – in real terms – to a negligible growth *per capita* by the terrible fertility of the Colombians. Overall unemployment is running (as of 1971) at 8.4 per cent; in Bogotá (which has nearly quadrupled in size over the past twenty-five years) it is up to 13.5 per cent and still rising, and some 400,000 of its inhabitants live in sub-standard housing. In this predominantly agricultural country, where 60 per cent of it is still owned by no more than 3 per cent of the population, land-hunger is growing among the peasants with their vast families, over half of whom live at below subsistence level. Colombia's dilemma is shared by most of South America. 'Of course, number one, we must have birth-control,' says the general; 'but we can't do anything until the Church permits the issue to become public.' The cause had suffered a devastating setback when the Pope's triumphant visit to Bogotá of August 1968 was preceded almost immediately by his encyclical broadside against the pill. 'Frankly', the General concludes gloomily, 'I think the future is dark.'

There is one more topic, more specifically in the general's orbit but which tact persuades us to skate lightly around. For all its tangle of domestic, social, economic and political problems, Colombia is indulging in an unimaginable extravaganza of old-fashioned sabre-rattling against her neighbour, Venezuela. Short of oil, she has been hotting up a territorial dispute over oil-bearing offshore areas on the frontier, and to give teeth to her case had just ordered $50 million worth of French Mirages, plus two unproven mini-submarines from West Germany. Colombia can ill afford the hard currency; the sophisticated weapons and their maintenance seem bound to push up her defence budget, currently one of the lowest on the continent, and it is difficult to conceive what use they would be against Tiro Fijo and his men, or against gun-runners from Cuba – which must remain Colombia's greatest security problems. And worst of all, here are almost the only two western-orientated democracies remaining in South America, that once, briefly, comprised Simón Bolívar's dream of 'Gran Colombia', apparently poised to fly at each other's throats. One is reminded of Cardinal de Retz's dictum: 'It is easier to fight one's enemies than to get on with one's friends.' How often this has been true of the internecine past of post-colonial South America, and no wonder the State Department is depressed today!

We left Valencia Tovar feeling that we would hear of him again. Two days later, when a western ambassador expressed doubts to me about the prospects for political democracy in Colombia after the Wimbledon truce ended in 1974, I asked him if there were 'any bright young army colonels waiting in the wings.' 'There don't need to be,' he replied without hesitation, 'we already have a bright young general; his name's Valencia Tovar.' The extreme Left evidently agree; towards the end of 1971 he was wounded in an attempt by urban guerrillas of ELN to assassinate him which came close to succeeding.

The rest of the day fills up with various meetings with students and journalists. A group of university students conjured up by U.S.I.S. present an interesting ethnological cross-section; one, a diminutive figure who never once opens his mouth, seems to be pure Amazonian Indian. They are of the Left, but none are exactly red-hot revolutionaries. A dispirited exchange ensues on the academic definition of freedom. Bill translates into superbly mellifluous Spanish an old favourite – Ernest Bevin's 'Freedom is the right to go to Victoria Station and buy a ticket to anywhere in the world you bloody well want.' The Amazonian glares silently and looks as if he would like to reach for his blowpipe, while another murmurs 'In South America, the essence of freedom is to be *able* to buy a ticket at all.' Point to the students. The journalists – warm, critical of the U.S., some vastly erudite – throw up questions and arguments that were later to seem fairly stereotype. What is the U.S. going to do about Allende? Problem number one. Will he be allowed to get away with it? Another Bay of Pigs? 'Of course not.' Reading between the lines, one senses the journalists torn between a sense of gratification at a fellow Latin American's show of *machismo* in cocking a snook at the U.S. Goliath – as per Castro – and a genuine fear of an 'export of revolution' from Allende's Chile.

Why have the *Estados Unidos* allowed the *Alianza* to collapse, they continue? They answer themselves, almost to a man, that the *Alianza* failed because Kennedy was killed;

and John F. Kennedy was the only *Norte Americano* thoroughly to understand Latin America. It was a refrain one was to hear again and again. During his era, the U.S. had never enjoyed such goodwill – and would it ever again? Has the U.S.A. run out of steam? Does Nixon have any policy towards South America? Does he realize that Colombia is possibly the last best friend of the U.S. in South America? Why don't you invest more money in us? What are you going to do for us until A.D. 2000? Later, Bill remarks to me 'Sometimes one longs to ask "what are you going to do for *us* until A.D. 2000?" ' But smiling ingratiatingly he shoots back with 'Why should we put money into Colombia when so many of your senior citizens are investing theirs, illegally, in Florida and Switzerland?'[1] Fifteen-all.

Next morning we are bidden to the Presidential Palace. Outside the elegant building where once the *Libertador* held sway, the men of the Guard goose-step back and forth in a disquieting fashion, with incongruously dark faces peering out from under spiked German *Pickelhauben*. Unlike any of his predecessors, the new president of Colombia, Dr Misael Pastrana Borrero, is no politician. He is a business executive who had previously served as ambassador in Washington. Yet, as the last president under the Conservative–Liberal truce, none has required more political skill; and the bare six months he has held office have brought a series of successive tribulations. Because of the slow pace of reform under his Liberal predecessor, Lleras Restrepo,[2] and the necessity of feeding and housing yet another two-and-a-half million Colombians born during the past four-year presidential term, Pastrana inherited a grave backlog of social discontent. As it was, the jointly backed *Frente Nacional* came close to defeat, (with a slim majority of only 63,000 votes out of four million, including many abstentions), at the hands of ex-dictator Rojas Pinilla's ANAPO opposition and his supporters to the left. The *Anapistas* proclaimed an electoral

---

[1] According to one estimate the siphoning-off of capital by rich South Americans used to run to over $500 million a year.

[2] Lleras, like Frei in Chile, claims his (mild) agrarian reform programme was scuppered by the resistance of the big landowners.

fraud, and there were scenes of wild uproar and chair-smashing in Congress as Lleras made his resignation speech. Rojas's firebrand daughter, Senator Maria Eugenia, a darling among the wretched slum-dwellers of Bogotá whose condition she had indeed done much to alleviate, was carried out screaming. With the ever-lurking fear of a return to the dread days of the *Violencia*, Pastrana imposed a 'state of siege', a favourite Colombian device for dealing with civil disorder. There was a wide feeling that the authority of the National Front governments was broken, and that Pastrana would have to move much quicker than Lleras if anything were to be salvaged of Colombian democracy by the running-out of the 'Wimbledon' truce in 1974. With the wealth of reform legislation he has to effect before 1974, the omens are not encouraging. The Colombian parliamentary system hardly helps, in that the passage of major bills requires a two-thirds, not just a simple majority in Congress, so that often they do not get through at all. Possibly in preparation for the renewed scramble in 1974, divisions appeared to be widening between Liberals and Conservatives, and – according to one pessimistic western ambassador – party loyalties within the civil service often make it impossible to get approved legislation carried out. 'And what can you think of democracy,' he added, 'in a country where Congress works for five months, and only three days a week?'

So President Pastrana heads a weak government, propped up to a large extent by Valencia Tovar and his brother officers of the Colombian army, and he is not himself generally regarded as being made of steel. The president is a handsome, young forty-seven, with completely European but not particularly strong features, and has a fresh look as if he might just have come from Los Lagartos, the smart Bogotá country club. He greets us affably, then after a minute or two of banalities, he sweeps Bill off into his inner office saying that he has a very private message for *el Presidente* Nixon. Bill shrugs his shoulders helplessly – you do not argue with presidents – and as far as I am concerned, that is the end of the interview. In some frustration the ever-attendant Dino and I sit chatting desultorily in the office of the presidential private secretary. May we go and see the famous room where Bolívar saved his life by jumping out of the window, while his courageous mistress, Manuelita, held his would-be assassins at bay? No, we must wait until *el Presidente* has finished with Señor Buckley. The best part of an hour passes before they re-emerge. Dino murmurs, irreverently, 'He must think he's got more time than Lleras; fifteen minutes was the most Lleras would ever spend on an interview.' I am agog with curiosity to know what was said at this eyeball to eyeball session; is it a disclosure that Colombia is about to declare war on Venezuela? No, says Bill, later; he just wanted me to impress upon Nixon how vital the U.S. market was to Colombian coffee. Promise? Yes, promise. The U.S. government had refused to renew the price-fixing coffee pact, on which the whole Colombian economy was largely dependent.[1] 'I murmured something about that being Congress's decision, not Nixon's,' said Bill, 'and the president sighed, recalling that soon after he had arrived in Washington he found himself wondering why he had not been accredited to Congress, rather than to the president.' As for the problematic future ahead, President Pastrana stressed how strong the democratic tradition was in Colombia. In 150 years of independence, the government had been illegally overthrown only three times; adding (with a trace of a smile, reported Bill) 'Only for four years each, as if the democratic rhythm of the people overwhelmed the prehensile resources of the despot.'

At a lunch given by the U.S. Chargé d'Affaires, an intelligent and pleasant man called Stevenson, I found myself sitting next to Dr Pastrana's new foreign minister, Vásquez Carrizosa. He was soon chiding me for the outrageous lack

[1] For Colombia, whose economy is more wedded to agriculture than that of most other South American countries, market prices for her extremely high-grade coffee (of which she is the world's second largest producer) are of transcending importance. As of seven years ago, coffee comprised 83 per cent of all exports. Now, following a considerable amount of economic diversification, it still accounts for some 12 per cent of the G.N.P. Even more important, in view of Colombia's chronic problems of unemployment and over-fertility, is the fact that most of the coffee is produced by some 300,000 smallholders, or *minifundistas*. And of late the trend has been towards a world-wide drop in coffee prices.

of interest shown in Colombia by Britain. Where were the British goods we should be selling Colombia? The cars that we should have been building here, under licence? (Indeed where were they? I had seen U.S. monsters everywhere, Volkswagens and even tiny, under-powered Renault '4 Chevaux' struggling manfully against the altitude, but otherwise nothing British but a handful of dilapidated Land-Rovers. My friend, Professor Galbraith, remarks that his countrymen will do 'anything for Latin America, except read about it'; but British lack of interest goes further – we won't even try to sell them motor-cars). There was the minister for trade, Michael Noble, currently visiting Colombia but he was, claimed Dr Vásquez, 'the first to come since Independence'. ('Nonsense!' snorted H.M. Ambassador when I put this deplorable neglect to him some time later. 'We've had one out here each year for the past five!') I began to understand something of the prickliness of Latin American sensibilities that must, much more so, be the everyday preoccupation of U.S. diplomacy.

Most of the remainder of the lunchtime conversation was taken up with Allende, and the problems posed by his take-over in Chile. Colombia, traditionally regarding herself to be the U.S.A.'s closest ally on the continent, had gone along with her in having Cuba boycotted within the Organization of American States (O.A.S.), but now Allende had already driven a hole through this by promptly re-establishing relations with Castro, unilaterally. The Colombians were concerned that, if other Latin American powers follow Allende's example, the whole O.A.S. structure might collapse. In a subsequent article, Bill sums up, aptly enough, that Colombia is 'both distressed and awed' by Allende. 'Distressed because the leaders of both major parties in Colombia recognize that the Chilean way is not likely to produce any desirable result. Awed, because it simply isn't plain that it will prove possible, in the crucial years ahead, to resist the forces that are now convulsing Chile.' Then – a matter of vital economic importance to Colombia – there was the Andean Pact. An act of great inspiration and faith, at least on paper, the Andean Pact was – for once – a totally Latin American creation, free of any initiative by the U.S. Signed

49

in May 1969, after years of haggling, in the glorious old Spanish Main fortress of Cartagena on the Colombian coast, it was a kind of Andean Common Market, comprising Colombia, Ecuador, Peru, Bolivia, and Chile. Only rich Venezuela and muddled-up Argentina remained outside. Now, at least one eminent Bogotá banker present at the lunch felt that, with the way that the internal systems of Peru, Bolivia and Chile seemed to be heading progressively leftwards, Colombia would find it gravely disadvantageous to be shackled to such an outfit. Her hand would, of course, be strengthened if Venezuela would enter the Pact, but with a history of high protective tariffs – not to mention the present ill-humour between the two countries – this was unlikely. Colombia, in any case, as *the* predominantly agricultural nation of the five, was the odd one out, and it was probable that all the massive built-in 'exception' clauses would be made to operate against her interest. He for one hoped that Congress would refuse to ratify the Pact, before it was too late. To a European, it all sounded rather familiar. Above all, continued the banker, there was the question of foreign investment. One of the principal functions of the Andean Pact would be to fix common terms on which foreign undertakings could invest in the Five. Hitherto Colombia had been one of the 'most favoured' nations with foreign investors. But if Peru, Bolivia and – soon – Chile were frantically expropriating U.S. and other holdings, with little or no compensation, would not Colombia become tarred with the same generic brush and find herself deprived of the foreign capital she so badly needed to develop and diversify her economy? It was a point.

One of the U.S. diplomats present pointed out, mildly, that U.S. investment in Colombia had not altogether fulfilled expectations. The facts (according to Senator Fulbright) were that, under the *Alianza*, aid to Colombia had totalled $732 million between 1963 and 1968, the largest in all Latin America. In return, the G.N.P. had increased from $276 per person per year to no more than $295 – or less than half the increase aimed at by the *Alianza*; land had been found for only 54,000 out of 400,000 landless families; while the number of illiterates had actually risen from five to six million. It was not very encouraging, and, the way things were going in the world, it looked as if *all* countries in Latin America – including Colombia – should be prepared to expect a notable cutting-back of U.S. investment in the future.[1]

On the subject of 'good neighbour' relations, I note a curious piece of tactlessness in Bogotá, repeated in all the other countries we were to visit. The telephonists of the United States Embassy always answer with 'This is the American Embassy.' Given the touchiness that exists south of the border about who are the 'true' Americans, it seems an unnecessary irritant; how much resentment might be avoided by a simple change of nomenclature to 'United States Embassy'?

Somehow, between all the political talks and interviews, we find time to visit the Gold Museum, appropriately enough owned by the Bank of the Republic and housed in superb modern buildings. We are escorted by the director himself, Dr Gómez, who is marvellously informative and his enthusiasm totally infectious. I could have spent days there. Colombia was, apparently, the original El Dorado where the Spaniards landed[2] in their terrible quest for gold which eventually led them to Peru and the tragedy of Atahualpa and the destruction of a great culture. Most of pre-Columbian upland Colombia was inhabited by the Chibchas, who came to be known as 'Muiscas' (a corruption from the Spanish *mosca*, or fly), because they were so numerous – though not for long. The Chibchas seem to have lived a simple, unpretentious, rustic life. They left no great pyramids such as the sinister Aztecs built for their human sacrifices at Teotihuacan, none of the monumental masonry and bas-reliefs of the Mayans down in the jungles of Yucatán, none of the imposing cities of the Incas at Cuzco and Machu Picchu. Yet they must have

---

[1] Colombia did in fact ratify the Andean Pact. But it seems that the Pact is rapidly losing its teeth as one country after another seeks refuge in one after another of the 'exception' clauses.

[2] Or, as the Créole Bolívar savagely put it, 'vomited on to the coast of Colombia to convert the most beautiful part of the world into a vast and odious empire of cruelty and loot.'

been superlative craftsmen. With their elementary smelting techniques, they seem to have used gold almost as a base metal,[1] and the museum is full of simple porringers made by wrapping the gold around a calabash. There are beautifully proportioned gold vessels for sniffing coca, pectoral ornaments or stomachers with powerful, aquiline Indian faces impressed on the wafer-thin metal, and incredibly delicate tiny bird pendants. One pair of earrings is made like the most modern kind of mobile of falling, sycamore-shaped leaves, as light as air. Apart from the superb delicacy of most of the work, what impresses one is its intrinsic humour, and also the modernity of its conception. Here is none of the ghoulish Aztec preoccupation with death, terror and human sacrifice; even the zoomorphized anacondas and alligators have an almost benevolent look about them. There is a rodent-like figure which has a long curled tail, comic feet and a human head, bearded and with extraordinarily European features. (Could the mysterious white god of the Mexicans, Quetzalcoatl, have reached here too, in some distant era?) In their depiction of human beings, the Muiscas seemed to specialize in elongated wedge-shaped figures, delineated in thin gold wire that could easily have come from the studio of Dubuffet.

Dr Gómez takes us up to see his *pièce de résistance*. We stand expectantly before a blank wall. He presses a button, and with a Bond-like whir of electrical machinery the wall slides back, revealing pitch-darkness beyond. Nervously we enter, accompanied by a well-armed guard. There is the soft sound of Indian flutes and drums and slowly the lights turn up. We are in a room crammed, each square inch of it, with gold artifacts of every imaginable kind, nine thousand of them altogether. This, says Dr Gómez in a hushed voice, 'is what the Spaniards probably saw when they came to Eldorado. And, if this is what is left, just consider what they must have taken!' (And, I mutter to myself, have destroyed and melted down for their beastly baroque reliquaries.) But,

---

[1] One is reminded of Candide who, on arriving in Peru, discovered the roads paved with gold and eagerly scraped up some nuggets; then, when trying to pay for his lunch with it, he was laughed at by the Incas for 'offering to pay us with stones off the road'.

for my taste, the vault, overpowering as it is, is not the most wonderful thing in the Museo del Oro. This is a tiny raft, no more than eight or nine inches long, found in Cundinamarca just a few years ago, in perfect condition. Supposedly it shows the ceremony tradition during which the *cacique*, or chieftain, would be rowed out on to Lake Guatavita by his nobles, covered in gold dust, and then bathed in the sacred lake. The *cacique* sits in the centre of his little raft, bedecked in gold ornaments and towering over his suitably diminutive companions and oarsmen, each of whom is a Dubuffet figure made of the most delicate drawn wire. Every joint of the giant bamboo logs forming the raft is there, every leaf of the palm fronds with which the flies are swished off the royal master. Totally devoid of the sombre notes of an Aztec religious ceremony, there is something festive and joyful about the little scene; one thinks of Fragonard and a *fête champêtre*, or Renoir and his friends on a Saturday outing to Courbevoie. What luck that this miniature masterpiece somehow escaped the notice of the venal Spaniard!

We leave Bogotá on board an Avianca jet for Lima. Colombia's Avianca is one of the world's oldest (it was started by Germans in 1919) and possibly most efficient airlines. It has a marvellous tourist scheme whereby for $50 (or £20) you can travel unlimited mileage almost anywhere within the vast interior of Colombia. Its service is admirable. But there were two small hitches before we took off. First, in a manner that I was to discover was the rule more than the exception to flying in South America, I had been listed under my christian name instead of my surname; so that, lucky to get on at all, I found myself relegated from the luxuries of first class (and the contents of Bill's overflowing briefcase) to the steerage. Then, something was wrong with the plane. Mechanics started unscrewing the nose, there, right beneath our eyes, tethered as it was to the waiting room; then, with the nonchalance of a vet removing a stone from a horse's hoof, they extracted all the delicate radar scanning equipment. 'Oh, God,' groaned Bill, 'can't they at least do it out of our sight!' The prospect of flying over twelve hundred miles of twenty-thousand-foot Andes with defective radar was hardly enlivening. Dino and his ravishing artist-wife,

53

Rose, did their best to calm us down. Finally a new box of tricks was wheeled out, screwed in place with the same nonchalance, and off we go.

Sitting next to me is a distinguished-looking and charming Texan in his sixties, called Charles South. It turns out that he is the president of Avianca's rival line, Braniff, and that he too has been relegated from first class because of the usual booking error. 'But never mind,' says Charles South; 'they'll give us a marvellous lunch; you wait and see.' He is a rewarding companion, has spent most of his life flying in South America and still spends nearly half his working year hopping from one part of the continent to another. He tells me some hair-raising tales of piloting across the Andes in 'the old days' in D.C.3s. With their ceilings well below even the mid-sized peaks, they would thread their way up the valleys, 'on a wing and a prayer', hoping not to meet a storm at the top of the pass. Looking down at the savage protuberances thousands of feet below the great jet, it is hard to realize that 'the old days' were little more than two decades ago. Charles knows everyone and everything in South America. If I get as far as Paraguay, he promises an introduction to his old friend, dictator Stroessner. Of La Paz he warns me, 'Watch out for the altitude; I'd lay off the women for the first two weeks. It can really kill you.' He is deeply troubled by Allende's intentions in Chile. He thinks that he will deliberately introduce galloping inflation to ruin the economy, then move in with totalitarian powers 'to save the country'. Brazil and Argentina might intervene, if things get too bad, he believes. Lunch arrives. Charles South is right about it. Wine follows wine, and our tables are piled high with palm hearts and lobster. Suddenly the worst occurs. The pressure of his knife seems to activate a secret spring on my neighbour's table. The whole mess performs a somersault, covering his immaculate silk suit with a hideous melange of mayonnaise, red wine, and pisco sour. He takes it wonderfully well, and the stewardesses are deeply caring. But what a way of putting a rival *cacique* out of business!

3

'Everything's Locked Up'

Seen from above, the Colombian uplands south from Bogotá
look marvellously green and fertile, and with so much good
farmland in a country nearly five times the size of Britain and
only a third of its population one wonders how there could be
such desperately acute hunger. Then, disappointingly, the
land disappears in cloud. No sight of those romantic-sounding
great volcanoes of Ecuador: Cotopaxi and Chimborazo.
When the clouds disperse again, we are already over Peru
and a fantastical mountain landscape. To the east, and
climbing to their very crests, is matted green jungle with
great murky rivers running down towards the distant Amazon
down-slopes, so contoured that they might have been made
of crumpled paper. Abruptly, to the west, the mountains
become brown like Sinai, the desert reaching equally right
up to their peaks. Dry river-beds wind down them but disappear before they ever reach the Pacific, and stranded
troughs of multi-coloured but rainless cloud fill the valleys.
So sharp is the transition here that one could almost draw a
pencil line along the watershed of the Andes, where, evidently, in this vast continent less than ninety miles separate
the drainage basins of Pacific and Atlantic. Here, at a
glimpse, are the basic facts of life that account for Peru's
weird geography and so many of its problems. It is all the
fault of the icy Humboldt Current which – through obscure
meteorological causes only partly comprehensible to me –
performs, for almost fifteen hundred dreary miles of the
coastline of Peru and northern Chile, the reverse of what the
cosy Gulf Stream does for Britain. In the lee of the Andes
that soar to fourteen, sixteen, eighteen thousand feet straight
out of the sea, there is nothing but arid desert. Its Chilean

continuation, the Atacama, supposedly contains the driest spot on earth, where rain has *never* been recorded year after scorching year. In Peru, on the eastern slopes of the Andes, it never stops raining, so that more than half the country is encumbered by the most impenetrable, dank Amazonian jungle. South-east of Lima the Andes fan out and, in between desert and jungle, lie the valleys and plateaux over ten thousand feet high that formed the cradle of the Inca world and where today its descendants eke out a precarious living from the worn-out soil. During the 1920s the Humboldt Current actually failed over two seasons, so that torrential rains fell and the Peruvian desert blossomed incredibly; and archaeologists believe that when the early pre-Inca civilizations flourished along the coast – at about the beginning of the Christian era – the climate may have been different. Certainly only a few inches of rain annually would have changed the whole course of Peru's history, making it one of the most fertile parts of the continent. (Evidently, there is a grandiose French scheme to reverse a tributary of the Amazon up north and have it flow backwards towards the coast. What an ecological revolution this might achieve for Peru!)

Decanting at Lima, we are hit by a hot blast of desert air and the aroma of fish-meal and guano plants. Bill has meanwhile turned the first class section, as usual, into a private office, and I try to help him out with his eleven pieces of hand luggage. Seeing my predicament as I stagger across the superheated tarmac, the amiable Charles South summons up a keen young man from Braniff to help unburden me. There is the usual reception committee of U.S.I.S. officials and local newspapermen, plus the Californian wife of one of Lima's most distinguished citizens, Pedro Beltrán, and an old friend of Bill. After prolonged embraces between Bill and Miriam Beltrán under a cross-fire of diffuse conversation, a vast limousine removes us to the U.S. ambassador's residence. There, to our dismay, we discover that the luggage whisked off by Charles South's keen young myrmidon is missing; namely a package of whisky for the Chilean natives and Bill's ponderous briefcase. Anxious calls are made to the airport while we sit chatting to the ambassador, Toby Belcher. The U.S. Residence is an attractive pink colonial building with a garden, typical of the more prosperous *barrios* of Lima, filled with giant red-hot pokers, frangipanis, oleanders, aucuparias, yellow blossom trees, something like a gigantic fuchsia and many unnameable species; evidence of what water can make grow out of the Peruvian dust. In this mini-Shangri La, a predecessor of Belcher's used to keep a jaguar, a vicuña, a deer, a heron, two condors and a boa-constrictor, until the boa took to escaping and alarming the neighbours. A fountain dribbles away quietly in the patio, while the telephone hunt for the missing hand baggage becomes increasingly frenetic. It is evident that Embassy officials are convinced the briefcase was crammed with secret papers from the White House that Bill should have swallowed before reading; the security officer is alerted, possibly the F.B.I. and the C.I.A. too. Bill, however, remains imperturbable, helping himself to another glass of ambassadorial scotch. At last – after another two hours of discreetly disguised hair-tearing – the two pieces are reported located, intact, and precisely where the Braniff courier had dumped them; in the middle of the concourse of Lima airport.

At dinner we are joined by Miriam and Pedro Beltrán, who are to be our hosts in Lima. Don Pedro, now in his seventies, has an unforgettable face. Like the rest of the forty old ruling families of Peru, the Beltráns doubtless proclaim complete *pureza de sangre* of their Spanish descent; yet, perhaps just as a consequence of some osmotic process over the centuries, Don Pedro with his patrician eagle nose, high check-bones and deep black eyes reminds me of one of the gold masks of the pre-Colombian Chibchas. He has the charm and warmth of a disappearing world, and a great big laugh. Educated at the London School of Economics, he tells me of his adoration of England with the kind of simple sincerity that sends an involuntary glow through one. On a recent visit he had found London 'still the most civilized city in the world, and everything in England so unchanged. But why do you English have nothing good to say about it? Always running yourselves down . . .' Later, he continued flatteringly 'I think the British are the most humane people in the world,' and when I riposted – perhaps with a manifest scepticism – 'Oh, do you really think so?' he roared with delighted laughter; 'There, you see, that's just what I mean about the English; always depreciating yourselves!'

Don Pedro is owner and editor-in-chief of *La Prensa*, a leading independent newspaper of Lima and one whose journalistic standards are surpassed by few in South America. Cotton planter, banker and economist, he was once ambassador to the U.S. and holds honorary degrees at both Harvard and Yale. Ten years previously he had served as finance minister, and prime minister under the Prado administration; and apparently with some courage. On an official visit to Cuzco, he was warned by the Communists that there would 'be trouble'. His entourage, on observing the hostile crowds as the plane arrived, became so nervous that he ordered them to go into the city in cars. He himself went alone, on foot all the way, two miles uphill at ten thousand feet; in itself no mean achievement for a sixty-year-old, without the incidental accompaniment of demonstrators lobbing a steady barrage of rocks from behind Inca walls. ('Really it is quite easy to dodge,' says Don Pedro modestly, 'when you can see the rocks coming.') All the shops of Cuzco were closed in protest against Don Pedro's visit, but gradually they opened up out of admiration for this ministerial display of *cojones*. Although every inch the oligarch, Don Pedro apparently never ceased to press on the Prado government the urgency for reform, of the need to do something about the desperate plight of the six million Indians. He warned his colleagues that if they did not speed reform, sooner or later a left-wing revolution in one form or another would sweep Peru. Sure enough it came to pass, in 1968, under the aegis of General Velasco.

About a hundred and fifty years old, the Casa Beltrán is a show-piece of Lima's earliest Republican architecture. Standing on the corner of a street in the centre of the city, it is surrounded by a wooden mirador, so characteristic of Peru, which overhangs the pavement and links every room internally. It also somehow creates marvellous cross-currents in the torrid Lima nights. A tiny lift decorated with bright blue wallpaper, mirror and candle brackets whirs you up to a roof garden of a thousand potted plants, with a raffia pavilion to give protection from the sun and the dust-laden winds. The interior is largely furnished with French nineteenth-century pieces, in excellent taste, revealing the profound influence of French culture on Pacific South America in bygone years. Across the road, and opposite a square of diminutive prettiness, is San Marcelo, the city's oldest (1584) parish church. With twirly grey *salomonicos* supporting a heavily ornate baroque façade, the rest of San Marcelo (as a guide describes with charming euphemism) has, alas, been 'subsequently restored in a manner of little felicity'. The same, unfortunately, could be said about much else that has been perpetrated upon Lima over the years. In common with many denizens of the New World, the Limeños are great destroyers; colonial churches and historic houses have disappeared in dismal succession under the hand of zealous city planners, quicker even than Peru's frequent earthquakes can level them. Now the latest upon which the municipal axe is scheduled to fall is the Casa Beltrán; because it stands in the way of a road-widening project. It has been under threat for three years, and both times I was in Lima the controversy of Casa Beltrán was being widely aired in the press. With the progress-minded generals tilting the balance, it looks as if the battle will be lost – even though the Beltráns have offered to make the house a museum of the republican era.

They are gloomy about what the future holds for them personally, not very encouraged about how the rule of the military junta will turn out for Peru generally: 'We are going to lose our house, our hacienda in the country, and probably the paper,'[1] predicted Don Pedro, and Miriam told me on one side: 'I have taken down the pictures and put away the silver, and our most valuable belongings, so that they will be safe if ever we have to leave. That is South America for you . . . And, can you imagine, Pedro hasn't even noticed that anything's gone!' She pointed out how the manservant was whisking off our wine-glasses one by one to refill them behind the scenes, 'because the poor man is so embarrassed at having to keep the bottles in an awful rubber bucket instead of a silver wine cooler.' Don Pedro sees recent events in Peru in the light of English history, and as an impassioned

---

[1] He was right – see Chapter 16.

believer in liberal democracy he is deeply despondent. 'When our last three elections weren't rigged, and the losers accepted defeat gracefully, I was greatly encouraged. I thought we were learning, like the English during the age of Walpole – the man who really introduced democracy to England. And then this [the generals] happened . . .' We sit up talking most of the night, about England, about Don Pedro's beloved Walpole, about Peruvian politics, about Machu Picchu – despite an early start for Cuzco the next morning. Before leaving the Beltráns, Bill makes a diverting discovery; on asking the maid, in perfect Spanish, for his raincoat, he is met with total blankness. Suddenly the penny drops; she had never heard the word *impermeable*, or seen the thing – because it never rains in Lima! Instead, in winter, there is a depressing kind of heavy and cold 'Scotch mist', called the *garrua*, which comes off the Humboldt Current and provides a minimum of moisture to sustain plant life. Lima must be desperately unhealthy during those months; rheumatism abounds, and some 30 per cent of the population are asthma-sufferers – probably the highest incidence in the world. One early twentieth century traveller to Lima, Lord Bryce, found it during half the year 'never cold enough to have a fire, but usually cold enough to make you wish for one. It never rains, but it is never dry; that is to say, it is not wet enough to make one hold up an umbrella, yet wet enough to soak one's clothes.'

We return through the dreadful grey-brown Cairene slums that flank the airport, but take off late because of rainstorms at Cuzco. The 727 makes a wide sweep out to sea so as to gain altitude for crossing the Andes. Clutched in the embrace of the impossible mountains we can see tiny patches of cultivation. Cuzco, fifty minutes by air and still several days by road, in its narrow valley nearly as high as the look-out point on top of the Jungfrau, has been renowned as a graveyard for aircraft. We begin to drop alarmingly close to crenellated hills the colour of the tops of Perthshire moors; the great plane banks and winds its way down into the valley, reminding me of a madcap chase up twisting canyons in north-western Australia in a tiny Cessna, but this is a vast jet. Suddenly there is a violent deceleration and all the papers from my briefcase go shooting forward across the floor of the plane, to be rounded up by a kind nun and an Indian two rows in front. We get out, slightly gasping for breath in the cold, thin air.

Abruptly we are in a totally Indian world of mahogany, weathered faces and long Inca noses, the men with tall knitted earcaps, the women with their bowlers and babies slung over their backs. It is another planet, another age; the contrast with European Lima is extraordinary. Along Don Pedro's *via dolorosa* from the airport are new housing developments, more impressive than one might have expected. There are also the invariable slogans of '*Viva Cuba*' and a sign outside a shabby upstairs flat proclaims the '*Academia de Idioma Ruso*'. As in Lima, one notes immediately an almost complete absence of police or army; the generals must feel remarkably sure of themselves here at Cuzco. At the Savoy Hotel (slightly less magnificent than its London namesake) guests are provided with printed and terrible warnings of what the dread *soroche*, or altitude sickness, can do for you: 'stomach crapms [*sic*] . . . bloody expectorations . . . disminuation of mental facilities'. I had also brought with me a grim caveat from a British author who had recently embarked, rashly, with a hangover on the Huancayo railway, which is the highest in the world, climbing to nearly 16,000 feet; and then spent several days in a clinic suffering from what was charmingly diagnosed as *sufocación*. But in addition to this good advice, the U.S. Embassy had equipped us well with oxygen bottles like small green bombs and pills for countering this *soroche*, apparently peculiar to the Andes, which – at its mildest – can cause the most violent headaches. So obediently we flop on our beds for an hour or two sniffing (quite unnecessarily) at the green bombs – which provokes a delectable feeling of light-headedness – and I am able to enjoy Cuzco with facilities undisminuated.

Cuzco – Machu Picchu! The fulfilment of the dreams of a lifetime. To any half-human being they would alone justify the fifteen-thousand-mile trip; in the words of the Michelin rating, *vaut le voyage*. But for us it can be only a diversion of painfully few hours. A professor from the university, with strongly Indian features, comes to take us up to the Inca fortress of Sacsahuaman. Up and up we go, out of the Cuzco bowl into bitterly cold and rain-sodden moorland. The roadside is covered with clumps of wild lupin, giant broom and wild calceolaria of even brighter yellow growing out of Inca walls. But the only sensible trees are eucalyptus; the Spaniards in their rapacity hewed down the indigenous forests, and, until the eucalyptus was introduced from Australia sometime in the last century, the hills round Cuzco must have been bleaker than Wuthering Heights. We pass Indians plodding alongside their alpaca herds with the slow, studied tempo of a race that can count its riches only in terms of time. An elderly, wrinkled farmer (possibly no older than forty) is scraping away at an exhausted pocket of earth with a digging stick. Like the Aztecs, for all the extraordinary efficiency of their civilization in other ways, the Incas had neither the wheel nor draught-animals, and, even today, the digging stick, just a length of sharpened stick, remains the principal implement of agriculture in much of the Peruvian highlands, where the plough – let alone the tractor – has yet to arrive.

Sacsahuaman is extraordinary – in its own way more imposing than any Mayan or Aztec ruin – and, like so much left behind by the Incas, it is a mystery. In essence it is nothing more than a fortress, plain, unadorned and awesomely functional. Three massive terraces rise one above the other, running some four hundred yards in length broken up with a score of salients, ravelins, and demi-bastions so that the whole looks like the teeth of a giant saw. The ramparts are still fifty feet high, and must have been higher before the depredations of the Spaniards. But what really staggers one is the masonry-work. Each of the immense grey stones is cut into complex polygonal shapes, perfectly interlocking with its neighbours; one of them is some twenty-eight feet in height, and estimated to weigh 361 tons. The Incas used no mortar, and yet one cannot insert the blade of a knife into the joints. Some experts believe that the Incas could not, in the short period of their ascendancy, have evolved by themselves such a skill of stonemasonry; that they must have inherited it from some earlier civilization, itself swamped by the Incas and long submerged in the mists of history. But, apart from the sheer miracle of such a technical achievement for a people who had no iron-cutting tools, no wheels, pulleys or horses, and did not know about the arch, the truly mystifying thing about Sacsahuaman is the strategic motive for such a structure. At the peak of Inca power when Sacsahuaman was built, the principal threat would have come from primitive tribes from the Amazonian lowlands, equipped with no more powerful weapons than bows and arrows, whom far less Brobdingnagian fortifications could have kept at bay. Could it have been, as someone had suggested, that Sacsahuaman – the building of which supposedly required fifty thousand workers – was nothing more than a giant W.P.A. scheme to provide employment? Sacheverell Sitwell wondered whether the megalithic walls, which could so much more easily have been constructed from ordinary sized stones, were built on such a scale simply 'to instil respect and terror'. Perhaps so. Then was Sacsahuaman in fact just an early precursor of the deterrent, designed never to be put to use? In which case, when the Spaniards arrived with their secret weapon of cavalry, it certainly shared the fate of the Maginot Line and the U.S. Strategic Air Command, outflanked by German Panzers and the Vietcong irregulars.

From just below Sacsahuaman, the whole city of Cuzco, red-roofed, is laid out in plan down in the valley. Legend has it that when Manco Capac, the father of the Inca race, led them out of the Island of the Sun in Lake Titicaca, he carried a golden staff with divine orders to travel until he reached a place where the staff would sink of its own accord into the ground and there to found his imperial capital. This happened at Cuzco. The city now counts some hundred thousand inhabitants, and possibly when Pizarro's men arrived, in November 1533, its population may have been no less. Some chroniclers claim that, when the Spaniards first gazed down upon it, those roofs were clad with gold, the mighty stone walls polished to enhance its blinding glitter. It seems more likely that most houses were thatched; nevertheless that first sight was enough for Pizarro to write to Charles V: 'This city is the greatest and finest ever seen in this country or anywhere in the Indies. We can assure Your Majesty that it is so beautiful and has such fine buildings that it would be remarkable even in Spain.' One can gauge something of the Spaniards' excitement by recalling the truly astonishing march they had just completed. Only 130 strong and with no supply line, they had covered in no more than three months a distance (from Cajamarca in northern Peru) which in air miles alone measures over six hundred miles, but which also involved repeatedly crossing the line of the central Andes – alternately plunging into torrid, fever- and snake-ridden rain-forests, or freezing above the snow-line – and fighting much of the way. Though one may detest Pizarro for what he did to the Incas, it is impossible not to gasp at the steely endurance of those Spanish *tercios* of the Renaissance, so recently tempered in the bitter struggle against the Moors, and at the faith – as well as greed – that drove them on. The conquest of both Mexico and Peru will always stand high among history's great military feats.[1]

The sack of Cuzco was 'one of those rare moments,' as John Hemming writes in his superlative study, *The Conquest of the Incas*, 'when conquerors pillaged at will the capital of a great empire'. What they didn't loot had already been stripped by the Incas themselves, to no avail, in their attempt to ransom poor Atahualpa, or burnt by them during the great siege of 1536 which came so close to defeating the Spaniards.[2] On to the massive walls of the destroyed Inca temples the Spaniards grafted their cathedral and monasteries and palaces, outstanding tributes to the bigotry and destructiveness of Western man, but beautiful and interesting in themselves; that is, if one can forget what must once have lain below. But Cuzco makes one feel that the foundations of the lost world of the Incas (in terms of culture, as well as masonry) were too solidly built for them to be erased by either earthquakes or Spaniards. Everywhere in the narrow streets are to

---

[1] Of course Cortés and Pizarro were, by a strange stroke of double chance, both greatly aided by appearing on the scene at the precise moment in history when the native empires were riven by internecine disputes.

[2] The Cuzco coat-of-arms, granted in 1540, contained an orle of eight condors, in memory of the great predators that descended to scavenge the corpses of the Indians who died in the siege.

1 The 'small earthquake'; Allendistas dance a
victory *cueca* outside La Moneda, September 1970

2 The *Bogotazo*, 1948

3 The Chibcha raft in the Museo del Oro, Bogotá

4 (*above*) President Misael
Pastrana Borrero of Colombia

6 Father Camilo Torres

5 (*above*) General Alvaro
Valencia Tovar

7 President Juan Velasco
Alvarado of Peru

8 (*above*) 'Pity my tears, Pity my anguish'; Peruvian altiplano Indians

9 Peru: Chimbote earthquake of 1970

10 (*above*) Machu Picchu

11 Threshing on the Peruvian altiplano

12 (*above left*) Eduardo Frei
Montalva

13 (*above right*) Pablo Neruda

14 Salvador Allende
electioneering

15 *La explosión demográfica,*
Chile

16 *Momio* selects reading
matter, Santiago

17 *Toma* of a *fundo*, Southern Chile

18 The MIR leads the way. The inscription is in Mapuche

be seen the great grey walls with their strange-shaped polygonal components, running for hundreds of yards, straight as a ruler, topped by a clutter of colonial bric-à-brac. There are no bas-reliefs or pictorial adornments to be found anywhere, even in places unravished by the conquistadors (such as Machu Picchu); this restricts one's knowledge of what the Inca world was really like. Perhaps it was because the hard granite in which their masons worked – unlike the soft limestone of the Mayans – was too much for their puny tools. It seems to me, however, more likely that it was simply not in their nature. For the Incas were the Roman organization-men, compared to the Greeks of the aesthete Mayans. The organization they achieved during the single century their empire lasted[1] was quite breathtaking. At the time Pizarro erupted upon the scene, the Incas' Tawantinsuyu – or 'Four Corners of the Earth' – stretched nearly three thousand miles along the Andes, from southern Colombia into northern Argentina. It was linked by a magnificent system of arterial roads, possibly superior as an engineering feat – if one takes into account the incredible geographic difficulties overcome – to the achievements of Rome. By means of relay runners, so they say, fresh fish from the coast could reach the table of the Inca in Cuzco in two days; messages (and they had no writing) between Lima and Cuzco took only a day longer – still better going than any modern transport but the aeroplane.

Politically, the Incas seem to have achieved a kind of Utopian Communism that has certainly never been attained by any Marxist society. It was authoritarian; the Inca himself was attended with godlike magnificence, but he and his nobles 'took their duties seriously and never degenerated into an idle and parasitic class'; nor were there any of the murderous religious rites associated with the Aztec hierarchy. Conquered peoples were permitted to continue to worship their own local deities within the general framework of the Sun-cult, while any tribute exacted was always in the form of labour contributed for the common good. In admiration, an

---

[1] A hundred years before the Spanish invasion, they were little more than a hill-tribe controlling the Cuzco valley.

early conquistador wrote: 'The Incas governed in such a way that there was not a thief, not a criminal, nor an idle man, not a single adulteress or woman of evil life in the kingdom.'

Inca policy was very much directed towards the general welfare of the people. Elaborate checks and balances suppressed any resort to tyranny or corruption of the local authorities. All land was communally owned and farmed. It was divided into three parts; one belonging to the Sun (the proceeds of which went to supporting religious institutions), one to the Inca (to provide revenue for the state), and the third to the local community. The labour of agriculture was sublimated to a semi-religious festival; the peasants working to the music of flutes and songs, and evidently with a song in their hearts that would be hard to find today in the sombre lives of Peru's Indians. Despite their lack of an alphabet, most meticulous records were kept, to a large extent directed towards stockpiling vast reserves of food to guard against the climatic uncertainties of Andean agriculture, in storehouses the scale of which amazed the conquistadors. But nothing excelled the Incas' triumphs of irrigation, by means of which they managed to transform the desiccated, wind-swept *altiplano* into rich farmland. The Spaniards destroyed this complex system, and replaced it with nothing – as indeed nothing in South America since has really replaced the social technology of the Incas. They were the best planners the continent has ever seen, let alone Peru.

The centre of Cuzco is laid out around the Plaza de Armas, a square redolent of sinister memories of the conquest, the scene of the public executions, the burning of 'heretic' Indians and all the fearful charade of cruelty that was the Inquisition. Here, in 1572, they decapitated Tupac Amaru, a mild-mannered rebel who simply wanted to turn his back on the conquest and resume the traditional life of the Incas in some remote corner of the Tawantinsuyu. Subsequently, any Indian leader in revolt against colonial rule adopted the name of Tupac Amaru; until finally the last one was put to the most atrocious death in the Plaza de Armas as late as the end of the enlightened eighteenth century. First his wife and family had their tongues ripped out and then they were executed before his eyes, and finally the last Tupac Amaru was torn apart by four galloping horses, until he 'looked like a spider'. This appalling act of repression has its echoes in South America today; it is from the Peruvian martyr that Uruguay's accomplished urban guerrillas, the Tupamaros, derive their name. They probably have no more Indian blood in their veins than I do, but traditionally a 'conscience' about the plight of the *indígenas* sooner or later becomes a banner of every white Latin American revolutionary. As a former Colombian minister of war, General Ruiz, once remarked, it was 'enslavement of the Indians by the Spaniards centuries ago' that is the root cause of contemporary guerrilla activity. When General Sucre sent news to Lima of the victory of Ayacucho, which completed the liberation of South America from Spanish rule, his emissary was stoned to death by Indians on the way. The act was symbolic; for double standards are involved. Bolívar proclaimed revolution in the name of the oppressed Indians; after Liberation, however, they found themselves as badly off under the Republican Creoles as ever under Spanish colonial rule. Haya de la Torre's Peruvian APRA rode in on the wave of promises to the Indians; then forgot about them. The Mexican revolution was carried out – and is maintained today – in the name of the Mestizo; yet the one section to be left out of the current economic 'miracle' of Mexico, condemned to miserable poverty, is that of the rural Indians. And now, in Chile, with great fanfares Dr Allende's UP has 'rediscovered' the under-privileged Mapuche Indians – but one cannot help wondering whether, when all the shouting is over, the Mapuches will find themselves any better off than before.

Certainly the plight of the Peruvian Indians, who comprise nearly half the population, will shock even the most blinkered and myopic visitor today. 'Outwardly agrarian life has changed rather little on the Andean uplands from Inca times until today,' writes Harold Osborne. 'But under the Incas the common man was contented and even gay; life seemed good. Since the fall of the Incas his existence has become burdensome, his life sombre and his character resentful and sad.' After the conquest, the Indians passed into virtual slavery under the Spanish *encomiendas*; at the beginning

67

of the eighteenth century Jesuit pressure brought about their abolition, but the Indians simply passed into the tutelage of a (often corrupt) *corregidor* and a state of feudalism continued until well into the post-1945 era. In fact, if one may believe the British Anti-Slavery Society, in 1970 Peru (with Bolivia and Ecuador) was still one of three western hemisphere countries where slavery continued to exist. Around Cuzco, only one child in three is said to reach adolescence, and tuberculosis is rampant. The state of mind of being a modern-day descendant of the once-proud Incas is portrayed in moving sadness by one of Peru's leading young poets, Carlos Germán Belli:

> My mother, myself, my two brothers
> and many little peruvians
> dig a deep hole, deep down
> where we hide,
> because up on top everything's owned
> everything's locked up,
> sealed tight,
> because up on top everything's taken:
> the shade of a tree, flowers,
> fruit, a reef, wheels,
> water, pencils,
> so we prefer to sink down
> into the bottom of the earth,
> deeper than ever,
> far, far away from the bosses.
> Today Sunday,
> far far away from the owners,
> among the feet of small creatures,
> who write, sing, dance,
> who speak beautifully,
> and red with shame
> we want only to disintegrate
> into tiny little pieces.[1]

The present military junta is supposed to have Indian affairs very much at heart; but can it move rapidly enough?

[1] *Segregation No. 1*, tr. Maureen Ahern Maurer, *Tri Quarterly* No. 15, 1969, Evanston, Illinois.

Meanwhile, the one piece of private property even the poorest Indian seems to possess is a transistor radio, and the air is full of Communist (Soviet) propaganda in Quechuan and Aymaran. But just how fertile is the ground? Shortly after we left Cuzco, an intriguing news item appeared in Pedro Beltrán's *La Prensa*. In the countryside nearby, a *batalla* had taken place between two Indian villages, the participants numbering some two thousand. The two teams were fighting for the 'virgins' of the losers – who themselves came out in all their finery to watch the battle. The winners were, by tradition, granted a week to decide whether to accept their booty, or to take a ransom in cattle and remain celibate for another year instead. On this particular occasion, at least three deaths (one an apparently still ardent male of forty-five) and twenty injured were reported. It was an annual event dating back to Inca times, which the authorities find themselves powerless to prevent. Such is the remoteness from the modern world of the Peruvian Indian that sociologists sometimes wonder whether either Marxist philosophy or the reforms of the generals will ever make an impact.

The night before moving on to Machu Picchu we have a dinner-party, at the Savoy. The best onion soup I have tasted anywhere in the world, in little earthenware pots topped with a crust of meringue, reinforces a growing conviction that one of the great cuisines of this world is Peruvian. Our guests are half-a-dozen of the intellectuals of Cuzco; the rector of the university, a couple of newspaper editors, an engineer and a radio 'personality'. The conversation is good and unconstrained, and there is laughter. Bill admits later that one would hardly expect to find an equivalent standard in a small, provincial, North American centre; not for the last time, I feel more as if I were in Europe, than in the New World, let alone in the capital of a very remote culture. My neighbour, the owner of *El Comercio* newspaper (circulation five thousand), is César Lomellini, a thirty-five-year-old bachelor with a sardonic expression who claims a bed once slept in by Bolívar. Like General Valencia Tovar in Colombia, he is soon expressing to me primary concern about Peru's 'demographic explosion'. 'The government won't take a stand, they are afraid of losing popular support,' he says. 'So here in Peru

69

family planning has to remain a matter of private enterprise, very private!' There is much general talk about the success or failure of the military junta – and without any of those nervous over-the-shoulder glances sometimes to be found under dictatorships. There are complaints at the extreme centralization of the present government. Cuzco has also suffered from the remoteness of Lima; until the railway came through in 1870, its European community was probably the world's most isolate, and no president of Peru ever bothered to visit Cuzco until 1940. Now, they say, things are worse than ever before. All local government officials, from mayors down, are appointed by the generals in Lima, and – since the dissolution of parliament – there has been absolutely no local representation. The central bureaucracy of the junta gives the appearance of being desperately overloaded, and decisions come through with heart-breaking slowness. Yes, but one has to admit that *things* are being done; but fast enough, in a community where still only one child in three reaches adolescence? Such is the view from Cuzco.

The train for Machu Picchu grumbles off at an ungodly 7 a.m. It is crammed with tourists, and we find ourselves wedged between two dour French-Canadians, dressed up as Indians. The train struggles asthmatically out of the Cuzco valley. The gradients are too steep for conventional Swiss loops, so from time to time the locomotive halts in a siding, then reverses up the next slope. Up and up at a snail's pace, past dreadful mud-brick hovels in ravines; scraggy patches of lima beans, wretched-looking dogs, children defecating by the railroad, black pigs feeding on endless garbage heaps. We reach 12,300 feet, according to Bill's inseparable altimeter: a new country of rich highland valleys, willows and poplars and bright red earth, like the so-called White Highlands of Kenya. In Switzerland we would be well above the eternal snow-line. Strangely, there are also agaves and cactus, and aboriginal escallonia trees – among the last survivors from the flora of pre-Columbian times. Mauve fields of potatoes. The train hoots incessantly to warn Indians off the line. A wonderfully rich plateau at Izcuchaca (11,000 feet). A large, well-fenced farm, cattle, prosperous-looking horses; obviously a grand *hacienda* belonging to a (still) rich *patrón*.

Suddenly the dirty red stream alongside the tracks begins to boil. We are descending rapidly, diving in among the hills. Indians with wonderful faces wave and shout imprecations at the train. Strange, sparse vegetation on the hills; weird tufty things like the prehistoric 'black-boys' of Western Australia. 10,500 feet; still higher than the top of most ski runs the average European will ever reach, but the vegetation is already getting lush. Sheer canyons hem us in; possibly where the Spanish relief force was ambushed on its way to the siege of Cuzco.

A moment of tremendous excitement: at Pachar, with a great rush of turbulent grey-brown water, the Urubamba sweeps into our little red creek, swelling itself with other clear, white-green torrents that hurtle down from the canyon heights, and absorbing them all forever in its rush to join the Amazon far away to the east.

> Rivers fall on you like birds, you are covered
> with pistils the colour of conflagration,

marvelled Pablo Neruda. And what a river! Never anywhere have I seen anything like it. A few miles lower down, the Urubamba goes mad; exploding over black boulders the size of houses, and throwing up waves twenty feet high. No canoeist could survive a minute in this turmoil, and one feels that by dangling in as much as a toe one would be sucked under. I find a note from my travel agent: 'It is important to remember that the rainy season in Peru lasts from December through to March and it has been known for the railway line through the valley and gorge to be washed away! I shouldn't let this deter you . . .' In fact, the following month the last coach of the little train fell a hundred feet down into the gorge, seriously injuring ten passengers. About the same time I was to meet some broken-spirited American tourists in La Paz who had spent a grim night, without heat, light or food, marooned when the track had been inundated. In retrospect, I wondered how Bill would have coped with such a disruption to our impossibly tight schedule. Glancing up from an article he appears to be typing off a French-Canadian knee, at the frantic, ochreous waters, he comments; 'Why, there's more pollution in the rivers here than in the Hudson!'

71

Eight thousand seven hundred feet. Brilliant yellow broom gives way to unknown trees festooned with Spanish moss. Silver alpine plants like giant starfish cling to the upper rocks. With astonishing suddenness we are in the Amazon rain forest, an impenetrable tangle of trees festooned with creepers. Parasites growing upon parasites upon parasites. Within – happily unseen – ring snakes, *coralitos*, cascabels, bushmasters and fer-de-lances, ranging from three inches to fifteen feet long; maggots that bore into the skin and eat one alive; umbrella ants that carry off injured humans piecemeal to fertilize their fungus plantations; finger-long *canero* fish that intrude themselves into any aperture of the human body, expanding poisonous barbs so that they cannot be withdrawn. And so on, in this Garden of Eden, a bare seventy miles from the cold highlands of Cuzco, all the way until the terrible river debouches in the Atlantic three thousand airmiles further down the line. Only a couple of hundred miles away, the country rates as 'unexplored', and just a few years ago Peru's number one guerrilla leader, de la Puente, maintained a *foco* on a frozen height nearby, called the Bare Plateau, for six months – until wiped out by the Peruvian army. We pass a hanging footbridge, suspended precariously above the torrent – unchanged from Inca days, it could be the prototype of the Bridge of San Luis Rey – then all of a sudden we are at Machu Picchu station. There is a stampede for an insufficient number of buses, frantic exhortations of 'Over here the Indiana party.' The 1,500-foot ascent, 'up the ladder of the earth . . . through the barbed jungle's thickets'.[1] Hairpin upon fearful hairpin, until the ancient Mercedes boils, and conks out. Alarmingly, the driver restarts it by rolling backwards with slipped clutch towards the precipice. We survive, and suddenly we are there – where no conquering Spaniard ever set foot.

At the top of the 'ladder of the earth', as improbable and fantastic as Jack-and-the-Beanstalk country, the lost city sits astride its saddle of rock. Not a stone of it can be seen from the Urubamba gorge; which is of course why the Spaniards never discovered it. Fifteen hundred feet below, but still just

[1] Pablo Neruda, *Canto General*.

72

audible in the hush of awe that the city imposes upon its most insensitive intruder, the river forms a tight horseshoe embracing it on three sides. So sheer is the fall at almost every point that a stone dropped would, one feels, plummet straight into the Urubamba. Great puffs of steam sweep up from the valley, adding a touch of inferno to the scene, dizzying the brain, and melting into low cloud that obscures the peaks. Gradually as the morning goes by it disperses, revealing on every side emerald mountains that look as if they had been cut by some mad sculptor's spatula, and that, in their geological pre-pubescence, have never been tamed or modulated by the forces of erosion. On the more distant peaks there are even patches of snow. Up from the saddle of the city rises the great hook of rock of Huayna Picchu, a miniature Matterhorn that to the very top of its nine-thousand-foot pinnacle has Inca terraces cut in the almost perpendicular face. They make the steepest vineyards of Switzerland seem like Wiltshire. Every pocket of cultivable earth a few feet square on these incredible heights was worked to sustain the city's population of perhaps one or two thousand people, and these giddy terraces – like the walls of most of the houses – are still in almost perfect repair.

As with so much of the history of this vanished civilization which had no writing in which to set down its affairs, the past of Machu Picchu is full of mystery. Who lived here? How many? When? Why did they abandon the city? And what was it even called? Nothing whatever is known from Spanish sources because – in its incredible fastness – it was never discovered by them, or even heard of. Hiram Bingham, the American explorer who came upon it in 1911 – apparently led by an eleven-year-old Indian boy – died convinced that it was Vilcabamba, the last redoubt where the unhappy Incas tried to maintain their world after the conquest. Machu Picchu had been unaccountably abandoned many hundred years before Bingham's arrival (possibly as the consequence of some dreadful epidemic), but the discovery of a preponderance of females among mummies exhumed led him and others to believe that they were vestal virgins of the Sun, and that therefore this was also a sacred city. In a masterly piece of detective work, John Hemming, however, now assures us that the real site of the legendary Vilcabamba is deeper down in the jungles, at a place now called Espiritu Pampa. Yet even he cannot identify Machu Picchu, or explain its essential mysteries.

Although the awe of that mystery, coupled with its amazing position, has manifestly silenced even the 'Indiana Party', people have mixed feelings about the actual city itself. Sacheverell Sitwell thought that the setting was enough – you should have a quick look, a kind of one-night stand, and then move on. John Mander suggests that 'culturally, it should be classified rather with Hadrian's Wall than the Parthenon', dismissing it scathingly as 'a common-or-garden hill-fort'. Some hill, some fort! And to Christopher Isherwood, a more sensitive visitor, the buildings of Machu Picchu because of their modest scale 'must have resembled municipal washrooms or public tombs'. But they all seem to me to have missed the point. To begin with, Machu Picchu was obviously never a fortress; there are no traces of anything like the great bastions of Sacsahuaman, and anyway invisibility must have been its surest defence. Although there are some superb examples of Inca stonework, it is true that the imperial majesty of what was Cuzco is lacking, and Isherwood is correct in noting the small scale of the houses. But what impresses me about the city of Machu Picchu is its entity, wonderfully intact, as a place where simple people lived. Above all this is the glorious triumph of the human spirit, the miracle of the will to live in liberty, that Machu Picchu represents. What immortal resilience, what determination just to survive, must have driven the last Incas up to this olympian refuge! (And did they then merely desert it, or just die away out of sheer, national despair when, with Tupac's death, they realized their race was forever doomed?)

'El reino muerto vive todavía.' says Neruda with total simplicity in The Heights of Machu Picchu.

On a ledge above the city, carpeted with wild strawberries and giant vetch, I sit a long while just looking at the crimson wild gladioli pushing out of cracks in the walls below; acanthus-shaped ferns and slenderest bamboos that bend out gracefully over the abysm like trout rods; alpacas grazing thoughtfully along the intact terraces where Inca

74

maize once grew. A figure in a white *impermeable* comes into sight, scurrying furtively down stone stairways. It is William F. Buckley; like Sacheverell Sitwell, enough is enough, and he is heading back towards his typewriter to deal with Clare Luce and legalized abortion in the U.S. We fly back to Lima from Cuzco in a morning of bitter cold, after the customary confusion about reservations.

4

Generals to the Left

An English visitor of sixty years ago tells how, shortly before his arrival, the president of Peru was discovered intact at the bottom of a pile of dead rebels outside his own palace. We arrive at the Presidential Palace, straight off the 7 a.m. plane from Cuzco, and, while waiting for our appointment, I reach inside my well-rounded brief-case for a camera to photograph the sumptuous courtyard and the magnificent cuirassiers guarding it. In the best F.B.I., corner-of-the-mouth manner, Bill reproves me, claiming that he has just seen one of the praetorians reach towards his revolver. Furtively I push the camera back into the bag, fearful that the green, bomb-like oxygen bottle might roll out at the same time. But in fact, in Lima as in Cuzco, the generals show little sign of being worried about bombs, or rebels. There is remarkably little military presence, and one does not have the feeling of the police state. Perhaps it is because the junta is so completely secure in its tenure at the Presidential Palace.

We might just as well have taken the later, more leisurely plane, for the functionaries tell us that President Velasco's hatchet-man, Señor Augusto Zimmermann, with whom we have an appointment, is sick. He has also not been informed of the interview. A diplomatic illness? I was beginning to get attuned to the precariousness of appointments in South America; but obviously one should have been prepared. The universal plea to anyone you want to turn up within an hour of the pre-arranged time is ¡hora inglesa!. Should you not therefore be suspicious of a people who regard the modern-day British as norms of reliability?

Consoling ourselves over the default of Señor Zimmermann, we lunch out at the Waikiki Beach with John Utley, a young freelance American journalist recently married to a Peruvian girl. Enormous Pacific rollers burst on an uncomfortable beach of shingle, just like Brighton. Surf-boarders are balanced skilfully on their crests, though the water of the Humboldt Current is ferociously cold; deceptively so, because within an hour the tropical sun inflicts a painful burn. Waikiki was once a men-only club (Peru traditionally being the most male-orientated Latin society west of Jerez-de-la-Frontera), which used to allow members to sneak in only girls between the ages of sixteen and twenty-one. Finally the wives objected, and the junta administered the *coup-de-grâce*.[1] The beach has now been handed over to the proletariat, and only the clubhouse and pool behind it remain as a last uncertain stronghold of the besieged Forty Families. John Utley takes a relaxed and rather philosophic view of what the generals are doing in Peru. In South America, generally, he says, people tend to say things and take up violent positions much as a matter of form; but in fact, to a large extent, life goes on as before.

Such is the uniqueness of the Velasco junta, not just within the Latin American context, that it is still not easy to evalue precisely what it means, or which way it is heading – even after three years of power. There have been generals before in Peruvian politics, but they were never left-wing revolutionaries; and there have been revolutionaries who were never generals. In the 1920s there emerged Haya de la Torre's APRA, the first South American party to preach violent revolution to the under-privileged peasantry, and for many years it was a powerful dissident force on the Left, but each time the *Apristas* looked as if they might be coming to power the army intervened – or else, in their equal detestation of APRA, the oligarchs would form a temporary alliance with the Communists. Eventually APRA ran out of reforming zeal and became partially assimilated by the oligarchy. Peru's last general-president, Odría (1948–56), moved in

[1] With a puritanism that seems dear to most military men when they come to power, one of the first things the generals also did was to arrest Limeños making love in public parks; they also banned the carnival, on account of the injury to life and limb its celebration causes each year.

77

when the civilian government proved itself incapable of handling *Aprista* violence, and presided over a period of remarkable prosperity (for the few, and largely assisted by the Korean War boom); then he obligingly moved out to make way for carefully supervised elections and the Prado government, in which Pedro Beltrán served. In 1963, after a nullified election the previous year and another brief intervention by Odría, Fernando Belaúnde Terry came to power with his moderate-left Acción Popular party, formed in 1956. Belaúnde, an architect, gained considerable support from the expanding coastal middle class and worked hard to arouse a sense of self-advancement among the sierra Indians. He launched a visionary plan for a peripheral jungle highway,[1] running along the eastern slopes of the Andes, that would connect with Bolivia and Ecuador and open up great new areas for settlement by the land-hungry, as has been done in Brazil. He stabilized the economy, began the nationalization of the U.S.-owned oil industry, and generally gave new hope by his reform-mindedness. But the accumulated sea of troubles was as vast as the Pacific. Out of 1,600 towns in Peru, Belaúnde discovered 1,200 lacked potable water, electricity and sewage. Half had no access to roads. The statistics of land ownership were the most inequitable in all South America; 9 per cent of the total number of landowners possessed 82 per cent of the land, while some million peasants had none at all. This factor, coupled to a birth-rate almost as crazily out of control as Colombia's, is the root cause of the appalling slums that ring Lima in every direction, growing all the time at a terrifying rate. Down from the hills where they can find neither land nor a living wage, the Indian and *cholo* (half-breed) peasants pour into the city slums which – though they may be the most fetid and dreadful of the whole continent – still offer prospects of a better life than the one abandoned in despair in the mountains. The contrasts of wealth have always been staggering in Peru, and there were many easy ways of making money for the 'haves': the family plantation hundreds of miles from Lima, speculation in fish-

[1] A combination of political pressures and lack of funds prevented Belaúnde from ever starting it.

meal shares or in a new supermarket catering to the needs of the expanding middle classes.

Then, in 1963-4, there were some of the most serious outbreaks of peasant revolt in recent Peruvian history, followed by the sporadic appearance of various guerrilla groups. It was a warning that the patience of the Peruvian *indígenas* was running out. Uncorrelated, all these *focos* were swiftly and brutally crushed by the Peruvian army,[1] while at the same time revolutionary zeal was manifestly diminished by Belaúnde's promulgation of a limited land reform. Inadequate as this was, the hopes it instilled sufficed to show that – in the 1960s – even a half-hearted land reform could halt the drift to the extremism of the far Left. But, as was the story with President Frei in Chile, and so often elsewhere in South America, many of Belaúnde's reforms were blocked by a hostile, conservative Congress. Early on the morning of 3 October 1968, he was woken up by his daughter shouting: 'Papa, I think we're being surrounded by tanks!' 'Nonsense, my dear,' he replied, 'they're garbage trucks.' But the generals had arrived, and a career of promise ended.[2]

General Velasco, the army C.-in-C., a fifty-nine-year-old of lower middle-class origin who had risen from the ranks, declared his immediate motive for intervention was to save the country from 'over-permissive encroachments of foreign investments upon Peru's economic resources'. He cancelled Belaúnde's agreements nationalizing the U.S. International Petroleum Company forthwith, and expropriated the oilfields instead; thereby settling at one blow an issue bedevilling Peruvian politics over the past half-century. The junta then went on to seize the agricultural land belonging to another U.S. company, Cerro de Pasco, parcelling it out to *indígena* groups, and extending fishing rights to the two-hundred-mile coastal limit, much to the annoyance of *Yanqui*

---

[1] Led by General Velasco, their chief-of-staff. It is worth noting, *en passant*, that Peru spends nearly a quarter of its national budget on the armed forces, more than double the proportion spent by Colombia.

[2] Belaúnde was subsequently accused of corruption, which seems unjust, in that he now has difficulty even in scraping together a livelihood by teaching city planning.

tunny-fishermen, several of whom were arrested and fined. Relations between the U.S. and Peru (which had already become cool following Belaúnde's nationalization of I.P.C. and U.S. aid cuts after Peru had incited displeasure by buying French and British military aircraft) fell to several degrees of frost, and there was nasty talk about invoking the Hickenlooper Amendment.[1] Peruvians, by and large, were delighted, and even some U.S. diplomats were privately admitting that the I.P.C. through its exploitativeness and general insensitivity to Peruvian feelings rather deserved what they had got.

A few months after the dust had settled an experienced Reuter's correspondent wrote with some cynicism:

North Americans hear tumbrils, young Peruvians hear the trumpet of revolt, but the present writer could hear only the tramp of marching feet – the same booted feet that have dominated Peruvian history since the establishment of the republic 150 years ago.

But the junta, so far, have proved him wrong by showing that they are not going to stop at being beastly to *gringos*, that they intend to strike once and for all at the oligarchs' traditional sources of power, that what they have in mind is nothing short of the most radical structural reform in Peru's history. For the first time they imposed effective penalties on tax evasion and, rather high-handedly, granted themselves powers to inspect bank deposits – thereby hitting at that South American plague, the flight of capital to numbered Swiss accounts. They enacted the most rigorous agrarian reform bill yet seen on the continent, and with it they nationalized water supplies – the lifeline of coastal agronomy. Because of their service in the interior, the Quechua-speaking army officers are more closely acquainted with the needs of the Indians, and it was declaredly in their interest that the land was to be reapportioned from its vested owners. They pegged the cost of living impressively during their first years in

[1] At the time of Velasco's takeover, U.S. investments in Peru totalled over $600 million, in book value; her share of Peruvian imports was 31 per cent, and of exports 35 per cent.

power; they struck at the inefficient plethora of foreign motor-car manufacturers, permitting only four out of thirteen to continue in business. They reopened relations with Eastern Europe and let it be known they would welcome investment from the Communist world.

General Pedro Richter Prada was President Velasco's chief of intelligence, and before we went to see him we were informed that, as a former member of COAPA, the junta's all-powerful executive inner circle, he was more closely involved in administrative workings of the government than his present post might imply. (This would seem to be substantiated by the fact that, several months later, he was given the key appointment of minister of the interior in place of the rather tactless General Artola.) General Richter is a vigorous figure in an army bush-shirt; the top of one finger is missing, and a silver bullet sits on his desk, but the significance of neither is vouchsafed to us. For a chief of intelligence, he speaks with remarkable openness on a whole range of subjects. He reveals that among other European countries he recently visited Poland and Czechoslovakia. He feels that in agriculture they were 'going backwards', and their model was certainly not for Peru. Communism, he considers, represented 'the negation of man', which is quite unacceptable in South America; certainly in Peru. It is in humanistic values that the present government is essentially concerned, he assures us. Is there any specific country on which President Velasco's would like to model itself? No, none; because Peru is unique. But one senses that a choice might lie somewhere between Yugoslavia and Gaullist France. 'Peru stands for *neither Communism nor Capitalism*,' he says, resorting to the favourite slogan of the junta.

Lighting up a large capitalistic cigar, Bill questions the general about the future of U.S. investments in Peru; getting the reply that the 'cold, calculating capitalists of the U.S.A.' cannot any longer expect to derive the same interest on their money as in the past. Instead, they must consider more universal motives for investment in South America, on account of the 'enormous danger' to the U.S. of ferment and agitation there. But he believes that U.S. private capital will re-enter Peru, under the junta's new set of rules for investment (as per the Andean Pact). Explaining these, the general picks up a box of matches: 'Now, suppose you start a match factory with $2 million of capital. You can take out $4 million of profits, and then you have to sell 51 per cent of your shares to Peruvians; from then on, for ever more, you can continue to take out 49 per cent of the profits.' Slamming down the matches, he 'looked up as pleased as Plato might have been on finishing the last sentence of *The Republic*', as Bill commented later, adding with heavy scepticism: 'And meanwhile there'll be a shortage of matches in Peru!'

We turn to internal security. The guerrillas are well under control, says General Richter, and to some extent he echoes the reasoning of Valencia Tovar in Colombia. It is true that, as in Colombia, the official Communist Party (P.C.P.) seems to be imposing restraint on guerrilla activities. But the guerrilla groups have in the past made serious tactical errors by attempting to set up 'free territories', which could be pinned down and smashed by the Army. They had never gained much support from the politically unconscious Indian peasants, and now – claims the general – by its 'structural reforms' the government has effectively eliminated what support there had been; a little as Valencia Tovar had hoped might be the result in his novel, *Uisheda*. So confident indeed was the junta that it had just released and amnestied the Trotskyist guerrilla chieftain, Hugo Blanco, who had been serving a twenty-year prison sentence.[1] There were in fact few political prisoners of any hue still held in the grim Fronton penitentiary.

---

[1] Significantly enough, while playing Robin Hood to the under-privileged peasants in the Machu Picchu area, Hugo Blanco made the mistake of killing a policeman and from then on he became a fugitive, with the peasants repeatedly turning informer on him and his men. It is of interest to note that Blanco was the son of a lawyer; de la Puente, whom Richard Gott rates 'the most important guerrilla leader produced by Peru, and he ranks with Che Guevara and Camilo Torres as among the most impressive intellectuals of the Latin American revolution', was the son of a well-to-do Catholic landowner; while a third guerrilla leader, twenty-one-year-old Javier Heraud (betrayed and killed in 1963) was a prize-winning poet and 'typical product of the Peruvian upper classes'. All this is very much in keeping with the generally bourgeois background of today's guerrilla leaders of Latin America.

Not everybody we spoke to, however, entirely agreed with General Richter about the junta's success in 'containing' the extreme Left. Several seemingly well-informed Western observers expressed serious concern at the less tangible advances being made by the orthodox Communists, within a kind of benevolent semi-truce granted by the junta. Since its advent, the P.C.P. has been perhaps even more meticulous in its moderation than its comrades in Colombia. Consequently the junta has devoted its energy to persecuting that traditional Peruvian whipping-boy, APRA. Although the P.C.P. is officially outlawed, paradoxically it is permitted to operate quite openly and maintains a vigorous headquarters, plus its own newspaper, in Lima. Since the autumn of 1969, under the averted gaze of the regime, it has achieved almost total penetration of the Peruvian mining unions. It had also assumed control over the Bankworkers' Union, previously held by APRA, and when – in June 1970 – armed Marxists came to occupy the union headquarters, there was no intervention by the government. In the universities, although (as elsewhere in Latin America) the divers factions are disunited, most student federations have come to be controlled by the P.C.P., the pro-Castro MIR or the Maoist *Vanguardia Revolucionaria*. A university reform enacted by the junta in 1968 limited harassment of the state universities by these leftist students; but in the long run it will prove to have forced some of the previously non-committed students into alignment with the Left. Since the resumption of relations with Eastern Europe, there has been the usual surge of Soviet cultural and propaganda activities; including the Moiseyev Ballet, the Moscow State Symphony, and the Moscow Circus which occupied the Lima *Plaza de Toros* for an entire month. The Novosti Press Agency has vastly expanded its propaganda output, and it can be presumed that more clandestine forms are receiving a similar boost in funds from the U.S.S.R.

Loans and investments and promises of such have been pouring into Peru from the Communist world. But there may be disappointments when it comes actually to delivering the goods. According to one Lima government official, during the catastrophic earthquakes of 1970 a Soviet promise to dispatch

83

immediately sixty-five supply planes at ten-minute intervals collapsed when the twenty-second plane had straggled in after weeks of delays and breakdowns. Meanwhile, once the first rude shocks have passed, economic relations between Peru and the U.S. seem to be improving. A deal acceptable to both sides was worked out over the nationalization of the I.T.T. holdings, and some U.S. mining concerns have already shown enough restored confidence to begin reinvesting in Peruvian development schemes – under General Richter's 'rules'. While threatened British car manufacturers were transplanting installations to Chile – out of the frying-pan into the fire, as it soon turned out – Ford took a relaxed view and simply 'mothballed' their entire plant; reckoning that they could afford to wait until the Peruvian climate improved. There is no doubt that the junta has been shaken by the accelerating Marxist tempo of their neighbour under Allende, and their apprehension seems to be edging them slightly back to the Right, towards the lee of the rejected *Yanquis*; at the same time, the U.S., desperate for any friends in Latin America, may well come to find there are less attractive bedfellows than the Peruvian generals.

But who, in Peru, supports the junta; to what extent is it succeeding or failing in its ambitious plans to reconstruct Peru; and will it ever give way to return of civil, democratic government?

On my second visit to Peru, returning from Chile, I was taken out to have lunch with a middle-class family (let us call them Fernandez) at their weekend house on the coast near Lima. Father Fernandez was a civil engineer, working for the government, and – perhaps at least partly motivated by personal frustration at his lack of advancement under the oligarchs – had welcomed the advent of the generals. His daughter, very pretty and slender with an Inca nose, worked as a secretary. The house was filled with a throng of people, at least forty, and all related – teenagers, plump matrons, and tiny infants. A tape-recorder was going full blast; the noise was appalling. At a signal the family descended on tables laden with exotic dishes of *cau-cau* and *ceviche* (uncooked fish) with the rapacity of starving seagulls. The guests were left to fend (badly) for themselves. I could not remember where else I had ever seen quite such a display of unbridled greed. Wandering away down to the beach, to watch the cormorants and dolphins playing in huge waves close to the beach, I wondered to myself whether the poor hungry *indígenas* of Cuzco would, in the long run, be better off under the neglectful oligarchs or the greedy Fernandezes of this world. Back at the beach-house, sated teenagers were already jumping, in an amazing digestive feat, to the blaring tape-recorder – so conversation was difficult. I gathered however that Señor Fernandez was now somewhat disenchanted with the regime. He wanted to sell his seaside house, but could not – because there were no buyers, on account of the uncertainty of life in Peru. His job involved assessing land and property values for the government. As a result of some intra-ministerial jealousy he had been wrongfully dismissed, and only just reinstated after a year's unemployment. But perhaps his principal stigma against the rule of the generals was the hamstringing bureaucracy which had led to increasing slowness in getting their intentions carried out.

The two most far-reaching domestic measures taken by the junta have been the land reform bill and the scheme to give Peruvian workers a participation in industry. Belaúnde's land reform of 1964 excluded the rich coastal sugar estates; partly because they were so efficient, but also because their owners were so influential. No one now escapes from the junta's reform, which leaves a working farm-owner with a basic area of only 380 acres, or five hundred if he can prove he farms efficiently and will pass on 10 per cent of his profits to his employees. Compensation for land expropriated is part in cash, part in long-term government bonds. Radical as it is, the junta's land reform cannot be compared with the socialist confiscations practised in Cuba and Eastern Europe, or what may prove to be the ultimate aim of Allende in Chile. The basic area permitted to private owners is large enough for the continued running of coastal cotton plantations on a profitable basis, and the government has avoided the fundamental error of splitting up efficient units; instead, they are maintained intact as co-operatives on a profit-sharing basis. In less than two years up to the spring of 1971, already nearly nine million acres of land has been 'reformed'. But in 1971 two clouds appeared on the horizon. First the government, by stepping in to cancel an arrangement already sanctioned, renegued on a 'private parcellation' scheme whereby owners could carry out their own land partitions, thus causing a collapse in confidence among collaboration-minded *patrones*. Secondly – and more serious – there was an increasing spate of slowdowns in the reform machinery because of the shortage of technical staff – the unseen canker gnawing at the heart of most of the junta's projects.

Under the General Law of Industries of July 1970, the junta requires all large domestic and foreign companies to hand over 10 per cent of the gross profits each year to the employees, and to earmark a further 15 per cent for investment, or for stock to be shared out among the employees. It is a scheme certainly more reminiscent of early measures taken by Dr Adenauer's Germany than by a Marxist regime, but there are doubts as to whether – in the long term – Peruvian workers will be satisfied with what it really gives them. Partly because of the success of President Velasco's austerity programme – the meatless days, the stern restrictions on imports and currency exchange – but also supported by the prevailing good prices for fishmeal and metals, Peruvian trade figures have boomed since the junta took over. On the other side of the balance sheet, as Velasco himself admitted while I was in Peru, fresh foreign investment essential to his ambitious $3,000 million development programme has not come in as fast as hoped. There have been signs of serious stagnation in the economy's growth prospects – to a large extent, again, attributable to the excessive, centralized bureaucracy of the regime and the creeping paralysis this induces. One disquieting sign has been the rapid rise in the number of Peruvians trying to leave the country; according to Ambassador Belcher there had been, over the previous year, an 80 per cent increase in the application for U.S. visas – and not only from members of the oligarchy but from the professional middle classes as well. Perhaps even more ominous have been recent incidents when slum-dwellers seized private land in their impatience at the junta's resettlement programme. At El Salvador, ten miles from the centre of Lima, the police fought for two days in May 1971 to dislodge some fifteen thousand squatters. Inevitably there were shootings, and a young unemployed labourer was killed. The Suffragan Bishop of Lima, Mgr Bambarén, preached a powerful sermon on behalf of the squatters, was arrested by Artola, General Richter's predecessor at the ministry of the interior, but almost immediately released. The squatting continued. About the same time, Velasco admitted that it might take thirty years to complete his reforms; but will the firebrands of the Left and Peru's vast and ever-growing mass of have-nots give him that amount of time?

Velasco's prediction undoubtedly has the ring of a life-sentence, but there are two opposing views about the junta's intentions for its own future. Pointing to the precedent of General Odría, foreign observers reckon that one day the generals will file off back to their regiments, installing a 'reliable' civil regime behind them; especially if they find the intricacies of modern statecraft increasingly beyond the ken of military lore. But most Peruvians, and of course particularly the oppressed oligarchs, feel that the generals will not go quietly. A clue to their intentions often produced is the press law promulgated by the junta, which – at face value – has the appearance of being one of the most oppressive in South America. So far two leading Lima newspapers, owned by Ulloa, the junta's most hated enemy among the oligarchs (now in exile in Madrid) have been expropriated, and are now run by and for the regime. Its next target was Enrique Zileri Gibson, an outspoken critic of the regime in his magazine *Caretas*, as well as one of South America's liveliest journalists. *Caretas* was banned temporarily after the 1968 *coup d'état*, and just before I reached Lima it had been fined $20,000, crippling for its slender resources, on charges of obscenity and 'publishing matter offensive to the revolutionary government'. The first charge related to a caricature of a nude Nixon sporting a G.O.P. elephant's head in lieu of a phallus; the second, *inter alia*, to an article alleging that the government was opening the mails, using a special device imported from Eastern Europe to do the job inconspicuously. But when I met Enrique Zileri at a Lima reception – effervescent, uninhibited and unashamed – he

87

seemed remarkably unworried; and in fact an appeal later reduced the fine to $3,500. It seems unlikely that the junta will attempt to drive Zileri out of business; comment in the other Peruvian newspapers remains surprisingly unrestrained and a further point of interest is that Z, the film so damning of the Greek colonels, was passed by the generals of Peru – although it was banned by the then military leader of neighbouring Bolivia, left-wing General Torres. The impression one has is that the bark of the Peru Junta towards the press may be worse than its bite – while, as will be seen later, possibly the reverse could be said of Allende's Chile.

My own instinct about the Peruvian generals is that they will emulate Greece's enigmatic Papadopoulos and be with us for quite a time yet. For better or for worse. And then what? A man being tipped strongly in 1971 as a possible successor to the generals was Luís Bedoya Reyes, a lawyer in his mid-fifties, and a former mayor of Lima, but not tainted with having been one of the discredited *ancien régime*. He had been brought into close contact with General Velasco when, following a tragic aircrash at Cuzco in which his sixteen-year-old daughter was killed, Velasco had attended the funeral. With Bedoya we began by talking about Allende. He blamed the left wing of the Chilean Christian Democrats for destroying the right-of-centre, and thus bolstering the strength of the Marxist parties. If Allende does badly, he foresaw that Chile would regain her political stability; but if he does well, then the regime would stay forever and transmit itself to other countries. 'Then you [turning to Bill] might just as well give up.' But he thought the only course the U.S. could adopt was *manos afuera* (hands-off), because the more outside interference the more firmly Allende would be consolidated. Peru he thought would never return – any more than Argentina – to the democratic system existing before the military junta, 'because there were so many errors'. Yet he feared the 'Peruvian experiment' might prove much more injurious to democracy than Allende. Why? Well, because, in contrast to General Odría, the takeover by the junta had been so complete as to weaken or destroy all the other traditional pillars of Peruvian society – the oligarchy, the Church, the political parties, even APRA – leaving only the army: 'And when that is discredited, what will be left?' Peruvian 'militarism' was paralysing the will of the people, and there were even military circles who felt strongly that the generals should 'disengage' before failure, so that the army could at least preserve itself as a respectable force. 'Otherwise, if the junta fails to satisfy popular demands, we shall have anarchy like Bolivia; and then beyond that there remains only Marxism.' This erosion of the conventional sources of strength in the country was, he was convinced, a terrible danger.

5

The England of South America

Another flight; this time the last leg to Chile. More desert, followed by white-capped Andes, then we sweep down over Lake Titicaca to put in at La Paz. The flat grey altiplano of Bolivia, with meandering rivers that seem to lead nowhere; miserable farms and bleak tufts of grass; not a single tree. Suddenly, as we are about to land, a blinding rainstorm reduces visibility to a matter of inches. The first sight of La Paz: a starved black dog limping along the runway and the unremoved remains of a previous aircrash. To acclimatize passengers to the thirteen thousand feet of La Paz airport, the highest in the world, the plane carries out strange manoeuvres with its pressurization system. Instead of pumping air into the cabin, the normal procedure, they let it out as from a balloon, with a nearly audible hiss. Almost at once one feels strange pains in the lungs, pressure behind the eyeballs. There is another painfully long take-off, worse than Cuzco, but this time fortunately the plane is empty. Only a handful of passengers seem to be making for Chile. We fly on into the desiccated wastes of the Atacama, where the nitrates and copper wealth, the past and present *raison d'être* of Chile, lie. Vermilion peaks engulfed in the blue-purple haze of evening, an occasional crown of snow – and beyond, Argentina. A glimpse to port of the supreme ragged tooth of Aconcagua; a sudden burst of prosperous farmland, and then we are down at Santiago.

The customs officers – our first contact with Dr Allende's Chile – are solemn, slow-moving women. There is something about such female officials that inevitably makes one think of an East European People's Republic. They comb through our luggage with the studied meticulousness of a British speedcop producing his breathalyser. Entering Santiago at night, it seems an austere grey city, empty except for immense slogans in praise of Allende painted on every conceivable surface. (A Communist body, the Ramona Parra Brigade – named after a girl martyr of the time of the Ibañez dictatorship – apparently dedicates itself exclusively to this agreeable task of orthography.) It reminds me of Belgrade, twenty years ago. Then, the next morning, as the seductive Chilean summer sun appears bringing with it throbbing traffic jams and tremendous bourgeois bustle, it is no longer Belgrade but Milan (too bustling to be Naples) or San Francisco.

Sunday morning: a large hired car with a Japanese-Chilean driver arrives to take us down to the coast to see the great poet, Pablo Neruda.[1] With us comes Selden Rodman, friend and American translator of Neruda, and a wonderful Chilean friend of his, Nena Ossa. Nena, divorced with two sons at college in the U.S., is one of Chile's leading woman journalists, writing for a lively conservative weekly called PEC. At the recent elections she voted for Alessandri's National Party; but, like millions of other Chileans, she went to bed one night living in a Christian Democracy – the most liberal and well-ordered in South America – and woke up the next morning in a Marxist state. Her whole world has gone, or is going, to pieces, and she remains of course an outspoken opponent of Allende and his policies. Yet – and despite her immersion in it, and particularly the shock of the recentness of it all – she manages to maintain a remarkable degree of detachment from the Chilean scene. We soon discover a superlative sense of humour, and with a laugh that would dislodge any bird off any tree she recounts all the current jokes about what – to her and her world – is unmitigated tragedy. There are, for instance, now only two classes of Chileans: *los tuvos, y los tienes*.[2] 'I was certainly never a *tiene*,' says Nena gaily; 'but there is no doubt that under

[1] Since then he has deservedly been awarded the Nobel Prize. The only other South American writer to be so honoured (1945) was also a Chilean; the poetess Gabriella Mistral.

[2] From the verb *tener* – to have; meaning, literally, 'the he-hads and the he-hases'.

Allende I am going to be *tuvo* in no time at all.' She warns us that when we get to Isla Negra she will have to 'hide on the floor of the car'; because of a critical article she had recently written about Neruda, coupled with publication of an old poem which PEC had dug up. Then Neruda had been scoring off an old rival in love who, to his disgust, had accepted an ambassadorship:

> If you are born a fool in Rumania
> you follow a fool's career.
> If you are a fool in Avignon
> you are known for what you are
> by the old stones of France
> by the schools and by the disrespectful kids on the farms.
> But if you are born a fool in Chile
> soon they will make you an ambassador.[1]

Nena republished the verses because Pablo Neruda had just been nominated Allende's ambassador to Paris. He, sharing the vanity of a Picasso (whom he resembles in more than one way), was in no way amused.

By the time we get back to Santiago late that night, Bill and I have both lost our hearts to Nena and her joyous laugh.

The road to the coast passes through country that is remarkably like Spain. First, flat Castilian plains, cattle grazing in hungry stubble fields turned to gold and umber by the Chilean summer; then hills of wild rocks and burnt scrub like the Guadarrama; finally, as we approach the coast, it is the green and sienna richness of Andalusia round Arcos-de-la-Frontera. I am transported totally from the other-world bizarreness of Colombia and Peru, back to Europe; a sensation that was to recur over and over again in Chile. With what ecstasy of recognition Pedro de Valdivia and his small band must have first viewed Chile, so incredibly far from Spain, yet so close.

Pablo Neruda's house at Isla Negra, seventy-five miles south of Valparaiso, sits on a rocky promontory battered by the Pacific. The violent sea and the elements are all round him – and his poetry:

[1] From *Canto General* (1950).

92

Antigua noche y sal desordenada
golpean las paredes de mi casa:
sola es la sombra, el cielo
es ahora un latido del océano
y cielo y sombra estallan . . .[1]

La ola viene del fondo, con raices
hijas del firmamento sumergido.
Su elástica invasión fué levantada
por la potencia pura del Océano . . .[2]

Even when he writes of age wrinkling his forehead, it is in terms of 'waves battering, tripping themselves to death.'[3]

Leaving Nena curled up in her hiding-place, we announce ourselves. Neruda has no telephone, therefore had not been warned of our visit, and we have obviously not chosen a good moment. The great poet is affable enough, but his afternoon is filled up with official appointments, briefings for his new post. Selden is not to be put off lightly: 'Don't worry, we'll wait, Pablo.' 'No, it's hopeless today; could you not come back tomorrow?' 'Impossible, I'm flying to Switzerland.' Bill and I begin to feel embarrassed, but Selden persists: 'Well, when can I at least see Matilde?' 'I'm afraid she's in the bath.'

Ultimately, we are taken on a tour of the property by a Uruguayan architect friend of Neruda's. Neruda spent his early years in Temuco, in the south of Chile, where his father was a railway-worker. His sympathies have been consistently with the Left, and the Spanish Civil War led him – like Picasso – firmly towards the Communist Party, and he was in fact its preliminary candidate for the 1970

[1] From 'La Noche en Isla Negra.'
>The ancient night and the unruly salt
>beat at the walls of my house;
>lonely is the shadow, the sky
>by now is a beat of the ocean,
>and sky and shadow explode . . .

[2] From 'La Ola'.
>The wave comes up from the bottom, with roots
>that are daughters of the submerged firmament.
>Its elastic invasion was mounted
>by the pure potency of the Ocean . . .

[3] From 'Alianza' (Sonata) (*Residencia en la Tierra I*).

elections. Though always a humanist in his poetry, he only seldom beats the bass drum, and his physical surroundings contain little to indicate the dedicated Marxist–Leninist. They are, in fact, positively bourgeois. Outside, in the garden, sits an old English steam-engine and various ships' bells suspended from trees and a tripod scaffolding. Inside, the bookshelves are filled with every work by James Hadley Chase – apparently Neruda's favourite author – and the rest of the house is crammed with beachcombers' bric-à-brac, mixed together with a few good things; but all collected with love. There are ships' figureheads, bottles containing crucifixes and other oddities, bottles in the shape of violins, politicians and Eiffel Towers, Indian masks and a bidet painted with roses. The bare joists are inscribed with lines from Neruda's favourite poets (other than himself). Some seem rather mundane. And there is a bar clad with bottle-ends and split bamboo. In sum, if one had been told Isla Negra was the dream-child of a stockbroker from Haywards Heath or Yonkers, who had made good and settled in Nassau – well, one would not have been surprised. Neruda and his third wife, Matilde, an elegant red-head with the remnants of a once considerable and sensuous beauty, join us for a minute from time to time. He has a prosperous paunch, the smooth baldness of a boiled egg, and eyes that tell of a life of indulgence. In our brief snatches of conversation he neither says nor does anything to dispel the stockbroker image. Later, Rodman relates how Ilya Ehrenburg once scolded Neruda for his bourgeois greed when, at the Dôme in Montparnasse, he capped a lucullan lunch by grabbing a vast plate of oysters from a passing waiter. *'Mais Pablo, tu es barbare!'* remonstrated the shocked Russian; to which Neruda retorted amiably, 'Ehrenburg, *you* are a victim of Western corruption.' In Chile, Neruda has a reputation too (again, not unlike Picasso) of being greatly attached to material wealth. It is all a little difficult to equate with rigid, orthodox Marxism[1] – plus the lyricism of an angel.

[1] In line with the outstandingly orthodox Chilean Communist Party, Neruda alienated a part of the idealistic youth among his admirers when, in 1968, he endorsed the Soviet rape of Czechoslovakia.

The net impact is, I must admit, disconcerting. But then who would expect the ethereal spring-song of the thrush to burst from such a drab-coloured, shapeless bird?

As Selden Rodman says, Spanish-speaking South America has three things in common: 'a nostalgia for Iberia, a distrust of the United States government, and the poetry of Pablo Neruda'. He adds that the special genius of Neruda is his 'capacity to project his own personality, unflaggingly over the years, as a particular person who feels, sees, eats, drinks, suffers, enjoys, loves, dreams, laughs, dawdles, gossips . . .' Neruda is, undeniably, a magician; often his magic is untranslatable, but you do not have to know a word of Spanish to be bewitched by the sheer music of such lines as:

> *Galopa la noche en su yegua sombría*
> *desparramando espigas azules sobre el campo.*[1]

or:

> *Mientras el viento triste galopa matando mariposas*[2]

The sensuousness of his love poems is immensely potent; I can think of no poem in any language where the anatomy of a lost love, so simply stated, comes across with such burning sadness as in *Tonight I Can Write*:

Tonight I can write the saddest lines
. . .
I no longer love her, that's certain, but maybe I love her.
Love is so short, forgetting is so long?[3]

And can there be any more loving ode to a cherished wife than his to Matilde?

[1] From 'Inclinado en les Tardes' (from his earliest *Veinte Poemas de Amor*, 1924; written when he was twenty, they sold a million copies across the world).
[2] From 'Juegas Todos los Días'(*Veinte Poemas*).
[3] (*Veinte Poemas*). The Spanish reads:
  Puedo escribir los versos más tristes esta noche
  . . .
  Ya no la quiero, es cierto, pero tal vez la quiero.
  Es tan corto el amor, y es tan largo el olvido.

You are the one most beautiful,
the wind has most tattooed
like a little southern tree,
like a hazel tree in August,
you are as succulent for me
as a baker's full of bread,
your heart is made of earth
but your hands are celestial.
. . .
I owe you autumn by the sea
with the dankness of roots
and the mist like a grape
and the elegant country sun:
I owe you this silent valley
in which sorrows are lost
and only joy's corollas
rise to the forehead.
I owe you everything . . .[1]

The other thing about Neruda is his deep, fervid and umbilical attachment to the soil of Chile – a very Chilean characteristic, as I was to discover. He has been called the Whitman of South America. But perhaps the best epitaph to the complexities of Neruda is to be found in the simple line:

And I sing because I sing because I sing.

Around Pablo Neruda in his Isla Negra has formed the nucleus of a colony of Marxist intellectuals. After redeeming Nena from her hiding-place, we lunch off delectable *corvina* (a particularly succulent kind of Pacific sea-bass) in an open-air *taberna* with Nicanor Parra, in the galaxy of Chilean poets perhaps second only to Neruda. Parra was also a party member, who revolted after Czechoslovakia, but he remains a loyal supporter of Allende's coalition. Afterwards, overcome by Chilean intellectualism, wine and midsummer, I flop in the sand and there comes seeping over me an irrational, perhaps premature, sense of warmth towards Neruda's and

[1] From *Estravagario*, 1958.

Nena's Chile – which means such radically opposed things to each. Bill goes off to pursue an intense dialogue with Miguel Rojas Mix, a university professor and expert on German medieval art. He too is a dedicated Marxist, glowing with enthusiasm about the intentions of the new Allende government, and Bill returns palpably impressed: 'That's the most attractive and honest Marxist I have ever met. His purity is child-like. He *truly* disbelieves, for instance, that the government is putting pressure on *El Mercurio* for ideological reasons.'

We move on to Valparaiso, Chile's great seaport. Alternately known as 'Pearl of the Pacific', or a 'filthy rose' (by Neruda), it is a fascinating hotchpotch of architecture and character, a Topsy-like port that has just grown. The comfortable houses of sea-dogs and shipowners, with a strong English influence like everything else to do with maritime Chile, rub shoulders with dilapidated shacks that seem about to collapse down the steep cliffs where they have sunk their insubstantial roots (as in fact, many subsequently did in the catastrophic earthquake of 1971). Much of even the semi-prosperous houses is constructed of wooden clap-boarding that looks as if it has not seen a coat of paint for a generation. There is something about Valparaiso that is unmistakably of the Pacific; perhaps it is those once-opulent decaying timber buildings that remind me of the Alaskan port of Skagway, that ghost of gold-rush days; or the precipitate upper streets that give startling marine panoramas in every direction, so like San Francisco. But there is none of the rooted sadness of Skagway; in fact Valparaiso this summer exudes a positively festive air. Gay bunting, portraits of Allende, the ubiquitous slogans in praise of the *Unidad Popular*, festoon the main square around the Intendencia. It is here, to this cheerful, pseudo-rococo little city hall, that the Chilean government moves for the summer season; here where Dr Allende is framing his first momentous bills for the new Socialist Chile. A statue of Arturo Prat, Chile's great martyr-hero in the triumphant War of the Pacific against Peru, gazes thoughtfully into the windows of the Intendencia; possibly the only naval hero ever to have his back turned firmly on the sea. In the port are several venerable warships of the Chilean navy, passed

97

on from either Britain or the U.S.A. (Nena murmurs, with a shudder: 'I suppose soon there will be Russian ships here!') On the quay, a typical Sunday scene: strolling groups of ratings and officers off the ships, in extraordinarily British uniforms; fat, jolly ladies selling gas-filled balloons and candy-floss. Tinted gold by the wonderful light of late afternoon that seems to belong exclusively to the Chilean summer, it is a joyful scene. But these plentiful crowds do not emit quite that astonishing intensity of Latin noise you would hear in similar circumstances in Spain, that of a million starlings. Chileans seem to take their pleasures more restrainedly.

A brass band, followed by a small procession, passes through the streets. It is nothing to do with Allende; just the Methodists on parade, a glimpse of the remarkable mixture of sects and strains that make up this most polymorphous of Latin American countries. This is also a reminder that we have to find a Catholic mass for Bill. But, although it is six o'clock and a proper time, round and round the meandering streets we whirl, in vain. Church after church is shut; some looking as if they have been closed since the expulsion of the Jesuits. Only the cathedral is open and celebrating mass;[1] an instructive first indication that in Chile the Church no longer exerts the influence that it does in either Peru or Colombia.

After mass, we drive to Viña del Mar, the seaside resort just a few miles out of Valparaiso, to dine with an architect friend of Nena's. We talk about our visit to Neruda, and he plays us a record of Neruda himself reciting 'Machu Picchu', with a deep resonance and the almost sacerdotal solemnity of a priest incanting mass. The pot-belly, the aroma of bourgeois well-being, vanish. Before returning to Santiago we make a slow circumnavigation of the Summer Residence at Viña, where Allende is at this very moment living. Since the assassination of General Schneider a few weeks earlier, *el Presidente* has surrounded himself with a strong bodyguard – largely composed of 'black berets', youths from the extreme

---

[1] The cathedral, too, suffered serious damage during the 1971 earthquakes.

left MIR. But if we expected to see tanks and machine-guns poking out of windows, we are disappointed. There is not so much as a sentry on the gate, the *miristas* are well out of sight, and all is perfect peace.

Chileans are themselves rather fond of stressing the paradox that they are economically underdeveloped, but politically overdeveloped. The validity of this is something one can appreciate after one day in Chile, and it stems from a mixture of racial, geographical and historical factors. As a very Germanic visitor once remarked, 'Here . . . in the extreme south . . . the inhabitants have become Nordic again!' It is true; because although the 2,650-mile-long tapeworm of Chile embraces the equivalent of every climate from the Sahara to Lapland, it is essentially a temperate country. People can think rationally, without the passions and distortions that over-exposure to the sun or altitude can induce, as in Colombia, or Peru, or Bolivia. And the people themselves are different. There was little intercourse between the Spanish invaders of Pedro de Valdivia and the warlike, unyielding Araucanians; so there has been little *mestizo* blood, with all its schizoid drives, divided allegiances and passions, to mould the political character of Chile; and, although Drake and wicked Sir John Hawkins both 'called in' on Valparaiso, virtually no Negro slaves were imported into Chile (and those that were the winter climate killed off). Also the wild, harsh and sensuous Spanish stock, with its incapacity for moderation or compromise, has been greatly diluted over the years with the various influxes of immigrants from different parts of the old world. Tough and independent-minded Basques formed a major and vital part of the Iberian content; then came educated Germans, getting out from under Bismarck's iron boot, to the south of Chile; Yugoslavs, fleeing Franz-Josef, still further south; Welsh sheepmen fleeing from Wales, down in the wastes of Patagonia and Tierra del Fuego; and Irish, Englishmen and Frenchmen everywhere else. Even the names of the founders of the Christian Democrat Party – Eduardo Frei Montalva, Bernardo Leighton, Manuel Garreton Walker – read like an ethnographic chart of Chile; and, of course, there is that great founder figure, with the name that provokes ignorant *gringo* mirth –

Bernardo O'Higgins. It is perhaps just this subtle mixture of blood that explains why the Chileans are so complex, interesting and civilized – and have such appealing women.

From the earliest days, when the far-reaching reconnaissances sent out by Pizarro found none of the Eldorado gold in Chile, it remained an underprivileged backwater of empire, a world away from Spain, administered by a captain-general, who in turn took his orders from viceregal Lima. Neglected, Chile existed chiefly off the land of its fertile central valley. When it came, the spirit of revolt found the land – metaphorically – even more fertile. The Chileans, between 1810 and 1814, liberated themselves; then royalist forces intervened, crushing their new-born independence. In 1817, San Martín, the Argentinian liberator-hero, made his remarkable, Carthaginian march across the Andes (one of the few times in history Chileans have felt gratitude towards an Argentinian). Simultaneously, at sea, that eccentric freebooting British naval genius, Lord Cochrane, whose statue graces many a Chilean plaza, pulled off feats that rank high in the history of combined ops. The rest was left to Bernardo O'Higgins, who then established the Republic, was unable to achieve a balance between conservatives and liberals, and finally – like Bolívar and every other South American *libertador* – was sacked for his pains. There was a brief interregnum of chaos (as in everything Chilean, mild by comparison with chaos elsewhere in Latin America), followed by an 'autocratic republic', followed by a Liberal Republic. For sixty years Chile went about governing herself sensibly and peacefully. A constitution created in 1833 endured until 1925; a longevity which, declares Régis Debray, makes 'countries like France look like banana republics in comparison'. The rival liberals and conservatives came to terms with each other, without recourse to such *violencias* as ravaged Colombia. The rapid consolidation of independence under Portales, coupled with Chile's isolation, came to lend her a greater homogeneity than most of her neighbours. Then, between 1879 and 1883, Chile won a great war against Bolivia and Peru combined. Out of the War of the Pacific she suddenly emerged from her backwater as a major South American power, annexing a large strip of northern desert, which was to become the future source of most of her riches, and problems (and incidentally depriving poor Bolivia of her access to the sea).

During the 1830s a series of mineral strikes, silver and coal, that had eluded the conquistadors, began to alter the agricultural complexion of Chile. In the last decades of the century, discovery and exploitation of vast nitrate deposits, the richest in the world, lying in the surface of the annexed northern territories, suddenly gave Chile an immense boom. But it was a one-crop prosperity. By 1864 some 70 per cent of Chilean exports (by value) were minerals; by 1881 the figure had risen to over 78 per cent. Germany was one of her best customers. Then came the First World War, and blockade; necessity led a German scientist to invent a process for making nitrates literally out of thin air. Almost overnight Chile's one-crop riches vanished. Next came fabulous copper finds; but, again, Chile was to suffer the experience of being painfully at the mercy of the whims of international demand, and saw the cream of her products skimmed off by foreign entrepreneurs – notably *Yanqui*.

The internal stresses provoked by her triumph in the War of the Pacific led to Chile's one and only civil war, in 1891. An authoritarian centralist-minded president, Balmaceda, tried to curb the powers of Congress so as to be able to push through certain radical and progressive measures. Paradoxically enough, one of Balmaceda's principal objectives tallied exactly with that of Allende eighty years later: the prevention of foreign interests possessing control over Chile's mineral resources. Led by the navy, the armed forces rose and ousted Balmaceda. Again, by Latin American standards, it was a very tame civil war indeed; and Balmaceda had the considerateness to end it by discreetly shooting himself. Congress emerged supreme, democracy flourished, but the lack of strong executive powers led to inefficient and torpid administration. It was characterized by one president (Ramón Barros Luco, 1910–15) when he identified 'two kinds of problems: those which have no solution and those which solve themselves'. Hand in hand with the escalation of 'unsolved problems', labour unrest mounted. Then in 1920 a strong man appeared on the scene, Arturo Alessandri

Palma, grandson of an Italian immigrant, nicknamed the 'Lion of Tarapaca' (his desert constituency) and described by one U.S. ambassador, Claude G. Bowers, as 'the most consummate politician in South America in his heyday'. When Alessandri was thwarted by Congress over a rather modest reform programme, in 1925 he rewrote the constitution, which had been in force for nearly a century. By laying hands on the sacred Chilean constitution – which really is the national Penates, far more so than anywhere else in South America – Alessandri established a precedent which was to become very important when Allende came to power; as, too, were the various measures to strengthen the Executive incorporated under the 1925 constitution.

It separated Church and State and provided that the president should serve for six years and not be able to succeed himself. He appoints his own ministers, and also has the power directly to appoint the powerful *intendentes* who run each of Chile's twenty-five provinces, within the framework of a strongly centralized 'unitary government'. The president is commander-in-chief of the armed forces, and in a time of emergency he can obtain extraordinary powers to apply censorship, temporarily suspend Habeas Corpus rights, and take police action otherwise unconstitutional. If Congress should not be in session, the president can, by himself, declare a 'state of siege' to utilize these special powers until Congress can be convened. Of particular contemporary significance are the facts that: 1. There is no vice-president who automatically succeeds on the death of the president; 2. There is no vote of censure capable of bringing down a government, and a president can only be removed by an impeachment with a two-thirds majority of Congress; and 3. The president cannot call an election, and the constitution makes it almost impossible for him to resign – or run away, as did Quadros of Brazil. Therefore, there are virtually only two ways of changing a Chilean government in the midstream of its six years; by revolution, or by bumping off the president. Congress consists of a senate and a chamber of deputies, elected on a rota of eight and four years respectively. As in the United States, it is quite possible (indeed, normal, as in the experience of Allende in 1971) to have a Congress in opposition to the Executive. The Chilean judiciary is completely independent of both president and Congress, and has been widely respected for its integrity. There is also a unique institution, the *Contraloria*, a kind of supra-party guardian of government laws who supervises their legalities and sees that they are properly enforced. In sonorous terms the Alessandri constitution guarantees to all Chileans the:

protection of labour, industry, and the works of social welfare, especially as referring to sanitary dwellings and economic conditions of living, in a form to give each inhabitant a minimum of well-being adequate for the satisfaction of his personal necessities and those of his family.

Alas, in practice, this has proved to be so much lip-service; which is one good reason why Dr Allende is in La Moneda today. The 1925 constitution also offers a right much cherished by Chileans, and one that needs to be noted in passing:

Freedom to express without prior censorship opinions, orally, or in writing, through the medium of the press, radio, television or in any other form. . . .

Chile was the first (1811) nation of the western hemisphere to abolish slavery (for native-born Chileans) and the first to inaugurate a comprehensive system of social security.[1] The Chileans are justifiably proud of their social achievements and constitutional stability over the years; which, together with their reputation for non-violence, has often gained Chile the nickname of 'the England of South America'. (A rather less desirable common characteristic that might now be added is economic stagnation.)

During the 1929 slump, Chile, now so dependent on U.S. markets for sale of her raw materials, was disastrously struck; suffering more severely and for longer than perhaps any other Latin American country. In three years exports declined in value by over 80 per cent. A mild dictatorship established by General Ibañez was overthrown by the army

[1] Now one of the most extensive in the world, its inflationary cost is also one reason for Chile's current and recurrent economic problems.

in 1931, and after a period of confusion Alessandri was returned for a second term, until 1938. Alessandri brought back political stability, but once again essential economic reforms stagnated because of factional divisions within Congress. It was in those hard, depressed years of the thirties that many young Chileans turned towards Socialism and Communism, and from them stemmed the power, cohesion and organization of the Communist Party, the strongest on the continent, and one of the most rigidly orthodox in the world.

For a brief spell during the turbulent year of 1931, an army colonel called Marmaduque Grove – who was as colourful as his name – came to power at the head of a left-wing junta which ruled for a hundred days as the 'Socialist Republic of Chile'. Grove was then exiled to Easter Island, 2,400 miles away in the Pacific, where a boat called about every six months. He managed to escape, however, and be re-exiled, several times; then eventually helped found a Popular Front composed of the Radical, Socialist and Communist parties. In 1938 its candidate, Pedro Aguirre Cerda of the Radical Party, won the elections by a mere four thousand votes, thereby bringing to power the first Popular Front government in the New World. It lasted until 1942, and in fact provided one of the most energetic administrations of the century, stimulating industry and launching impressive programmes of house and school construction.

At about the same time, on the international scene Chile with its large German population was fiercely divided by pro-Axis sentiments. In 1938, a group of young 'Nazis' seized the social security building overlooking the Moneda in an abortive coup, and sixty-two of them were massacred by the *carabineros*. Chile was in fact the only South American nation never to declare war against the European Axis powers, and only did so against Japan in the spring of 1945.

From 1942 the Radicals, cut loose from the Popular Front, ruled for ten years; ten years of inefficiency, galloping inflation and vast expansion of the bureaucracy. Then the disgruntled electorate brought back Ibañez, the old dictator of 1927–31, with one of the biggest majorities in Chilean history. But Ibañez as a constitutional president seemed to have lost his steam; after a brief flirtation with Perónism he spent most of his time coping with endless cabinet crises. Once again, the economy stagnated and inflation soared unchecked; on a basis of 100 in 1940, it had reached 2,887 by 1955. At times it looked as if the army might intervene again, in exasperation, as was the established norm in most other South American countries; and indeed as it had done briefly and restrainedly between 1924 and 1932, the only time in the century it did so. But the army stayed its hand.

One now comes to the two elections that set the trend towards Allende's Marxist Chile; 1958 and 1964. Over the ten previous years the Communist Party had been banned (under what was known by them as the 'Accursed Law'), but the ban was lifted in 1958, and two new forces then appeared on the scene: a Communist-Socialist alliance called the *Frente de Acción Popular* (FRAP), headed now by Dr Salvador Allende, and the newly formed Christian Democrat Party (PDC) under Eduardo Frei. Both factions stood on platforms demanding basic reform, and the vast number of votes they jointly received was indicative of growing Chilean disenchantment with the old order, and of the general shift to the Left. As it was, Allende with 352,915 votes lost by only some 35,000 to Liberal Jorge Alessandri (387,297), son of the old 'lion'; while Frei collected 255,168 votes. Despite the leftward swing, Alessandri's victory through this division of the votes meant that Chile had its first declaredly right-wing president since 1938, and a businessman's government. With the oligarch's traditional technique of buying off the opposition, Alessandri offered reforms but without teeth; a weak agrarian reform bill was put through, but it resulted in the redistribution of only five big properties. No less than Ibañez, Alessandri proved himself incapable of coping with Chile's endemic plague, inflation. In 1964 alone the cost of living rose 61 per cent and the escudo was devalued several times; of 35 million acres of land suitable for cultivation, only 7.5 million were in use; one-third of all Chileans had no purchasing power at all and were all but unemployable. For all the stability and political sophistication of Chilean governments over the years, economically the already yawning gap between the *tienes* and the *no-tienes* gaped still wider.

The 1964 elections showed an even more marked decline of the rightist parties. Before the results were announced, airlines were heavily booked by panicky *tienes* preparing to take flight from a Chile gone Marxist under ·Allende. But they were a little previous; for, with a sweeping majority of 56 per cent, Eduardo Frei became the first Christian Democrat president in the Americas. Allende, this time a rather uninspiring candidate, lagged behind with 39 per cent, and a Radical, Julio Durán, got a bare 5 per cent. Over the preceding six years the electorate had expanded vastly from 1,750,000 to nearly three million, with many of the first-time voters representing the new rising middle class.[1] Some Chilean sociologists believe that it was the mass of this middle class, which after being frustrated in its yearnings to become identified with and absorbed by the oligarchy, threw its weight behind Frei's promises of social 'revolution in liberty' – with a Christian, as opposed to a Marxist, wrapping. Certainly either the parcel or the wrapping drew Chilean women of all classes, who first received the vote in 1949, and of whom 63 per cent voted for Frei as against 32 per cent for Allende.[2] In the U.S., Kennedy liberals were triumphant; here, at last, in Latin America was a government which looked like conforming to the *Alianza* principles.

Frei was born in 1911, son of a Swiss immigrant who worked as an accountant on the Chilean railways. Brought up in middle-class surroundings he became a lawyer, then journalist and finally a professor at the Catholic university. In 1952 he had been approached by Ibañez to form a government; then Ibañez withdrew the offer. But it was enough to establish Frei as a national figure. Five years later he was elected to the Senate, and in 1958 the Christian Democrats asked him to run for the presidency. An austere-living Catholic, Frei is a man of great energy who spends much of

[1] Literacy has always been one of the chief qualifications for enfranchisement in Chile.

[2] Possibly human sympathy played some role in these figures, in that just before the election Frei lost his much-loved sister, killed in a car accident when returning from a public meeting where she had spoken for him.

his free time immersed in serious reading. He is tall and spare, has a rugged face with a massive, beaky nose, that has a touch of de Gaulle in it. Standing squarely in the political centre of the Christian Democrat Party (which he himself created), he was a fervent admirer of Konrad Adenauer and – supposedly – his party received substantial funds for their electoral campaign from their opposite numbers in Western Germany. Frei's Christian Democrats had indeed a distinctly – and uniquely international flavour; they maintained close contacts with sister parties elsewhere in Latin America, and looked towards an economically integrated continent that might assume a third position between capitalism and Communism.

Despite his remarkable personal victory, Frei was hamstrung initially by a 'lame duck' Congress. In the chamber of deputies his party held only 23 out of 147 seats; then the congressional elections of 1965 brought him an absolute majority, something not achieved in Chile for over a century. But he could not gain control of the conservatively orientated Senate, a fact which was to plague his legislation throughout his term of office. Nevertheless, the first half of Frei's administration – aided by a benevolent Washington – was accompanied by notable economic success. In his first year of office, the deadly rate of inflation was cut from 38 per cent to 25 per cent, and the country's internal debt was reduced dramatically. By importing tax experts from the United States, tax evasion (which used to run at something like 50 per cent of all collections) was stringently reduced. Chileans were induced to work harder – by such devices as replacing the traditional three-hour lunch-cum-siesta with a 9 a.m. to 4.30 p.m. straight-through working day. Over the three-year period, 1964–7, Chile's G.N.P. rose by 19 per cent, compared with a target of 15–16 per cent, and copper production went up 14 per cent. In those years Chile was exporting about $450 million dollars worth of goods annually and importing about $600 million; the difference being made up by foreign loans, principally from the U.S.A. 'The problems of Latin America are not Fidel Castro', declared Frei. 'The real problems which must be dealt with are misery, ignorance, and poverty. Ignoring them is to invite

Communism to enter, whether from Cuba or elsewhere.' It was on these three targets that Frei concentrated his energies. To clear the awful *callampa* urban slums (literally 'mushrooms', but perhaps more aptly dubbed *villas miseria* in Argentina) he built 360,000 new dwellings, and tripled the number of schools; he introduced the first effective land reform, expropriating 1,224 private holdings and redistributing them to the landless; and he 'chileanized' the copper industry, 85 per cent of which was then controlled by three giant U.S. companies, Cerro, Kennecott and Anaconda, to help pay for his social reform programme.

The copper companies, paying the highest mining taxes in the world, were currently contributing to Chilean government coffers more than all other sources of tax revenue combined. But they still managed to make vast profits. Like most underdeveloped producers of raw materials these days, Chileans watched resentfully as their future heritage was steadily scooped away; so that the principle of 'chileanization' was almost universally popular. But it was over his 1966 copper bill that Frei began to run into major political trouble. Under a compromise with the U.S. the Chilean government was to take over holdings ranging in scale from 51 per cent downwards; production was to be increased dramatically, to make Chile the world's biggest copper extractor, but of the investment required to achieve this end Chile was to find one-third, and the cost of the purchase of the shares would be bound to make a big hole in Chile's national budget. In return for their co-operation, the U.S. companies were to be guaranteed against expropriation (a scrap of paper, as it later turned out). Both Left and Right opposition parties, however, turned and rent Frei for having given too much away; the FRAP wanted nothing less than complete nationalization, with Allende's Socialists as usual going farther than the Communists in their criticism. Shortly afterwards, at by-elections in Valparaiso, the FRAP increased its share of the votes from 19 per cent to 28 per cent. Then there were prolonged strikes for higher wages in the mines, and at one point Frei was forced to send in the troops and several miners were killed. The Left howled with rage, and it was allegedly in revenge for these shootings that, in

June 1971, Pérez Zujovic, who had been Frei's right-hand man and was now the Christian Democrat leader most acceptable to the National Party was assassinated by left-wing extremists. Castro, from his lofty pinnacle of morality, commented acidly of Frei: 'He promised revolution without blood and has given blood without revolution.'

But it was Frei's agrarian reform programme that encountered the most savage storms. The Right attacked it for going too far, the Left for not going far enough; and for a long time conservatives in the Senate were able to block legislation. Basically (and more will be said about this later) the bill provided for the immediate expropriation of privately owned farms over two hundred acres, or any that were 'poorly cultivated or entirely neglected'. But when Frei announced that, in fact, only 2 per cent of Chile's 260,000 estates would be affected, the Landowners' Association publicly congratulated itself in *El Mercurio*. Disappointment at the slow tempo of the agrarian redistributions provoked resentments that Allende was to make good use of in the 1970 elections. Because of the structural changes Frei's reform imposed on the basic laws governing private property, he had to push through an amendment to the constitution. The blocking tactics he encountered in Congress persuaded him towards the end of his term to effect another amendment of outstanding political significance today. This was one streamlining the use of the *plebiscito*, an instrument already incorporated under the 1925 constitution. As a result of Frei's amendment, a president finding his legislation thwarted by a hostile Congress would be entitled to appeal immediately to the nation by means of a *plebiscito*, or referendum. To get his amendment accepted, Frei had to renounce any benefit from it, postponing its promulgation until after the 1970 elections. His successor, Salvador Allende, was thus to find himself handed a ready-made weapon of inestimable value.

After half-term in 1967, the dice seemed progressively loaded against Frei. The Marxist parties within the FRAP split over specific issues – with the more moderate Communist Party actually supporting Frei on agrarian reform, the Socialist Party refusing to co-operate, in principle, with a 'bourgeois' government and going so far at their General

Congress in 1967 as to call for 'violent means' to achieve revolution. But the internal splits were far more serious within the ranks of Frei's own Christian Democrat Party. Progressively at each by-election its popularity began to wane. In the 1967 congressional elections, Frei's 56 per cent was scaled down to only 36.5 per cent, with Allende's Socialists moving from 10.2 per cent to 14.3 per cent. Indicating a protest against too rapid change, the right-wing parties jointly increased their share of the votes by 3.6 per cent; while as a protest against too little change, the FRAP gained 6.6 per cent. Frei himself received a grave personal rebuff that year when the Senate, aggrieved at his treatment of it, refused to authorize him a prestige trip to the U.S.A. Then the budget ran into a large deficit, and Frei had to reduce public expenditure, his reform projects suffering as a result.

Next, the cruellest of unanticipated misfortunes, Chile was stricken with one of the worst droughts in its history. Electricity and water were rationed in Santiago, in the country hundreds of thousands of cattle died, and one-third of agricultural production for 1969 was lost. The country had to import vast quantities of food; as a result of which inflation once again took over, with the cost of living rising by 20 per cent in the first five months of 1969 alone. The armed forces began to show increasing restiveness with the government's policies, with two regiments actually mutinying on grounds of poor pay – an almost unheard-of thing in Chilean history. The Communist-controlled unions began to step up pressure, through strikes and excessive wage claims, to wreck Frei's reform programmes, and there were disquietening accounts of discoveries of large armed camps of would-be revolutionaries in the countryside, belonging to a new extremist body, the MIR. In 1970, an official of the agrarian reform was killed in a dispute in which the right-wing were involved. Tensions were rising. At last, the economy showed signs of slowly improving,[1] but it looked as if it

[1] One of Frei's outstanding achievements, helped by high copper prices, was to turn a balance of payments deficit of over $4 million in 1964 into a surplus of $183 million in 1969.

might be too late to help the Christian Democrats at the autumn elections of 1970; and meanwhile inflation still kept galloping ahead, reaching an increase for the year of 40 per cent, the world's worst except for South Vietnam.

Frei could point with pride to the fact that whereas, in 1965, 25 per cent of Chilean national wealth was held by 5 per cent of the population and 2.5 per cent by the poorest 20 per cent, by 1970 the slice of the rich had been reduced to 20 per cent, and that of the *no-tienes* at the bottom of the scale increased to 5 per cent. But was it enough? Allende violently attacked Frei's record; he had promised to build 360,000 new housing units, but had fallen short by 100,000, and there was still a deficit of 440,000. It had been the same with every government over the past thirty years. Frei had promised to provide land for 100,000 out of Chile's 350,000 landless families, and he had resettled fewer than 30,000. And so on.

Three days before the 1970 elections, a Chilean contraband-runner, the *Puelche*, foundered in heavy seas off the coast of Peru. According to the Lima press, Peruvian rescuers were amazed to see the politically minded Chilean smugglers solemnly filling out improvised ballot slips, then putting them overboard in bottles in the hopes that somehow their votes might be recorded, before actually abandoning ship themselves. The episode was symptomatic of the intense interest aroused during the elections, which resulted in record low abstention figures.

In the line-up, Allende was making his fourth bid at sixty-two, this time at the head of an expanded left-wing coalition, calling itself the *Unidad Popular*, and consisting of the Communists, Socialists, Radicals, Social Democrats and MAPU (*Movimiento de Acción Popular Unitaria*, a breakaway fraction from the Christian Democrats, headed by Frei's former chief adviser on agrarian reform, Jacques Chonchol). Jorge Alessandri, the president of 1958–64, led the National Party, a new amalgamation of Liberals and Conservatives created since the disastrous defeat of the Right by Frei; while Radimiro Tomic took over the Christian Democrats from Frei, constitutionally barred from succeeding himself. Tomic, of Yugoslav origin, was formerly ambassador to Washington.

He stood to the Left of Frei in the party, and was regarded by many moderates as politically unreliable; although a fiery orator, he was a far less attractive personality than his predecessor. If Frei had been able to stand, he would probably have brought the Christian Democrats through to victory again. As it was, neither he nor Tomic helped each other; Frei, misguidedly, stood back in Olympian disdain during the campaign, refusing to counter-attack the Marxists and leaving all in-fighting of that kind to Alessandri's Nationals, content to rest on the 'positive' record of his own achievements; Tomic, on his side, torpedoed his own party by repeatedly criticizing Frei for not having gone fast enough.

Alessandri-the-younger was now seventy-four, and a bachelor – never exactly an advantage in a *machismo*-minded Latin American country. He came over poorly on the new medium of television, often appearing with shaking hands, and the Left had little difficulty in lampooning him as a senile reactionary; which, in fact, he was not. Nevertheless, until almost the last minute the pollsters were giving him the best odds. Although the actual election was a model of fairness, the various campaigns were fought with no holds barred. The U.P. circulated songs impugning Alessandri's virility; the Nationals responded with posters showing a Russian tank outside La Moneda, with the caption 'Czechoslovakia 1968; Chile 1971. We never thought that this could happen!' It was a replay of the 1964 Christian Democrat posters of a Russian soldier and Santa Claus, which put the question: 'Who do you want to knock at your door this Christmas?' But this time it was overdone and rebounded. Allende, on the other hand, fought his campaign with all the skill and confidence of a seasoned veteran. His Communist allies, operating the most highly organized political machine on the continent, proved themselves capable of getting thousands of supporters and hecklers on to the streets at very short notice. Allende himself appeared cultured, urbane, witty and elegantly dressed: to wavering non-Marxists, an almost reassuringly bourgeois figure. Could such a man really impose a Red Terror on Chile? To his own side he struck, above all, the image of a man in a hurry, playing on all the compounded impatience and frustrations of the slum-dweller, the landless, the underprivileged, and the impetuous young. Again and again he castigated Frei for his essential contradiction in speaking the language of revolution 'while maintaining an old-fashioned bourgeois image'; for arousing the revolutionary appetites of Chileans, and leaving them unsatisfied.

There was some substance to Allende's charges. After the elections, a gloomy Frei confided to a friend that he was now regarded as the 'Kerensky' of Latin America; the man who had opened the door to Marxism. And one could recall the famous dictum of de Tocqueville: 'Patiently endured so long as it seemed beyond redress, a grievance comes to appear intolerable once the possibility of removing it crosses men's minds.' Or, in the assessment of Régis Debray: 'it is impossible in Latin America today to initiate a bourgeois democratic revolution without rapidly unleashing a process of socialist revolution; it is impossible to avoid the second while waving the flag of the first.'

It seems hardly fair to say of Frei, however, that he opened the floodgates to revolution in Chile. If Frei had not offered reform, the flood would certainly have attained tidal-wave proportions. As it was, he and his Christian Democrats were to a large extent frustrated by the intransigence of the vested interests of the right wing. In the tragedy of Frei, one is reminded of the Weimar Republic's Stresemann when, in despair at all his overtures being rejected by the French, he lamented: 'if they could have granted me just one concession, I would have won my people But they gave nothing . . . That is my tragedy and their crime.'

When the votes were counted after 4 September, Allende just squeezed in with a majority of only 39,000 votes over Alessandri; 36.3 per cent of the poll compared with Alessandri's 34.9 per cent and Tomic's 27.8 per cent. The total number of votes received by Tomic was roughly half what Frei had won in 1964; it was also curious that Alessandri actually had a higher share of the votes than when he had won the 1958 elections (with 31.6 per cent), while Allende's was less than it had been in 1964 – although then there had been only two main electoral contestants. So out of this splitting of the vote brought about by the three-cornered fight, with a tiny 1.4 per cent majority Salvador Allende woke up to find himself the world's first Marxist president to be voted in through a democratic election.

According to one of the idiosyncrasies of the Chilean constitution, Congress has the last word in ratifying the popular choice of the new president. After a period of six weeks from the elections, it meets to choose by secret ballot between the two candidates with the biggest popular votes. It has in the past consistently selected the electoral victor; but there is no ruling convention that it should do so. Thus Alessandri – although before the elections he had declared he would abide by the choice of the electorate – now tried to do a complicated and somewhat shady deal with ex-President Frei. Because Allende had only gained little more than a third of the votes, the combined National–Christian Democrat majority in Congress could, constitutionally, declare the elections null and void, proposed Alessandri; he himself would serve as an interim president, pending fresh elections in which Frei would once more be eligible to run (in so far as he would no longer be succeeding himself) – and, presumably, win. It was all just within the constitution – just. But the party was outraged by the idea, and rejected it. Instead the Christian Democrats went to Allende with a pledge of their support, in exchange for certain (not entirely substantive) guarantees that he would respect political and civil liberties. The net result of Alessandri's manoeuvre was to widen the breach between the two main opposition parties, and to enrage the Left at what seemed like blatant dishonesty by the candidate who claimed to stand for probity.

On his election, Allende predicted that 'between 3 September and 4 November, Chile is going to feel like a football being kicked about by a Pele'. It was no exaggeration. During this six weeks' incubationary period tension mounted in Chile. Members of the bourgeoisie began to flee in waves, before the portcullis of a Red dictatorship slammed down for ever; the Left went daily in fear of a right-wing or military coup that would sweep away their legitimately elected president. Then a terrible thing happened. On the morning of 22 October, two days before Congress was due to have its secret ballot, the commander-in-chief of the Chilean army, General René Schneider, was driving from his home to his office. His Mercedes was cornered, in Tupamaro fashion, by four cars. Some well-dressed young men getting out of them apparently tried to kidnap the general. He resisted, was shot in the neck and stomach, and died in hospital three days later. It was the first time since the killing of Portales 140 years ago that there had been even an attempted assassination of this kind in law-abiding Chile, and the whole country was deeply shocked. Although a number of arrests were made, and blame was cast squarely on the right-wing lunatic fringe, there is still some mystery about both the motives and executors of the Schneider killing. Schneider, it was said, had angered the extreme Right by the army's refusal to intervene 'to save Chile from Communism', but it is not quite clear in what way the assassins planned to exert pressure by kidnapping him. Such an incredible folly was the killing that there was also a strong, though unsubstantiated, belief that the actual assassin (still unapprehended) had been a left-wing *mirista*, acting as an *agent provocateur*. Certainly, in its repercussions, the killing played superbly into the hands of the Left. On 24 October Congress voted solidly to affirm Allende's presidency; the army closed its ears, and heart, to right-wing clamouring for an anti-Marxist *Putsch*, and declared itself dedicated only to maintaining its traditional role as guardian of the sacred constitution.

On 4 November 1970 Dr Allende officially began his six-year office as *El Compañero Presidente* of Chile.

6

Allende's Ninety Days

For the next few days we rush round Santiago in a frenzy of study and cross-examination; interviews from 8 a.m. until lunch; talking lunches; more interviews; seldom time for a bath in the evening, just a burst of Rightguard right and left, then dinner – sometimes at 2 a.m., worse than Spain – and more talk until the large small hours of the morning. Chilean energy is enormous; and their capacity for political intellectualizing possibly even greater than that of the Greeks. (They must also be the most legalistically-minded people in the world: instead of erotica, small boys at street corners jostle you to buy white papers of 'the latest law'.) The pace would be killing, were it not for two things: much of the tempo of the serious, after-dinner conversations is maintained by the women, whose compelling charm and beauty prohibit one from nodding off – and the climate. During much of the year Santiago can be unpleasantly cold and smoggy, but now in these midsummer weeks there is day after exquisite day of sunshine, hot but so dry that you never perspire; followed by wonderful golden evenings that bring in a cooling Pacific breeze so punctually at five o'clock that you can set your watch by it. Nevertheless, each morning when Nena telephones to enquire solicitously, 'Are you still alive?' I am not quite sure.

Our first meeting is with Eric Schnake Silva, a lawyer and Socialist vice-chairman of the chamber of deputies close to Allende. His office is grubby, but he is expensively dressed – like his leader – and friendly. On his wall is the inevitable picture of Che, plus one of two rhinos copulating, with a caption of 'Make Love not War!' I wondered whether this pachyderm rhapsody could in any way be symbolic of the relationship among the U.P. partners, and Schnake begins by defining some of the common denominators and differences. During the 1930s the Popular Front had been dominated by Soviet-orientated policies, he explains; now it is no longer so, and internal issues call the tune. In broad strategic terms, the Socialists and the Communists have shared the same domestic programmes these past fourteen years. But on foreign policy they were not always in accord. For instance, Allende and the Socialists wanted to restore relationships with Red China (and they did), while the Russia-loyal Communist Party opposed it. In 1968, the Communist Party had wholeheartedly supported the Soviet invasion of Czechoslovakia (one of the few to do so); the Chilean Socialists and Radicals condemned it. The Socialists had also intervened, recently, on behalf of Jews about to be sentenced to death in the Soviet Union. It was Allende's intention to line-up with the Third World (whatever that might mean, these days), not with the Soviet bloc – or any other. As far as the socialization of Chile was concerned, however – and make no mistake – the two U.P. partners would go ahead together, and at full steam.

'We are a land of *terremotos* [earthquakes],' says Schnake, 'and now we are about to have an economic *terremoto*, far greater than the real thing.' The biggest earth tremor was going to come about over agrarian reform – because the *campesinos*, who believed now they could 'realize their dreams in one day', were – in their 'elation' – colliding against the diehard *latifundistas*. Every day the papers were, indeed, full of it, and it was a theme that would recur again and again.

Cristian Casanova, permanent secretary and spokesman in the foreign ministry, comes of a wealthy oligarchic family, regarded by those with whom he had grown up as a 'playboy gone bad', admiring of the reputation of his great namesake. His walls are festooned with posters of European ski-resorts; he tells us that he would like to talk as an 'individual', not as an official – then proceeds to say, spiced with a touch of bombast, little that we cannot read in *El Clarín*. I have met his type before in other government offices across the world. He begins by reiterating what Schnake had said about the

U.P.'s aversion to world blocs in principle. Would Chile now leave the O.A.S., as a consequence of her prompt resuming of relations with Cuba? No. 'This is a free country,' he says (parroting Allende), 'and we are going to stay in the organization until expelled.' U.S.-Chilean relations' would, he thinks, remain all right. 'There will be no Bay of Pigs, because we hope the U.S. will recognize the difference between us and Cuba.' Nor does he see Chile 'exporting revolution' to her Latin American neighbours, as the State Department evidently feared. In the event of leftist revolutions in Peru, Bolivia or Argentina, was there a danger of Chile becoming, like Tunisia during the Algerian War, a haven for guerrillas? No, Chile would 'by no means allow her territory to be used as either a refuge or a hopping–off place'. Of course, there was Chile's well-known tradition of granting asylum to political exiles, and he points out that only a few days previously twenty-three right-wingers had arrived from Bolivia after an abortive coup. 'And they will be able to stay here happily, like any leftists – if they can find work and not interfere.' Meanwhile of the Chilean *tuvos* who had fled after September, '99 per cent have already returned – to make a little profit on the shoulders of the Chilean people through the exchange rates,' claims Casanova. Would the returning self-exiles be persecuted? Naturally not; not even Agustin Edwards[1] – though 'He was no patriot, and has been organizing a campaign from abroad against Chile. Why,' says the ex-playboy scornfully, 'Doonie could come back and swim, and play golf – all the things he used to like to do – and even have dinner with me, as he was a good friend of mine.'

Allende speaks of this being 'the most confused' time of his country's history. He does not exaggerate, and if it is confusing for the highly intelligent, sophisticated Chileans, how much more so for a European *gringo* on a few weeks' visit? Out of all the talks, newspaper reading and less tangible impressions, one element is immediately distilled above all others: a sense of extreme shock. For the Left, for the joyful supporters of the *Unidad Popular*, it is the shock of euphoria

---

[1] The former owner of *El Mercurio* (see Chapter 1).

combined with not quite realizing that they have *arrived.* 'Doesn't it remind you a little,' says Bill, 'of the mood of 1917 Russia that John Reed described in *Ten Days that Shook the World*?' For the opposition, it is sheer, numbing shellshock; bemused, they just do not know what has happened to them, how it happened, or what is now *going to happen.* As with the shock that follows the sudden severing of a limb, it is the astonishing speed with which Allende is moving, already, that most intensifies it. For one elected with a slimmer than forty-thousand majority, a polygenous coalition and a hostile Congress, the self-confidence of the man is astounding; he behaves almost as if he were looking forward to a life tenure. Foreign journalists are suddenly waking up to the realization that here is one of the most astute political tacticians on the world scene. Allende is just celebrating his first ninety days in power, and what he has already accomplished makes Harold Wilson's famous hundred days of 1964 look like the progress of a crushed slug. The intervening year since I left Chile has seen the birth of few developments that were not conceived during those first ninety days. Of course, as a motive for proceeding with such extreme speed, Allende knows he has the winged chariot of Chilean history at his back. Traditionally after the first halcyon year or two of a new regime, the mercurial Chilean electorate becomes speedily disenchanted. This is what happened to Frei. So, to get through the radical parts of his revolutionary programme which are bound to produce unpleasant repercussions, Allende has to move with utmost celerity – and before the defeated opposition can shake off its shock.

Allende declares that his goals are primarily political and only secondarily economic. But the two are closely intertwined. The endemic, inherited economic problems are simply immense. One Chilean writer (Aníbal Pinto) designates Chile's as 'a difficult economy'; but with her spidery length and no breadth, her tenuous communications and tiny domestic markets so remote from the centres of world commerce, this is a superlative understatement. (As an example, down in Temuco I was later shocked to discover that lemons cost considerably more than they would in England although they grow only a few hundred miles further north.)

On the economic scene, Allende seems to have three broad objectives: to set right the social injustices of the past; to prime the stagnant economy; but, above all, to break once and for all the political power of the oligarchs and their bourgeois supporters by striking at their economic foundations. Within Allende's first cabinet, the Communists were immediately placed in control of the economy (which suited them very well indeed) by allocation of the key ministries of finance, labour and public works;[1] while the minister of economics himself, Pedro Vuskovic Bravo, now described himself as an 'independent Marxist', although in the past he was known to have very close ties with the P.C.Ch. (Communist Party of Chile). As Señor Vuskovic explained to visiting journalists, what was basically wrong with the Chilean economy was the chronically small number of consumers. According to him, out of a total of nine million Chileans some eight million – the wretched poor of the *callampas* and the landless peasants – had no spending power and were thus virtually non-consumers. At the same time, the other economic evils which Vuskovic claimed to have inherited from the Frei regime included: 1. Inflation of 30-35 per cent per year; 2. An increase in the national income of only 2.7 per cent over the previous three years (0.8 per cent for 1970 alone), which was roughly swallowed up by the growth of population; 3. Unemployment (for 1970) of 6 per cent, plus 'under-employment' on so massive a scale that the real figures might be something more like 20 per cent; 4. A decline in industrial capacity usage from 81 per cent in 1967 to 75 per cent in 1970. (Particularly to blame here, in the eyes of the Allende government, were the numerous foreign-controlled companies, whose tendency on a stagnant market was to raise prices rather than output.)

To tackle these ills, the U.P. immediately undertook a major redistribution of incomes; a policy that was also, of course, very much in keeping with Marxist philosophy.

[1] Minister of finance was Americo Zorilla Rojas, member of the Central Committee of the P.C.Ch. The predominant Socialists kept for themselves the sensitive posts of foreign minister (Almeyda) and the interior (Toha) – plus the ministry of housing.

There was an all-round wage increase to meet the previous year's rate of inflation, the lowest paid workers receiving a cost-of-living plus 5 per cent increase. The increases went as high as 40 per cent, with some workers in specialized industries actually getting as much as a 65 per cent rise. At the same time, DIRINCO, the government price-fixing agency, rigidly barred any concerns from passing these wage increases on to the consumer. The effects of all this will be seen later, but it suffices to say, in passing, that it was hardly designed to cost Allende votes. Equally popular early measures were the provision of school-children with a daily half-litre of milk,[1] a free pair of shoes for Christmas, and a promise of free summer holidays for the outstandingly bright ones at the presidential palace in Viña del Mar. The government also promised to create 180,000 new jobs during its first fourteen months, and build a hundred thousand new housing units.

As could be expected, the U.P. brought in with it comprehensive schemes of nationalization, and these too it set about implementing with great celerity. Vuskovic envisaged the new, reformed Chilean economy falling into three 'areas': first, a 'social area' of total state control; then a 'mixed area'; and finally a completely private sector. Out of Chile's some 35,000 industrial concerns (meaning any business that employs more than four employees), the government declared that it was only interested in taking over the 120 most important companies. (This drawing of the line, thought Bill, made it sound as if 'the one hundred and twenty first largest company is engaged in selling goldfish'; for, so the U.P. economists claim, 3 per cent of Chilean enterprises control half the country's industrial resources.) But, in fact, by the end of Allende's first year in office 187 firms had already passed under state control, and businessmen still remaining in the 'private sector' were beginning to feel that they had little guarantee that they would not be swept up in some future

---

[1] As Allende himself declared passionately after the elections, half of all Chilean children under fifteen suffered from malnutrition, while 600,000 were, he claimed, actually mentally retarded because of inadequate protein nourishment. But, because of agricultural short-fall, the daily pint of milk has now been dropped.

netting operation. Compensation terms were heavily weighted in favour of the least wealthy entrepreneur; the smallholder would be paid in cash, the middle-sized holder in part cash and part short-term bonds, while the bigger fish would have to wait much longer for their money in long-term bonds. A number of factors combined greatly to ease the U.P.'s nationalization programme, without recourse to special legislation in Congress, where it lacked a majority. First of all, through loans or participation of one sort or another, the government in fact already financed something like 50 per cent of all private enterprise. Then it seemed a fair certainty that many of the less robust private concerns would be simply driven to the wall by the combination of massive wage increases and price freezes; thereby making them easy pickings for state takeover. No doubt this was all a built-in consideration of the Vuskovic-Zorrilla policy, its goal being, as the latter put it while I was in Santiago, 'to defeat definitively the dominant class in Chile.'

But no weapon in the nationalization armoury proved to be handier than an obscure, half-forgotten law dating from Marmaduque Grove's brief Socialist Republic of 1932, seldom invoked since then, but now dredged up by some bright U.P. lawyer. This was a law which, in legalistic language, provided for 'the intervention of the central power in all industries producing basic necessities which infringe on norms of functioning freely established by the administrative authorities'. In plain English, it meant that a government *interventor*, or arbitrator, could be imposed upon a business that could not meet its obligations, or where there were allegations of 'financial irregularities'. The law could be – and was – interpreted by the Allende government with the widest latitude, and applied in almost any situation of internal discord. It conformed admirably to 'the Leninist principle that it is necessary to squeeze every possible use out of the limited instruments afforded to the exploited masses by democratic bourgeois republics,' says Allende's 'Boswell', Régis Debray, with glee. In the ensuing week I was repeatedly to come across examples of the *interventor* at work. Here are two. One was a factory processing animal food, 80 per cent U.S. owned, whose workers appealed for an *interventor* on the grounds that the management had refused to supply its products on credit to agricultural co-operatives demanding six months' credit, and that, as a result, the plant was unnecessarily working at only 60 per cent capacity. The management denied the charges; but an *interventor* was installed, the owners summoned to the ministry of economics and told that they had been expropriated. A second was the case of the Christian Democrat *Ercilla*, Chile's reputable leading weekly with a format not unlike *Time* magazine. In December 1970 *Ercilla* had been forced to cease operations for three weeks because of strikes by Communist-controlled unions. An *interventor* was brought in, who promptly awarded a wage increase of 60 to 70 per cent. Zig-Zag, the parent press, claimed that this would put up its overheads by 140 per cent, and pleaded to go bankrupt. This was refused by the *interventor*, and Zig-Zag was forced to continue running at a heavy loss, while draining the blood from its other, healthier children.

The *interventor* was also used as a means of taking over the private banks; 'an unexpected Christmas present', as Debray puts it. Nationalization of the banks was a high U.P. priority:

for [Debray again] it cuts off at its source the economic power of the monopolistic bourgeoisie, taking from it its ability to arbitrate credits and loans, depriving it in the long term of its control of the means of production, communication and political propaganda.

Here, too – without the passage of any fresh legislation – the government was showing considerable adroitness in knocking the banks off one after the other, with stunning rapidity. It was seductively offering to buy shareholders' shares at roughly twice the prevailing market prices, but on deferred terms, and – of course – the stick with the carrot was: 'If you don't accept our offer, we *may* then take the shares for nothing anyway.' Meanwhile, some of the tougher nuts – after being submitted to the *interventor* – were finding themselves placed under control of the Central Bank, on account of allegedly 'irregular' operations.

On one nationalization issue, Allende could feel assured of

widest support in his otherwise hostile Congress. This was the final swipe at the nearly $1,000 million U.S. investment in the Chilean copper companies. It was essential – both economically and politically – for Allende to strike the toughest possible deal with the Americans. To pay for his extensive social reform programme, he had to get the maximum value out of the vast copper royalties; and he could not let himself be burdened, as Frei had been, by paying off large sums of compensation. Also, the tougher the deal, the more likely Allende would be to get a larger popular backing in the country to face other, politically trickier issues. On the other hand, if he was too aggressive towards the copper companies, there was always the danger of provoking an infuriated U.S. into imposing Cuban-style sanctions; which could prove disastrous to Chile's economy, even allowing for substitute aid and assistance promised by her new friends in the East. Within his second month of office, Allende had sent a constitutional amendment to Congress to complete the copper takeover begun by Frei, his first major piece of legislation. He declared that the companies would receive compensation over thirty years at 3 per cent annual interest; but he warned them that payments would be suspended if they tried to disrupt the process of nationalization. 'This is not aggression against the United States,' Allende told cheering crowds, and added the assurance: 'We are going to pay compensation to their firms.' But, as it turned out in the course of arduous bargaining, after Allende's negotiators had made various deductions for excess profits and back taxes, it began to look as if some of the U.S. shareholders were going to end up with a negative sum of compensation. (By mid-1972, the issue was still unresolved; but clearly it will be a major test case in U.S.-Chilean relations, as well as of Allende's *machismo* at home.)

Allende's second major act of legislation, a proposal in early January to set up 'neighbourhood tribunals', was equally a test case in purely domestic terms, but it aroused very different reactions in Congress. As a preliminary to the U.P.'s declared aim of judicial reform, to replace 'bourgeois justice' with 'socialist justice', these 'neighbourhood tribunals' were to have powers to try (and, apparently, to survey) Chileans suspected of committing 'minor social offences'. Such offences would embrace cases of drunkenness, public nuisance and wife-beating. The judges were to be over eighteen, otherwise no professional qualifications would be required, and they would have power to impose forced labour of unspecified duration. Such 'neighbourhood tribunals' had been instituted by Khrushchev in Russia, then dropped, and they had chilling implications of Cuban practice which were particularly repugnant to Chileans, with their long and proud judiciary traditions. For the first time since its electoral defeat, the parliamentary opposition was stung out of its paralysis and let it be known in no uncertain terms that it would fight the 'neighbourhood tribunals' tooth and nail. A few weeks later, Allende withdrew the bill – rather than face a first certain defeat in Congress. The episode sidelighted his sensitivity as a political tactician, and it may well be that Allende was also using this relatively minor issue as a kind of barometer to gauge the climate of Congress.

The reaction was hardly encouraging to him. Sooner or later he would reach a limit of the structural reforms he could achieve by means of such old-established laws as that of the *interventor*; then, constitutionally, he would have to go to Congress for new powers – and, in all probability his more revolutionary proposals would be defeated by the combined opposition majority. How then, Chileans of every political hue were asking with anxiety, was Allende going to get parliamentary support for his reforms? How would the U.P. return itself to power in six years' time, so as to ensure survival of the 'revolution'? Would there indeed be any elections in six years' time? This was what worried the opposition, despite Allende's 'Statute of Constitutional Guarantees' pledged to the Christian Democrats. For when had an entrenched Marxist regime ever permitted itself to be voted out of power?

The most informative exposé of Allende's political intentions, perhaps the closest thing to a *Mein Kampf* to come out of Chile so far, was provided in the series of interviews between Régis Debray and Allende. Debray, released from his Bolivian prison under an act of amnesty by President

Torres,[1] had been expelled to Chile about the time of my arrival, and was currently closeted with Allende. Although a fellow Marxist, Debray was a dedicated apostle of the Castro–Guevara school of 'armed revolution', and throughout the long taped interviews he plays the role of *provocateur*, baiting Allende to admit that – sooner or later – he will have to resort to 'unconstitutional' means, and reach for his gun. In these dialogues are to be found the fundamental contentions between the opposing sets of revolutionaries of Latin America today. They are extraordinarily revealing. 'The popular forces have not conquered power, they have merely taken a few forward lines of fortifications in the direction of power,' declares Debray in an introduction that is perhaps the most penetrating analysis yet written by that otherwise rather erratic pen. 'The path from polite hatred to open hostilities is shorter than either side had thought,' he predicts ominously; 'today there is a bizarre state of truce . . . which may be broken any day.' So the 'popular forces' must begin 'to take their future into their own hands, if they do not want their enemies to steal it away from tomorrow by brute force, or to sneak it away as usual – e.g. by an electoral conjuring-trick in a few years' time.' By complying with Chilean constitutional form[2] the U.P. would hamstring itself – 'because the real settlement of accounts has merely been postponed'. For instance, under another less helpful law inherited from the 'old regime' it is forbidden to sack permanent civil service officials; which means that the bourgeois administrative structure remains intact. But, says Debray, provocatively (and rather bossily) to *el Compañero Presidente*, 'revolution is the destruction of the machinery of the bourgeois State and the replacement of it by another, and none of this has happened here. What is happening, then?' He gets a testy response: 'What country do you think you're in?' Then

[1] Debray had been arrested by the Bolivians on a somewhat nebulous mission to cover the guerrilla *foco* of his idol, Che Guevara, in 1967 (for which Che was not particularly grateful), and sentenced to thirty years' imprisonment.

[2] As Debray notes acidly on page one, the key word in Chile 'is not Revolution, or Justice, or Liberation, or Proletariat, but Legality, the tabu term, the obsessional *leitmotif*.'

Allende goes on patiently to explain what a 'lot of things' his government had already achieved in its few weeks of office, by employing constitutional machinery: 'And we said that we would take advantage of what openings there are in the present constitution to open the way to the new constitution, the people's constitution. Why? Because in Chile we can do it.'

Allende now becomes explicit. He reminds Debray of the *plebiscito* law thoughtfully amended by his predecessor President Frei,[1] enabling the president to by-pass an obstructive Congress by means of a referendum:

If we put forward a bill and Congress rejects it, we invoke the plebiscite. I'll give you an example: we propose that there should be no longer two houses in Congress, the proposal is rejected by Congress, we hold a referendum and win. Hence the end of the two house system, and we now have to go to a single house, as we had proposed. And who are the people going to elect to this house? The representatives, I would presume.

So here, in a blow, Allende would be gaining the enabling majority he requires by means of this single-chamber 'people's assembly'; he would probably also be gaining the power to alter the constitution as he wished in the future, which would include, if such were to be his intention, the right to postpone *sine die* the next presidential elections, should the needs of 'the people' dictate it. And all this *could* be attained, as Allende points out to Debray, once again by employing purely constitutional instruments. In other utterances shortly after his accession, Allende made it abundantly clear that he was not speaking hypothetically – that the single-chamber 'people's assembly' was a definite blueprint of the U.P. There were to be important municipal elections in April 1971, and while I was in Chile it was generally assumed that, if – as Allende hoped – the U.P. got a strong majority, it would then proceed at once with a *plebiscito* to get the single chamber. (But in fact, though it increased its lead, the U.P. total vote fell just short of 50 per cent. So rather than risk a critical defeat, Allende held his hand.)

Allende's Communist allies, for one, certainly did not

<hr>

[1] See Chapter 5, page 109

expect to be shoved out of power in 1976. The veteran P.C.Ch. leader, Luis Corvalán, declared pointedly of the U.P. electoral victory a short time afterwards: 'The situation is not irreversible, but we must make it so.' There were various paths towards achieving this, other than through the immediate utopia of an acquiescent 'people's assembly'. In his interviews with Debray, Allende stressed the need to 'organize' the Chilean proletariat. Only 20 per cent of Chilean workers, for instance, were organized; previous governments had restricted the growth of the CUT (the Single Workers' Union) by refusing it legal status, and this would have to be put right. 'We must organize the masses, we must organize the homeless, the unemployed, we must organize our women,' said Allende.

The Chilean eighteen-year-olds were to cast their votes for the first time at the municipal elections of April 1971, and, electorally, there was always a prospect that the U.P. might ensure its re-election by further broadening the franchise, to embrace, for example, wider classes of the semi-literate at present not entitled to vote. Finally, there is always the sinister, menacing possibility that Allende and the U.P. might find themselves 'forced' to assume dictatorial powers to meet a threat to 'national security'. Pressing Allende to recognize the inevitability of civil war, fomented by a right-wing coup, Debray queries: 'If they go outside the law, will you also go outside the law? If they hit out, will you hit back?' Allende replies: 'If they deal us an illegal blow? We'll return it a hundredfold, you can be sure of that.' Debray persists. 'But the time will come when the class enemy will go outside his own laws, and this is already happening'. Allende, in one of his more sombre and explicit statements, replies: 'To begin with, we are going to contain it with their own laws. Then, we shall meet reactionary violence with revolutionary violence, because we know that they are going to break the rules.'

Certainly one of the simplest ways of resolving his parliamentary impasse would be for Allende to *provoke* an abortive right-wing coup – and crush it, with the forces of Chilean constitutional morality on his side. But it is highly improbable that he will make the first illegal move himself.

Allende resists (I think genuinely) becoming the object of a 'cult of the personality'. In different variations, he repeated to Debray: 'I am not a Messiah, nor am I a *caudillo*.' But Nikita Khrushchev also held the same view, and because he possessed an abundance of personality, *malgré soi-même*, he was rapidly turned into a cult; which is why, as much as for any other reason, he was replaced by the grey triumvirate of Brezhnev–Podgorny–Kosygin. Allende is already an established international figure; he gets more foreign press coverage than any other purely South American figure since Perón. At home, it is to a large extent his personal charisma – however much he might deny it – which brought the U.P. to power in 1970, and then increased its lead in the municipal elections of the following April. He is a more than parochial figure, likely to be with us for some time (provided one or other set of extremists does not get him); therefore it is important to know something about him.

The quality of Allende that most persistently seemed to baffle the compartmented, Gallic-Marxist mind of Debray was his bourgeois attributes. His grandfather was a Grand Master of the Freemasons, his father and uncles professional men, who, nevertheless, were committed militants of the Radical Party. Allende's own early upbringing was conventionally *petit-bourgeois*; he went to university and qualified as a doctor. While at university he was sent down for taking part in a student protest against the Ibañez dictatorship. Then, following the fall of the ephemeral Socialist Republic of Marmaduque Grove,[1] Allende, then a young doctor at hospital in Valparaiso, was arrested for making an inflammatory speech. His father died painfully of gangrene while Allende was in prison, and at the funeral 'I made the promise that I would dedicate my life to the social struggle.' In 1933 he became one of the co-founders of the Socialist Party.

Starting with the 'very hard and very dull' job of carrying out autopsies, Allende continued to practise medicine, but was henceforth never out of left-wing politics; deputy for Valparaiso, minister of public health under Aguirre Cerda in 1940, aged thirty; senator, then appointed to the august

[1] Whose brother was a brother-in-law of Allende.

129

role of president of the senate (1965-9); four times presidential candidate. It was these implicit contradictions of a double life that Debray found irreconcilable.

DEBRAY: How is it that a man from the petite bourgeoisie – with all those parliamentary, masonic, ideological and social ties – can carry out a consistently revolutionary line of action?
ALLENDE: . . . I have always worked with the masses. I am aware of being a grass-roots Chilean politician and very close to the people. Remember, Régis, a great majority of revolutionary leaders have been drawn from the ranks of the middle and lower middle classes.

Barely satisfied, Debray explains that it was true, yes, that in Chile 'nearly all the leading figures in the working-class parties have also been leading figures in the bourgeois Parliament.' But Chile, of course, was peculiar, and Salvador Allende the 'living exemplar' of its double life.

As well as being deeply involved in grass-roots provincial politics, Allende managed to travel widely, in particular to the countries of the Communist world. In 1953 he was in Red China, only four years after Mao's seizure of Peking. He visited North Korea and North Vietnam, as an official guest, and claimed to be one of the last politicians to meet Ho Chi Minh – whom he greatly revered. He was also one of the first to arrive in Cuba after Castro's triumph. Of Castro, he says to Debray: 'From the first moment, I was impressed by his immense intelligence – an incredible phenomenon that sweeps all before it like a sort of human cataract,' but their friendship had been punctuated by various 'fundamental and violent disagreements'. He felt great affection for Che, and proudly showed all journalists visiting his house a copy of Che's *Guerrilla Warfare*, with the autograph: 'To Salvador Allende, who is trying to obtain the same result by other means. Affectionately, Che.'

In Havana, at the Tri-Continental Conference of 1966, it was Allende who conceived the revolutionary O.L.A.S. organization,[1] as an anti-body to the U.S.-dominated O.A.S.,

[1] Organization of Latin American Solidarity; it came to very little, in fact.

130

essentially a guerrilla front with a basic creed of continental armed struggle against 'North American imperialism'. When the surviving guerrillas of Che's Bolivian *foco* were exiled to Cuba via Easter Island, Allende insisted on travelling with them on the first leg of the journey; risking censure as president of the senate. Until 1971 at any rate, he made little secret that his relations with the extreme Guevarist MIR in Chile were close. After various assassination attempts which he alleged had been made against him around the time of the Schneider killing, and out of mistrust of the 'bourgeois' police, he appointed a group of young *mirista* 'black berets' as part of his personal bodyguard. The MIR also provided him with 'intelligence' on right-wing conspiracies, for which he publicly thanked them. When there was a serious confrontation (in December 1970) between *miristas* and Communist Youth at Concepción University, culminating with the killing of a twenty-three-year-old *mirista*, Oscar Arnoldo Rios, it was Allende who personally mediated. Liking to think of himself as a man of action, rather than a theoretician, the image of a gun-toting revolutionary was also obviously not repugnant to Allende personally; he describes to Debray, with some relish, how during one of the right-wing 'attempts' on him he had 'had to come out shooting to frighten them away'.

Allende likes to be known as *el Compañero Presidente*, which has a racier, 'off-to-the-hills' connotation than the stodgier, title of *camarada* with its P.C.Ch. connotations.[1] Yet everything about his personal life is deeply rooted in bourgeois

[1] Following the 1970 elections, much mirth was made by opposition wags at Allendista jargon. Nena's PEC published a strip cartoon, showing a small boy rushing to his father:
'Papa!'
'What's this "Papa" business? You're supposed to say *"camarada"*.'
'Yes, *camarada*.'
'That's better.'
'Mama says . . .'
'What do you mean "Mama"? What you mean is *la compañera*!'
'*La compañera* says that the baby . . .'
' "Baby"? You mean "the future of Chile"!'
'. . . *La compañera* says that the future of Chile has just soiled its nappies.'

habit. His clothes are expensive and trendy; his pudgy, owlish features and neatly trimmed moustache have a flavour of *Gemütlichkeit* about them. In Santiago he has a small but comfortable house in the fashionable upper-class district of Providencia, its compact living-room is filled with pre-Columbian ceramics and neo-impressionist paintings; later he surprised Chileans by purchasing a house for the President's official residence in a thoroughly *momio* suburb of Santiago. He enjoys high living, and his taste for mistresses is an open secret throughout Chile,[1] with Allende himself doing little to dispel this happily *macho* image and telling journalists proudly 'I have been accused of everything, except being a thief or a homosexual!' Señora Allende is a sophisticated and attractive brunette, very *simpática* even to political foes, who works away in support of her husband – like so many Chilean women, unobtrusively but effectively. On the other hand, his daughter Tati (who is said to have even more influence over him than his wife) is a close friend of Fidel Castro, and recently married one of Cuba's top diplomats; while his nephew, Pascal Allende, is a leading *mirista*. But in sum Allende's predominantly bourgeois attributes (and those of a good number of his fellow socialist parliamentarians) combine to cause deep suspicion among the out-and-out revolutionaries, while, at the same time, to good social democrats like Professor Hugh Thomas, the fact that Allende has mistresses, and doesn't suffer from the accumulated bitterness of years spent in gaol, as was the lot of European Communist leaders of the 1940s, encourages the hopes that here we may yet have a cosy Harold Wilson or a Roy Jenkins, rather than an Ulbricht or a Gottwald.

There is a favourite Chilean saying – *otra cosa es con guitarra* – meaning, it's one thing to talk about playing the guitar, and quite another thing when it's actually in your hand. But, after those first few weeks in office, there was absolutely no mistaking the firmness of Allende's grasp on the guitar, nor the subtle skill with which he was fingering

---

[1] While I was in Chile Allende was ardently wooing the conservative Chilean navy, and the *chiste* made the rounds that his current mistress was called 'Marina'.

the strings. I thought of trying to see *el Compañero Presidente* myself, but it would necessarily be a formal affair and by the time I had arrived in Chile it seemed that he was just about punch-drunk with interviews, repeating the same things to the journalists – who were assiduously rewriting each others' thumbnail sketches of the great man. I would have quite liked, however, to have had a chance of judging his charisma (that overworked word that politicians so love to use about each other!) for myself. It would not be easy to arrange; but a member of the British Embassy fixed an appointment for me with the private secretary, down in Valparaiso, with the hint that – if he liked the look of me – he might insinuate me through the side door of the presidential *despacho*.

In Valparaiso, chaos. Every single taxi in the country appears to be parked, in a demonstration, on the square in front of the pretty little *intendencia*, covered with painted slogans of 'Chilean *taxistas* for Allende'. The rest of the space is occupied by other trades union deputations, the enthusiastic and the purely curious. When I squeeze my way through to the entrance, a *carabinero* takes away that fatal briefcase with courteous tranquillity; otherwise, no sign of nervousness, or – again – of the *mirista* 'black berets' watching out for a potential assassin. Upstairs, more chaos, and a harassed female soldier tells me that the secretary is attending a *reunión* with *el Compañero Presidente*; would I return in half-an-hour? I leave, buy a copy of Che's *Diaries*, have a pisco sour, and return. By now the throng has doubled, and there is a palpable air of expectancy. This time with considerable difficulty, I reach the postern door, and start up the stairs again. Half-way up I am met by an avalanche of journalists and supplicants, surrounding the compact, cocky and dapper figure of the president, on his way home for lunch. He nods, murmurs a few words lost in the general hubbub, then passes on. That was my interview with Latin America's man-of-the-hour. Meanwhile, the secretary too has disappeared somewhere into the crowd, lost for ever.

After this rather frustrating experience, I take a train back to Santiago. My Chilean friends had warned me against it; I had replied that according to the North American guide-books, Chile was renowned chiefly for its women and trains ('the only thing they both have in common,' a cynical man growled in my ear, 'they're always full of people!'). The train calls itself an 'express', but the first-class ticket (my sole concession to my friends' cautioning) costs the suspiciously low sum of fourteen escudos ($1 U.S., at the official rate). Before we leave Valparaiso the aisle in the first-class coach is densely packed. A jolly, plump matriarch seeing off her daughters is carried on to Viña, laughing; '¡no importa nada!' We stop at every single station to Santiago, and at each one more returning holiday-makers surge in, while nobody gets out. At one major halt, another train is parked in the siding, and all its occupants, mostly youths with rucksacks and bulky sleeping-bags, clamber in through the windows, singing lustily. At any moment, I feel, the sides of the coach will physically burst outwards; except for the suffocating heat, it is like the rail scene out of *Dr Zhivago*. I wonder idly what the second class of a non-'express' on a weekend (this is a Monday) would be like. Here was a demonstration, graphic and formidable, of *la explosión demográfica*.

But the patience and good humour of the passengers is boundless. A sweet-faced thirteen-year-old opposite me takes the slobbering infant (known in Chile, onomatopoeically, as a *wah-wah*) from a peasant standing, or rather pressed upright, in the aisle and holds it on her knee in fulfilled contentment for the nightmare journey. Her father, next to me, is a railway engineer. He is, in a quiet way, without being over-demonstrative, for Allende. 'At least give him a chance, and he'll build us more railway coaches!' We all laugh. And certainly there is already more money to spend, and prices are being kept down. His wife nods agreement, but – obviously a religious woman – what worries her is that sooner or later '*They* will begin interfering with the Church. After all, that's what happened in Cuba, isn't it?' The son, who is still at high-school is buried behind the Marxist *El Clarín*, and is disdainful of getting involved in a family argument. But it is evident from his occasional interjections that he is rather sympathetic to the firebrands of the MIR. Many of his classmates would like, when they get to university, to 'go into the country' where the *miristas* are busy 'liberating' farms for the peasants. The daughter, preoccupied with her bor-

134

rowed *wah-wah*, is totally uninterested in politics; it is just good to be alive, to be in Chile, on a summer's day.

We pass through some rich-looking farms in the Central Valley. Maize and tomatoes. A few wretched hovels. Cattle grazing in arid stubble fields. No signs of any modern agricultural machinery. A *campesino* standing up on top of an ancient rake towed by a ragged horse. Endless Allende – U.P. slogans painted up on every wall, even on every prominent rock in the fields. 'The paint companies were the only people to make money out of the last election,' remarks the railwayman. The outskirts of Santiago; miles of dispirited *callampas*, and even more wall artistry by the industrious Ramona Parra brigade. At last, after three-and-a-quarter hours to cover 100 miles we arrive. The passengers burst like shrapnel into the station. There is a box at the exit marked '*Señor pasajero*, please deposit your suggestions here.' Nobody does. I stagger into an antique taxi, dazed and crumpled, but feeling that possibly I have indirectly and intuitively learned more about Chile on the Valparaiso 'express' than I would have done in half-an-hour of formal interview in the *intendencia*. The taxi-driver is of French origin; his parents left Grenoble in 1920. He is, perhaps surprisingly, an impassioned Alessandrista, and he passes me a copy of the (conservative) evening tabloid, *La Segunda*. There had been a shoot-up between the police and five VOP[1] terrorists. 'Look, the country is going to the dogs,' comments the driver. 'Within two years the army will move, you will see, they will have had enough.'

---

[1] *Vanguardia Organizada del Pueblo*, a left-wing extremist break-away group from the MIR, even further way-out and held responsible in the summer of 1971 for the assassination of Señor Pérez Zujovic, Frei's former minister of the interior.

7

After the Earthquake

The army will move. A familiar old maxim in just about every Latin American country – *except* Chile. And this is a major issue – one of several – which divides the opposition more than ever before. The extreme Right, and a good part of the respectable Right, the Alessandristas, hope that the armed forces *will* intervene, and sooner rather than later. The Christian Democrats, as in most things, are split. Frei's supporters say they would approve intervention only if Allende shamelessly violated the sacred constitution; something which it seems he is unlikely to do. The left wing of the Christian Democrats, who tacitly support much of Allende's domestic programme, say they would oppose a move by the armed forces under almost any circumstances.

Frei was sulking in retreat somewhere up in the Atacama Desert, refusing to speak to anybody. Tomic had declined an interview with Bill, rather churlishly, on the grounds that they 'had nothing in common'; to which Bill replied acidly that Señor Tomic was wrong, 'after all, we *both* lost an election.'[1] Silence. But we went to see Onofre Jarpa, president of the National Party, and obvious successor to the played-out Alessandri. Most shades of *momios*[2] regard him as the only possible rallying figure of the whole opposition. Jarpa is blue-eyed and fair skinned, a substantial man of fifty. Quiet-spoken and manifestly dejected, he does not immediately strike one as a magnetic personality; but, like so many

[1] Referring to his hopeless but gallant challenge in the New York mayoral elections, when he ran against John Lindsay.
[2] 'Mummies', a rather engaging term of opprobrium coined by the U.P. for anyone of the *ancien régime*.

Chileans, he is still suffering under the trauma of the U.P. electoral avalanche.

For Jarpa and his party the supreme fear was that Allende would lead Chile into Marxism, inexorably and irrevocably. The danger was growing all over the continent, not just Chile. There was an urgent need, he said rather vaguely, for a multi-national organization to combat Communism throughout South America. Was it not too late? He shrugged his shoulders. In Chile, the process of Marxist penetration had been going on for a long time. For instance, it was ex-President Frei who had let in sixty left-wing professors persecuted by the military regime in Argentina. Here in Chile they had promptly done much harm by spreading Marxism in the universities. What were the chances of the Nationals and Christian Democrats joining forces in opposition? The National Party leader sighed, and said (not with the utmost conviction) that he would like to see a 'dialogue' between the two groups, but there was no mutual trust – even less than before the elections. On the other hand, he saw no chance of the Socialists and Communists splitting within the U.P.; except for Allende, the Communists were rapidly dominating the coalition. The root trouble in Chile, politically, and what made it easy for the Communists to dominate, was that the poor – sadly – no longer believed in democracy. With reason, they were saying 'What's it done for me?' The coming municipal elections[1] were all-important, because Allende, if he won, would regard the verdict as a tacit *plebiscito* of approval for his policies. But Jarpa felt that, already, Chileans were beginning to 'reject' Communism, and that the opposition parties would win in April – though again he said it with little conviction. And the army? Even though this government was 'doing illegal things,' the National Party was opposed to any kind of military *golpe*, said Jarpa, 'because then all parties become abolished'. In any case, he did not think the armed forces would move. The senior officers tended to be socialist-inclined (their juniors were the impatient ones), and Allende was playing a very cautious hand. 'But after April, then it will begin.' Probably there would be

[1] In April 1971.

purges of the top brass unsympathetic to the regime. Meanwhile the Nationals would try to organize themselves for the fight – constitutionally, of course – as best they might. For instance, they were on the verge of launching a new national newspaper, *La Tribuna*,[1] into which Jarpa and his family were putting a large part of their own capital. (But how sensible a venture was it, one wondered, when there was already a perfectly good newspaper of the conservative opposition, *El Mercurio*, in a shaky position because of lack of financial support?)

Two young men of the right, 'Pedro' and 'Juan', came to lunch at our rooms in the Carrera, very privately. It was just as well, because if we had lunched in the elegant restaurant encrusted around the swimming-pool up on the roof the whole of Santiago would have learned every detail of the plans and intentions of the right-wing activists. Both were passionately indiscreet, highly intelligent, patriotic – and desperate. In their mid-twenties, they had worked energetically for the Alessandri youth movement during the elections, but now they felt that there was nothing to be gained by sticking to constitutional paths. There had to be a *golpe* by the anti-Marxists. One, Pedro, had fairish hair and strangely smoke-coloured eyes that lit up with the true light of the fanatic. Both were firmly convinced that, now once in power, the U.P. would never let go. They would find some dodge or other. After all, since 1917 when (except for Bela Kun in Hungary) had any Marxist regime let itself be ousted? Of course it was different in Chile (everything was always different in Chile), because it was the unique exception where Marxism had not come in on the bayonets of a Red army. But the U.P. was developing other means of seizing total power by force. Did we not recall what had set the final spark to the Spanish Civil War? Communist *brigadas del amanecer* (dawn brigades) had taken to terrorizing 'bourgeois' public figures, and their families in their own homes. Meanwhile the leftist government of Manuel Azaña just looked

---

[1] *La Tribuna* was in fact started in March 1971. During the troubles following Castro's visit in November 1971, it was banned temporarily by the government.

aside. Provocation had culminated with the leader of the opposition, Calvo Sotelo, being dragged from his house one night and murdered. The right wing reacted; the civil war began.

In the murder of Calvo Sotelo, Pedro and Juan saw frighteningly close parallels with what was happening in Chile. Here Marxism was at work 'with two hands'; with one hand, the Allende government operating in all constitutional respectability; with the other, clandestine groups perpetrating violence and armed illegality under the benevolently averted gaze of the government. In fact, the *miristas*. One of the very first acts of the U.P. had been to release forty-three *miristas* imprisoned for various deeds of violence – against the decision of the *contraloria*. (One of the 43 released men was later involved in the killing of Pérez Zujovic.) Now, particularly in the south, the MIR had started evicting land-owners from their property, or were inciting the peasants to do so; and the *carabineros* had received strict instructions from the government to stand aside. Sooner or later, there would inevitably be bloodshed, and it seemed clear to Pedro and Juan that the government was deliberately aiming to provoke the anti-Marxists 'to go outside the law' to protect their property, to start a half-cock rising which it could then crush, at the same time granting itself 'emergency powers' to perpetuate its hold over the country. One bad sign was the recent triumph of Senator Altamirano, just elected Secretary-general of the Socialist Party: Altamirano represented the activist, aggressive wing of the party, and was an outspoken apostle of 'provoking an *enfrentamiento*'.

(This notion of the Left provoking the Right into an *enfrentamiento* was to be heard repeatedly in Chile, outside U.P. circles. And, indeed, indirectly it gained some support from the Debray–Allende dialogues – which had not yet been published at the time of our lunch. 'A subtle and dangerous game is being played in Chile,' admits Debray, 'each of the existing camps sticks to its corner of the woods, *waiting arms at the ready to see which will make the fatal blunder, which will break cover before the other.*' 'Yes,' says Allende; 'we shall wait for them to start it. We are vigilant . . . we shall meet reactionary violence with revolutionary violence, *because we know that they are going to break the rules.'* [Author's italics])

Quite fatalistically, Pedro and Juan too *know* that this is how it will happen; and in their heart of hearts they *know* that they will lose. They are despondent at the sense of resignation among the traditional leading classes of Chile; at the mass flight, since the elections, of so many 'responsible' figures – like Doonie Edwards – who should be staying to 'fight it out', one way or another. They are despondent that the army will not act – until it is too late. And, because of its fingers burnt in Vietnam, the U.S. is of course impotent to help its friends; anyway, a *Yanqui* intervention or economic sanctions would only consolidate all Chileans behind Allende. Worst of all, time – in every sense – seems to be completely on Allende's side. So the Right is caught on the horns of a dreadful dilemma. If it does nothing for too long, the Marxists will have so entrenched themselves – in the civil service, in the unions, in the armed forces – that nothing will be able to budge them. Alternatively, if it acts precipitately – and *unconstitutionally* – the chances are that it will lose, and the Altamiranists will have achieved and won their *enfrentamiento*.

The two young men tell us indiscreetly about their 'plans'. They are horribly amateurish – and, as the U.S. ambassador, Ed Korry, was to tell us later, 'hopelessly blown to the government'. Not surprisingly. But they are totally dedicated. 'Some of us will have to die,' says Pedro of the smoke-coloured eyes, with quiet sincerity. 'One must fight before it is too late.' Momentarily I could see those eyes glaring back at the firing squad. It was a disturbing lunch.

Next morning on my way back to the Carrera, I came upon a military 'happening' just outside La Moneda. Uniforms seemed to be converging from all directions, accompanied by large crowds. For a brief instant I wondered whether the army, inspired by Pedro and Juan, could be about to lay hands on *el Compañero Presidente*. Inquisitively, I asked a nearby captain what was happening? He seemed to read my thoughts. 'Nothing,' he replied, defensively, and rather squashingly. 'It's only the *carabineros* changing the guard. They do it every forty-eight hours.' The arrival of bands and the *carabineros* close- and open-order marching dispelled any remaining doubts. Khaki-clad, they looked like the British army, and their drill was every bit as smart as the Brigade of Guards.

For all its pride in having won every war it ever fought, Chile is a singularly unmilitary country. Its defence budget (as of 1965) comprises a tiny 1.8 per cent of the national budget (compared with much wealthier Argentina's 17 per cent). The efficient navy that patrols Chile's extravagantly long coastline and maintains a long-established (and very British) maritime tradition, numbers only 15,000; the Army 38,000. But the key force is the 25,000 strong *carabineros*. An autonomous police militia not unlike Spain's *guardia civil*, they are commanded by an army general but are (in theory) directly responsible to the minister of the interior. They perform all the normal police duties, such as traffic control and the maintenance of public order, plus the more far-reaching criminal prevention tasks such as those carried out by the Canadian 'Mounties'; they teach at schools in the outback, and they are also equipped with heavy weapons, armour and light artillery. They have a reputation for utter incorruptibility, and are the most widely respected police force in all South America. No anti-government *golpe*, of Right or Left, could conceivably succeed without the support of the *carabineros*. Although their members tend to be somewhat right of centre, traditionally the corps holds itself icily aloof from politics and politicians. It is this quality that has distinguished the Chilean armed forces as a whole from those in the rest of South America. With the exception of that brief period in the turbulent 1920s and 1930s, they have never been subject to the mystique of being an olympian kind of watchdog of the nation's political morality, holding a virtual power of veto over the head of every government. In Chile, notes Debray perceptively, 'one calls for a lawyer when there are problems to be solved, whereas in other countries they call for the army'.

Down in the south of Chile, I later met a *carabinero* major – a typical professional serviceman – who was prepared, discreetly, to be drawn out on the possible involvement of the forces in politics. Though he disapproved strongly of the way the government seemed to be letting the MIR run amok, particularly in that part of Chile, he would certainly not be willing to take part in any *golpe* by the armed forces. 'After all,' he said, with some feeling, 'opposition politicians never showed any interest in the armed forces in the past; so why should we bail them out now?'

But, with great astuteness, Allende now *was* showing an interest. If anything the *chiste* about 'Marina' being his new mistress was a mild under-statement, in that he was making equally flattering advances to all the other services. For the first time in some forty years, units of the Chilean army had the previous year mutinied over service conditions. The *carabineros* were also poorly paid, and worked long hard hours. All this Allende promised to set right soon after coming to power; and to an impressive extent he has already fulfilled his promises. He wooed the top brass with a warmth never shown by Frei, seldom missing a military occasion, and adding a blandishment irresistible to most military hearts – the offer of new, modern arms and equipment. He had also wielded the stick, purging, on various pretexts, a number of 'awkward' senior officers after the Schneider assassination. General Viaux, the man whose regiments had mutinied and who had been implicated, allegedly, in the assassination, was still imprisoned in a disagreeable gaol in the red-light district of Santiago.[1] One of Allende's very first acts was to stand down the mobile riot-squad of the *carabineros*, the *grupo movil*, a much-hated target of the Left on account of its strike-breaking actions and evictions of squatters.[2] A more sinister trend, at least to all opponents of the U.P., was the apparently steady insinuation of Cuba-trained security men into key jobs in the *investigaciones*, Chile's F.B.I., starting with thirty-two-year-old Eduardo Paredes, recently arrived from Havana, who was appointed its deputy director immediately after the Schneider killing.

There was much talk in the U.S. before we left of a purposeful assault by Allende on Chile's hallowed freedom of the press. To what extent was it true? If one can judge

[1] He was subsequently sentenced to twenty years imprisonment.
[2] One such eviction, the so-called 'Puerto Montt massacre' of 1969, resulted in eight deaths and twenty-seven wounded.

from the ubiquitous Santiago newsstands,there is an abundance of freedom of all kinds; sleazy sex magazines rub shoulders with scurrilous political broadsheets of both ends of the spectrum, and you can buy such *Yanqui* imports as *Time* and the *Miami Herald* without difficulty. After Uruguay and Argentina, Chile has the third highest newspaper readership in Latin America. Like Harold Wilson and the British Socialists, Allende has always complained that – because of the monopolies of the wicked press barons (notably the Edwards family) – the 'popular' cause has never been properly represented; and therefore, freedom of the press was illusory. But a breakdown of the media shows that he has less to complain about than Mr Wilson – and very soon after the U.P.'s election the balance began to swing radically in its favour, for reasons that will be shown.

As of January 1971, there were five Marxist dailies with a national circulation: chiefly the shrill-voiced, pro-government 'independent', *El Clarín*, with the largest readership of the five (110,000); the stylistically anaesthetic official government paper, *La Nación*; the P.C.Ch. *El Siglo*, as ponderous as any organ of the Kremlin,[1] and *Puro Chile*. Most influential of the left-wing weeklies was the pro-Castro *Punto Final*, edited by Manuel Cabieses (who was expelled from the P.C.Ch. in 1966 for Castroite 'deviationism') and which first published the Debray-Allende dialogues. Of the non-Marxist press there were notably also five national newspapers: three 'independents', headed by the conservative Edwards – owned *El Mercurio*, with a circulation of 140,000, the largest in Chile;[2] and two pro-Christian Democrat dailies,[3] chiefly the newly launched *La Prensa* (30,000). *La Prensa* has speedily acquired an influence out of proportion to its modest circulation, and while I was in Chile it was producing much of

---

[1] *El Siglo* is so docile to Soviet policy that when the U.S. carried out its abortive commando raid to release P.O.W.s in North Vietnam, it waited three days until *Tass* gave permission to publish the (no-longer) news.

[2] The Edwards empire also owned a powerful network of provincial newspapers across Chile.

[3] At the time of writing, reduced to one (*La Prensa*) only.

the liveliest and most resourceful journalism on the opposition side. (Jarpa's *Tribuna* had not yet started.) Then, among the weeklies there was the Christian Democrat *Ercilla*, whose difficulties have been touched upon already; on the (respectable) Right there were *Sepa*, *PEC* and *Que Pasa*.

In Chile there are no oppressive controls over the press – such as those in Peru under which Zileri Gibson was groaning; or those in Brazil, where the editor of one of the two leading conservative dailies has been arrested no fewer than twenty-five times; or the unchecked mob-rule of Bolivia, where, in the turbulent year of 1970, one newspaper owner was blown to pieces and another simply thrown out by his typesetters. In the white-heat of the election, Allende went on record as promising to put out of business his bitter enemy, *El Mercurio*. But, so he later assured Régis Debray, he had no intention of imposing any press law. There were, however, other ways; subtler, indirect – and *constitutional*. Allende went on to explain to Debray that, instead of suppressing the hostile, 'bourgeois' media, 'We are going to co-ordinate our own, we are going to increase them.' The U.P. was also going to set about educating the journalists 'so that even when they are working for bourgeois companies and they see that their employers' policy is against the Popular government, they are, by their presence in these companies, an element of resistance against the bourgeoisie.' The implications of this last were particularly clear and menacing. Already since Allende made his declaration of intent to Debray much has been put into effect. Soon after the elections 'committees of people's unity' began to show their heads inside opposition newspapers; 'bourgeois' journalistic comment was met with threats of industrial action by the unions; and, (according to Professor Hugh Thomas) on one provincial paper in the south, *El Sur*, the printers actually took to adding their own comments – known as *coletillas*. Later in May 1971 Allende went as far as creating his own 'Assembly of Journalists of the Left' composed of U.P. faithfuls – apparently excluding the rest from La Moneda press conferences, a rather ominous development in the light of East European experiences.

There were also occasions when the government gave the impression of harassing the opposition press (always, though, within the framework of existing laws), and, on the other hand, of protecting its own. In March 1971, for instance, the editor of *PEC*, Marcelo Maturana, was arrested and held under investigation for ten days on some trifling charge of having 'leaked' details of a meeting between Allende and the service chiefs; and during the 'saucepan' demos at the end of the year, *Tribuna* was summarily suspended for infringing the 'emergency' regulations The contrast with what happened, in February (1971), to the Communist *Puro Chile* is instructive. *Puro Chile* had been closed down for three days by court order after it libellously accused three opposition senators of conspiring against the government. Nevertheless *Puro Chile* appeared as usual the next day, calling itself *Dulce Patria* – both being phrases from the Chilean national anthem. The banner headlines proclaimed PURO CHILE in huge letters, and then – in much smaller print – 'did not come out today'. A photograph showed the editors convulsed in laughter at the excellence of the joke; which was evidently shared by the government, in so far as it just looked the other way in the face of such manifest derision of a judicial ruling.

But, as with his policy of nationalization, the best weapons in Allende's armoury for bringing the hostile press to heel were economic ones. It has already been noted how the Christian Democrat publishing house of Zig-Zag, the biggest publisher of educational books in Chile, but already financially shaky, was bankrupted by impossible union wage claims. The government *interventor*, however, refused to allow it to go into dissolution. Negotiations dragged on, each turn of the government screw increasing both the humiliation and the drain on the funds of the parent company as well as its publications. In the end, after a personal plea to Allende, Zig-Zag was simply taken over by the government, making a very useful addition to the U.P. media. As an eleventh-hour rider, its president, Señor Mujica, beaten down by the negotiations, was required to sign a letter declaring that he had in no way been subjected to any kind of duress. *Ercilla*, Chile's leading weekly news review, somehow managed to survive the collapse of its own printing press; but found itself confronted by two new weeklies, launched by the State. The principal new product of the captive Zig-Zag press, called *La Firme*, had also contrived to make off with a useful part of its staff. *PEC* and *Sepa*, the two conservative weeklies comparable to *The Spectator* or the U.S. *National Observer*, were also struggling against mounting financial problems. Since the September 1970 elections, *PEC*'s circulation (12,000) had actually risen; but it was losing money, its private support was gone, and each week it was expected to put up the shutters. Both struggled on, however, attacking the U.P. in articles often of high quality, and quite fearlessly.

The new product of the former Zig-Zag press, *La Firme* (Chilean slang, virtually untranslatable, for 'the real truth'?) was to sell for the ridiculously low sum of 1.50 escudos as a kind of comic strip written in a peculiarly vulgar form of vernacular, evidently aiming for the lowest common denominator of semi-literates or adolescents. Strongly Marxist propaganda, it was quite clearly directed at arousing hatred against the propertied classes, and each weekly issue had its own specific 'know your class enemy' target. The first issue dealt with agrarian reform, and explained how the big *latifundistas* came to own so much land; starting with the Spaniards stealing it from the Mapuche Indians. A bloated modern landlord was shown in his huge car, gazing proudly out over neglected land and declaring: 'This year I don't intend to plant anything – why should I let it obstruct the sunset?' Crude, but effective. Another issue, anatomizing 'the monopolies', depicted a banker telling a Poor Little Man: 'There is very little money around, so we can only lend money to people with money!' It ended in basic instructions to workers: those in state 'monopolies' must develop a sense of responsibility, and improve productivity; those in 'private' concerns must prevent the wicked owners from sabotaging them before they can be expropriated. Yet another, entitled 'What is behind the news', was largely an attack on the veracity of the Edwards press, revealing its vested interests and exposing thereby the motives for its 'unreliability'.

The arch-enemy of the U.P. is, and remains *El Mercurio*. Allende's attack on it was one of the most instructive examples of his strategy of 'indirect approach' – such as would have warmed the heart of the late Sir Basil Liddell Hart. First a U.P. 'cell' within *El Mercurio* spoke up, opposing the paper's line and claiming to represent *all* its employees. This was promptly shot down by the management – but the threat had been registered. Next began the process of undermining the powerful paper's financial props. A suit was filed against the Banco Edwards, alleging 'irregularities' which violated Chilean banking regulations. Chiefly, it concerned the obtaining from a North American bank of a one-million-dollar loan which the government claimed was improperly secured. Banco Edwards countered that the loan was perfectly legal, and had the Central Bank's authorization. An *interventor* (the familiar story) was installed. The bank president, a prominent Chilean industrialist and son of a former presidential candidate called Jorge Ross, was arrested and brought before the *investigaciones*, not primarily on matters relating to the bank, but on the apparently dubious charge of illegal possession of arms. Although Banco Edwards and *El Mercurio* were quite separate entities, linked only within the Edwardses' holding company, the paper possessing no more than a 10 per cent holding in the bank, the U.P. ran a powerful press campaign to attempt to associate *El Mercurio* with the banking 'scandal'. The government then went so far as to send in ministry of finance inspectors to attach the accounts ledgers of *El Mercurio* and its subsidiaries. Simultaneously, demands were made for the immediate payment of a quantity of tax arrears; while, in the course of his protracted investigations the *interventor* froze all dealings by the bank.[1] This greatly exacerbated the financial stresses and strains already existing within the *Mercurio* group, which included an unprofitable publishing offshoot, the Lord Cochrane press. Like Zig-Zag, the Edwardses had been disallowed from liquidating Lord Cochrane, and they were also lumbered with a huge, extravagant new printing-press – *El Castillo* – with a capacity far in excess of demand. One of the last acquisitions of Doonie Edwards before he fled from Chile, *El Castillo* was supposedly one of the most modern presses in the world; but

[1] Banco Edwards was subsequently fined $550,000.

its over-ambitious capacity had locked up in it a large part of the group's credit resources.

Perhaps the most serious blow of all, however, had been the government's immediate withdrawal of all official advertising, such as the results of state lotteries, etc. This had reduced *El Mercurio*'s own revenue at once by 33 per cent, while at the same time the post-election wage increases had sent production costs up by 40 per cent. The paper was almost crippled, its forty-eight pages reduced to a mere twenty-four to twenty-six (though some Chileans thought this belt-tightening noticeably improved its editorial standards). The progressive nationalization of private industry posed a further, more serious threat to *El Mercurio*'s advertising revenue. In the absence of Doonie Edwards, nominal control passed to his sister, Sonia, a close personal friend of Senator Altamirano and with pronouncedly leftist views. Under the shock of all this, for the first few weeks after the elections *El Mercurio* performed some strange editorial gymnastics and gave the semblance of being crushed in spirit.

El Mercurio proudly claims to be the oldest newspaper in the whole Spanish-speaking world, and its offices in Santiago reinforce the boast. One is instantly carried back to the London *Times* of two decades ago; there is the same miasma of aged sub-editors, dead but unburied at their posts. In the fusty boardroom dominated by a large Laszlo portrait of an Edwards ancestor, I am greeted by Fernando Léniz, the newly appointed managing director of *El Mercurio*, a slender man in his forties with nine children, who reminds me (the resemblance is purely physical) a little of Fleet Street's Peregrine Worsthorne. Léniz does not come from an oligarchic family and gives the impression of being a man of caution and compromise, certainly no fire-eater, hedging many of his remarks with a 'but, on the other hand. . . .' With him is Rene Silva, *Mercurio*'s chief leader writer, renowned as a mandarin stylist, a slow-speaking figure of perhaps sixty who, too, might have come straight out of Printing House Square, and Arturo Fontaine, who has been responsible for some of the more outspoken recent leaders. Fontaine confirms that 'strictly speaking we are not being persecuted; we can write anything we want. It's just a matter of pressure.'

148

The pressures are, everyone admits, very strong. They are unhappy about the attack on Zig-Zag which does seem, indirectly, to threaten freedom of the press. 'But we are not being much helped by some of our "friends" abroad,' interjects Léniz. For instance, just the previous day at a conference in Rio of the Inter-American Press Association (S.I.P.), its president – a Brazilian journalist called Nascimento Brito – declared outright that 'the liberty of the press no longer exists in Chile', adding that El Mercurio would perhaps last no more than four months under such an atmosphere of 'government repression'. 'This was very bad for us,' says Fernando Léniz, because it seems to reinforce the accusation that El Mercurio was organizing an international campaign against the government. He shows me a strongly worded telegram he is about to despatch, protesting against such foreign 'interventions'. Meanwhile, at home the paper is now counter-attacking fiercely; at the moment, on its own account particularly against the U.P.'s attempts to implicate it with the Banco Edwards 'scandal'. 'We are not defending the Banco Edwards, per se.' Léniz assures me. 'What most alarms us in the nationalization of the banks is that all fiscal powers will become centralized in the government.'

The policy of El Mercurio is now to fight at every turn what looks like an infringement of legality, in any form. It is lashing out at the government's interference in the judiciary; first, in its release of the forty-three convicted miristas, and secondly, in its attack on the Chilean supreme court over the Morales case.[1] In common with the Christian Democrat press, El Mercurio is also condemning the government for its failure to respect existing agrarian laws, by permitting the miristas to take the law into their own hands with their seizures of properties down in the south. 'Our view is simply

[1] In November the military prosecutor had demanded the withdrawal of parliamentary immunity from Senator Raul Morales, a right-wing Radical, on the grounds that he had been implicated in the Schneider killing. The Court of Appeal approved the application, but was overruled by the Supreme Court on the grounds of insufficient evidence against the senator. It was then attacked violently by various U.P. spokesmen, calling for a substitute for 'bourgeois justice'.

this,' explains Léniz. ' "If you don't like the law, change it – otherwise enforce it." '

Whatever the political colour of its policy, and the occasional stodginess of its style, it cannot be denied that – journalistically – *El Mercurio* has the highest standards in Chile, and perhaps in South America. Its tone of high seriousness and its wide coverage of non-parochial news would place it in a top league in either Europe or the U.S. But, with much more limited resources, it is the Christian Democrat *La Prensa* that is producing some of the most dynamic journalism. Its reporters scooped the MIR seizures in the south; and later they were greatly to embarrass the government with details of ministerial involvement in shady copper trafficking. The editor of *La Prensa*, a young man rather pleased with himself called Patricio Silva, has no sympathy with the problems of either *El Mercurio* or Banco Edwards. The government was 'absolutely right' to investigate the latter; certainly there had been 'irregularities' and 'illegalities'. There is no *direct* pressure on *La Prensa*, but indirect pressures, yes. Fortunately its union chapel is not Communist-controlled. 'And if the government *did* take over *La Prensa*, it would go broke in ten minutes!' he laughs. Slightly reluctant to talk much further about U.P. interference with the press, Silva expands freely on the 'scoops' *La Prensa* has been getting on *mirista* activities in the south. The situation is very bad, anarchic; it is difficult to see how the government is going to handle it, how they are going to get the MIR hotheads out of the farms they were occupying. 'You should go and talk to Pablo Hunneus, our reporter who's been down there.'

In the world of broadcasting, the advantages seem much more favourable to the Left; and the influence of the media is growing all the time. It is reckoned that more than nine out of ten Chilean homes have at least one radio, and there are some 120 stations throughout the country. Out of twenty-eight in Santiago alone, twenty-four were already (as of January 1970) reckoned to be firmly under left-wing control. There are four TV stations, all subject to some degree of government pressure. One is state-owned, though operating nominally under an independent TV authority, while the other two belong to the universities and have traditionally been orientated towards one or other faction of the U.P. (Channel 9 to the Communists, Channel 13 to Chonchol's MAPU).

I lunch with Maria-Eugenia Oyarzun; formerly correspondent of the deceased Latin-American edition of the *Economist*, she now gives two radio commentaries each week. She terms herself an 'independent radical' and is widely respected for her courage and intelligence – and presumably for her looks, too. She is a big, handsome woman in her late thirties; wide shoulders and imposing bosom, red hair tied back in a bun, and beautiful but forceful features. Immediately she sits down her presence dominates our corner in the restaurant of the Carrera, but she is agreeably unaware of it. She is one of those Chilean women who seem to have just that much more than the men, and it is difficult at first to concentrate on what she is saying. However it emerges that in broadcasting it is the same old story of 'indirect pressures'. Government representatives, she says, tell the individual broadcasting companies 'we won't upset your business – provided you just sack so-and-so . . .' To comply with the government's demands for 'fairness of comment', even the non-Marxist companies find themselves having to give the Communists ten minutes' space 'at the peak time of day'. She is convinced her mails and telephone are being tampered with. 'But I am going to stay and fight it out.' She looks as if she means it, and would give a good account of herself.

A strange charivari of films are on show in Santiago, and there appears to be no visible censorship. But the Communist Party is reputedly urging that Costa-Gavras's film *L'Aveu* (*The Confession*) with its unflattering references to Stalinism, should be banned from Chilean screens. (As it was, later the treatment of *L'Aveu* became something of a *cause célèbre*, both on independent TV and because *PEC* published large parts of the script, publicly daring Allende to explain why the film was not shown in Chile. Finally, in a superb piece of stage management which showed off his 'indirect approach' to its best advantage, Allende produced Costa-Gavras himself, who declared helpfully in front of Chilean television cameras that he quite understood why the film might be considered unsuitable for release at such a 'delicate' period;[1] that he knew of no attempt at censorship and blamed 'neo-imperialists' for trying unfairly to make political capital out of his film! By comparison it is worth noting that in Peru – with its much more *overtly* oppressive press controls – the Generals permitted the showing of Costa-Gavras's other film, *Z*, despite its unfriendly allusions to military dictatorships.

Nowhere in Chile is the ideological battle being waged more vehemently than in the universities. As in most Latin American countries today, it is the students who are the most militant political force. Comparatively speaking, educational standards are (or used to be) high in Chile. The medical school of the University of Chile used to be, for instance, rated the best in Latin America. The general illiteracy rate is 10 per cent, which is low by continental averages, but it has not shifted since the 1940s. No tuition fees are paid in the state universities; nevertheless, only a minute fraction of Chilean undergraduates come from the working classes – substantially less than 5 per cent. Professors and lecturers are miserably paid,[2] sometimes receiving less than the cost of the taxi fare to and from classes. So most of them have to work part-time at other jobs to make both ends meet; hence they are less involved in university life even than the 'remote and ineffectual dons' of Oxford or Cambridge. Little fresh research gets done. Running of the universities has, to a large extent, been left to the politically mesmerized students, with education taking a poor second place to the struggle for control in the student bodies, the ousting of an unpopular rector, and the gaining of power on the *consejo*, or governing body. A foreign research student described to me the working of the *consejo* at Santiago's University of Chile (40,000 students) – which he rated 'the most politicized university in the world'. In the *consejo*, 'Four out of twenty-five members are students, and they have the power to select or reject professors. Because of the passionate hatreds – academic as

[1] *The Confession* was, in fact, finally shown *after* the critical April 1971 municipal elections.
[2] £30, or $75 a week would be a fair salary for the head of an *instituto*; a major department, or faculty, at the University of Chile.

well as political – that exist between the professors on the *consejo*, the four students can usually swing it completely. Their principal weapon – to bring the university out on strike.' Because of the frequent close-downs – as well as the necessity of the students to devote time to earning a livelihood – it is not unusual to find undergraduates still working for a degree in their early thirties. Five years ago it was estimated that the wastage in university hours meant that – despite the slave wages paid to staff – it cost roughly twice as much to produce a doctor or engineer in Chile as in London or Paris. (It must be considerably more, now, in these turbulent times.)

The trend among the students, as everywhere else in South America is leftwards. In all but one (the Catholic university) of the seven Chilean universities, the majority are reckoned to support Allende, and it is probably true to say that higher education has been 'controlled' by Marxists already for the best part of a decade. It is the Altamirano-wing Socialists and the MIR who currently create most of the noise;[1] but one has the feeling that, as in so many other spheres of Chilean life, it is the orthodox Communists who, quietly and methodically, are making the most headway, gaining the positions of influence that will count over the very long term. The *Juventud Comunista de Chile*, for instance, numbers nearly half the total membership of the P.C.Ch. Among others it heads the most important of the university student federations, that of the University of Chile.

Claudio Veliz is (or was) director of the Institute of International Studies within the University of Chile, and he is something of a Chilean institution himself. Barely forty, Veliz can already look back on a remarkably full academic life: Harvard, the Sorbonne, the London School of Economics, St Antony's College, Oxford – and, perhaps above all, ten years at Chatham House from which he had recently returned. Many are the distinguished works on Latin American problems that bear the caption 'edited by Claudio Veliz':

[1] The MIR have controlled the student federation at Concepción University for several years; in December 1970 there was a shoot-up between Communists and *miristas* resulting in the death of a twenty-three-year-old *mirista*.

153

The Latin America Handbook, Obstacles to Change, The Politics of Conformity (two titles that indicate where the heart of the editor lies); and so on. An excellent skier and swimmer, married (for the third time) to an elegant and intelligent Chilean aristocrat, he cuts a rather sophisticated cosmopolitan figure. But he is far from being, politically, of the Right; on the contrary. He is bitterly critical of the Chilean bourgeoisie, of whom he says in one of his books that 'Programmes of fundamental institutional change, if left to the reforming zeal of the urban middle-classes of Latin America, are unlikely to succeed.' For this reason among others he was to the left of the Christian Democrats. In 1970 he backed the U.P., and, while I was in Chile, there was talk of his being appointed Allende's ambassador to the Court of St James (certainly, Doña Isabela would have made an exquisite ambassadress). Bill and I find Veliz in his university office, his trim black beard a-bristle with rage. 'Look, I have to get out of this bloody place. Let's drive up into the mountains and talk.' We drive furiously for half-an-hour, up and up. Eventually we stop off the road, on a hillside at Lo Curro. The view over Santiago and towards the Andes is incredible. Already that indescribable gold of evening is beginning to touch up the distant snowcaps. The air tastes wonderful and I remark banally how hard it is to think of political strife in such surroundings. Veliz pays no attention. 'I have just handed in my resignation, again, for the *n*th time. But the rector says "don't, that's exactly what they want."'

'*They*', basically, are the *miristas*. 'These mad kids want to turn us into an institute of anti-imperialist studies.' The Institute had been going four years, and Veliz had fought throughout his stewardship to model it on Chatham House – to make it completely above politics. Even Richard Gott, who wrote *Guerrilla Movements in Latin America* in Veliz's Institute and whose views are openly sympathetic to the *mirista*-style revolutionaries he describes in his book, praises its impartiality as 'perhaps the only centre in Latin America – or indeed elsewhere – where it would have been possible to engage in this type of research in a completely free and unfettered manner'. Now every attempt is being made to Marxify the Institute. Veliz did not blame Allende; but the U.P. victory *had* 'generated a certain effervescence'. At first Veliz had not taken the pressures too seriously; now he was beginning to. 'And, you know, we're all getting what visitors to Germany in the early Hitler days used to call the *deutsches Blick*; that look over the shoulder to see who may be listening.' His slim budget of $45,000 has already been halved, but what most infuriates him is how – under the university charter – even the lowest grade non-academic employees of his Institute are granted a voice in its policy. The porters (who are Communists) can, he says, vote on decisions by the governing body; 'And, imagine, the cook has half a vote and that's usually the casting one!' Thus on her vote may depend whether the Chilean Institute of International Studies remains independent – or becomes a centre for Marxist propaganda.

In fact, matters have taken a different course; two months after I left Chile Veliz arrived at the Institute one day to discover that he had been locked out. *Mirista* students had simply moved in and taken over the building, placarding it with hostile slogans directed at Veliz personally. He has not, to this date, been allowed back in – though nominally still the director – nor have the occupying students been chased out. Almost simultaneoulsy, Veliz was arrested by the *investigaciones* at seven in the morning and questioned for three hours on charges of illegal dollar manipulations – which were never pursued. A letter I received from a mutual friend in Santiago said:

Fortunately he has all kinds of proof of the inaccuracy of the accusations, but it just simply destroyed him. . . . The core of the matter is that he is for Boenninger (Christian Democrat) to be elected Rector of the University, and against the U.P. candidate. . . .[1] The sad part of his affair [Claudio's] is that it so clearly shows the unscrupulous Marxist methods already rolling on so effectively.

Since then, Veliz has apparently given up the unequal struggle and decided to follow in the footsteps of thousands of

---

[1] The election was a week or so later, and Boenninger *was* elected.

thousands of other Chileans and accept a teaching post in Australia.

The picture one gets of the orthodox, Soviet-line Communists entrenching themselves within the universities silently and efficiently behind the U.P. façade seems to extend to the key sectors of the trade unions and the civil service. It is also one of the most disquieting features of Chile under Allende; because, once entrenched, the Communists will be much the most difficult to dislodge. Already by the time of the 1970 elections, the invisible power of the P.C.Ch. was out of all proportion to its 16 per cent of the electoral vote. After the Italian and French Communist Parties, the Chilean with some sixty thousand well-disciplined members is reckoned to be third strongest in the Western world, and one of the oldest.[1] During the elections over 80 per cent of the Popular Front committees swiftly organized for the campaign were Communist-led. On the *consejo directivo* of CUT(*Central Unica de Trabajadores*) the 'single trades union' which controls perhaps 70 per cent of organized labour in Chile, fourteen out of twenty-seven seats are held by Communists, only seven by Allende's Socialists. Its president is a Communist deputy. The P.C.Ch. also has the most efficient network at grassroots levels in the *callampa* slums, and among working journalists of the Left. Because of its superior, long-standing organization it alone can provide the expert civil servants required to carry through Allende's 'revolutionary' programme, and he is being forced to promote them. At the same time, while under the Constitution permanent civil servants cannot be sacked, their lives can be made intolerable in devious ways, and they can be passed over for promotion. This is happening with 'opposition' civil servants; thus, in addition to the three ministries controlling Chile's economy which Allende handed to the P.C.Ch., their men are also beginning to appear in the key secondary roles, as heads or deputy-heads of departments. One civil servant echoes what numerous other Chileans were to tell me: 'Suddenly one finds oneself coming up against faceless Communist functionaries at all levels.' There may be something about the cautious, scientific approach of the

---

[1] It celebrated its fiftieth anniversary in 1972.

Communists, as opposed to the adventurousness of the Socialists, that in the long term is most acceptable to the Chilean mentality, where it would not be to, say, the fiery Cubans. Will Chile in fact turn out to be the first real triumph of the Khrushchev doctrine of 'peaceful coexistence', · to 'bury' Capitalism by means of the subtle penetration of bourgeois institutions, instead of Maoist and Castroist violence, or the dogmatic rigidity of Stalinism?

The Communists infuriate the more flamboyant Altamirano Socialists and the MIR by the protean aura of 'bourgeois' respectability with which they cloak their burrowing activities. Clearly they are out to impress the marginal Chilean voter by their good, democratic, and – of course – constitutional behaviour.[1] But it seems likely that the masterminds in the Kremlin also have a broader vision, and have their eyes on Italy and France. What could be more conducive to the successful formation, and election, of new Popular Fronts in these two countries than the success of a *Unidad Popular* coalition in Chile of which the dreaded Communists prove to be the best citizens? This is certainly the view of one of Frei's ambassadors, a man with the mobile eyes of a practised diplomat, just returned from one of the top posts in Europe. For this reason, he thinks that the P.C.Ch. is *genuinely* interested in the democratic success of the U.P., and may act as a restraining influence on the left-wing Socialists and *mirista* hotheads. In the wake of Allende's victory, there was much fearful talk both in the U.S. and elsewhere in South America that Chile might 'export revolution' to her neighbours; but what if she were, in fact, to export the 'revolution of the polling booth' to the Old World instead?

In no way did Allende act more swiftly and audaciously than in re-aligning Chile's foreign policy. Within ten days of

---

[1] Though this appears, so far, to have paid off only in part. At the highly significant municipal elections of April 1971, the Communists, to their vexation, increased their vote to just 16.6 per cent while the Socialists leap-frogged over them to get 22.3 per cent. The Socialist successes however, to a large extent must have reflected Allende's own personal popularity rating.

his coming to power, and without consulting Chile's partners in O.A.S. (once designated a 'whore-house' by Castro), he restored relations with Cuba; thereby effectively driving a breach through the six-year-old U.S. boycott. Day by day Castro himself was expected to pay a triumphant visit to Chile.[1] Next, early in January 1971, relations were resumed with Mao's China; shortly afterwards I spent the evening with the young Chilean, Sergio Silva, who was about to go to Peking as Chile's first *chargé d'affaires* – enormously exhilarated at the vast new horizons he would be opening there. Then, having suggested at first that there might be only an exchange of consuls, Chile sent a full diplomatic mission to East Germany. It was a risk, because the Federal Republic was one of Chile's biggest copper customers and had provided her with 355 million Deutschmarks of aid over the past decade. But Chancellor Willy Brandt did not sever trade relations; any more than the U.S.A. would send in the Marines. Allende expected relations with Washington to become strained, particularly when the hard terms of his copper bill became known, but coolly he calculated that there would be no direct intervention, or blockade *à la* Cuba; as he explained to the faithful Debray, it was with this in mind 'that I have maintained that victory through the polling booths was the way to pre-empt any such policy, because this way their hands are tied'. Debray agreed: 'It means that any intervention would have no legitimate justification.'

And what prospect for British relations with Allende's Chile? At the most elevated levels of the British Embassy in Santiago, one encounters the rather mystical and mystifying belief that, in some marvellous way, Britain's commerce will prosper through the U.S.A.'s discountenance, that British firms will move into the vacuum left by the departing *Yanquis*. But one British businessman with long experience in Chile told a correspondent of *The Times* shortly after Allende's election that already 'We come up against the idea that we are not welcome. The new government's long-run aim, I think, is to run private enterprise slowly into the ground.'

---

[1] In fact, for one reason or another, this was postponed until Allende's first anniversary in office.

Certainly if, in its habitual lethargy, British enterprise was unable to scratch the surface under Chile's old capitalist regimes, how much more favourable are the terms it is likely to get from Allende's Marxist nationalism? *Le défi anglais?* Hmm . . . But belief persists, and no doubt provides the U.P. with a useful divisive weapon when dealing with *Yanqui* enemy number one.

It is, in fact, at the British Residence that we pass Bill's last evening in Chile. The Velizes are also there, and the newly arrived ambassador, a charming and cultured man, leads the conversation in great sweeps of history from Napoleon to Hitler, away from Chile. I am sunk in a torpor of exhaustion, the kick-back of just a couple of weeks of hanging on to the Buckley coat-tails, and contribute little. Just before we leave, Bill's eagle eyes light upon a piece of paper absent-mindedly left by the telephone – the list of dinner guests. It reads, *inter alia:*

Alistair Horne	Author
William Buckley	Companion

'*Compañero Bill*'! I feel that honour is, to some extent, paid back for that snub in Colombia's Presidential Palace! We move back to Nena's tiny but cosy house, where most of the friends we had made in our short time in Santiago are gathered. There is some mirth at the expense of *El Compañero Bill*, his sobriquet in Chile for ever more. Another 3 a.m. night, and the Chileans have hardly begun to talk before we leave. The next (or, rather, that) morning there is the usual confusion about flights. Bill is off to Rio for a thirty-six-hour stopover; then on to Switzerland, via – I believe – Saigon and the South Pole. At 7 a.m., U.S.I.S. rings to warn him 'The plane is several hours later. No hurry.' Then, at 7.30, 'The plane has arrived, we're calling for you in twenty minutes.' A desperate struggle to round up the innumerable boxes of pills, typewriters, tape-recorders and sheaves of paper; complicated financial transactions over the bill. Poor Nena arrives, notebook and pencil in hand desperately trying to complete an interview with Bill for *PEC* which she has been pursuing the last week in odd minutes in taxis, elevators and through bathroom doors. Finally the *compañero* departs, bleary-eyed, making little sense and for the first time showing the strain of the trip. I tell him he should at least be able to get some sleep on the plane. But, as always his resilience is miraculous; I get a letter later saying: 'A hell of a long flight to Rio! I wrote four columns on it.' There suddenly seems a vacuum in Santiago. When Nena telephones her usual cheery matutinal greeting, 'Are you still alive?' the answer is *NO*. Bill's exit leaves me feeling like a collapsed soufflé. It is how it was when they let all the pressurization out of the plane at La Paz.

8

The Struggle for the Land

Nena takes me down to the coast to spend the weekend with a friend of hers, 'Jaime', who has a flat on the sea at Con-Con. Jaime is a real *tuvo*; in his early forties, he was proprietor of his own boat-building company and had built up from scratch an aircraft sales firm which he valued at U.S. $800,000. 'But as of September 1970, it's worth at most $100,000, and I'm likely to lose the lot anyway.' He is surprisingly cheerful about it all, and explains why. A few weeks after Allende's victory he was driving his E-type Jaguar down to Con-Con, missed a bend, and ended up in the living-room of a very surprised *campesino*. Both he and the *campesinos* were quite unscathed and spent the rest of the night drinking and laughing together. It could only happen in South America. After he paid them for the damage and said *adios* to the ruins of ten thousand dollars' worth (by Chilean values) of E-type, he felt – he assures me – 'The most marvellous sense of liberation. You just don't know how worthless material things are, until you lose them.' I believe him. He means it. Jaime has also been a great playboy, leaving few beds unturned in Santiago. He has less sense of time than any Chilean I know (and that is saying something); there always seems to be another girl, or something, to be fitted in on the way between somewhere and somewhere else. When we go to pick him up at his flat, right opposite the intersection where General Schneider was assassinated, he is not there – by an hour-and-a-half. It is midnight when he takes us for 'an early dinner' at the smart, *momio* golf club, Los Leones. The club has a totally, expectedly English atmosphere, and is rather empty. The club servants look dejected; how much longer will they have employment there? There is a long table of young, beautiful people, and like young, beautiful people all over the world they fill the air with carefree chatter. Elsewhere, in sharp contrast, sit small groups of the middle-aged, with furrowed brows and heads close together, talking in low tones and pausing whenever the club servants approach. Jaime voices my thoughts, 'I wonder where they'll all be, where we'll all be, next year?' Finally, well after midnight, we set off in Nena's car, the oldest German Taunus in existence. By rights it should have given up the ghost years ago, but – like every animate object in Chile – it responds amazingly to Nena's touch, and we wheeze and rattle over the mountains to reach Con-Con at a modest 4 a.m.

Morning brings the sun shining hotly out of an orientally pure sky, marred only by a distant grey strip of fog that defines the Humboldt Current. Slow patrols of black pelicans ponderously skim the sea. At high tide the Pacific laps right up against the terrace of Jaime's microscopic flat. He makes me lean out over the parapet to look at a curiously smooth boulder set in the wall below. The sea has moulded it into the shape of a pair of perfectly rounded female buttocks. 'It's a very sad story,' says Jaime, in his gravel voice. 'You see once upon a time there was a beautiful Swedish girl, running away from her cruel husband, in a terrible storm; and – poor girl – she plunged straight into this wall and got turned into stone.' He tells his fable with such conviction, almost with tears in his eyes, that I wonder whether, Hans Andersen-like, a kiss would restore the unhappy Scandinavian to life; but a first swim persuades me that one would be much more likely to be turned to stone oneself. It is an experience not to be repeated. Con-Con's deceptively Mediterranean-tinted water is bitingly cold; worse than Peru, about on a par with the British seaside. But the Chileans seem not to mind. A plump lady who passes by at low tide, collecting huge black and silver whelks, in her excitement gets her slacks drenched by the icy waves without apparently noticing. In one corner of Jaime's terrace there is a strange tree with large leaves and gold tassels for blooms. It comes from Robinson Crusoe Island. 'I

162

believe it's a bread tree,' says Jaime, 'but it doesn't produce any bread; perhaps it needs a mate.' From behind the bread tree there appears from time to time a ravishing *Chilena* with high cheek-bones and immense brown eyes like a loris. She is the wife of Jaime's next-door neighbour, a Santiago lawyer. Behind the flat are pretty villas with white, pendent moon-flowers and feathery *aromo* trees growing in the gardens; tiny fish boutiques sell *congrio* and *corvina* and abalones straight out of the sea. There are steep sand dunes like ski slopes down which the children slide with wild shrieks of joy. At night we dine, terribly cheaply, off tasty *anticuchos* (a kind of kebab) barbecued at an open discotheque, which is filled with surpassing pretty sixteen-year-olds (Lolitas, Jaime calls them), evidently with a huge capacity for enjoyment. Over the weekend they drift cheerfully in and out of Jaime's flat; he affects not to know who they are or how he met them. It is a rapturously Arcadian setting, with no suggestion of the 'revolution' that besets one at every turn in Santiago; the only intrusion of politics is the shout of '*Mercooo-rio*' of the newsboys in the early morning.

The next day I start writing my first article. Jaime, when he is not flirting gently behind the bread tree with the loris, is discussing his future with Nena. Divorced from a Brazilian beauty, he is about to marry a French countess. 'My future mother-in-law wants to send out pompous wedding invita-tions, and asks me how to "designate" myself. Señor Jaime Rodríguez doesn't sound nearly snob enough – so what title can I assume?' I suggest the Conte de Con-Con; that would sound very good in French. He pretends he cannot make up his mind, but is clearly much in love with his absent countess. He has decided, however, like thousands of other Chilean *tuvos* – to get out. 'It's the last weekend I shall see this flat,' he says without any sentimentality, 'I may start an aircraft company in Miami – no, I think I'll go to Europe. No, I'll sail round the world while the money lasts. I won't get married, after all . . .' 'Jaimecito! Don't be so irresponsible!' protests Nena. They sit down and draw up a list of their friends and acquaintances across the world, giving them two- and three- star ratings, like a *Guide Michelin*. After the Lolitas, unsmiling men come and go, taking a hi-fi here, an ice-box there, books and armchairs. Jaime is selling everything. 'We are all going to become White Chileans,' he says gaily; 'you know, opening restaurant doors in Paris! It's funny, compared with the Argentinians [whom, in common with most Chileans, he rather despises for their boastful vulgarity] we never had much money; and we never worried about it. But now I suppose we shall have to worry, and it's so sordid.' Nostalgically, he goes through his photographs of girls and aeroplanes, and beneath all the gaiety there is a deep sadness.

After the September elections, Chileans left the country in droves, panicking lest, once Allende was confirmed in office, no one would be permitted to leave. Some twelve thousand left in September, and another seventeen thousand during the first fortnight of October. In one week, before the government stepped in, there was a run of U.S. $87 million on the banks. Allende declared it to be part of a right-wing conspiracy, but in fact it looked like sheer, unpremeditated panic. Most of the 'refugees' went just across the Argentina frontier from Santiago, to Mendoza, where they lodged in discomfort and dislike, and after November the tide gradually began to flow back. The attitude of mind of the Chilean self-exiles falls into two quite sharply differentiated categories, says Nena: those who go to Argentina or Spain do so because they want to continue to lead the life they have always led; and those who go to Australia, because they want to make a complete break and are searching for a 'new frontier'. Many of the middle-class Chileans I met were undergoing a bitter spiritual struggle within themselves: whether to stay, and face dismal prospects; or go, and leave a land they adored, its beautiful climate and their warm friends. 'It's something we have to be thinking about all the time,' an opposition journalist told me. 'But how hard it is!'

Bill, one day before he left, went gliding in the Andes (apparently, an incomparable experience); his pilot, of German origin, told him as they dodged from one thermal to another that when Allende came to power he had asked his accountant what he was worth:

One hundred and fifty thousand dollars [he said]. So, well, I thought; Look: I own a membership in this gliding club, where I

164

am a part-time instructor. I have my little business. I have a small airplane. I go fifteen times a year to ski at Portillo, with my wife and son. I have a sailboat, two cars, a swimming pool and a house. Where else can you have all of that with capital of only one hundred and fifty thousand dollars? So – I decided – I'll repose my faith in the army.

But, selectively, the less optimistic elite of Chile were still continuing to leave. The Australian consul in Santiago told me that his office was getting emigration enquiries at the rate of five hundred a day. They were having to bring in extra 'vetting' staff from elsewhere on the continent. 'And the emigrants who're coming are the best material Australia's getting anywhere in the world. All professional men.' It seemed a grim choice to me; to be Red in Chile, or dead in Australia! Some of the foreign communities were also dispersing; in Bolivia I was to meet a British missionary who told me that he was increasingly depressed by the virtual disappearance of his flock. From fifty British families it had dwindled down to twelve; most of them workers on the ore railroads, they were leaving because of fears that they would no longer be able to transfer their pay back home.

The steady drain of skilled copper mine technicians, doctors and lawyers is bound to have a serious effect on the Chilean economy eventually, and one wonders how long Allende can afford to let it go on, without placing restrictions – a kind of bureaucratic Berlin Wall – on foreign travel.[1] On the other hand, the fate of the Chilean self-exiles abroad hardly encourages the remaining *tuvos*. 'If I lie naked in the main square of my hometown, even my enemies will throw me a coat,' said one Chilean landowner. 'But I am not sure that I could expect the same treatment in Buenos Aires.' The Jaimes will return;[2] the Nenas won't leave. And why? Because – like the native *amancai*, the saffron-coloured alstroemeria which grows wild in profusion but transplants badly – the Chilean has an umbilical attachment to his

---

[1] He did, (see Chapter Sixteen).
[2] He did, too – plus countess.

land, stronger than anything existing elsewhere in South America.

> In Chile now, cherries are dancing
> the dark mysterious girls are singing,
> and in guitars, water is shining
> The sun is touching every door
> and making wonder of the wheat.
> . . .
> I have no wish to change my planet.[1]

says Neruda at his most poignant; and nine million other Chileans agree with him.

Meanwhile, at Con-Con, I note a small item in the press about another kind of exile; seventeen right-wing Bolivians expelled by left-wing President Torres and who had sought asylum at Arica, in the north of Chile. Claiming that they were in 'desperate straits' because they had no funds and no undertaking from the Chilean government to extend their fifteen-day resident permits, they have now seized the Bolivian Consulate to hold a hunger strike there. So much, I thought, for Cristian Casanova's assurance to us a week or so previously that they would receive the same treatment as the welcome left-wing exiles!

It is the beginning of February. What occupies the Chilean press most – more than Allende's economic programme, his political problems with Congress, even more than his struggle with the press itself – are stories of the troubles down in the southern provinces, the 'bread-basket' of Chile. What is happening down there, declares the Castroist *Punto Final*, 'constitutes the trial-by-fire of the Chilean revolution' which, over the next months, 'will define' its course. And, in summing up on his first ninety days in office, Allende admits that his 'most difficult problem . . . is still the conflict in Cautin'.

The problem is, basically, all about agrarian reform. Although real poverty is perhaps nowhere as desperate in Chile as elsewhere in South America, land hunger has long been a gnawing evil. When Frei came to power, it was said that

[1] From 'El Perezoso', *Estravagario* (1968).

between 2 per cent and 5 per cent of landowners possessed 75 per cent of the land, and there was only an average of two-and-a-half acres per person to go round, about the lowest on the continent. A few of the large estates in Chile still harked back to the original grants of land made by the conquistadors, which had never been broken up into smaller units and still operated like medieval serfdoms. The *inquilinos* – or tenant-labourers – were paid very low wages, receiving temporary assignment of a marginal plot of land in lieu of higher wages. They were, says Claudio Veliz

the group with the fewest possibilities, expectations or opportunities of improvement. Their only real chance of breaking through the social and economic barriers which surround them is by moving to an urban area.

In the past when the vote was not secret, the *latifundistas* were able to exert considerable political pressure by threats of dismissal; and still, to some extent, the tradition of political patronage continues. Much of the land was inefficiently farmed, or sometimes left waste altogether; because the landlords either lacked, or were unwilling to spend, capital on expanding cultivation. One statistic has it that, before Frei, 21 per cent of all the irrigated (i.e. the best) land in Chile was kept fallow. Under Frei's fiercely disputed reform laws, inefficiently worked land could be expropriated; so could the property of any one farmer adding up to more than two hundred acres of irrigated land – or its larger equivalent in less fertile areas. This was calculated to be the minimum area from which a farmer could derive a living. The owners of 'reformed' land were paid compensation at a rate of 10 per cent down on the value of acreage, and the rest in deferred bonds over twenty-five years. But, for a variety of reasons (not least of all Chilean legalism), under Frei – as has already been seen – the practical application of the agrarian reform moved at a far slower tempo than expected. When Allende came to power, his new minister of agriculture, Cuban-trained Jacques Chonchol – whose love for the *latifundistas* was about as warm as Spiro Agnew's for the Black Panthers – made it clear at once that he intended to accelerate Frei's programme out of all recognition. Every week long lists of *fundos* due for immediate 'reform' began to appear in the Chilean press. Their acres, rich and poor, were to be parcelled out among landless *campesinos*, or among the miserably underprivileged half million Mapuche Indians who can claim their lands were 'usurped' by the whites back in the 1880s. Or the land will be aggregated into super-collectives. In any event, things were really on the move.

But for the young firebrands of the MIR, they were still not moving nearly fast enough, down in the province of Cautín particularly, where poverty and land hunger were most extreme. They did not accept, for one thing, that the dispossessed farm-owners should receive any compensation whatever. So, taking advantage of the uncertainty and paralysis which existed in the countryside since the U.P. victory, the *miristas* began moving in on the farms themselves. Their technique, evidently, is to stir up and organize the *campesinos* and Mapuches, operating in small armed groups. Then they swoop down on the *fundos*, often in the small hours of the night, evicting the owners and their families at ten minutes' notice and with nothing more than the clothes they can grab. Next they set up their own 'revolutionary' administration on the seized property. According to the opposition press reports, the government is not intervening to check these illegal seizures, or *tomas*.

The south was clearly where the action was, so after Bill's departure I decided to go down there, and in Con-Con I persuaded Nena to come with me. It was the happiest idea I ever had; she knew everyone, and every door – government, opposition, and even *mirista* – was to fly open at the sound of her laugh. In some mystic way the right people were always on tap, and everything she organized seemed to work. It looked as though the Taunus might prove a greater liability than the MIR, so I hired a Chilean-made Peugeot auspiciously bearing 'Providencia' (a suburb of Santiago) on its number-plates. But first we set off for El Arrayan in the foothills of the Andes – along the rushing Mapocho river, up into country where perennial sweet peas, hydrangeas, purple hebes and six-foot-high pelargoniums seem to grow wild – to see Pablo Hunneus. A good-looking young sociologist – by no means a *momio* reactionary – who had turned journalist only a few weeks previously, it was Hunneus, working for *La Prensa*, who had just produced the most detailed reports of what was happening down south. His house is full of the impedimenta of the intellectual who has travelled: Samurai helmets, pre-Columbian pottery. Chickens dart about loose in the yard.

Pablo Hunneus reckons that at least 86 *fundos* (and he has made a detailed list of them), embracing an area of 400,000 acres, have already been taken over by the MIR and its M.C.R. (*Movimiento de Campesinos Revolucionarios*) allies in the two provinces of Cautín and Valdivia alone. Groups of the *miristas* were being led with great efficiency by a mysterious figure called 'Comandante[1] Pepe', who – a little like Strelnikov in *Dr Zhivago* – was roaming the countryside at will, carrying out *tomas* and establishing revolutionary committees wherever he went. He describes how he had found 'Pepe', up in wild mountain country close to the Argentina frontier, by checking through local *carabinero* files. All Pepe's *tomas*, he noted, were concentrated in the same area, on consecutive dates. He believes that the strategy of his group was to form a *foco*, in case of a coup by the Chilean right wing. The various *mirista* groups seemed to be quite autonomous; operating without orders from above, on the 'broken pyramid' principle. Hunneus gives us the names of the properties which have been seized – Poco a Poco, El Vergel, Las Tres Hijuelas, Carranco and so on – and then shows us on a map where Pepe himself has last been seen. The latest report are that some fifty armed men have descended out of the Andean forests to seize a series of properties around the village of Liquiñe. It looks forbidding country. The social conditions of the labourers there are bad, says Hunneus, but the *carabineros* are getting fed up with their orders to stand back: 'We're a very legalistic country, and their job is to arrest anyone carrying a gun.' Meanwhile, in self-protection, property owners are beginning to import *metralletas* from over the border: 'Very crude weapons, they seize up after one magazine.' But the situation looks menacing. The government has been enraged

---

[1] The self-appointed rank has a Castroist derivation.

169

by Hunneus's articles and has formally declared (of the Comandante) 'We don't know anything about the existence of this person.'

We leave Santiago late one afternoon, after the usual Chilean delays – in the form of an extended lunch given by the hirer of the Providential Peugeot. Amiably, he is more concerned for our safety than that of his car, and warns us to be prudent; the *miristas* are a tough lot, and their counterparts in Uruguay still have Ambassador Jackson sequestered in some hole in the ground. So I deposit in Santiago my diaries and any other document likely to encourage the *miristas* to think they might have their hands on a worthwhile hostage – except for the 'pull' of a jacket of *The Terrible Year*, my book on the Paris Commune shortly to be published. There are no signs leading out of Santiago, and even Nena gets gloriously lost. But when we find the Pan-American Highway it is straight and empty and we make rapid time. South of Santiago the Central Valley is only twenty miles wide; between eroded foothills lie prosperous farms and nectarine orchards; great fields of sky-blue vetch and then, suddenly, a bowl full of acre upon acre of sunflowers. The effect of that golden evening light, so uniquely Chilean, on this sea of giant yellow heads tossing gently in the breeze, is quite magical. The Andes become lower; Nena explains that, in pre-jet days, this used to be one of the old flight routes across to Argentina. We pass some *asentamientos*, marginal land parcelled out under Frei to landless *campesinos*. They are generally identifiable by the poor husbandry; much waste ground, weeds, gigantic *zamora*[1] thickets, and uneven patches of wheat. The chief trouble here seems to be that, when these land redistributions were made, they were not accompanied with adequate credits for the new owners to purchase such necessaries as fertilizers and weed-killers.

The outskirts of the towns along the route are marked by the invariable *callampas*, euphemistically renamed '*poblaciones marginales*' by President Frei as being less offensive to

---

[1] The European blackberry, which was brought over to Chile for hedging and has since run wild, often growing to fifteen feet high; about as evil as a pest as the rabbit in Australia.

the dignity of the poor. But they are still the same old grim slums, without water, electricity or sewage, and multiplying all the time as the inexorable *explosión demográfica* brings in fresh waves of landless *campesinos* from the country – just as everywhere else in the continent. What is the reason for the particular misery of the South American slums? One explanation is that, whereas the rise of Europe's cities during the nineteenth century was closely related with industrialisation, here it is taking place without any industrial revolution. Occasionally one passes a well-built *Alianza* housing estate; but the frequency ratio between the one and the other is disproportionately small. Allende admits that his housing officials encounter difficulty in persuading the individualist-minded Chileans to abandon their *callampas* for multi-storey co-operatives. And there, right in the middle of a wide, dried-up river bed, we come across one particularly atrocious shanty settlement; Nena explains that the residents have repeatedly been moved, out of the danger of seasonal floods, but back they come again. Often the rehoused *callampa*-dwellers return because they will not, or cannot, pay for such luxuries as power; or they try to steal it by tapping overhead high tension lines, and are often electrocuted.

As night falls, we are stopped several times at roadwork diversions by tired little figures with oil flares, giving contradictory instructions. Why don't they use automatic traffic signals, I ask Nena? 'Because it provides employment,' she says simply. We reach the motel at Salto de Laja after midnight. It is closed. There is only a guard standing gloomily, half asleep, in a small box. He assures us that we have no reservations. Nena assures him we have. The poor man makes an unconvincing attempt to read the accommodation chart, then says we can have one room with ten beds. Gently, Nena helps out with the chart and we get what we want. The illiterate nightwatchman, the lonely torpid figures out on the Pan-American Highway; they represent one of the worst curses of Chilean economic life – not unemployment, but underemployment.

I sleep badly, dreaming that I am being devoured by ticks; it is a combination of the itching after-effects of sunburn from Con-Con and of reading Che's diaries, with their

171

terrible descriptions of starvation and voracious insects and ticks in the Bolivian jungle. There is the roar of a tremendous cascade, a little Niagara, behind the motel. The morning brings sad, boreal skies:

> The day of the luckless, the pale day appears
> with a cold heart-breaking smell, with its forces in grey,
> with no bells on, dripping dawn from everywhere:
> it is a shipwreck in a void, surrounded by weeping.[1]

We have left the mediterranean world of Santiago and are already in the south, on a latitude roughly equivalent, I suppose, to New England. The vegetation along the roadside becomes increasingly familiar: cotoneasters, orange montbretias, and yellow hypericum, all growing wild. There are oaks and elms and chestnuts in the woods, and well-kept plantations of Oregon pine. Here in the south the combination of strong sun (when it shines) and a hundred inches of rain a year bring the pines to maturity in twenty years; it is a forester's paradise, which is perhaps one reason why so many Germans settled here. All the way to Temuco, the capital of Cautín, nearly five hundred miles south of Santiago, it never stops raining. Fields of wheat with that jaded, grey look suggestive of a bad English summer stand still unharvested. Nena assures me we should be able to see several volcanoes, but their cones are so completely enveloped in the swirling rainclouds that I teasingly tell her she is inventing. Temuco is a town of wooden buildings, instead of the brick and adobe of further north. There are many pure Indians hanging around under doorways, in the rain. The apparently slow, sleepy tempo of life reminds me of some of the northern Canadian communities I visited, many years ago.

Apart from *miristas* and Mapuche Indians, this part of Chile is also distinguished by its large German community. Our first visit is to the *alcalde*, or mayor, of Temuco – Germán Becker, who is as German as he sounds, although his family have lived in Chile for over a hundred years. A blonde, blue-eyed son of fifteen leads us to the *alcalde*'s office, where we

---

[1] Pablo Neruda, 'Weak with the Dawn', *Residencia en la Tierra II*, 1933.

have a complicated trilingual conversation; principally between the *alcalde* and myself in German, in Spanish when he wants to make a point for Nena, and English when he becomes indiscreet. He too is fair-complexioned, with slightly protruding teeth, and speaks with characteristically German precision, interpolating frequently a 'one-must-define-what-that-means'. His grandfather came out from Hanover in 1865 and was given a strip of *Urwald* (virgin forest) by the government, which he cleared. Out of the 200,000 to 300,000 Chileans of German descent, Becker says, about seven thousand live around Temuco. They are mostly farmers, or own small industries producing farm machinery. All the children go to German schools still, and are bilingual in Spanish and German. Becker himself has been to Germany four times since the war, and visited the G.D.R. in 1966; it had worried him that, though they were 'still the same Germans, now they had completely accepted Communism'. He had also travelled to Russia the previous year – which had not pleased him very much. He has served as *alcalde* seven years, and is vastly proud of the stadium for thirty thousand people which he had copied, in miniature, from one built in Hamburg to replace war destruction. During the past presidential elections, he had run the campaign in Temuco for Alessandri, who received his strongest support in Cautín.

On the subject of the present 'troubles' on the land, he begins cautiously but warms up as he goes along. He personally farms 950 hectares (just under 2,500 acres), which he bought thirty years ago. Yes, he has had 'difficulties' recently on his *fundo*, but will not specify. It is also true that the *carabineros* have received quite definite instructions not to defend property owners from the MIR: 'They only come after there has been an "incident", to note what action was taken. They write down the details and don't do anything. They won't even come when rung up and told "We are threatened by force." ' Yet, in December, they *did* come when an owner took back his farm from the *miristas*.[1] The

---

[1] Later we were to hear more detail of 'Rucalán' *fundo*, as it was called. The owner, Señor Landarretche, was instructed by the *interventor* that henceforth he would now have to employ thirty-eight workers on his 800

173

toma had taken place at between two and three in the morning, and the *miristas* allowed the owner and his wife to take a few clothes in a car, and get out. When he came back with a gun, the *carabineros* 'arrested him and reinstated the "squatters"; then brought in an *interventor*, so that all his assets are frozen and he can't sell anything. Mind you,' Becker adds, 'the *carabineros* are very unhappy with the role they have to play.' He deplores the mischief that 'agitators' are creating among the Mapuche Indians, for whom he has little admiration. The Mapuche have never been much interested in clearing virgin territory; they only keep sheep on odd patches of land, and few ever work properly. Drunkenness is a terrible problem: 'There is no race in the world quite so bad.' Had he ever been to the north of Canada? No. And there are no 'interdiction laws' forbidding the sale of drink to *indígenas* in Chile.

He is pessimistic about the immediate future in Chile. 'There is no doubt about it, we are a Communist country already! You can't compare Chile with East Germany, however, because everybody works there, but not here,' he adds with irrepressibly Germanic overtones: 'We Germans are so disciplined, so at least *Kommunismus* is working over there . . . Here everybody wants to take, but not to work. In the past the Chileans never discovered a system for making people work, so for these reasons the future must be worse here than in East Germany.' Have any Chilean Germans left for the Federal Republic already? 'Yes, and many are thinking of doing so, but are just waiting to see how things turn out. I have seven sons, they will all leave – and so would I if I were younger.' The fifteen-year-old was going to the U.S.A. next year. 'We have all worked fantastically hard, – and now . . .' The *alcalde*'s cautious formality leaves him: 'We built up everything from nothing . . . people abroad just don't know what is happening here in Chile . . .'

Jacques Chonchol, Allende's minister of agriculture and

---

hectares, instead of the existing six. He declared that this was 'impossible'; so the MIR evidently moved in again. The *fundo* was renamed *Campamento Che Guevara* and the familiar signs of '*Tierra o muerte*' have appeared outside it.

currently one of the most powerful men in Chile, has set up a kind of 'Battle H.Q.' here in Temuco. We go there to try to arrange an interview. The offices are filled with harassed supplicants, being bossed about by cocky, mustachioed young men. Chonchol himself was leaving town, but a friendly secretary is charmed into setting up an interview for the following week.

Raul Gallardo is the fifty-five-year-old editor of the local Christian Democrat newspaper, *El Diario Austral*, which has been taking a strong line against the *tomas* and the government's tacit encouragement of the MIR. He confirms the 'non-intervention' orders transmitted to the *carabineros*: 'Just the other day a *fundo* was taken a hundred and fifty yards from a *carabinero* post, and they did nothing.' That afternoon he has received reports of three more *tomas*. Yes, the *miristas* are armed, and have been for some time; he has no evidence that any owners possessed *metralletas*. The MIR is also being helped by some four thousand 'revolutionary students' working in Cautín alone on 'summer vacation jobs'. They have received three million escudos from the government to finance this work, which consists of 'cultural activities', such as the *alfabetización* of the Mapuches, under cover of which, in fact, these students are assisting the MIR with their *tomas*. *El Diario Austral*'s line has already invoked the wrath of the government, and intramural threats of industrial action by the printers' unions – an example of totally improper political interference with press freedom. Gallardo himself has had a Molotov cocktail thrown at his house during the election campaign; he was at the paper, but his son and niece had a narrow escape. The episode, he claims, has never been investigated. Nerves are bad in Temuco; both Alcalde Becker and Gallardo tell us that Cubans and North Vietnamese, and possibly also North Koreans, have been seen at work in the area, or in the streets of Temuco. But Gallardo admits that none have been interviewed by any of his journalists.

A specialist in agronomy, Gallardo expresses deep concern at the longer term consequences that both the *tomas* and Chonchol's accelerated reform policy will have on Chilean food production, worries that we were to hear constantly repeated by big and small farmers over the next days. Because of the weather, harvests are going to be bad in any event; perhaps 50 per cent down on the previous year. But, because of the uncertainties of the future, many farmers are neither sowing seed for next year nor spending money on fertilizing their fields: 'And in this hungry land, you have to use a lot of fertilizer.' But the situation has the worst effect on the cattle farmers, because breeding stock is being killed off. Out of fear of the MIR *tomas*, owners are selling off herds in 'catastrophe sales' at 30 to 40 per cent below normal values. Superb breeding stock is being slaughtered, stock which has been carefully bred to be acclimatized to Chilean conditions. 'It's a long work, and now it's being thrown away.' Chile will have to import new stock, with all the cost that that involves. Gallardo reckons that 1972 is the year when the food problems will hurt. There is likely to be a milk shortage, and he thinks Allende 'will have to import milk to keep his political promises of a free pint a day for school children'.[1]

Whichever way one looks at it, Chile's food production policy in the past makes little sense. During the Frei era, U.S. $100 million was spent every year on imports of which three-quarters was for foodstuffs which Chile could have produced herself, while so much cultivable land was either left fallow or waste. In criticizing previous performance the U.P. agronomists undoubtedly have a case; but the big question is, with their own crash programme – even though they might rebalance 'social justice – will they radically improve Chile's food production? Or the opposite?

We dine at the Hotel Central in Temuco. Pablo Hunneus on his first visit had found it a hive of *miristas*, but now the bar is full of locals very quietly playing *cacho* with dice and drinking pisco. No women. Nena says plaintively 'this is typical Chile – men who like the company of men, and don't care to talk to women!' I reassure her that it happens in England too. It is still raining. Masculine umbrellas are drying round an elderly wood stove, stamped 'Made in Rendsburg', a fine old relic from the Kaiser's Germany.

---

[1] Before the end of his first year in power Allende was forced by economic circumstances to withdraw the 'pint-a-day'.

Outside is a travel poster from the *Bundesrepublik*. The restaurant is a large, obviously once opulent room, built somewhere at the end of the last century. The ceiling is crumbling, and the room is almost empty. Once again, it reminds me of those collapsed gold rush towns of the Yukon. Where, one wonders, has the wealth of Temuco gone? Two young men arrive and dine together at the far end of the restaurant, with heads close together in low conversation. Obviously *miristas*. Nena goes to chat them up. 'No, they are only poor tourists from Puerto Montt, running away from the rain and heading north!'

Across the road from the Central, Temuco's really chic hotel, the Frontera, is something out of yet another world. At lunchtime an electric organ thunders out the *Badenweiler Marsch, Preussens Gloria* and other fine old Wilhelmian favourites to a lot of nice old ladies who might have been lifted from Wiesbaden Spa. Thomas Mann would have felt wonderfully at home. No suggestion of *miristas* here. Our own much more modest, cosier lodgings are owned by a Chilean with a magnificent name that leaves few fields of human endeavour unembraced: Abelardo Velasquez Pizarro. I address him as Don Abelardo, which seems eminently suitable, and pleases him. He declares glumly: 'The weather hasn't been like this for twenty years,' and is a little discountenanced when I tell him that's what they always assure tourists to England, too. But Don Abelardo is a mine of local information, and after half-an-hour's conversation becomes totally dedicated to Nena, patiently making call after call for her to places and people it seems probable that only a carrier pigeon could reach. He insists on accompanying us when we go to see a *población* in the town, because 'they might throw stones at you.' But in fact, with his trim businessman's moustache Don Abelardo looks much more the part of the respectable bourgeois. The *población*, in a muddy outskirt of Temuco, is festooned with bunting and Chilean flags, a sign that it is on land recently seized by squatters. So far there are nothing but temporary shacks, such as the potting sheds you would see at the bottom of an English allotment. A young man with no front teeth comes to talk to us, quite open and friendly. He comes from the poor port of Saavedra, worked in

a soda fountain, but is now unemployed. At present he is acting as custodian to the 'properties' of the *población*. Two hundred families have established their claims here, by putting up
these shacks and teepees, but none live here yet. Don Abelardo
is sympathetic towards the squatters, who – he says – seized
the land a short time ago from a landlady notorious for
demanding high rents for very poor quality accommodation.
Small children from the *población* happily wolf down some
chocolate found in the car: 'We all go to school,' they tell
us – except the youngest who admits, proudly: 'I go to
Church and sing.' The rest laugh, and no stones are
thrown.

On to Valdivia. It is still raining. We pass flooded valleys
with tree-stumps sticking desolately out of the water. They
are a left-over from the terrible earthquakes of 1960, which
ravaged Valdivia and caused thousands of acres of surrounding farmland to sink beneath sea level. On its broad, placid
river, Valdivia itself (population 96,000) must once have been
a charming place, but now it still looks a little like London
after the war; great empty gaps, temporary pre-fabs and
shells of wrecked buildings. A town that seems to be even
more asleep than Temuco. It is very cold. We stay with
Matilde, a friend of Nena who created her own ballet
company, which is now attached to the university; a slender
brunette with an alive cat-face and hoarse voice – probably
from over-use. When she and Nena and a third girl-friend,
Cecilia (who insists on calling me '*gringuito*'), chat together in
their machine-gun Chilean shorthand, I cannot understand
one solitary sentence; they might just as well be conversing
in Mapuche. There is an atmosphere of delightful disorganization in the house; no hot water, and a spring out of
my mattress sticks into my back like a *mirista* .38. But Matilde
is a wonderfully warm hostess. Raimundo, eight, asks me at
once, '*Sprichst du Deutsch?*' while his flirtatious and devastating
older sister, Barbara, ten, critically announces that I speak
Spanish like a German. They both go to a German school,
run by German professors – according to Matilde (who is
pura Chilena) the only good one in Valdivia.

Looking out over Matilde's fence at the houses with their
high gables and neat, tidy gardens, I feel I might be in some

part of northern Germany. Three years as foreign correspondent in Adenauer's Germany makes the intense Germanicism of this remote corner of the world quite fascinating for me. Chile's Germans seem to have imposed their stamp so much more distinctly than any of her other minority groups and to have lost none of their roots. Originally the German 'colonists' emigrated in two waves. The first was comprised of Liberals who left following the revolution of 1848; the second, encouraged by the material successes of the first wave, came in search of prosperity in the 1880s. Drawn by its temperate climate, they established themselves principally down here in the south, with Valdivia – then a frontier town of two or three thousand people – as capital. By and large the German settlers were small farmers and artisans, and with characteristic hard work and efficiency they carved farms out of the dense *Urwald*, much of which had never been inhabited previously even by the indigenous Mapuches. They created the industries from which the south prospered, and remained largely isolated from the rest of Chile. Their ethnic ties with the *Vaterland* remained strong. In both world wars, their sympathies were openly with the German cause; the Battle of Coronel, just off the coast here, where Admiral Graf Spee's squadron triumphed over Cradock in 1914, is still a vivid memory to older Valdivians. In the Second World War, Chile – largely because of the domestic German influences – was the only South American nation not to declare war on the European Axis powers.

After 1914 immigration from Germany dried up, and the Second World War brought about a final severance between Chilean Germans and the *Heimat*. Today in their common plight (as the vast majority support either the Christian Democrats or the Nationals), they like to plead complete identity and integration with their fellow Chileans, and vigorously deny that there still exists any such phenomenon as a 'German colony'. Yet, in Valdivia, nearly half of trade and industry is still in the hands of Chilean Germans. The names are everywhere; Juan Kaiser, Alb. Haverbeck y Hijos, Gildermeister and Holzapfel, Germán Becker and Ernesto Wagner; in the homes, the prints of Blucher at Waterloo, the trophies of superb stags' heads inscribed

Waidmannsheil 1964!, and the Mauser sporting rifles. On the *fundos*, the superbly cared-for forestry plantations bear the special hallmark of German expertise. The children (like Raimundo and Barbara) go to German schools, and they are still bilingual. Up to this generation, they intermarried almost exclusively; other Chileans thought them rather stand-offish – and *vice versa*.

Now the barriers are falling, slowly. A middle-aged lawyer, Federico Saelzer, whose ancestor, a mill builder, had come from Kassel four generations ago and prospered in the building trade, tells me that, out of eleven among his children and their cousins, only one had married another German. Once again, he insists on the non-existence of a 'German colony'. When I gaze around the room, however, at the *Gummipflanz* in the corner, the sparklingly dustless Biedermeier furniture, the well-tended roses outside and the ochre stucco of the exterior walls, the lady of the house with bright blue eyes and white hair tied back austerely in a bun, sitting rather stiffly – *sehr korrekt!* – I feel myself in a room of Bad Godesberg. But of many years ago. We speak in German, and Frau Saelzer tells me she thinks very few of her compatriots have returned to Germany since Allende: 'And how can we? This is our home. We have nowhere to go.' Señor Saelzer says that he has made only one trip to Germany: 'I felt very happy there – *nicht fremd* – but I felt that I came from another country.' His brother has just heard that day his *fundo* is on the list for expropriation.

It is interesting to gauge the reaction of 'real' Germans to their Chilean counterparts. With Matilde I meet Helga Bornemann, the wife of a West German forestry expert who has spent four years at El Austral university in Valdivia. She is pertly pretty with the quick-mindedness and practicality of today's typical young German. She adores being in Chile: 'The people are so unbelievably warm and open-hearted; what's happening to them is tragic, and yet they continue to laugh . . .' But it is the 'other' Chileans among whom she prefers to mix. 'With these German-speaking Chileans, it is like living in the Wilhelmian era; they don't read anything new, and in many ways their thinking is a hundred years behind the times.' And of course there *is* a 'German colony';

worse, they are a positive 'clique'. 'It's rather boring how one meets the same people again and again in their houses.'

There is indeed an atmosphere of *Buddenbrooks* that hangs heavily over Valdivia. The 'golden years' were the 1880s; then life began to deteriorate after the opening of the Panama Canal in 1914, which turned this part of Chile's coast into an economic backwater. Then came the catastrophic earthquakes of 1960. The German-owned industries – shoes, tanneries and breweries – were destroyed and not rebuilt. To an extent the fortunes of Valdivia are reflected in those of the Haverbeck family. Marilita Allende is a Haverbeck, Valdivia's leading family, and once enormously prosperous. Nicanor, her husband (no relation to *El Compañero Presidente*), is very much a Latin Chilean. She has a certain, distinctly German formality at first acquaintance. They have a large house, stairs carpeted with puma skins, heavy Teutonic dark oak furniture in the dining-room, on the wall a family tree of *Stillfrede von Goettingen* dating back to the sixteenth century. Marilita's great-grandfather came out in the 1860s, having married the 'wrong' person in Germany. Her mother, evidently, still lives like a *grande dame* of Imperial Germany, maintaining the standards of a vanished world. In 1938 the family was given a present of superb German deer by Reichsmarshall Goering. Marilita has family links in West Germany, but finds it *unsympatisch*: 'It is becoming so materialistic.' Over the generations the Haverbecks built up a large fortune: ships, newspapers covering the whole of the south, several *fundos*. Then the father became senile, and lost his grip. The earthquake of 1960 inflicted a mortal blow; shipping sank in the harbour and was never replaced. The papers began to totter, and were sold to the Christian Democrats after the 1970 election. Now Chonchol is about to administer the *coup de grâce*; while we are in Valdivia the press reports that the Allendes' 8,000 acre farm at Allipen north of Temuco is listed for expropriation. Nicanor is flying to Santiago, in the hopes that he can save something by giving all his workers the freehold on their houses and by handing the deer park (populated with the descendants of Goering's gift, and unique in Chile) over to the university.

We pay a brief visit to Nicanor's small dairy farm just

outside Valdivia. This he *may* be allowed to keep, as its acreage comes well under the expropriation line. The pasture is lushly English, and supports one cow per acre. Overhead *jote* buzzards are spiralling, and occasionally a kind of dun-coloured goose that Nicanor calls a *vandurria* flies past squawking. The fields are surrounded by great steaming woods where *laureles* trees (could they really be cousins to the humble, boring bush cultivated in England?) rise a hundred feet towards the watery sky. In the crotches and notches of the lesser trees grow, symbiotically, scarlet *copigue* parasites, the national flower of Chile. And down below in the rough grass there are brilliant saffron clumps of *amancai*. Afterwards we dine together, rather tensely. Also present is an army major and his wife; he is sleekly smart, unmistakably a military man. We talk of the elusive Comandante Pepe. The major has heard of him, is certain he exists, and reckons that he may have five thousand men. However, 'We could round them up tomorrow, if we didn't have strict orders from the government not to'. He believes the MIR has a 'school of indoctrination' somewhere up in the mountains where Pepe is operating. They chose Liquiñe because it is very isolated, and very, very poor. 'It all started well before September [1970].' The major is frankly frightened. We go along with him to call in on the house of another local farmer. After the representative of law and order has left, our host brings out a large Mauser revolver from under his bed, and half-laughing says: 'That's Chile today!'

Nicanor Allende, an Alessandrista, is very bitter about the Christian Democrats. He says: 'I feel I could get along with the Communists – but *never* the Christian Democrats. It's they who started the rot, they who laid down the laws that the U.P. are using today.' He and another Valdivian friend of Nena's, Joaquin Holzapfel, typify the disastrous schism within Chilean opposition politics. Holzapfel, a Christian Democrat, was the *intendente*, or governor, of Valdivia province under Frei, and we spend an evening with him and his cheerful large family at their farm some miles out of the city. He has a slightly glazed look after a heavy wedding party that afternoon and, *in vino veritas*, vents his spleen on the Nationals. 'If they want to make peace with us, then it's up to them to make the first move.' It is the first time I have seen Nena angry; she weighs into the ex-*intendente*, then whispers to me: 'Now you see how hopeless we all are. How on earth shall we ever get Allende out!' As a diversion the son takes me to inspect the *fundo* 'armoury'. And what does the 'armoury' consist of? A gun cupboard with a handful of antique shotguns and rifles, all German – and an old German cavalry sword. 'You see, we're ready for the MIR!' he says proudly. The farmers round Valdivia were already taking anti-MIR precautions, sending out joint patrols at night. (Were they armed with German cavalry swords, I wondered?)

In the party is a young man with Anglo-Saxon looks and an even more English name: John Raby. His ancestors came from Durham, but he speaks English with a strong Chilean accent. He trained as a veterinary surgeon at El Austral and is currently the vet at the slaughter-house. He is moderately pro-Allende: 'I know it's selfish, but as a professional man I expect to be all right. And at lease Allende *is* doing something for the poor – so I am optimistic.' But he adds that typical Chilean qualification – 'just as long as he remains legal'. He believes in Chonchol's agrarian reform: 'But there is bound to be a slump in production. It's a revolutionary process, and like all revolutionary processes it's bound to be unjust.' What worries him most is the fate of the small farmers who are also being dispossessed under the expropriations.

The next day we set off in pursuit of Comandante Pepe.

9

Comandante Pepe

It is Saturday, 6 February, and the rain has stopped at last. As we head north-eastwards towards Liquiñe up on the Argentina frontier, that wonderful Chilean sun comes out again – and everything looks different. Suddenly, crossing over a rise, there is the first of the Chilean volcanoes, the existence of which I had refused to believe on the way down. Villarica has a constant small wreath of cloud and perhaps smoke, that floats around such a perfect white-clad cone superimposed upon a sky of unnaturally delicate, exsuccous blue, that I tell Nena it must be a fake, that it really couldn't exist after all. 'Yes,' she laughs, 'I got up very early this morning and painted it up there!' One painted volcano succeeds another; Choshuenco across a rippleless lake with the Xanadu-like name of Panguipulle. Their snows seem so close; in fact the snow-line descends to less than two thousand metres, far lower than it would be in Switzerland in mid-summer. When I stop to photograph Villarica, a swarm of green parakeets, *choroyes*, flies screeching into an oak tree. We climb up from the lake through rugged foothills and a few small hamlets. There is an extraordinary tranquillity in these Chilean villages; jolly children, but none of the voices raised in argument or animation to be found elsewhere in the Latin world. We descend to another utterly still, deserted lake, Calafquen, with the Argentinian volcano, great Lanín, beckoning in the distance at the far end. The emptiness of these silent lakes and rich green mountains is almost unimaginable. No weekend villas or restaurants, no Coca-Cola signs; only an occasional small farm, an ox-cart with wooden wheels; *campesinos* on horseback, bat-like in their copious black *mantas* that almost envelop the horses as well, or else walking endlessly from nowhere to nowhere, all smiles and quiet courtesy. We never pass a car, nor a *carabinero* post. It is as Switzerland must have been before Wordsworth began its ruin, and the cuckoo-clock trade brought prosperity and population.

At Panguipulle we stop for petrol. There is a MIR slogan painted on a rowing-boat at the water's edge. The garage attendant points to Choshuenco volcano, glistening white across the lake. 'The MIR have seized the ski *refugio* there. They say they're fighting among themselves.' Yes, he does know Comandante Pepe, he claims, and he is definitely still up at Liquiñe. The *miristas* are everywhere. They have also taken boats belonging to a fishing lodge. Looking out across the placid water it is hard to believe that, in the midst of all this sublime beauty, discord, bitterness and violence might be just around the corner. But there was no doubt we were well into the heart of MIR territory.

The south of Chile has been a favourite hunting-ground of the MIR ever since it began life some five years ago in the anthropological department of Concepción University. The leading revolutionary hotbed in the country, it was here that South America's first international Tupamaro convention took place, quite openly, only a few days ago. Tupamaro spokesmen explained that they had come to Cautín because this was 'where the situation was tensest', and where there was going to be 'an armed confrontation between farm owners and *campesinos*'. The MIR likes to look on itself as Chile's Tupamaro equivalent. It has indulged in minor kidnappings, bank robberies and thefts of arms. One of the first *mirista* coups in Santiago was pulled off under the Frei regime in January 1970 by twenty-eight-year-old Victor Toro. Armed with pistols and *metralletas* he led three thousand men and women from the *callampas* to occupy a two-acre unoccupied site close to the centre of the city, where they set up a 'paradise commune'. With the presidential elections ahead, the government showed reluctance to evict Toro and his supporters; thus a violent confrontation was avoided. Toro was recorded as boasting: 'We do not promise. We *do*!' So far there have been shoot-ups, but no Tupamaro-style killings yet; the MIR appears to have been building itself up for the *Walpurgisnacht* to come. The *miristas* largely share the same social origins as their Uruguayan counterparts; they are middle-class misfits, more akin to the bomb-throwing anarchists of the nineteenth century than today's scientific Communists, and with no clear-cut political objectives. (A working-class fraction, the VOP actually broke away from the MIR because its members found themselves 'embarrassed' by the social *chic* of the *miristas* – as well as finding them insufficiently bloodthirsty.) The MIR has the same broad aim as the Tupamaros, as was once chillingly defined by the Brazilian guerrilla leader, Carlos Marighela:

It is necessary to turn political crisis into armed conflict by performing violent actions that will force those in power to transform the political situation in a country into a military situation. That will alienate the masses, who, from then on, will revolt against the army and police and blame them for this state of things.

Where basically the two sets of extremists differ is on methods: the Tupamaros operate solely in the urban areas, the MIR principally in the countryside, but with ramifications in the cities. The MIR's heroes are Mao and – more passionately – Castro and Che, and it goes along with Debray's Cuban-influenced view that the cities are 'lukewarm incubators' and that 'the mountain turns bourgeois into proletarians, while the city changes proletarians into bourgeois.'

How can an inhabitant of these cities [asks Debray], however much of a Marxist-Leninist he may be, understand the vital importance of a square yard of nylon cloth, a can of gun grease, a pound of salt or sugar, a pair of boots? . . . Any man, even a comrade, who spends his life in a city is unwittingly bourgeois in comparison with a *guerrillero*.

But there is little doubt that, in recent years, it is the urban Tupamaros who have registered the most notable successes in South America. So the MIR is on its mettle.

Allende remarked mildly to Debray:

The revolutionary struggle may be found in the guerrilla *foco* or in urban insurrection; it may be the people's war and it may be an insurgence through the polling booths; it depends on the content it is given. . . .

But the MIR does not see it at all that way. It is impatient with Allende, and a little distrustful; and profoundly opposed to the 'soft' policy of Chile's official Communist Party (P.C.Ch.), believing that only violent, armed revolution can liberate Latin America. Its polarization is symptomatic of the ideological struggle being waged today throughout Latin America, cutting across national frontiers, between the various Marxist groupings – Castroists, Trotskyists, Muscovites and now the so-called *pekinistas*. 'Infantile disorders' is how the orthodox, Soviet-line parties dismiss Guevarist-*mirista* activities; for, stated the Central Committee of the Peruvian Communist Party (August 1965), echoing Lenin:

the guerrilla movement in itself cannot engender a revolutionary situation . . . [it] can develop only when a revolutionary situation is maturing. . . .

Che's thesis was the direct reverse of this. As long ago as January 1959, deeply influenced by the recent successes in Cuba, he declared:

There must be agrarian revolution, and fighting in the country-side and the mountains. The revolution must be taken from there to the cities, and not started in the cities without overall social content . . .

Régis Debray dotted a few of the 'i's some years later:

The conquest from the enemy of a small area of fertile land belonging to the *latifundistas* is better propaganda for agrarian reform than a hundred illustrated pamphlets on Ukrainian *sovkhoses*.[1]

[1] Debray, *Le Castrisme; la longue marche de l'Amerique Latine*, Temps Modernes, January 1965.

Che was martyred while attempting to prove his thesis, and so far it has met (in sharp contrast to the, admittedly local, successes of the Tupamaros) with disastrous failure everywhere outside Cuba; nevertheless it is the philosophy which the Chilean MIR pursues with complete fidelity.

Shortly after Allende's election, the MIR formulated its own clear-cut policy statement, some of which is worth outlining here. Like Debray, it stressed that between the electoral triumph of the U.P. and power itself 'there is an enormous gulf; and in this are inserted everything from right-wing conspiracies and manoeuvres to pressures pushing the Popular Unity towards conciliation with the parties representing the interests of the ruling classes.' The capitalist state apparatus had to be destroyed, and this made inevitable an 'armed confrontation between the ruling classes and the workers'. The MIR predicted that Allende would, however, govern by legal means – which involved governing 'with the capitalist state intact'. He would be confronted by two alternatives; if the U.P. intended 'to satisfy the workers' aspirations, it will be obliged to break absolutely the legal fetters upon it [or] it will be forced to conciliate, to affirm itself with the middle strata and the bourgeois reformist parties.' What the MIR leaders most dreaded was any such conciliation between the Christian Democrats and the U.P. because that would make 'the strategy of armed struggle . . . appear unwarranted'. So the Christian Democrats must be struck at and provoked at every opportunity.

As the road winds precipitously up into the Andes, it becomes appallingly rough, little more than a logging track. Apart from being a small lumber centre, Liquiñe (4,500 inhabitants, of which two-thirds are Mapuches) used to have a thermal spring; but, judging from the road, it must have been patronized more by Argentinians from across the border, where access is easier, than by Chileans. Blackened spikes cover many of the mountain slopes, a sombre reminder of the terrible droughts of two years previously. The 1960 earthquakes also apparently wreaked appalling damage, making it look 'like a bombed area', cut off for a long time from the outside world. Rumours were rife afterwards that, in the terrible conditions prevailing, the Mapuches had ritually sacrificed a child to appease the devil-god, Pillan. The mountain rises sheer above the track, and often it is partly blocked by landslides of rock and earth. Perilously rickety (and easily demolished) bridges lead it over Andean torrents. Where the slopes have not been ravaged by fire or earthquake, dense primeval forests and bamboo jungle thrive, lightened occasionally with flashes of colour from wild fuchsia trees. It is as impenetrable as the Aberdare Mountains of Kenya, the home of Mau-Mau. A wilder, more desolate place it would be hard to imagine. During the winter months, apparently, deep snow isolates it completely, and at every twist of the track one reflects what ideal guerrilla terrain this inaccessible, inhospitable country presents. Occasionally black and white pigs run out into the road, and there are small enclosures of impoverished sheep with flocks of *tiuques*, brown-and-white hawk-like birds, feasting off their ticks. But otherwise hardly a sign of life.

We pass slowly through a deserted Liquiñe, on up towards the frontier, just a few miles away. Not a sign of *miristas*. Total bucolic peace. At the *carabinero* frontier post, we are informed that all is quiet; but the *carabinero* sergeant adds, meaningfully, 'too quiet'. He will not be drawn out as to the whereabouts (if any) of the elusive Comandante. We stop for a picnic lunch close to the border, and even closer to the snow-line. It is bitterly cold. Below us there is a rushing mountain stream, on the other side an apparently abandoned sawmill. Stacks of wood, turned grey with the years, have been piled up haphazardly, and apparently forgotten. The whole neighbourhood exudes a miasma of neglect, of slow death. One red car passes us, full of children: an Argentinian family on holiday, feeling very brave at tackling the unspeakable road. No, they have not been stopped by any *banditi*; they turn pale, and hurry on. Cold and depression begin to settle in, accompanied by a feeling that we too should hurry on – that we are on a wild-goose chase.

Eventually, after further wanderings up by the frontier, we come upon a roughly painted sign:

CARRANCO
Territorio Liberado

It is a timber property which Pablo Hunneus had informed us had been seized two months earlier. The entrance is barred, but across the barricades we converse with the *campesino* 'guards' who at first are not obtrusively welcoming. Then they are joined by a middle-aged man with a large tumour on the side of his face. His name is Humberto Velozo, he had worked twenty years at Carranco, and he was now *el presidente* of the seized property. Gradually, Velozo becomes friendly and informative. Yes, certainly there was a Comandante Pepe. It was he who had 'helped' the *campesinos* to take over Carranco. Without him they would not have known how. Was he there now? No, but he had been there a few days previously when the *campesinos* had started fighting among themselves, because each had wanted to be *presidente*. Pepe had knocked their heads together. This all-powerful figure had also, says Velozo, kicked out the *interventor* sent by the government – because he had seemed too favourably inclined towards the boss, Señor Etchevarry. Pepe had then insisted on being sent an *interventor* from Neltume (another seized property), who was 'one of us'.

Carranco had been the first *fundo* in the neighbourhood to take itself over, aided by Pepe and his men: 'because we were braver and more decided,' says Velozo. He was armed only with a machete at the time of the takeover. 'I am not a *guerrillero*,' he explains, 'but a religious Evangelist.' And as such he had taken part in the *toma* because the land was not strictly speaking private property, but 'state land' under licence to Señor Etchevarry. So he could not be accused of theft. They would abide by what the government decided, but if the boss came back, and tried to retake the property by force, then the *campesinos* would 'fight to the death'. Why had they taken over Carranco? Well, Señor Etchevarry was an absentee landlord. Pay was bad, houses worse, there were long periods of seasonal unemployment and the workers were not permitted to keep their own animals. Before the *toma*, there had been seventeen families living on the thirty thousand acres at Carranco, now there were 168 souls in all. Wages had been increased and all-year employment promised. There was also a school now being built at Carranco by 'revolutionary' students on vacation. Velozo's companion,

an old man with few teeth, keeps interjecting with a sad nod
'*La necesidad tienes cara de hereje.*' (Necessity is shameless.)
But where was the cash coming from to keep Carranco
going? Well, in some roundabout way *el presidente* thought
the *fundo* had received $10,000 (U.S.) from Chonchol's
organization to 'keep them going'.[1] Also they were now selling timber to a nearby co-operative. The government just
'looked sideways' at that. Finally, now thoroughly amicable,
Velozo tells us where we can find Comandante Pepe. He is at
a *fundo* called Trafun, some twenty-five miles away which he
and his group of *miristas* had occupied just two nights previously. On leaving Carranco we give a lift to a boy who had
worked there for ten years, and was walking the ten kilometres down to Liquiñe – because his horse had no shoes.
Passing a truck on the way, he points out: 'That's the boss's
chauffeur driving; but he is working for us now.' We set off
across even more appalling roads, up mountains covered by
more of the most impenetrable bamboo rain forest I have
ever seen. A few paces inside it and one would be totally lost.
Could any conventional army in this world winkle out
guerrillas established in the hills up here? It was real
Guevara country. We pick up an old man heading for
Trafun. He complains all the way of some unspecified illness,
which the doctors can't cure; 'Just a *dolor de cabeza*, they say.'
No, he didn't know anything about Pepe; only about how
much his head ached. At last the road reaches a settlement
and finally comes to an end in another barricade, draped
with flags – the certain sign of a *toma*.
It is Trafun. This time the men on the barricades look far
more menacing than at Carranco. One is fingering a revolver
barely concealed beneath a blue shirt. What does the *com-
ãñero* want? I explain with a dry mouth that – a mild pre-
varication – *el presidente* Velozo had sent us. We want to see
Comandante Pepe; was he there? Possibly, but who was I?
We tell Blue Shirt that I am an English historian, that I am
touring Chile studying a great moment of history. This lady
is my interpreter. That evokes interest, there are some whis-
pered exchanges; then Blue Shirt asks for proof. I remember

[1] This was later confirmed.

191

that I have with me, among my papers in the car, the jacket for *The Terrible Year*. Blue Shirt sets off with it into the interior of the camp. Ten minutes later what looks like the Hosts of Midian appear, walking rapidly, half-running towards the barricade. I begin to wish we could get into the car and beat a dignified withdrawal: the thought of a prolonged sequestration as hostages of the MIR at Trafun, or possibly worse, is not particularly appealing. And what would they do with Nena, if they discover that in fact she is an eminent *momio* journalist, not just an interpreter? But she shows total equanimity; in any case, retreat is out of the question.

At the head of the multitude is a smallish man dressed predominantly in black. Black trilby, black leather jacket with a fur collar, black knee-boots, black hair, black moustache, lively black eyes and freckles, over-tight jeans held together with string, an automatic and a large bowie knife slung from a rawhide belt. He looks every English boy's image of a Latin-American outlaw. Yes, he is the legendary Comandante Pepe. With him is a pretty girl – brown eyes, poor complexion – whom he introduces as Valentina. Pepe speaks with nervous rapidity, almost a stammer, occasionally punctuated with an asthmatic cough; he suffers from the same affliction as his hero Che. Every movement exudes animal vitality, and immediately his total authority over the surrounding *campesinos* is apparent. 'No,' he laughs, 'I am not a *Cubano*,' as some of the opposition papers were suggesting. His real name is Gregorio José Liendo, he is twenty-six, and (as might have been expected) of *petit-bourgeois* origin. His father ran a dairy business near Punta Arenas in the extreme south of Chile, where constant fierce winds, snow and ice produce a hard race of men. He went to university first in Santiago, then Valdivia, where he studied agronomy. He first joined the P.C.Ch. Communist Youth Movement, then – on finding it too easy-going – became a *mirista*. He had spent four years 'working on' the *campesinos* in the Liquiñe area, starting when still a student at university, and he had just married a local peasant girl. Valentina – who spoke good English with a strong American accent – told me that she too came from a bourgeois family. She had been sent to school in Maryland, on an 'exchange' – which she enjoyed.

19 The author: behind, Villarica volcano

20 Chilean faces

25 (*above*) 'Che lives' – a Chilean MIR parade

26 Lautaro

27 'The People of the Land':
Mapuche Indians

28 Señora Lemonao

29 Student power, University of La Paz. A list of professors and students who 'betrayed university autonomy'

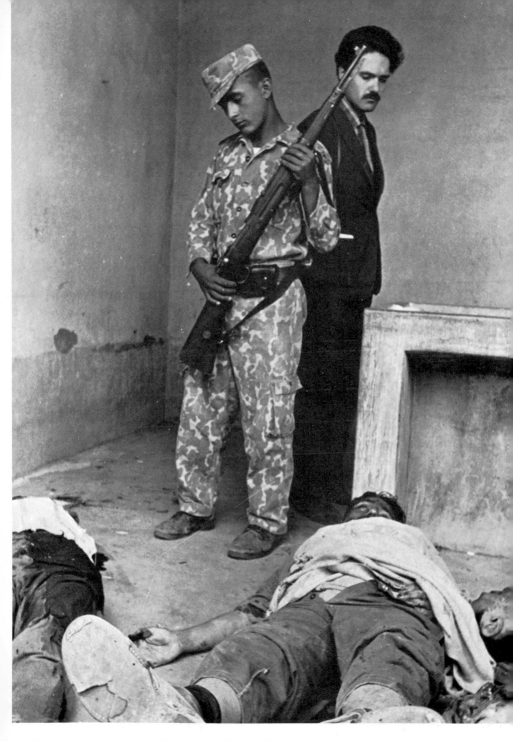

30 Student defeat, dead Teoponte Guerrillas

31 The witch-doctor's stall; La Paz

32 Anti-American demonstration during the Barrientos era, La Paz

She became a Socialist on her return, then – when an anthropological student at Concepción – turned to the MIR out of impatience with Frei. She is now twenty-three. After a few awkward and suspicion-laden minutes conversing over the barricades, both Pepe and Valentina become quite cordial. Pepe seems to regard me – a *gringo* from England, an historian to boot – as a rather comical object. We take photographs of the men manning the barricades, and then they invite us into the camp. Rather apprehensively, feeling a little like Daniel, we enter. Inside the *fundo*'s administrative offices, where papers are scattered everywhere, we resume the conversation with a throng of wide-eyed, silent *campesinos* gazing in through the windows from the outside. They are the faces of good, simple peasants, with occasionally the fierce, rather frightening oriental features of a pure Mapuche. The *fundo* covers about 125,000 acres, says Pepe; there are some 130 families in it, each averaging six to eight people (a figure which in itself gives an idea of the *explosión demográfica* that is the fundamental factor behind Chile's land-hunger). The *fundo* belonged to a Señor Kunstmann, a Chilean of German descent, who lived chiefly in Valdivia. The reasons for the *toma* were much the same as those given at Carranco. The average wage of the *campesinos* was eighteen to nineteen escudos a day.[1] 'We will take you up to see Herr Kunstmann's house,' says Valentina, 'and afterwards by comparison you will see how one of his labourers was expected to live.' The *miristas* who had seized the *fundo* number only ten; all are in their twenties, all students from Concepción. They were now organizing Trafun and busily engaged in indoctrinating the *campesinos*. In keeping with the Castroist principle of 'armed propaganda', their slogan was 'Let's arm the peasants for the fight!' Valentina says she expected to stay about a year, because 'There is so much to teach these people.' This again was in line with the Castroist doctrine which frowns upon the typically Soviet *aparatchik* who descends on the peasants, 'gives an unintelligible speech, and then returns straight away to render his report to the party or to the leaders in the

[1] Approximately 50p or $1.25 at prevailing official exchange rates.

city'. We were to learn later in Liquiñe that Pepe had in fact been working for several months before he could *concientizar* (a favourite *miristas* word, meaning to make politically conscious) the workers at Trafun to the point where they were prepared to seize this vast estate.

We move up to Kunstmann's house. Vigilant *miristas* in black *mantas* are on guard outside; inside, one of them is on crutches, his leg bandaged. The thought passes through my mind, then, that he might have been shot in a recent confrontation. The house is certainly no pleasure palace, although the *miristas* obviously expect us to regard it as such; just a comfortable, working farmer's dwelling, like a Swiss chalet, with very few traces of luxury. I ask Pepe and Valentina if they were now living there. 'No, we have allotted it to the *campesinos* who live in Trafun. We are sleeping on the floor in their houses, like them, so as to share their lives fully.' Valentina says she has forgotten what it is like to sleep in a bed. Pepe uncorks a bottle of Herr Kunstmann's wine for us; but none of the *miristas* will join us. 'We have given it up. Alcoholism is such a problem up here and we must set an example,' they explain puritanically. We talk about the agrarian reform. I ask whether, in dispossessing small and medium landowners, the 'revolution' would not simply perpetuate social injustice in Chile by creating yet another class of landless poor. 'Possibly,' replies Pepe. 'But remember that for centuries a minority has abused the majority in this country, and now it is the turn of the majority to abuse the minority, and there is bound to be injustice in the process.'

The conversation turns to general matters. Pleasantly enough, Valentina tells me she believes that only violent revolution can sweep away the bourgeois structure of all South America, and *Yanqui* colonialism. Inevitably there would be killing eventually. 'We are in agreement with the Allende government, in that we believe that the old laws need to be swept away; but the way they are doing it takes too long.' She despises the gentler techniques of the P.C.Ch., and the new left-wing governments of Bolivia and Peru she regards as 'just other forms of imperialism' – because there has been no basic alteration of the political structures there. Another *mirista* interjects: 'In Peru they are just transferring things from one pocket to another; they clamp down on the International Petroleum Company, then they allow other *Yanqui* companies to open hotel chains.' A third *mirista* with a wispy moustache adds, sardonically, that if Chile got Soviet economic aid that too would be 'just another form of imperialism'.

Valentina is a red-hot, pedantic doctrinaire, a carbon copy of what one might meet on the campuses of Berkeley, or the Sorbonne, or the London School of Economics. In answer to my question, 'Don't you agree that the population explosion is the number one problem in all South America?' she gives me a half-hour lecture going back to pre-Spanish times, on the evils of 'colonialism'; then finally agrees that birth-control is a good thing. Her facts are not always accurate; she is, I note *en passant* – among other things – unaware that Argentina was not a signatory of the Andean Pact. She is a starry-eyed ideologue, totally sincere and dedicated, but seeming to regard the *campesinos* as little more than political symbols in the struggle for Marxist victory. Her only concession to feminity is a touch of mascara round the eyes. Pepe, on the other hand, is a romantic of immense attraction and charm, such as one can find only in Latin America, and manifesting a deep human involvement with the *campesinos*. He turns the heat on me: what is my interpretation of History? For the first time since we have been inside the *fundo*, I feel slightly nervous as to how things will turn out; particularly for Nena's sake. But her guise as my 'interpreter' pays a double service; it gives me twice as long to think up my responses. A little glibly I reply that there could only be one view of History – that is the Truth. Expectedly, Pepe says that there is a Marxist and a bourgeois truth; which do I embrace? I reply, dodging, that that is nonsense; that when it comes to writing history only absolute truth counts. Pepe changes tack:

'What do you want for Chile?'
'Justice.'
'Justice for whom?'

And so on. Do I agree that economic development is the most important motivating factor in history? What about the Paris Commune? I disagree; immediate political events

195

were what sparked the Commune. Pepe insists that it had been motivated solely by economic injustice. I tell him – as light-heartedly as possible – that that interpretation was invented by Karl Marx after the event. As we talk and talk, Pepe asks: 'Do you mind if we bring in some of these *campesinos*. It's good education for them!' More and more peasants fill the unknown Elysium of Herr Kunstmann's salon, watching with spellbound incomprehension the Comandante's performance of re-educating a *gringo* bourgeois. The whole bizarre performance reminds me of what used to be known in my American schooldays as a 'bull session'; yet all the time one cannot quite be sure that the 'bull' may not turn nasty. I try to study the *mirista* faces. Some look just like schoolboys, out for the excitement; one or two have disagreeably vindictive sneers, and one could, without difficulty, imagine them operating as dispassionate killers; and most of them impart a sense of dangerous determination. Privately I cast my mind back to the two young right-wing extremeists, Pedro and Juan in Santiago, and by comparison these *miristas* seem just that much more fanatical – and fearful. They are also rather better organized – and armed.

Finally Pepe says:

'Do I have the impression that you are not a Marxist?'

'You could be right!'

Then, almost in a whisper:

'But if you were a Chilean of my age, you would be with *us*, wouldn't you?'

'Quite possibly.' But 'as a half-baked romantic, not as a Marxist,' I think privately to myself.

By now things are very free and easy, and Pepe does not seem to be worried by my dialectical shortcomings. I am intensely glad that Bill is not with us, but I cannot help thinking how much he would have enjoyed Pepe as a human being. He would certainly be better company on a desert island than a Cristian Casanova, or a Chonchol – or even Valentina, who I suspect would be a bore. 'Why don't you stay the night,' Pepe says laughingly, 'and we can *concientizar* you!' We both decline politely, Nena adding: 'He has to write.'

'He can do it here.'

'No, he needs peace.'

'Ah!'

It is already dark. We leave Herr Kunstmann's 'palace' to visit a *campesino* dwelling, on the way encountering a man with a dead white face, wearing a jacket with an artificial fur collar. It is Kunstmann's ex-manager. Was anyone going to Valdivia, he asks pleadingly? No, laughs Valentina. 'We can't let him out yet – he might say something bad about us to the *carabineros*!' Unable to help, we leave the poor man, 'Looking,' as Nena remarks later, 'like a human being abandoned on the moon.' One feels instinctively more sympathy for this casualty of the 'revolution' than for the Kunstmanns of this world; as an employee, he had probably just done his best for the boss – now what? It was the end of a way of life. As a man trained, presumably, to be nothing but a farm manager – and therefore a 'class enemy' – what possible future could he expect in a Chile of the Pepes and the Valentinas?

The *campesino* house is a wooden shack; the interior is hard to see in the dim candle-light; there is no electricity, no running water, no lavatory. In two squalid rooms, a man with five years' service on the *fundo* lives (or exists) with his wife and six children. One bed, in which all but one of the children has been born. (And yet, there on the wall is pinned a clipping of Neil Armstrong landing on the moon!) 'At least we have a wooden floor,' says the owner apologetically. 'Some don't.' It was how one imagined the Russian muzhiks to have lived long before 1917. Here was the human background to what brought the MIR in, and the Kunstmanns out, in Chile 1971. I feel less guilt about Herr Kunstmann's wine.

At about this moment I ask a now warmly amicable Pepe the sixty-four-dollar question: is it true, as the papers say, that he is concentrating in this unapproachable area, not solely because of its poverty and backwardness, but with the object of developing it as a future base for guerrilla operations? He laughs and says, 'Look there are no *guerrilleros* here!'

But he adds, significantly: 'Historically there is bound to be a counter-reaction against the Allende government, a right-

197

wing coup. As a *mirista*, as a Marxist, my historical view is that the longer time passes, the more difficult it will be to reverse the popular processes – therefore the right wing will have to react sooner rather than later. And if you see a man about to hit you in the face, you don't just stand there waiting for the blow, do you? Of course, we will defend ourselves, *hasta la muerte*; but we must organize, and we feel that there is not much time. It is likely that there will be a right-wing coup within the year.'

He firmly believes that the army, when the crunch comes, will support the exploiting oligarchy, because the officers belong to a class hostile to the workers. The role of the MIR is to organize the workers against the moment when the inevitable reaction comes. To Pepe the highest form of Marxist activity is that of the 'militarists', such as Giap and Che. 'There is no such thing as peaceful coexistence – it is just not possible in South America.'

Several times Pepe repeats with chilling emphasis: 'Civil war in Chile is inevitable.'

Pepe produces an astonishing figure, which he assures me is correct. Instead of the 400,000 acres of *fundos* under MIR control, which Pablo Hunneus had given us, Pepe claims that the overall figure is now nearer *one million*. The area stretches in a more or less solid, mountainous belt close to the sensitive Argentina frontier all the way from Cautín in the north down to Osorno. Within it there are evidently other 'Strelnikovs' like Pepe at work, building up large *mirista* empires on their own initiative, energetically and efficiently. It seems reasonable to accept that the *miristas* have not reached a stage of establishing an armed guerrilla stronghold in the Liquiñe area,[1] or of creating anything like the independent Communist state of 'Marquetalia' which flourished in Colombia for nearly fifteen years. If the Allende government is so far, at least tacitly, on their side, they do not need to. But should things change, Pepe and his men seem well on the way to having created a base – far sounder than anything

[1] Although some six weeks after my meeting with Pepe, one of his men evidently told a Christian Science Monitor correspondent that it was Pepe's aim to 'create a new *Sierra Maestra* around the Liquiñe *foco*'.

Che Guevara achieved in the Bolivian jungles, and with the *campesinos* on their side (something Che never achieved) – from which it would be extremely difficult to dislodge them. In the unpredictably turbid state of present-day Argentina, it is also not inconceivable that a *foco* at Liquiñe could at some future date link up with a similar Guevarist-controlled area on the other side of the adjacent frontier; strategically, a good enough reason alone for the *miristas* to have selected Liquiñe.

A battered truck takes us out of the *fundo*. Its brakes are doubtful, the driver explains that the servo is not functioning. There are women and children clinging to it on every side. Their exhilaration is unmistakable, as is the impact that Pepe and his *miristas* make on the *campesinos*. Possibly disillusion may set in when it transpires that the Pepes cannot give them the material paradise they feel they have been promised. But meanwhile he has given them more: a sense of individual dignity and importance; and whatever happens in Chile they will never now be able to accept the conditions of the past. There is also no mistaking the imposing personal influence of Pepe. 'No *interventor* we dislike will set foot in any farm we have seized,' he tells us proudly, and then sets off to *concientizar* another occupied *fundo*.

He bids us a cheerful farewell: 'When you get back to Europe, don't forget to put a flower on the grave of Karl Marx for me! and please greet my good friend Jacques Chonchol when you see him. He was here two weeks ago.'

Safely back in Liquiñe at the tiny *hosteria* which once served the thermal baths, we dine with the manager, Julio García, who never draws breath, but speaks in so low a conspiratorial whisper that it is quite hard to follow him. He fills us in on quite a few points. The owners of the two seized properties, Kunstmann and Etchevarry, were very different types. Etchevarry was absent frequently; 'one sensed trouble brewing there'. Kunstmann was often on the *fundo*, and did a lot for his workers, says García. He had known the MIR was at work, and offered to hand the *fundo* over to CORA (the organisation in charge of agrarian reform), to satisfy his employees' demands. But, according to García, the *campesinos* at Trafun had said, 'No, we don't want you to go.' The MIR kept on working at them. He claims that Pepe had held frequent meetings in the Liquiñe neighbourhood, preaching 'revolution' with bloodshed and killing, and there had been quite a few incidents.[1] García then rambles on into a long, tedious political dissertation, and is hard to shake off. Meanwhile, a happy young 'bourgeois' couple are dancing cheek to cheek in one corner of the tiny dining-room to ancient tangos on a gramophone, obviously and incongruously in total oblivion of the doings of Comandante Pepe.

The next day, Valentina takes us to visit another group of twenty-eight university students who are doing 'summer work' among the *campesinos*. They all come from the FER (Federation of Revolutionary Students), an affiliation of the MIR, and are equipped with handbooks on 'How to communicate with the masses' in their hands and slogans of '*La Tierra para el que Trabaja!*' on their lips. Their function of improving hygiene and literacy is closely intertwined with the work of Marxist *concientización*. Over two thousand such students, aged fourteen to twenty-four, were apparently engaged on similar holiday tasks throughout the Chilean countryside that summer. Here at Liquiñe they are settled in the school building. All of them are sleeping on the floor in one room, holding discussion groups on how to get at the *campesinos*, laying their plans. One of the male students is drying his socks, dangling them one by one in front of a wood stove. There are bossy signs pinned to the walls – 'Compañeros against dirt' – 'Use the ash-trays' – 'Keep clothes tidy'. All the students come from Concepción or Talca. They receive money from the government for their summer work, in addition to extra funds from Concepción University. They say they are getting more help now under Allende, and better transportation. They find the *campesinos* very grateful for

---

[1] What García didn't tell us, in his extreme caution, and which we were to learn a few days later, was that his own son had been in a car with the owner of *Fundo* Neltume when the latter had been involved in a shoot-up with the *miristas*, early in December. One *mirista* had been hit in the leg (could it possibly have been the young man on crutches at Trafun?). It was evident that García was too frightened to disclose the episode to us.

their help. Valentina stresses the tragic lack of schools in the countryside. The children leave school at an average age of twelve, and Cautín area has the highest proportion of illiteracy in the country. The lack of roads makes school attendance very difficult indeed; so there is a crying need for boarding schools, but no government has been prepared to make the necessary expenditure. (Nena whispers: 'Not true. A lot was done under Frei.') The next most grievous problem, says Valentina, is health; she stresses that one of the principal jobs of the MIR and its associates of the M.C.R. and the FER is also to teach the *campesinos* how to work. 'For instance,' she adds proudly, 'already we have doubled timber production from the mill at Trafun.' 'And if you cut down *all* the trees, what then?' She shrugs her shoulders.[1] Valentina does not believe that the about-to-be dispossessed farm owners will sell or slaughter their cattle: 'The *campesinos* will not allow it.'

As we leave her, she says: 'There are 25,000 of us now – next year there will be 50,000 – the year after, 100,000, all out among the *campesinos*, spreading the revolutionary word.'

That day, a small helicopter flies overhead. It is Allende's minister of the interior, José Toha, who – in response to Christian Democrat pressure – has come down to make an assessment of the stories about *mirista tomas*. He inspects the area cursorily from his helicopter, lands briefly at Neltume, but not at either Trafun or Liquiñe; then returns to announce that absolutely nothing irregular is going on 'except for some isolated cases where farms had been seized for motives based on owners not fulfilling their responsibilities'[2]. That same day there are reports in the local press of two more *mirista tomas*.

---

[1] Two weeks later, the Liquiñe *miristas* approached our friend Bornemann, the German forestry expert from Valdivia University, asking for advice on how to run the saw mills. His advice was 'If the present *mirista* plan is followed, the timber resources of the south will be finished in less than two years!'

[2] Less than a year later, Toha was impeached by a motion of the opposition in Congress, on five counts, chief among them was his permitting 'illegal armed groups' to operate in the south.

10

In the Shadow of
the Volcanoes

It is, one has to admit, with perhaps a touch of relief that we
leave Liquiñe and its savage hinterland. Back down the
spring-breaking track and its sheer hairpins and out of the
oppressive bamboo jungles; through rugged foothills to Coñaripe, a small town evidently wiped out one night when Villarica erupted seven years ago; across a ford filled with
rough black lava boulders, the site of where Coñaripe used
to be. Down on a deserted cove of Lake Villarica we eat the
rather stale remains of yesterday's lunch under a *boldo* tree.
The grey, shingly beach is pure lava from the volcano. An
old man in a brown poncho, with a happy smile and terrible
teeth, wanders down to the strand to potter round with his
boat. We discuss the virtues of the *boldo* trees. There are, he
says, a male and a female, the leaves of one or the other is a
potent anti-aphrodisiac, much used by the Mapuches – but
he doesn't know which, so that's not much help. Around the
edge of the water are small private holdings, happy and
prosperous little farms. The contrast with Liquiñe is hard to
credit. That evening we go into Pucón, and dine at a large
holiday hotel. It might be somewhere at Harrogate or the
Wörther See: table after table of bored, unsmiling bourgeois
holiday-makers with their children, eating together in vacu-
ous silence; totally, unbelievably oblivious of what the
miristas are doing up at Liquiñe just sixty to seventy miles
away; their minds no doubt preoccupied with such pressing
problems as when the waiter will bring the next course, and
whether the rain will spoil the fishing tomorrow. There they
sit, resentful of any change or discomfort, like the good

bourgeois all over the world. (I find myself thinking like a *mirista*; perhaps Pepe had been successful in his *concientización*.)

Fernando Léniz of *El Mercurio* and his own private *explosión demográfica* – all nine children – are at a holiday house by the foot of the volcano, near Pucón. He is very disinclined to believe our story about Pepe and his activities; especially that we ever managed to get into Trafun. I asked him why *El Mercurio* hadn't sent one of their own journalists to do just that. He looks surprised. One sees another aspect of the weakness of the Chilean opposition press in the face of the U.P. There is a certain lethargy and unimaginativeness among Chilean journalists, who tend to live on hand-outs and press conferences; even on a newspaper of such outstanding quality as *El Mercurio*. Léniz says something about it being a question of expense, but not very convincingly. When we finally persuade him that we have indeed seen the *miristas*, and describe them to him, he says, soberly and reflectively: 'You know, I don't think I could shoot at them. They are decent young men, and I am not sure that just conceivably they are not doing what's right for Chile. Anyway, I *am* sure that I am not sure enough to be prepared to shoot them down. I would rather get out.' I tell him that, having met Pepe, I rather agree; but would *he* hesitate to shoot us? I doubt if Valentina would. In retrospect Léniz's view seems typical of the middle-of-the-road Chilean; in his determination to avoid violence, at all costs – and thereby avoid the 'provocation' which the Debrays claim to be inevitable – the Lénizes may prove to be the salvation of Chile. Or its ruin.

A daughter of Léniz comes in from having skied on the volcano in the morning, and is about to go swimming in the lake. She suggests we try it too; there is a ski tow at the top of the volcano and equipment for hire. It would be nice to be able to say that one had skied on a Chilean volcano in *their* mid-summer. Léniz also urges us to visit the Flor del Lago *fundo* belonging to Ernesto Wagner right across the lake from him, a magnificent estate which is imminently about to be expropriated. We take their advice on both scores. The volcano is hidden in cloud. At the bottom the mechanic from the ski lift hitches a ride up with us. He says it only operates between October and April; during the winter there is too much snow, and it is abandoned. There are few tourists this year. Too much snow and bad weather. The mechanic says that there were plans to extend the tow up to 2,700 metres – well up into the eternal snows. The plans have been shelved because of the political situation; he wouldn't be surprised if the *miristas* took it over. The uncertainty about the future rather disgusts him, and he does not know what will happen to his livelihood. On the bottom of the slopes we pass through wonderful great woods of *coigue*, a kind of rough-barked beech. Escallonias with white flowers. Then out into the open, into a dead black lava belt, with scatterings of an azalea-like shrub called *notro* springing right up through the clinker, with brilliant vermilion blossoms. The mechanic says gloomily that they should all have been out in October, but the season has been so bad that the *notros* kept flowering throughout the summer. There are great gullies of black lava left over from the 1949 eruption. The sinister coloration and the burnt smell remind me of the Aegean island of Santorini. Up on the snow-line lonely auracaria pines stand like solitary sentinels, with their feet half in the snow, half in the lava. They are Chile's national tree, and Nena is very excited to see them, but outraged when I remark that, since Darwin brought them to England, as the humble 'monkey puzzle', they have become the symbol of every suburban garden. When the sun comes out, in brief snatches, the sharp contrast between the white of the snow and the black of the harsh lava is quite blinding. Then it begins to sleet, and snow; the coldest snow I think I ever remember. The ski lift is not functioning; it is a great frustration. So we retrace our footsteps and invite ourselves to visit Ernesto Wagner.[1]

He is a Chilean German in his late forties, whose mother's family came out from Germany in 1850; his father, some fifty years ago. When his father bought the *fundo* soon after his arrival, it was completely uninhabited, densely

---

[1] Almost exactly a year later, Villarica erupted disastrously, the molten lava turning the snow into floods in which a score of people lost their lives. What could be more symbolic of the inherent, explosive instability of Southern Chile than the blowing up of this great big beautiful volcano?

covered with primeval rain-forests. In the last century it was also the site of the last battle fought against the Araucanian Indians, or Mapuches. Wagner himself had an unusual upbringing. Sent off (aged sixteen) to be educated in Germany by his father, he was caught in 1939 and spent the war in Nazi Germany. 'It's from those days that I hate any kind of ideology,' he says; 'being at school and having to say *Heil Hitler* in the mornings!' When the end came in 1945, he was in Pomerania, working on a Bismarck property; then made his way to the Swiss border to arrive three days before the capitulation. In 1953 he married a Gräfin from Salzburg, Gabriella; a typically robust and energetic Austrian woman dressed in a leather skirt and pigtail done up in a bun. Ernesto Wagner is nervous, and rather suspicious about us. He explains that recently some bogus 'French journalists', with 'what sounded like Brazilian accents' had rung up and wanted to see the *fundo*, and take some photographs – especially of the house. Given the proximity of Liquiñe and Pepe, it is easy to understand his nervousness. Flor del Lago was the nearest proximation to a seignorial hacienda that I was to see in Chile. The Austrian-style house, with its interior courtyard that you drive into under an arch, zebra skins in a sumptuous hall, walls crammed with big-game trophies from Mozambique to the Yukon, might easily be a small *Schloss* in the Tyrol or Carinthia. It is far more luxurious in every sense than Kunstmann's 'palace'; but then, as we quickly discover, Wagner's workers' houses are also infinitely superior to what we had seen at Trafun. Some (but not all) houses had electricity; there was a small hydro-electric plant for the main house.

The property is, as Leniz suggested, quite exquisite and superbly cared for. It consists of 4,000 hectares (roughly 10,000 acres) of which 700 are arable, and 1,800 forest. Wagner employs 130 people and says: 'We could do it with thirteen, if we were allowed to.' There are three schools on the *fundo*, and 2,000 head of cattle. There are great forests of overpowering *rauli* trees – apparently Chile's most useful indigenous timber tree, and also related to the beech – and more *coigue. Zorzales,* Chilean thrushes, sing in the dark undergrowth with their distinctively drawn-out, plaintive note. Fallow deer run through the forest in front of the car. There is also a kind of elm, a big tree with white flowers, which, Gabriella says, produces 'the best honey you can imagine'. These virgin forests are what all·the property was like when Wagner's father took it over; now much of it has been replanted with well-grown belts of Oregon pine. There are rich fields of oats, but the wheat is still unripened. Wagner says gloomily that the rape crop has been completely lost and that the yields on other crops are likely to be halved because of the bad harvest. He confirms what we had heard before; that many farmers in the province were simply not planting or cultivating any more, because of the political uncertainty.

In a clearing we come upon a charming small wooden church. Gabriella explains that it was built in 1965: 'Ernesto and I pledged to build it if Allende did not win the 1964 election. We believed then that we must have been protected by God – so I built it to give thanks for Frei's victory – but what a cruel joke that was!' Now Flor del Lago is down on the next list for expropriation. Wagner quotes gloomily, 'Where Attila passes, nothing grows' as we skirt fields of sodden wheat. With Wagner is a nephew, a Teutonic, blond, blue-eyed young lawyer, who is also very right-wing. He talks wildly about the Argentinian army 'massing' up in the Andes opposite Liquiñe, and vaguely of something 'about to happen' on the Right inside Chile. Wagner remarks, hopelessly, 'I wish the Germans *were* organized in Chile, but they're not, any more than any other Chileans.' He adds, 'It is extraordinary to think that we are only twenty hours away from Europe, but a hundred light-years away.' His mind seems very much set on Europe, remote from Flor del Lago, or the problems of his *campesinos*. He becomes increasingly despondent as we drive through the *fundo*.

I ask him, as gently as possible, what he intends to do?

'If I could live on here in dignity, I would stay – but under Marxism? What can I do? I can't become a waiter – so I will have to leave.'

Apparently he won't fight expropriation – as Nicanor Allende and others are doing – but seems to have ideas of going to farm a property belonging to his wife's family in

206

Austria. Gabriella Wagner excuses herself, and hastens off to one of the *fundo* schools to teach sewing. Wagner says, 'I can't think why she still does – it's finished.' She – perhaps having gone through it all before in post-1945 Austria – seems just that much more devoted to the *campesinos*. After his wife's departure, Ernesto Wagner seems to become more broken. It is painful to watch. We hasten to leave, down a magnificent avenue of poplars planted by Wagner senior. As we drive round the lake, I remark to Nena: 'I feel that man has already left for Europe.'

'Yes. But what on earth can he do in Austria, except live on memories. The wife is much tougher – she'd fight. But he is a destroyed man; and he is only forty-seven.'

Ruperto Vargas, a friend of Nena's, runs a small shop which sells Mapuche arts and crafts in the town of Villarica. He is an expert on the Mapuches, speaks their language, and has spent much of his life living among them. They are notoriously shy and retiring and distrustful of all *huincas* (any kind of white); therefore it is no mean feat to be accepted. Vargas is deeply concerned by the present plight of the Mapuches, and, after a few minutes conversation with him, I suspect that he runs his shop more to help them than for what small profit he derives from it. The Mapuches (literally, 'the people of the land'), or Araucanian Indians as they are known historically, are a race unique among the indigenous Indians of Latin America. They were the only Indians who never capitulated to the Spaniards. At the time of the arrival of the conquistadors in Chile, the Araucanians had risen above the savage state and were about as far advanced as the Algonquins or Dakotas of North America. They had organized a kind of fighting confederacy of four tribes, but were in no way agriculturists or organization men like the Incas. Short and muscular, with broad faces not unlike some East Asiatic types, they were *par excellence* fighting men. One of their heroes, Lautaro, captured when fifteen years old, became head groom to Valdivia, the conquistador, and is supposed to have stolen from the Spaniards details of the deadly 'secret weapon' which overthrew both the Inca and Aztec empires – the cavalry horse. Hitherto the *indígenas* had regarded it in terror as a kind of centaur, rider and mount combined in one super-being. In their campaigns, the Araucanians were the only Indians ever to use captured horses against the invaders – with deadly effect. In Lautaro's rising, Valdivia was ambushed and put to death horribly; the details have never been verified but the not very *belle légende* has it that he was forced to swallow molten gold, after being told 'Spaniard, you came for gold; here it is!' Lautaro died in battle shortly afterwards, in 1557. Their efforts to 'pacify' the Araucanians (with the customary cruelty), cost the Spaniards more men than all their campaigns elsewhere in South America. The wars were waged with little quarter on either side, the Araucanians fighting back with a desperate, invincible pride. On Santa Lucia hill in the middle of Santiago there is a small monument to Caupolican, one of the few Indian leaders to be captured alive by the Spaniards. He was impaled publicly by his captors; his wife, Fresia, so disgusted that he should have allowed himself to be subjected to such an indignity, dashed their child down to the ground before his dying eyes.

All the time the Araucanians were being driven further and further south, into more and more inhospitable territory. Eventually they retired behind the Bio-Bio river and – in the words of Chilean historians – 'simply ceased fighting', without in fact ever being vanquished. This was to come, however, late in the nineteenth century. The Mapuche survivors were then progressively despoiled of their lands, one way or another, until the Chilean government provided them with sancrosanct *reducciones*. Protective laws prohibited the Mapuches from ever selling any of the *reducciones* land to *huincas*; but the laws also imposed a strait-jacket on them when it came to acquiring funds for developing their agriculture. As populations increased, too many Mapuches were to be found trying to scrape a living from land which had been too overworked. Figures fluctuate wildly on the total number of pure Mapuches in Chile today, but the upper limit could be about half a million. The biggest concentration of these, an estimated 190,000, is in Cautín. They represent 75 per cent of the province's population, but own no more than 25 per cent of the cultivable land; or something less than four acres per person, of which only 60 per cent is fertile. Thirty-seven per cent of the Cautín Mapuches are illiterate, they have the highest infant mortality rate in Chile, and 20,000 are unemployed. Many of them are chronically unable to better themselves; whether through genetic causes, or as a result of so many years of deprivation. Therefore, there is here undoubtedly a very serious social malaise in Cautín, which provides the backdrop to the activities of Señor Chonchol on one hand, and the *miristas* on the other.

Ruperto Vargas takes us to visit a Mapuche woman, Rosa, whom he describes as 'my best artisan'. We walk across planks laid over mud, through the yard of another house-owner. Ducks and moulting chickens dart about. At the bottom of the yard there is a leaky shack in which an old woman with pigtailed grey hair is eating a plate of beans as we enter; a kettle is boiling on the mud floor over a pile of charcoal, a dubious piece of meat hanging on a piece of string from the roof. The roof is made of tin, and there are large holes in both it and the crude planks that form the walls. Rosa lives and works in this shack. She makes her own dyes from roots and berries, and spins her own wool on a hand *huso* (spindle), talking all the time she twiddles it. Shooing the chickens out, she tells us that she works a whole month to make one coarse but beautifully woven *manta*. Through Ruperto, she sells her best quality *mantas* for a maximum of 450 escudos;[1] it is the most she can earn in a month. Yet she is enormously cheerful, and laughs all the time. She is sixty-five, and was brought up by her brothers and sisters. Her own house was wiped out in the 1949 eruption of Villarica volcano, and she lost everything. 'I never married – couldn't bear men – because they drink so much!' she says with a gusty, rather tearful laugh.

To what extent are the Mapuches responding to the agitation and promises of the MIR ? I ask Vargas. 'The Mapuches distrust all *huincas* so much,' he says, 'they will really jump on any bandwagon.' But he doubts that, if the crunch comes, the Mapuches would side with the *miristas*.[2] He stresses how

---

[1] A little over $30 at the prevailing rates of exchange.
[2] Since then there have been signs of the Mapuches becoming increasingly disillusioned with the MIR.

great is the population pressure in the *reducciones* and how grave the hardships among the Cautín Mapuches. But what they want is their *own* land. They do not want to live in communes, or co-operatives. This is the basic miscomprehension of the MIR; and it could also provide a serious headache to the government's official agrarian reform.

Two days later, through the kindness of Dr Hernán López, another Mapuche expert and agronomist of the Carillanca Agricultural Station, we were able to spend a morning with a second Mapuche family near Temuco. Francisco Lemonao works on the Agricultural Station as a labourer and lives with his wife and seven children in a *reducción* called Agustín Porma The children are clean and well fed, and have smiling, sweet faces They appear to be a completely happy family, living simply but without want. Inside their small compound, filled with fruit trees and flowering shrubs, there are three thatched huts; one in which the family live, one where the mother works at her loom, using yarn that she dyes herself like Rosa, and a third which houses the kitchen. The kitchen hut has a fire on the floor with a kettle hanging from the rafters; no chimney, and smoke filters through the thatch. But in the corner there is a modern-looking Aga cooker. Señora Lemonao explains that she bought it five years ago; however she prefers the old, traditional way of cooking. They make cider from their apples, which they prefer to wine. They have no electricity, and get water from their own well. All the time we are talking, *queltehue* plovers make a tremendous din. They are semi-domesticated birds, rendering great services to the Mapuches by way of mopping up undesirable insect pests; they shriek, evidently, because they regard us as intruders. But the Lemonao family are totally welcoming, and allow me to take some marvellous photographs – a rare privilege in itself, as the Mapuches tend to resent fiercely being photographed by any *huinca*.

Lemonao tells us something of the herbs and natural potions which still constitute most of the Mapuche medical remedies. For its various properties, the *canelo* or cinnamon has always been regarded by them as a 'holy' tree; and there is the *radal*, a kind of laurel whose juice is used 'when the blood doesn't flow'; and, of course, there is the *boldo* which we had already heard about. The elder Lemonaos are obviously still subject to strong superstitions. The children are thrilled with a transistor radio which they have recently bought, with their own money, and which they play at top volume incessantly. They tell me that they followed the course of Apollo 14 (which had just returned) with keen interest. But Francisco Lemonao looks disapproving: 'Each time the Americans send man to the moon,' he says, 'they upset both it and the weather.' Hernán López remarks that, statistically, he is right; it rained the whole time during the flight of Apollo 14, and the sun only came out the day of its return; the same had happened on previous moonshots.

There are fifteen families working in the village on an area of two hundred acres, of which Francisco Lemonao owns just four acres. He has five brothers, each possessing one ox. They get together to plough and work the ground, principally growing potatoes and raising pigs and sheep. Everybody in the *reducción* is related. He does not so much mind the idea of a co-operative, or living on land which he does not privately own. 'The important thing is to have food in the belly.'

'Is there much hunger, then?'

'Yes, but it is among those who have little intelligence and are lazy.'

Lemonao refers frequently to the 'lazy Mapuches' – especially the scoundrels who live in terrible tumbledown shanties at the entrance to the road up to the *reducción*. In the past they tried to exact a toll from Lemonao and the 'good' Mapuches at the *reducción*. Dr López had helped them fight against this inequity; which was one good reason why we were received with such warmth that day. Lemonao's idea of a co-operative in fact turns out to be a grouping together of only the good workers – and to hell with the bad. Because 'if all were grouped together in a co-operative, the good with the bad, that would only lead to fights'. He had not been bothered by the *mirista* 'students', as he calls them with a certain amount of contempt. They bid us a warm farewell in Mapuche:

'Peucallal.'[1]

We spend two nights at Nicanor Allende's fundo at Allipen, on the way back to Temuco. Allipen runs to 8,000 acres of good land, of which over a hundred are contained in the fenced-off deer park. According to one of Pablo Hunneus's articles, Nicanor Allende is regarded as perhaps the 'biggest of the big' among the Chilean *latifundistas*. At the moment he is away in Santiago, wrestling with the government for the survival of the *fundo*. The strain is telling on Marilita, who seems desperately nervous, heavily dependent on Chilean champagne. She talks at top speed, switching from Spanish to German to English – often in the middle of a sentence – so that it is not easy to follow her. The Allendes' house is an unpretentious working farmhouse, larger and grander than Herr Kunstmann's – but not much. It overlooks a small lake, and there is Llaima volcano framed by poplars in the distance. With its twin craters, one of which emits a constant fuzz of smoke, Llaima is not such a perfect cone as Villarica, but the sun of a perfect evening turns its snows to a delicate flamingo pink. We go out into the deer park and, in the gathering dusk, a large herd of fallow deer and stags with massive antlers bolt down into a ravine. Noisy flocks of *choroye* parakeets flutter into the chestnuts, trying to find a roosting for the night. A silent figure on horseback rides up with an ancient rifle hidden under his brown poncho – guarding against deer-poachers, or *miristas*? According to Marilita, unless Nicanor can persuade El Austral University to take over the deer park, and Goering's magnificent herd, they will be slaughtered. It is questionable whether he will be allowed to keep any part of the *fundo* for himself.

At dinner we are joined by Marilita's thirty-one-year-old son-in-law, Alfredo Millthaler, a corpulent Chilean German. The news that the *miristas* had seized Trafun from Kunstmann (whom he knows) also takes him by surprise, and he can't understand our shock at the living conditions of Kunstmann's workers. The timber business in Liquiñe was always a marginal enterprise, he says; no markets, no money. 'And you have just no idea what these *campesinos* are like. Give them a

---

[1] 'Goodbye, and may all go well with you.'

decent house, and they will always bring their pigs and chickens into it. For instance, in one house of mine, three times I gave the *campesinos* boards to repair the porch; each time they ripped them down for kindling wood, although there was a dump of wood just a hundred yards away which they were too lazy to use.' Alfredo declares that he is very happy that evening, for the rather surprising reason that at last he has been officially visited by an inspector of CORA; a pure Mapuche, and a Communist, who had spent six years at Patrice Lumumba university in Moscow. 'I am very contented he came today,' he explains, 'because it assures me of the lesser of two evils; if the inspector comes it means that CORA is *officially* going to take my farm, and that in turn means that they will at least pay for all the movable assets. Otherwise, as things are now, there will be an *illegal toma* by the MIR, like Trafun, where the owner is driven out with nothing.' Up till that day, Alfredo's *fundo* and one other in the district were the only ones which had not received a visit from CORA. To my surprise, it turns out that Alfredo is by no means one of the big *latifundistas*, like his father-in-law, and he runs his *fundo* by himself without a farm manager. The man from Patrice Lumumba has not encouraged him to think that he will be permitted to keep any of the *fundo*. So he too, with Pilar, Marilita's pretty twenty-three-year-old daughter, who has a nine-month baby and another on the way, will leave Chile. 'But where shall we go? I have two offers already; one from Windsor [Ontario] to teach riding, another from Germany. Pilar doesn't like the idea of going to Germany. But what's Canada really like?' asks Alfredo without enthusiasm.

The next morning brings a day of that wonderful dry Chilean sunshine; the west wind blowing cool off the Humboldt Current, moving the tops of the tall pines. Clear, clear, clear, air. Sounds of farm life; the lowing of cows driven past the farmhouse. The farm *administrador* comes and goes in a wide, flat-brimmed grey sombrero; a man with a completely Castilian face, and the grave courtesy that goes with it. Somewhere in the interior I can hear Nena laughing with Marilita; that wonderful rich and gay laugh. We ride out, the three of us through the *fundo*, through vast wheat fields

213

that remind me of the line from *Oklahoma* – 'The corn is as high as an elephant's eye'; and certainly it stands nearly as high as my horse's. Villarica and Llaima hover like gods in the far distance. There are fragrant cool woods of *coigue* and *canelo*, the sacred tree of the Mapuches, with clear brooks meandering among them. We ride through apple and plum orchards run to riot, picking fruit off the trees as we go, finally arriving at a wooden hut which Marilita lovingly introduces as the 'Palacio Allende'. She and Nicanor had lived in this converted *campesino* dwelling temporarily after the main house had been burnt by fire. It is surrounded by overpoweringly strong philadelphus and huge shasta daisies. We tether the horses, and crack a bottle of Marilita's Chilean champagne. She says, with passion, 'I adore this little place.' We loll about, gossiping and laughing about nothing in particular; enjoying with her the moment, for the moment. Unlike Ernesto Wagner, she expresses absolutely no maudlin regrets about the immediate prospect of losing it all. 'I cannot leave Chile, like Alfredo and Pilar,' she says, adding half-seriously: 'Do you think the government would let me run a motel here – don't you think I would do it quite well?' Popping another bottle of champagne, I reply: 'Yes, but you wouldn't make a profit!' 'I think perhaps I might teach riding!' Then, more sadly: 'Anything, anything to stay near this place and help the people.'

That afternoon we drive into Temuco for the interview set up with Jacques Chonchol. In the sunshine Temuco has ceased to be the Yukon, and is now run-to-seed California. A curious thing happens in Chonchol's outer office. While we are waiting to see him, I read and sideline *El Diario Austral*'s report of minister Toha's recent visit to the Liquiñe area. A functionary comes up and asks if he can borrow the paper; he returns a few minutes later with a completely clean copy. It seems rather a crude way of discovering where an interviewer's interests lie! Chonchol, who must be in his early forties, has an unusual background. He was born an orthodox Jew, then became a Catholic; now, though he still claims to be a Christian, he is in fact outspokenly Marxist. He studied agronomy at the University of Chile in Santiago, then went to Cuba and helped Castro organize his agrarian reform. Returning to Chile in 1964, he was made vice-president of CORA by President Frei, with whom he later fell out over political differences and the slowness of reform. He left the Christian Democrats and founded the splinter MAPU faction. Though considered an outstanding intellect, like many a theoretical ideologue, he has never worked the land himself. With curly greying hair, and eyes that dart rapidly about behind glasses, he is nimble-witted and answers articulately the questions I have carefully prepared.

I begin by asking him to compare his programme with the policy under Frei. The main difference, he says, is in the tempo. 'We shall make the agrarian reform enormously more rapid, and achieve in one year as much as Frei did in six.'[1] The reason for this acceleration is that the *campesinos* – now much more 'conscious' – have become more pressing in their demands: 'We couldn't continue to frustrate them.' Under Frei, only 5 per cent of the total fiscal budget went to agrarian reform; this is now being doubled, and – in real terms – development credits are being multiplied three to four times. But the serious trouble under the *ancien régime*, claims Chonchol, was more than lack of money; it was lack of political will. 'It is not just a simple redistribution of land that we are about,' he says, stressing the importance of the 'social aspects' of the 'agrarian revolution'. He explains that the Mapuches are the 'principal reason' why his ministry is concentrating on Cautín province, and why he has set up his 'battle headquarters' here. 'We will return the same lands as have been usurped from the Mapuches since the end of the last century,' he assures me. They will be given land as 'co-operatives'; there will be no *individual* property. Thinking back on the Lemonao family and the other Mapuches I had met, I wonder how happily they would fit into such a programme.

'What are you going to do with the new landless, the small farmers dispossessed under your *reforma agraria*?' Chonchol claims that the small owners who farm well will have no problem. He explains the technicalities of land reform; how

[1] In fact, by the end of 1971 Chonchol had already expropriated 2,700,000 hectares, compared with Frei's 3,500,000 in six years.

215

the owners receive 10 per cent of the value of the land now, and the rest over twenty-five years, at a rate of 4 per cent interest adjusted to meet inflation. The owner can still sell his 'inventories' – or movable assets; but Chonchol now wants to change the law, so that the 'inventories' too will be taken over on deferred payment. As regards the definition of who is or is not a 'good' farmer, Chonchol explains that a system of points is given to each *fundo* by his inspectors, but that the ultimate decision rests with him. I wonder just how politically 'subjective' such decisions might be. (Alfredo Millthaler – who it might be said was mildly prejudiced – remarks later 'They can get you on anything. "Bad" farming can mean not sowing enough grain, even on unsuitable land.') The owner, has several avenues of recourse, continues Chonchol; after his *fundo* has been 'registered' for reform, he may contest it (as Nicanor is doing now). Then that olympian figure, the *interventor* is brought in. The whole process now takes about two months.

I ask Chonchol whether he expects there to be a big food deficit in 1971. It is obviously a question he does not like, and he looks a bit shifty, but claims that the harvest will be *better* than last year over the country as a whole, and does not admit that there will be any food shortage. It is not true, he insists, that the *latifundistas* have been killing their cattle; because the abattoirs are controlled by the government, and it is illegal for owners to sell cattle to them without going through government control. So, in fact, the cattle just 'go round in a circle'; the owners may sell them, but they still remain alive, in somebody else's hands. Of course, it was possible that some unpatriotic *patrones* were driving their herds over into Argentina; but the ministry of agriculture didn't know anything about that.[1]

---

[1] I had already heard stories from many different farmers about farm owners threatened by expropriation selling their breeding stock to slaughterhouses, and later I put Chonchol's answer to one who raised cattle on a medium-sized *fundo*. He exploded, 'That's absolute nonsense. Look, I have room for six hundred milking cows, but I only had four hundred and I sold half of these, all in calf, last month for the slaughterhouse. Of course it is government controlled, but it's amazing what a little bribe under the counter can do.'

216

We arrive at the delicate issue of the MIR and the *tomas*
of property. I ask Chonchol, 'Why is the government not
intervening? Is the MIR 'helping your policy?' Yes, the
carabineros have been ordered not to intervene; but it is
because 'traditionally they were regarded as the forces of
repression, and today this government does not employ
repression . . . the *tomas* are an external manifestation of a
very profound problem; which is how to reconcile the
tomas with the acceleration of land reform'. He insists that
the *tomas* are a political embarrassment to the government,
because the *latifundistas* are using them as a political weapon
to fight the government, 'by creating a climate of insecurity'.
Of course, the stories had been 'much exaggerated in the
press. In terms of overall hectares,' claims Chonchol, 'they
were not very significant. Out of 25,000 farms in Cautín,
only sixty[1] had been seized, affecting no more than 20,000
hectares out of a total of 1,600,000.' The government would
like the *tomas* to cease. Chonchol himself is treating each one
individually; if the *fundo* was due for expropriation, it would
be expropriated. Otherwise it would be taken back from the
MIR and handed over to the owner – after the *interventor*
had been in. Is it true that the MIR have received government finance to maintain the properties they have seized
(e.g. the 150,000 escudos given to Carranco)? Yes, it is true;
but the money has been doled out to pay the wages and buy
essential food. He doesn't believe 'press reports' that the
miristas are armed; if they were, some *latifundistas* would
almost certainly have been shot already: 'The only people
who are armed are in fact the *latifundistas*.' Apart from the
episode at Rucalan, there has been no shooting. He does not
believe that there is any likelihood of there being a right-
wing *golpe*; it is only the right wing trying to create an
'atmosphere'. But if there were an attempted *golpe*, he says
menacingly; 'The only result would be, reforms would
come faster – and more will be taken from the *latifundistas*.'
It is 'nonsense' that the MIR are forming a 'free Chile'
around Liquiñe 'Of course the government would act if they

---

[1] Compare Hunneus's figure of 86 given to me several weeks earlier,
during which time a number of other additional *tomas* had been reported.

knew that *guerrilleros* were active there.' He admits that he has been at Liquiñe himself two weeks ago – 'And all was quiet.' He was also at Carranco – 'and all that'. I ask him the sixty-four dollar question: 'What about this Comandante Pepe?' Looking me absolutely straight in the eye, the minister of agriculture says: 'All inventions of the press . . . I doubt if this Pepe exists, but even if he does, he has little significance.'

I cannot help remembering Pepe's parting remark; 'Please greet my good friend Jacques Chonchol when you see him. He was here two weeks ago.'

I have been with Chonchol for nearly three-quarters of an hour, and at this point he is clearly nervous, as if he would be glad to get me out of his office I leave. Back at Allipen, Marilita does not join us for dinner. The number of empty champagne bottles had grown. They tell a tale of the stress and the anxiety, of what it means to be a *tiene* about to become a *tuvo* in 1971 Chile; of the waiting to learn whether you are about to lose every piece of property you have created and loved, or whether you will be permitted to stay and keep a fraction. The next morning we move to Lautaro.

I want to have a quick look at the Tres Hijuelas ('Three Grand-daughters') *fundo* outside Lautaro, reportedly seized by the M.C.R. allies of the MIR. At the beginning of December the *intendente* of Cautín himself had gone out to Tres Hijuelas to tell the occupiers that judgement had been passed in favour of the owner, and to order them to vacate it peacefully forthwith. He was politely told to go to hell by the M.C.R.; they intended to die on the barricades rather than give up the *fundo*, which they would only do as and when CORA expropriated it and handed the land over to the *campesinos*. The *intendente* withdrew meekly and reported the rebuff to minister Toha; ten weeks later Tres Hijuelas was still in the hands of the M.C.R. The country could hardly be more different from Liquiñe: wide open prairies, some of it rich land, and so empty one wonders how there could possibly be land-hunger here. No cars, and few signs of life at all except for an occasional group of pure Mapuches waiting patiently in the middle of nowhere. The road leads straight towards Llaima, which today is part-hidden in cloud, and

Argentina. At first we miss the turning to Tres Hijuelas, travelling many miles on beyond it until we find a solitary Mapuche boy to put us right. When we find it, the entrance presents a rather more imposing sight than either Carranco or Trafun. There is a banner redesignating the *fundo* 'CAMPA-MENTO LAUTARO – TIERRA O MUERTE – VENCEREMOS' and beneath a large picture of Che (see plate 26).

I reverse the car cautiously back towards the entrance, ready to make a speedy getaway. It is only a day or two since a West German journalist was set upon here and his camera seized, and I have accumulated too many valuable photos and notes now to risk losing them – apart from anything else. Just as we are about to halt, a man in a red shirt, making little effort to conceal a machete under it, moves towards us. Instinct and cowardice combine, and I crash the gear lever into first; but the gearbox of the Providential Peugeot ('French design, but Chilean execution,' Nena once laughed as I gnashed the gears for the hundredth time) has a tiresome habit of deceiving the driver. Instead I get into top and stall, and then narrowly avoid bellying down on a large rock. With a shaking hand Nena takes a (hopelessly blurred) photo, and we make off at top speed. After a mile or two, I notice in the mirror a cloud of dust gaining on us. It is the first car we have seen all day. The coincidence is too great, and I have a nasty feeling that the MIR is on my tail. I put my foot hard down and we rattle at a terrifying speed over the ribbed surface of the dirt road. Then, for the first time on the whole fifteen-hundred-mile trip, the Providential Peugeot begins to cough and splutter in its carburettor. The dust behind us seems to be catching up. Only a couple of kilometres away from Lautaro town does it fall back, and then disappear. I do not feel very courageous.

The last *fundo* in the south we visit belongs to Nena's friend, Nella Martin. It is close to the waterfall of Salto on the way back to Santiago. Nella, in her late forties, is severely crippled by polio, but – with her husband working in Santiago – she runs the *fundo* single-handed. Only four hundred hectares in size, it is listed for expropriation; but nothing has happened yet. Nella knows that in the neighbourhood there are 250 *campesinos* 'waiting' for a *toma* of the property, and she

219

has been expecting the MIR nightly for many weeks. Nena is horrified at how worn her friend looks: 'Yes, I am terribly tired. I go to bed early and then wake up at 11.30; listening to every noise. Then I have to work a full day on the farm . . .' Her son Juan Luís, aged twenty-three, is studying architecture at the university. A supporter of Alessandri, he too cannot conceive of any co-operation with the Christian Democrats. He gives a long speech on theoretical politics; is impatient with his mother's views, often interrupting her *'Mama, tu no entiendes la política!'* But she does, rather better than him. I ask Juan Luís what the opposition students at the university are doing. He is angered when Nella interjects: 'Nothing, they are doing nothing, just sitting on the beach!' Then he admits that, in fact, he is doing nothing. And he *is* bored, this vacation, at home. I ask him, rather priggishly, why he and his friends don't go out into the country to *concientizar* the peasants, like Valentina and the FER, during the vacations. 'Why?' he answers, in a note of incredulity: 'Because the vacations are for resting from exams.' Nena looks at me, and we are both thinking of the fanatical young students in the school-house at Liquiñe.

Towards the end of dinner, the dogs begin to bark. Nella, who has become quite animated and gay under Nena's expert treatment, suddenly stops talking. There is no sound but the croaking of bull-frogs and the ziz-zizzing of cicadas. Nothing happens; no one comes, but the evening is finished. As we leave, Nena is markedly dejected: 'I have never seen Nella like that,' she says: 'She's never, never given up.' It is what it was like in Kenya during the Mau-Mau, though admittedly without the butchery. This is how many hundreds of other wicked land-owners spent night after night in Allende's Chile, 1971.

11

'The Cowards are
Leaving . . .'

As we drive northwards back to Santiago along that endlessly straight lifeline of Chile, the Pan-American Highway, I try to form a few conclusions from what we had seen in the south. Of one thing there is no doubt: whatever the 'social injustices' committed in the past collectively by them, in the expulsion from their properties of the good and bad *lati-fundistas*, a human tragedy of major proportions was being enacted. The question was, how far would this counter-swing of the pendulum go? Out of the deprivation of those being deprived, would there emerge a better life for more Chileans, a real millennium for the long underprivileged Mapuches? Would Chonchol's reforms make Chile, in greater or lesser time, a more efficient food producer? Was the Allende government playing a dirty game with the MIR? Would the agitation on the land lead to the 'armed confrontation' so ardently sought by Debray and the *miristas*?

First of all, there appeared to be some division of opinion within the U.P. itself as to how to deal, ultimately, with the 'reformed' lands. Allende was on record as backing the continued existence of small and medium-small farmers; his reasons being no doubt part political, because he could reckon on the support of many opposition Christian Demo-crats for land reform (which, after all, they had themselves instigated), but not for collectivization. Despite all the panic and alarm, not *every* landowner was having his farm taken away – yet – in that February of 1971. There was, for in-stance, the ex-ambassador to France, Enrique Bernstein, (now permanent secretary of the foreign office) who had told

221

me in Santiago how he had returned from France expecting to find his 320-hectare *fundo* expropriated. The 'syndicalists' called for him, and three-and-a-half hours of discussion ensued. 'But as I had just had weeks-long negotiations in Paris with the Chinese over the resuming of relations I was in good training, and I just exhausted them! In fact, when it was all over they threw a party for me, composing impromptu *cuecas*[1] about my career in France.' So Bernstein will keep at least the major part of his *fundo* – but for how long? Repeatedly Chonchol has made it clear that he intends an end to private holdings, and for them to be incorporated into massive state farms. On these 'co-operatives' *à la* Chonchol, the individual workers will merely possess their own house and a *huerto* or allotment. And the majority of Mapuches – like the Lemonaos – seem to be making it equally clear that, although they want their 'usurped' lands back, this is not how they want them. So will the wretched Mapuches find that once again, like the *indígenas* all over Latin America ever since Independence, they are being swindled by yet another set of all-promising *huinca* revolutionaries?

Historical experience everywhere has been against collectivization of agriculture – in almost any form. Tito valiantly abandoned it, after a few early disasters; Russia plunges on, wastefully and inefficiently; Castro has reduced Cuban agriculture to a catastrophe. Can Chonchol, in his wisdom, succeed where the others have failed? In Santiago Gregorio Rosenberg, a Chilean Jew, Social Democrat and freelance agricultural adviser of some distinction, echoed much of what I saw myself in Cautín. The four hundred thousand *minifundistas* of Chile who tried to eke a living from small plots of land with no capital were in a bad way; unable to buy machinery and, with their next year's crops already pawned in advance for the purchase of seed and fertilizer, increasingly in debt. The new small farmers created under Frei's land reform were in just as precarious a state, because they had not been granted sufficient funds or credit to develop the land efficiently. Out of 150 small farms dealt with by an accountant known to Rosenberg, only seven were

---

[1] Chilean equivalent of the calypso.

actually reckoned to be making a profit. On the other hand, Rosenberg spoke in extreme gloom of the incompetence with which some of the already 'reformed' *latifundos* were being farmed, on a co-operative basis, by CORA. There was, for example, a milk and cheese co-operative in Cautín which had had finally to be closed down by the sanitary authorities, 'because of the filth and flies'. There was no resident *administrador*; it was run by 'advisers' living in the town. Some British agronomists had been so deeply shocked when visiting it three years previously that, while being followed round by a horde of CORA officials, one disgusted Briton had snapped: 'Why in hell don't some of these people go and clean up the cows, instead of trailing round behind us?' Rosenberg had himself recently gone to Israel and seen some of the prize kibbutzim there; there was a drift away from them, and in general the kibbutz philosophy seemed to be withering. 'And if Israel has difficulty with her kibbutzim,' asked Rosenberg, 'how on earth then can the individualistic-minded and in-efficient Chileans hope to succeed?'

Rosenberg was only one of numerous agronomists and farmers I met in Chile who disagreed emphatically with Chonchol's assurances that there would be no food shortage as a result of the accelerated reform programme, and the *tomas*. (And indeed events were to prove them all right, and Chonchol wrong; for by the beginning of 1972 Chile, with her great agricultural potential, was importing food at the rate of 280 million dollars a year, was buying chickens from France, and was forced to abandon Allende's 'pint-a-day' for school children for lack of milk.) Suffice to say that the causes for this slump in farm productivity lay chiefly in the loss of confidence among the frightened farmers who *were* (*pace* Chonchol) selling off their breeding stock, and who *were not* seeding and cultivating the land for the coming year[1] – which held so little promise for them. Over the longer term, concluded Rosenberg, if present trends were to continue,

---

[1] A typically crude cartoon in an issue of *La Firme* devoted to agrarian reform depicts a fat *latifundista* lolling back in his rocking-chair and gloating: 'This year I shall order them not to sow anything, so that they'll all die of hunger – ha, ha, ha!'

Allende was going to find that by the 1973 mid-term elections agriculture 'would have gone so bad' that his electoral chances would be slight; therefore 'totalitarian methods' were bound to be forced upon him before that date, on the agricultural front alone.

'The estate owners in Cautín are armed, and are provoking violent confrontations with the workers on the land. There is a serious amount of arms smuggling from abroad; dangerous subversive plots are being set afoot,' declares Debray in his *Conversations with Allende*, and the *Compañero Presidente* tacitly agrees – as indeed had Chonchol in his interview with me. But, after visiting Cautín, it is hard to go along with this thesis. The boot seems to be properly on the other foot. In the same exchange, Allende made it quite clear that a loaded 'revolutionary' justice was being, and would be, meted out to landowners who were the victims of *tomas*. He explains how 'the bourgeoisie made laws which were very lenient to people who occupied land [but] those who recovered their land received very harsh treatment indeed at the hands of the law.' Now the law is being turned around and applied to the disadvantage of the 'bourgeois legislators': 'the people occupying the land are the indigenous population, the Mapuche Indians for example', and they are being treated leniently (i.e. the carabineros are not permitted to intervene), 'while the people trying to recover it by violent means are the estate owners, who . . . are feeling the full weight of their own law.'

But in fact incidents like Rucalán, where the owner had returned armed and retaken his property, were without any doubt the exception rather than the rule – at any rate in 1971. In the dozen or so farms we had visited, the *patrones* had possessed little more than a rusty shotgun or sporting rifle, which they were far too frightened to use. I thought of Joaquin Holzapfel's ancient German cavalry sword, on the one hand; on the other hand, Pepe and his *miristas*, well-equipped with weapons which they were ruthlessly determined to use, if need be. Only a day or two after our return from the south, the Christian Democrat senator for the area, Ferrando, was actually held up by an armed band near Liquiñe, and over the ensuing months the MIR were to become increasingly active and audacious in their movements. It was sheer nonsense to say, as had minister of the interior Toha, that 'nothing irregular' was going on. There was no longer much doubt in my mind that the U.P. government *was* giving the MIR a free run in the south, *was* turning a blind eye on its activities. Typical of its line was an article in *El Siglo*, captioned 'Momios Invent Tomas of Fundos', which asserted derisively that a nun had simply 'mistaken for guerrillas students who were doing their voluntary work' in the neighbourhood that summer. Chonchol tried to deny Pepe's existence to me, although Pepe claimed to have seen him up at Liquiñe just two weeks previously; and shortly afterwards Allende himself – openly surrounded by his guard of black-beret *miristas* – dismissed Pepe and his group as '*muchachitos, buenos muchachitos*[1].'

Allende's motives in not bringing the MIR to heel were somewhat mystifying. Was there perhaps, after all, a grain of truth in what the two wild young men of the right, Pedro and Juan, had suggested that day in the Carrera; namely, that the government was using the MIR as the left hand of its policy, with the aim of provoking a half-cock uprising? As a founder member of O.L.A.S. – the clearing house for Latin American revolutionaries – and on the basis of his own declarations to Debray and others, Allende may well himself have been suffering from divided loyalties. But was he acting (or, rather, not acting) out of strength, or weakness? There were many Chileans who felt that he would never take action against the MIR until he had consolidated his position by winning the municipal elections coming up that April. On the other hand, there was Chonchol on record as saying: 'I welcome the agitation that we face today – as long as it is compatible with our resources.' And, indeed, over the short term it does appear that the MIR is *helping* to accelerate Chonchol's own expropriation by creating an atmosphere of panic among the *fundo* owners. I recalled Nicanor's son-in-law, Alfredo, declaring how 'contented' he was to have had the Patrice Lumumba inspector come that day – instead of the MIR, in the middle of the night. But, by allowing the Pepes to strengthen their grasp on the backwoods, perhaps

[1] 'Little boys, nice little boys!'

225

Allende may be building up – unintentionally – a grave conflict for Chile in the more distant future; leading the government 'into a cul-de-sac with no way out', as *La Prensa* commented. Possibly, in their despair, the 'brutal' land owners will arm – helped by friends over in Argentina.[1] Then there would be bloodshed.

Pepe's chilling words continued to ring in my ears: 'Civil war in Chile is inevitable.'

But could it really happen, here, among such a warm-hearted and historically unviolent people?

The long miles tick by on the speedometer. Pale yellow clumps of wild eschscholtzias with the lovely name of *dedales de oro* give way once again to the great glowing fields of sun-flowers. Nena prevents the journey from dragging with an ever-lively flow of conversation. There is always something she finds comical, or something to enthuse about. I remark with genuine admiration: 'You're marvellous – always laughing, and even in the morning!' She replies, surprised, 'But why not, life is so wonderful, isn't it?' Wonderful? She has just seen some of her closest friends about to be dispossessed; her whole world has been stood on its head, and the future for her can only be seen through a glass darkly, very darkly. And yet 'life is so wonderful'. I am filled with reverence. She talks with animation of her future plans (or fantasies?), of how she would like to start a summer school for children to teach them arts and crafts, the visual and tactile joys that they miss in the winter months. We stop at a stall to buy *choclos* (Chilean sweet-corn) and water melons, and start swopping notes on the nature of the South American and the Chilean in particular.

Nena raves about Gabriel García Márquez's great novel, *Cien Años de Soledad*; which, as she rightly remarks, is 'South America in microcosm', perhaps the one book that – although written by a Colombian about Colombia – almost all South Americans regard as being universal to the whole continent. (And of what modern European novel could anything comparable be said?) This strangely unreal, allegorical fairy tale does seem to embrace all the romanticism and

[1] This has in fact, now happened – see chapter 16.

226

fantasy, the frustrations and guilts, the passionate violence and irrationalism, and the hopes for identity of every South American; the schism between speech and action that is so characteristic (and so destructive) of the continent as a whole; the love of sonorous language, the sensibility to friendliness or insult, the open-handed generosity and the sense of personal dignity; above all the hope, and the despair. The Macondo of García Márquez is a mystical, savage but sadly beautiful and joyous place of complete unworldliness where it once rained 'for four years, eleven months, and two days' and where a man, in the eyes of his enraptured *inamorada*, is followed about everywhere by a cloud of yellow butterflies. There is the semi-educated, gullibly romantic paterfamilias, Jose Arcadio, who parts with all his money to an itinerant gipsy for such gimcracks as a magnet, a magnifying glass, a flying carpet, secrets of alchemy – and, finally, ice. 'This is,' he declares triumphantly, 'the great invention of our time;' and pays the gipsy another five *reales*, 'just to touch it'. Meanwhile, his rather more practical-minded wife, Ursula, is methodically rediscovering the forgotten route through the swamp which has isolated Macondo from the world for a hundred years: 'the route that her husband had been unable to discover in his frustrated search for the great inventions'. There is Aureliano Segundo who buys the first zinc sheets ever to arrive in Macondo, to roof his mistress's bedroom with them simply on account of the erotic sensations 'that the sprinkling of rain produced'.

In all the succeeding generations of Buendías the women, like Ursula, are stronger and more down-to-earth than their bemused males; a generalization I had already observed many times in Chile. In the end Ursula has Jose Arcadio tied to a chestnut tree for the rest of his life, to keep him out of mischief. Then the terrible, endless civil war (based on Colombia's *La Violencia*) begins, in which Colonel Aureliano Buendía 'organized thirty-two armed uprisings and lost them all' – as well as his moral principles. At the end of it, Aureliano admits in a moment of despairing lucidity. 'We fought all those wars and all of it just so that we didn't have to paint our houses blue.' A *gringo* banana company sets itself up in Macondo, and is (typically) blamed for the beginnings of decay within the community. 'Look at the mess we've got ourselves into,' they complain; 'just because we invited a *gringo* to eat some bananas.' The banana company pulls out, then the strong-willed, centripetal matriarch Ursula dies at an enormous age and Macondo collapses in total ruin.

García Márquez ends by echoing the deep pessimism that so many South Americans feel when they contemplate their place in the sun: 'because races condemned to one hundred years of solitude did not have a second opportunity on earth'.

'You really have to be a romantic to love South America, to understand it at all, even to tolerate all the dreadful things that are wrong here,' insists Nena, still talking about García Márquez. But the Latin American male is not as intrinsically romantic when it comes to his relations with women. 'They are romantic up to a point – and that point is their *machismo*. Oh, these Chilean men; they either want to make you, or to put you on a pedestal, or both. Then when they have you, one way or the other – or when they think *you* are getting interested – they run. They really don't want women – it's just to flatter themselves. These Latins – and basically they're all the same – they promise the moon to their beloved, and at the most give her chocolates . . .'

In Santiago there is a remarkable and discreet rendezvous – the Hotel Valdivia – that caters exclusively to the love fantasies of Chileans; and it is quite revealing. There are fifty-four diverse and exotic suites. The Cave is an eighty-foot long dim grey cavern carpeted with animal hides and festooned with realistic stalactites and stalagmites, and a vast litter tucked away in one rocky recess. There is a Petrified Forest in which to play hide-and-seek; a Cage Room for lovers with an 'O' hang-up; a Polynesian room with a ten-foot hammock; an Arabian room with mirrors and 1,001 cushions; a Psychedelic room, with the usual dreadful light effects; and, for those with a craving for back-seat rape, an Automobile room, hung with car accessories and photos of Indianapolis. The Valdivia does not just cater to rich *tuvos*, and prices are remarkably modest: The owner explains that 'the secret is volume'; it operates in three separate shifts, round the clock. South Americans are notoriously scornful about each other, and the Argentinians (about whom the Chileans are even ruder) sometimes use the word *chileno* when they mean a pickpocket, and *chilena* for a lady of easy virtue. The labels are neither chivalrous nor fair, but the Chilean women (apart from being probably the most beautiful) are certainly the most emancipated in South America; the divorce rate is astonishingly high, the illegitimacy rate runs at about 20 per cent of the population, and there is little doubt that a considerable number of man- (and woman-) hours are spent happily *en la cama* in Chile. Less happily, alcoholism is also a big factor in Chilean life; it has been said that 5 per cent of all Chileans over fifteen are alcoholics, and one in every ten adults dies of cirrhosis. To combat this, Allende has now launched a vigorous anti-drink campaign.

In other respects, the Chilean is, reputedly, a careful, meditative man, his ideas somewhat lacking in depth; perhaps all this derives from his isolation from the rest of the world. Nena also claims that he is devious, always searching for some hidden second meaning behind every proposition. (I wonder, momentarily, whether this peculiarly feminine trait could have anything at all to do with that silent pre-eminence of the women in Chile?) And what other readily identifiable characteristics? A felicitous sense of humour; as a U.S. ambassador once remarked, 'The Chilean chuckle is a safety valve.' And a tremendous, genuine warmth in human relationships, among family or friends. Two Chileans greeting each other can present quite an overpowering emotional demonstration; again, perhaps because of that particular sense of remoteness from the rest of humanity.

Nena is quite piqued when I comment on the small number of churches we pass, and their disrepair. So for the last hundred miles or so to Santiago she exclaims in each village: 'Look, there's one! And there are two, right opposite each other!' But, for once, the evidence seems to be against her: I cannot help recalling that on our first day in Chile, the only church in Valparaiso Bill could find open for Mass was the cathedral. One senses the physical presence of the Church much less in Chile than in, say, Colombia or Peru – or Spain; and its spiritual and material influence is certainly feebler. Chile is one of the three South American countries (Uruguay and Brazil being the other two) where the Church is disestablished. The Church is much poorer in financial resources than in Colombia where it is still estimated to own some 2.5 per cent of all urban and rural real estate, valued at about U.S. $100 million; by comparison, in Chile it owns less than 1 per cent of the lands, and the dioceses are universally poor. There were (as of 1960) calculated to be some three thousand Chileans per every priest, as compared with seven hundred Catholics to one priest in the U.S.A. Church attendance is low; ranging between a maximum of 25 per cent down in the rural south to 4 per cent in urbanized central Chile. Fernando Léniz of *El Mercurio* put the overall rate of 'proper churchgoers' currently at no higher than 3 per cent to 4 per cent. Of his family of nine, 'only my oldest daughter goes regularly,' he told me. 'My wife calls herself an R.C. but goes to church once every ten years. I refuse even to call myself one. The Church no longer has any influence in Chile.'[1] Divorce with remarriage is, of course, not recognized by the Church, but – as already noted – the rate is extremely high; for, *outside* the Church it is very easy to obtain. All you have to do, under Chile's wonderfully legalistic procedures, is to hire a lawyer and admit to having committed a mild perjury in filling out the original marriage form – such as giving a wrong address – and the union is annulled. Thus still more Chileans find a reason, or necessity, for living outside the Church.

It has often been said that, on an intellectual level, the Catholic Church in Spanish America never quite recovered from the expulsion of the Jesuits. Since then it has perhaps too little concerned itself with the material problems of man's life in this world, has all too little attempted to instil a sense of social responsibility among individual Catholics. This is one good, fundamental reason why throughout Latin America the Church is becoming increasingly divided between conservative traditionalists and the progressive, often 'revolu-

---

[1] The power of the Catholic Church in Chile is also somewhat diminished by the presence of over half-a-million Protestants, including many nonconformists.

tionary' priests impatient for reform.[1] In Chile there is nothing to compare with the 'Golcondas' of Colombia, heirs to Father Camilo Torres, or the Christian guerrillas of Bolivia (about which more will be said later), but the 'progressives' are growing in strength. In general terms, the Church can less and less be reckoned a force for political cohesion within the Christian Democrat party.

Perhaps the most encouraging aspect of the emancipation of the Church in Chile is its attitude to the key problem of birth-control. It seems grimly ironic that, just sixty years ago, Lord Bryce designated South America as the only continent capable of cultivation 'which still remains greatly under-peopled'. Today – with the exceptions of Bolivia, Paraguay and Argentina – the continent as a whole has one of the worst over-population problems in the world, and its overall birth-rate still remains the highest. Hopes of the progressive churchmen that a new, enlightened philosophy towards birth-control might be on the way received a devastating blow when Pope Paul's historic visit to South America in 1968 almost exactly coincided with his fundamentalist blast against the pill. It could hardly have been more disastrously timed. Nevertheless, in Chile where the birth-rate stands slightly higher than the continental average, some progress has been made – against odds. In 1964, *Revista Mensaje*, the Catholic periodical, actually came out in favour of pro-gestogene contraceptive pills as being no more than a substitute for 'the natural dynamism of nature' – then had its knuckles rapped by the Vatican. Chile also had the worst abortion figures on the whole continent; in 1961 they were assessed at *one for every two live births*. After some soul-searching, the Frei government's health service lauched a campaign to suppress abortion by providing special clinics; which – under the counter – also offered free contraceptive advice and devices.[2] There are a hundred such in Santiago alone and –

<hr />

[1] In guerrilla-torn Guatemala, for instance, one figure estimates that 40 per cent of the priesthood is 'progressive', and another 15 per cent outright Marxist.

[2] One of the greatest obstacles to birth-control in any so-called 'backward area' is lack of education. A Colombian woman who had attempted

if one can believe census projections – they have already made their mark in that, on the last count, there turned out to be a million Chileans fewer than predicted! The Church conveniently averted its gaze, and the editor of *Mensaje*, Dr Ochagavia, assured me in Santiago that if Allende were to introduce an official birth-control policy the Church 'would *not* fight hard against it'. So far Allende has not made any move, but were he to do so it might well turn out to be his greatest contribution to his country's well-being.

Almost as soon as I get back to Santiago, there is Jaime's gravel voice on the telephone. He has not left Chile yet, after all. His future mother-in-law, *madame la comtesse*, is growing impatient and he fears she may be coming to 'get him'.

'I am coughing – I am getting thinner – I'm sure it's cancer. Perhaps she'll let me off. . . . And *why* does a beautiful twenty-three-year-old girl want to marry an old man of forty-two? When you're over forty, you look at yourself in the morning and think you're a lion – but not because you're a beautiful king of beasts, but because you *smell* like one!'

It is not only his engagement-neurosis that plagues him; he has just heard that his ex-wife, a romantic fringe left-winger, has just been arrested by the police in Brazil. Not a very happy thought. But he cheers up as he talks. Had I heard the latest Santiago saying? '*Los cobardos se van, los tontos quedan*' (The cowards are leaving, the fools remain).

Even during the short time I have been away in the south, it is possible to detect in Santiago an increase in anxiety at the way things are developing. Tempers seem to be rising, and factional hatreds mounting; something which, Nena and others assure me, never used to exist in Chile. The Marxist radio stations are resorting more and more to personal abuse, couched in language that – to the Chilean – is often *grossero* or downright obscene. There are rumours in the air that the government may soon make it very difficult for people to leave the country; which naturally exacerbates alarm among

to run a clinic in Bogotá told me how one of her patients told her 'I forgot to take my pill one day, but my husband took it instead the next day. That will be alright won't it?' At least the Chileans with their higher standards of literacy may have a head start here.

the *tuvos*. Allende could well find a ready-made excuse to do this in the continued flight of money abroad, if there is any substance in the growing concern one hears on all sides at the country's economic state of health. Just how bad things really are, or are likely to become, is hard to gauge and there is much difference of opinion. A walk through Santiago gives one almost an impression of boom-time; the shops are full of goods at moderate prices, and full of people buying them – just as at Con-Con the restaurants and *anticucho* bars had been full of free-spending young people apparently having the vacation of their lives. Chileans remark on how there has never been so much money in circulation. So Señor Vuskovic's scheme to boost consumer spending *seems* to be working. On the other hand, how much of it reflects sheer anxiety on the part of the middle-classes to exchange money, which they feel may soon either lose its value or simply be taken away, for consumer goods which – in the way of other Marxified economies – may rapidly become as rare as hens' teeth? Already, because of demand, there is a waiting list for new cars. Television sets may be next. Although the official exchange rate of the escudo is pegged at fourteen to the dollar, any Chilean will willingly offer you thirty on the black market, and the ratio seems likely to widen.[1] But there are few tourists around to top up the supply of illicit dollars. According to one travel agent, where U.S. tourists used to come at the rate of 350 a month at this time of year, there are now 50.

All over Santiago there are partially completed and apparently abandoned buildings, despite Chile's crying need for housing, and the fact that unemployment in the construction industry stands at 28 per cent. Some of the part-completed units are already being occupied by squatters, desperate to get a roof over their heads before the harsh Chilean winter begins. The entrepreneurs have called a halt to work through lack of cash, or confidence, or both. It is a predicament which seems to typify the private sector at this moment, and it is difficult to see what, bar a resort to

[1] By January 1972, the official rate had climbed to 28 to the dollar, but free exchange reached over 80; six months later it had soared to *170*.

authoritarian measures, Allende can do to reverse the tide. The picture in the copper industry, on the health of which virtually the whole of the Vuskovic–Allende economic programme depends, is also not encouraging. Since November some three hundred key technicians have evidently left Chile, and production is reported to be running at 20 per cent below par. There is also much mystery as to how the heavy cost of Vuskovic's 'pump-priming' operation will be covered; or the budget deficit that it is bound to cause. A bright young liberal economist, Alejandro Foxley, reckons the government will be forced to print money in dangerously large quantities. This will lead to inflation and then, he tells me with great concern, Allende will either have to let inflation rip (which he is heavily committed to opposing) – or he will repress it; and this would mean a wholesale takeover of industries, accompanied by rationing. Inflation will also bring acute balance-of-trade problems. Foxley thinks it questionable how much imports can be purchased by copper profits; and what if a coming food shortage in Chile dramatically forces up those imports? He concludes that Chile's substantial reserves of nearly U.S. $380 million may only allow stability for a maximum of another eighteen months; but there will be a major economic crisis well before then.

This is not how Ed Korry, the retiring U.S. Ambassador, sees it. The accrued copper royalties, in his view, will last at least three years and give Allende all the fiscal flexibility he needs to Marxify the economy completely. There will be no economic crisis. Who is right? Korry or Foxley? *Vamos a ver*. Korry is an imposing virtuoso who speaks without pause for either question or comment; a former journalist, his despatches to the State Department are renowned for their literary quality. As United Press chief correspondent for Eastern Europe, he observed the 1948 Communist takeover in Czechoslovakia, and on the basis of his experiences – although by no means a right-winger – he openly expressed his misgivings about Allende's accession. This has not exactly endeared him either to the regime or its *aficionados*. (Graham Greene in an article[1] which, by extension, almost

---

[1] *Observer Colour Magazine* of 2 January 1972.

made Haiti's Papa Doc sound respectable and seemed to betray some of the symptoms of senility, accused the wretched ambassador of symbolizing 'outside aggression' – because, evidently, of the 'size and fatness of his earlobes'!) On my last visit to Korry, I find him in deep gloom. The expropriation of the copper companies is going to be total: 'They will sweeten the pill as much as possible so Congress in Washington can swallow it – but it will hurt.' He himself expects to be sacked within a month or two. And, just to complete his cup of woe, the Chilean foreign office are making ugly noises about declaring William F. Buckley, jr – currently somewhere in orbit between Rio and Switzerland (or is it Israel?) – *persona non grata* on account of his unflattering articles about the *Compañero Presidente*'s Chile.

Nena lends me the well-beloved antique Taunus to go to the U.S. Residence, and I do a terrible thing to the gears on the way back. The result is that it will not go into reverse; or indeed any other gear but top. So we grumble and shudder back to Nena's house and I wonder whether to throw myself quietly into the Mapocho river. But she is all-forgiving of this outrage to the loved one, and simply laughs: 'Don't worry! I'm delighted; if it hadn't been for this I would never have gone to the garage!'

On the day before my departure for the weird world of Bolivia, I lunch with friends from the British Embassy at their house wonderfully sited on a hillside outside Santiago. Across the valley the High Andes rise, smoky and mysterious, out of scorched foothills. One can just make out, nearly forty miles away, the eternal snows on the twenty-thousand-foot peaks. With binoculars on a clear winter's day, they say, one can see the skiers wedelling up at Portillo. For the hundredth time, one feels that it would take more than a 'coward' to be able to say goodbye forever to all this beauty, to all the warmth of friendship that is so uniquely Chilean.

The next morning as Nena drives me (always in top gear) to the airport the Chilean sun is just awakening the peaks of the coastal range with a soft pink kiss. The vast *callampas*, thousands of new wooden shacks covering many acres, seem to go on for ever. 'None of these were here six months ago,' says Nena. 'There were just green fields.' The walls are plastered with the expectant, hopeful tributes to Allende and the U.P. Will he be able to satisfy them? Or will he be swept away Kerensky-like by the Pepes and the Valentinas on a tidal wave of disenchantement?

There is a long queue at the Iberia desk; a slow, and muddly departure. A group of hard-faced French tourists stand ardently discussing a favourite Gallic theme; the cost of things. I think of Jaime's discovery of the worthlessness of material objects. More delays; the doors of the exit lounge won't open. A Mapuche walks very slowly out to the plane, carrying six rolls of lavatory paper. At last we embark. The jet's Muzak is playing the hauntingly melancholic second movement of Aranjuez. In the distance, as the jet wheels I can just recognize Nena on the spectator stand, a small figure in a white skirt and black top. I have a bad feeling of abandoning someone on a precarious life-raft, while climbing into the rescue ship myself.

12

'In Bolivia, a Fire is Nothing'

That first night in Bolivia the hotel caught fire. As an old Cuzco hand, on arriving at La Paz's two thousand extra feet of breathlessness[1] I had noted all the warning lights of *soroche* – the fluttering of the eyeballs, edging of the teeth, a certain light-headedness – and heeding them with respect had obeyed all the rules: no exertion, no alcohol, a modest dinner, early to bed and two sleeping pills. Remembering Charles South's advice, I had conformed – without hardship – to the 'internal regulations' (*sic*) posted up in my room:

Guests are prohibited by Law to entertain members of the opposite sex in their rooms unless chaperoned or under completely accepted social conditions. [Whatever those might be.]

Then, somewhere in the night and through the Tuinal torpor, I became vaguely conscious of the noise of breaking glass and agitated shouting. Bolivia's 187th revolution, and I was missing it! I struggled out of sleep and to the window. Flames were billowing from the upper storeys of the hotel above me, glass and other objects falling past to crash on the tin roof below. Briefly I wondered whether to be English, not panic and stay put until given instructions – or get out in a hurry. Then the lights went out and that decided me it was time to cease indulging in national fantasies. Into a suitcase I hurled a few clothes, my precious films and notebooks – plus, unintentionally, an open bottle of mineral water which was hardly a help to legibility – and groped my way to

---

[1] 12,400 feet above sea level; the world's highest capital.

237

safety. Water was cascading down the stairs, but if anything the fire seemed to be getting wilder. After I had gone down two floors, an iron hand gripped my chest. The remaining three I tottered down panting, a step at a time, feeling (with the exaggeration of terror) that the flames were descending faster than me.

In the small plaza outside, the other hotel residents were congregated. The fire engine (which had come all the way from La Paz airport up on the *Altiplano*) ran out of water – and there were no hydrants. However, an ancient Scot with thirty years experience of Bolivia assured me that – because of the lack of oxygen – the fire would peter out of its own accord. A serious conflagration in La Paz was virtually unknown; indeed, until recently it had been the only capital of the Western world to have no official fire department. He was right. By about 2 a.m. the flames began to flicker irresolutely, having gutted most of the top storey. The *patrona* then threw open a still partly flooded bar to provide free drinks for those of her guests that had not yet abandoned ship. I commented on her admirable *sang-froid* and she replied with a cheerful laugh: 'Well, if you live in a country that has a revolution every other week, a fire is nothing!'

In fact just the previous month an abortive coup by right-wing army officers had attempted to oust the current president, General Juan José Torres, who had himself come to power that way only three months earlier. For several hours that night the army commander, General Reque Terán, had been held a prisoner in his own headquarters. After the Second World War Mustangs of the loyal air force had made several passes at G.H.Q., firing harmlessly into the air but causing terrifying reverberations in the bowl of the cañon where La Paz is situated, the coup – like the Crillon fire – petered out. Had it been successful, it would have been the 187th revolution or *golpe* since Bolivia won her independence 145 years ago. Unkind wits in Chile dub their mercurial neighbour 'the long-playing record – thirty-three revolutions a minute'. Geologically speaking, the Bolivian Andes are said to be in a constant state of movement; in technical parlance, they are 'unstable' – which means that a road existing on Saturday may well have disappeared, disastrously, by Monday. There is hardly one in the country which is not blocked more or less regularly by landslides or floods. Then, too, it is said that in winter in La Paz you can get frostbite on one side of the main street and sunstroke on the other. Such elements of excess and instability are also symbolic of Bolivian social and political life.

Of all the countries of South America, Bolivia is perhaps the strangest and most fascinating. It is undoubtedly the most tragic. The parting words of the British Ambassador in Santiago, Toby Hildyard, to me were: 'You know you feel that there is a *possibility* of something being done in Chile – in Bolivia, nothing.' Geography and history have both combined to be intolerably unfair to Bolivia. After independence, General Santa Cruz, who was of Inca descent and probably the ablest leader Bolivia ever produced, wanted to recreate the old Inca ideal by means of a Peru-Bolivia confederation. But this was defeated by the joint opposition of Chile and Argentina, and for the ensuing decades anarchy, civil war and a series of tatterdemalion generals reigned over Bolivia, while Chile was solidly establishing constitutional democracy. The worst was Mariano Melgarejo, a one-time army pack-boy and a drunken brute who murdered a political rival with his own hands inside the presidential palace. Melgarejo was subsequently assassinated by the brother of his mistress; but not before his reckless policies had paved the way to the disastrous War of the Pacific which (in 1884) led to the loss of Bolivia's entire coastal region. It is the fate of Bolivia to be ruled by Melgarejos and to lose wars. Since 1825, her territorial losses to neighbours have totalled 492,155 square miles out of an original 904,952. The most recent took place in the Chaco War of 1928, the last conflict in the Western Hemisphere, when Bolivia rashly took on the warlike Paraguayans. One of the only campaigns of history in which a French-trained army actually beat a German-trained one,[1] it ended with poor Bolivia losing her access to the Atlantic as well as the Pacific.

[1] One of those in charge of training the Bolivians was the odious Major Ernst Roehm, later to achieve immortality in the Nazi 'night of the long knives'.

The territory left to Bolivia today still equals twice that of France, but to some extent it is composed of the tracts that nobody else coveted, leaving Bolivia the least homogeneous and most unviable country in South America. It falls into the three totally contrasting areas; the windswept and poverty-stricken Andean altiplano bordering on Peru and Chile, which contains 60 per cent of the population; the vast *oriente* to the north-east consisting of appalling jungles drained by the headwaters of the Amazon, and comprising nearly two-thirds of the land area; and the semi-tropical valleys round Cochabamba and Santa Cruz, potentially rich but only haltingly developed because of hopeless communications both internally and externally.[1] Perhaps Bolivia's greatest blessing is that, with a total population of somewhere over four million, she has the lowest density in all South America; at least no *explosión demográfica* here! But no other country of the continent still suffers so much from the depredations of the *conquistadores*. To provide forced labour for the silver and gold mines, they broke up the highly advanced agricultural system of the Incas – and replaced it with absolutely nothing. In the swampy Beni to the north, the Spaniards destroyed the wide causeways that the Incas had laboriously raised above flood level; now there are no roads, and the canals and causeways have disappeared. Even with modern agricultural methods, existence on the eroded altiplano seems to be a losing battle; a U.S. official report of 1963 stated that most of the small holdings there had reached the 'point of no return'. The indigenous Indians frequently subsist at starvation level, and not so long ago the expectation of life was thirty-two years – fifteen years below the continental average. The national average per capita income stands at around U.S. $100 a year, or one of the lowest in the world.

The conditions in which the agrarian *indígena* lives are frankly disastrous; he is without social security or medical care; he

---

[1] When the new highway to Cochabamba was opened by the president a few years ago, the city worthies greeted him; 'We have been waiting for you for three hundred years!'

33 Archangel at the
Oruro Carnival

34 The Oruro
Carnival

35 (*above*) Colombian cattle ranch; El Palmar

36 Luís, vet and the repaired bull

37 Towards a new *Violencia*? Cali, February 1971

38 Priest administers last rites; Cali riots, February 1971

39 *Pax Vobiscum* – Castro and Allende

40 The women of Chile disagree: The 'saucepan riots' of December 1971

inhabits inhospitable regions; his alimentation is wretched and his hygienic conditions compare with those of his animals, for the latter share his house and his food.

These words could have applied to the lot of the Indian under Spanish colonial rule; in fact they were written (by a Bolivian)[1] a generation ago, and circumstances have not altered recognizably since.

But the life of the Bolivian miner is even worse – and so it always has been. In the later sixteenth century, Potosí, whose great silver mountain made Spain rich on the slave labour of the Indians, was a glittering city of 150,000, smaller only than Paris, London and Seville. But it was hell, literally, for those who worked inside the mines. According to a contemporary description:

A man moves a load of two arrobas [50 lbs] fastened to his back with a cloth and they go up in threes. The foremost carries a taper attached to his thumb so that they can see, for there is no other light.

Out of seven thousand Indians conscripted in rotation by means of the *mita*:

no more than two thousand souls ever return, and the remainder, in part they die, and in part they remain in Potosí . . . when they want to return they have neither cattle nor food for the road.

Because of the poisonous fumes, even outside the mines 'No grass grows even for cattle to eat, and there is no wood to burn.' Since the hey-day of Potosí, many mines have become exhausted by the Spaniards, and they have never provided much benefit for the Bolivians. Today, silicosis is rife, and the miners are probably the lowest paid in the world. The tragedy of the Bolivian tin mines (which account for 80 per cent of exports) is that, economically, they cannot afford to pay more. Even when the world price of tin sinks to 70 cents a pound, Bolivia's competitors in Malaya and

---

[1] Jorge Pando Gutierrez, *Bolivia y el Mundo*.

Indonesia, with their easily-worked alluvial deposits, can still make a profit; whereas, at the current high price of $1.70 a pound, half of Bolivia's mines – where the ore has to be scraped and blasted out of the Andes at altitudes often higher than the summit of Mont Blanc – constantly run at a loss. Conrad in his novel *Nostromo* wrote of the 'San Tomé' silver mountain in his imaginary 'Costaguana' as 'hanging over the Campo, over the whole land, feared, hated, wealthy; more soulless than any tyrant, more pitiless and autocratic than the worst government; ready to crush innumerable lives in the expansion of its greatness.' This could equally have been a truthful description of the tin mines of Bolivia.

Before the Second World War, the disparity of wealth in Bolivia outpaced anything elsewhere in the continent; eight *latifundistas* owned one-tenth of the whole national territory; the tin millionaire, Simón Iturbi Patiño, whose income was alleged to equal that of the entire Bolivian budget, gave his daughter the world's largest recorded dowry. But service in the Chaco War had opened the eyes of Bolivia's wretched feudal Indians to how the other half lived – even in backward Paraguay.

Here were the basic ingredients of a chronic revolutionary situation. Whereas, however, in some Latin American countries (such as Mexico), revolution sometimes leads to better things, it never does in Bolivia – perhaps simply because her predicament is simply insoluble. In 1952, Bolivia underwent one of the most fundamental Latin American revolutions of this century. Dr Paz Estensoro and his M.N.R. swept away the Bolivian tin barons, nationalized the mines, and parcelled out the land of the big agrarian estates among the landless serfs. But over the next ten years a combination of bad times on the tin market and inefficient management reduced production by 40 per cent. The richest and most accessible ores were worked first, and nothing was spent on exploration or the development of new veins. Because of lack of working capital, productivity of the peasant small-holders slumped catastrophically. Because of the M.N.R.'s pledge to increase wages when there was no money in the till, inflation soared. In 1953, the Boliviano converted at 60 to the dollar; within three years the free-rate reached

11,885 to one. By 1964, the army had had enough and moved in, putting in power an Air Force general with great dash and *machismo*, Barrientos, who spoke fluent Quechuan and was a skilful manipulator of the Indians. Under his strong-man rule, and with much U.S. aid, Bolivia began to show signs of restored equilibrium. But still the burning dis-content in the mines (where, to balance the books, Barrientos cut the miners' basic wage from $30 to $20 a month) con-tinued. Several times they erupted in revolt, and on each occasion there ensued dreadful massacres of the miners by the Bolivian army. At the same time, mineral concessions granted to U.S. companies by pro-American Barrientos provoked mounting resentment among Bolivian nationalists.

It was on to this scene that Che Guevara and his *Ejército de Liberación Nacional* (ELN) burst in 1967, thereby really put-ting Bolivia back on the map whence Queen Victoria had once removed her in a fit of pique.[1] Che considered that Bolivia with its 'oppressed' miners and peasants and its borders touching on five different countries was ideally suited as a starting point for the 'continental revolution'. His strategic aims were far from modest; he would 'create a second or a third Vietnam', he told the Tricontinental Conference. Brazil and Argentina would be forced to inter-vene; which would crack their military regimes at home. The U.S. would also be drawn in, and in trying to fight guerrillas in Latin America as well as in Indochina it would be com-pelled to introduce a dictatorship at home, leading ultimately to the inevitable disintegration of the bourgeois state predic-ted by Marxist prophets.

Apart from his posthumous success as a pop idol and a sales gimmick for T-shirts – Che in fact proved to be one of the greatest flops of modern times. This is not the place to re-explore Che's campaign, or to analyse the errors that led to the final disaster, but one may briefly summarize some of

[1] The story goes that a British minister, after apparently offending Bolivian susceptibilities, had been sent out of La Paz strapped across the back of an ass. Outraged at this slight to imperial dignity, and realizing that there was no way a gunboat could reach Bolivia, Queen Victoria simply ordered the country to be struck off the map.

them. Drawing on his triumphant experiences in Cuba in a manner close to arrogance, he would operate by establishing guerrilla *focos* in the countryside, while eschewing the cities. Che selected the wild, jungle area south of Santa Cruz. He had no tangible tactical objectives. In his own book, *Guerrilla Warfare*, he stresses the need for the *guerrillero* to 'have a good knowledge of the surrounding countryside . . . naturally also, he must count on the support of the people.' Both these principles were breached fundamentally by Che. He never investigated just how inhospitable is the terrible Bolivian hinterland, as well as lacking in the means of sustenance for even a small body of men. Mostly Cuban 'foreigners', his group did not gain support from the *campesinos*. They learned the wrong Indian dialect – Quechuan instead of Aymara – and, as a Peruvian *guerrillero*, Héctor Béjar, has noted previously, in predominantly Indian areas the *indígenas* 'identify Spanish with the boss'. Such is the extent of Bolivian peasant xenophobia that those around Santa Cruz in any case tend to regard even miners from the north-west as 'foreigners'.

So Che's Bolivian recruits were mainly of fairly low calibre. One who, when captured, was interrogated as to his motives, produced an almost music-hall response: 'If you had a mother-in-law like mine, you too would join the guerrillas!' When Che's lieutenants were trying to *concientizar* another peasant, they promised him: 'When the ELN triumphs, you will have tractors, schools and even a university,' and got back the baffled question: 'What's a university?' About a third of the Bolivians deserted and went over to the other side; it was the information from such peasants, whom Che had come to 'liberate', that led to his final rounding-up. Although some of the miners came out spontaneously for him in 1967, they were savagely repressed by Barrientos with more than a score of deaths, and Che – with his strategic understanding blinkered by the Sierra Maestra – never attempted to organize any effective support system in the towns. Nor did Che get the backing of the official Communist Party, to whom he pridefully refused to subordinate his operations. The encounter, down at the Ñancahuazú *foco*, between Che and Mario Monje, secretary general of the P.C.B., is perhaps the outstanding interlude in the whole Che saga. Monje delivered three conditions for supporting the guerrillas, which included:

The setting up of a broad political front in the country . . . which would organize a single revolutionary command. . . . The revolutionary plan for Bolivia should be related to mass experience and consciousness and should not be based solely on the guerrillas . . . anyway the military leadership should be subordinated to the political leadership.

I.e. Che to take orders from Monje. In his diaries, Che accuses Monje of being 'evasive at first and later on treacherous. The party is now taking up arms against us and I do not know what it will lead to.' Here, in a nutshell, was the basic confrontation between the two sets of Marxists persisting throughout Latin America today: Pepe versus Allende.

In almost all his tactical handling of the campaign, Che was hopelessly amateurish, resembling more a fish *out of* water than the famous prescription for guerrillas laid down by Mao. He was not helped by the arrival of the Marxist adventurer, Debray, whom he swiftly sent packing, but who – when in captivity – according to the Che diaries 'revealed more than necessary'. Starved, diseased, betrayed, himself crippled with asthma but heroic to the end, Che and his group were out-manoeuvred and finally cornered by Bolivian army 'Rangers' hastily trained by U.S. counter-insurgency experts, and then 'liquidated'. Substantively, Che's mission was a disastrous failure, and it symbolized the failure of the rural guerrilla movement in South America as a whole. But Che – of course – was to become an infinitely larger-scale figure in his martyrdom than in his life. In the course of my wanderings, I had the good fortune to talk at length to General Zenteno Anaya, whose division had captured Che and subsequently carried out the execution order. With that soft-spoken, gently courteous manner typical of many Bolivians, so much in contrast with the tempestuousness of their backdrop, Zenteno, when I found him, was retiring ambassador to Peru and is now the Bolivian commander-in-chief. He had never before discussed the death of Che with anyone, but showed me unpublished documents and photos taken by himself. (Among other things, they seemed to disprove Castro's contention in his preface to the Che diaries that his executors had brutally machine-gunned Che 'from the waist down', so as to conceal signs of the deed, and had left him in prolonged agony.) I asked Zenteno one question: did he now think it had been a mistake to kill Che?

'I did not think so then; but now – yes, absolutely.'

Over the short term, Che's eleven months' campaign did succeed in shaking the Barrientos regime, and from 1967 the pressures mounted. The end of Barrientos – as with so much of the Bolivian scene – reads like pages of Ian Fleming. There was a mysterious, somewhat unbalanced personality called Antonio Arguedas, minister of the interior under Barrientos as well as being a close personal friend. Barrientos loaned the captured Che diaries to Arguedas (who, according to a reliable informant in La Paz, also had Che's hands, pickled, in a bottle), and he promptly forwarded them to Castro. When the truth became known in Bolivia, Arguedas admitted under interrogation that he had also been working for the C.I.A. over the past three years. Subsequently he took refuge in the Mexican embassy, where several attempts were made to bump him off, and then fled to Cuba; whence he has never been heard of since. But the Arguedas scandal thoroughly rocked the government. There were violent riots in La Paz, and more trouble in the mines – with the army leaders now becoming increasingly restive at the revelations of the extent to which the C.I.A. had been involved in the anti-Che operations, behind their backs. The mood in Bolivia began to swing passionately against the U.S. Then, in April 1969, Barrientos, who had always been proud to claim that he had survived eight assassination attempts and four plane crashes, was himself killed while piloting a helicopter. At the time, it was reported that he had flown unwittingly into a telegraph line; since then, however, there have been repeated allegations that he was in fact shot down. In the Bolivian press accusing fingers pointed at his successor, General Alfredo Ovando Candía, and over the ensuing months there were a series of unexplained but seemingly linked murders that looked like part of an elaborate silencing operation. It reached out as far as Hamburg when, in April

1971, the Bolivian consul-general and former intelligence chief was shot by a woman disguised in a grey wig. The mysteries, still unresolved, have been considerably thickened by repeated allegations that both Barrientos[1] and Ovando were involved in an arms deal worth U.S. $50 million to purchase weapons in Europe and pass them to Israel. This was hotly denied in Israel; yet the curious fact remains that, in a country as far removed from Middle East interests as could be imagined, Israel maintains an extremely active embassy, including a substantial military mission, and supplies Bolivia with generous financial credits. Suspicions have long persisted that remote Bolivia may be one of the principal channels through which the supply of weapons to Israel has circumvented the arms embargo.

After a further period of instability, Ovando, commander-in-chief of the army during the anti-Che operations, took over. An enigmatic, shadowy figure, Ovando promptly went far to the Left, motivated (so several Bolivians told me) partly out of a sense of acute guilt at having given the order to execute the wounded Che. Taking a strongly anti-American line, he expropriated U.S. mining companies, and re-established relations with the Communist bloc. In what had for five years come to be regarded as perhaps her most reliable satellite in Latin America, the U.S. suffered a major defeat. After Peru, Bolivia was the second of the Andean countries to go seriously left. Throughout his brief career Ovando, however, seemed unable to keep pace with the forces to the Left of him – notably the miners' unions and the students. During the summer of 1970, there was a fresh outbreak of guerrilla activity; this time organized by the left-wing students of La Paz University, about which more remains to be said in the next chapter. On 9 October, after

---

[1] It is also perhaps worth noting that Barrientos, though penniless on coming to power in 1964, was discovered (in a style familiar to Latin America) to have amassed property worth $10 million on his death five years later. The mystery has been further thickened recently by reports from Bolivia that Altmann/Barbie, the German whom French investigators claim was the S.S. chief in wartime Lyons, was also in some way implicated in the Israeli arms deal.

Ovando had been in power just a year, General Miranda, a 'Barrientista' and then commander-in-chief of the army, launched a right-wing revolt against him. The army was split, and the country teetered on the brink of civil war; the U.S. State Department declared the situation 'the most dangerous in South America'. Miranda and Ovando agreed a temporary truce, and then the left-wing students ran amok – revealing themselves to be better armed than ever before. A professor of medicine was machine-gunned leaving a hospital; police stations were overrun; the two leading newspapers of La Paz were taken over; U.S. embassy offices through the country were sacked. Finally, after those Second World War Mustangs of the Bolivian air force had dropped a few dummy bombs on the presidential palace, Ovando was deposed in favour of another general, forty-nine-year-old J. J. Torres. He was of poor parentage and largely Indian extraction (unusual for a president of Bolivia, although it is the country with the biggest Indian proportion of any in Latin America). He was also pronouncedly left-wing – having been sacked as commander-in-chief by Ovando for over-praising Castro. Miranda took refuge in the Paraguayan embassy; and Ovando – following the other conventional path open to unseated Bolivian rulers – was sent to be ambassador to Spain.

The eccentricities of Bolivan history are well matched by the weirdness of La Paz's setting. Sixty years ago, Lord Bryce remarked: 'In no capital city have I felt so far removed from the great world,' and the sensation persists today. As you drive from El Alto airport across the flat bleakness of the altiplano, past the parked Mustangs waiting to swoop like hawks on some new uprising, there is no sign whatever of La Paz. Then suddenly it is there, beneath your feet, roofs of its hard-won Bolivian tin glistening like silver below, in a great hole, fifteen hundred feet deep that resembles a vast open-cast nickel mine. Why here? one asks. At the entrance to the city there is a large statue of John F. Kennedy; not very far away, a sign advertising 'Bank of America', and immediately behind it an even more imposing one with armed fists breaking out of chains, and in large capitals 'We are liberating ourselves – at last.' The street *graffiti* of La Paz are even more eloquent than those of the Ramona Parra brigade in Chile. *'Revolución es Dignidad!'* they proclaim apologetically; and *'Alfabetización es Revolución!'* In the main street, there are still signs left over from a past era (all of four months ago: 'Long Live Ovando – The solution will not come from the mountains [i.e. Down with the guerrillas!] – Ovando will strangle Yanqui Imperialism – Bread, Shelter and Work with Ovando'.

High up above on a butte inside the canyon and deplorably dominating the city are hoardings 'PEPSI COLA – BUBBLE UP – CRUSH'. In the middle of the Plaza Venezuela there stands a monument to Columbus, inscribed *'Navigare Necesse est, Vivere non Necesse'.* For a country where there is no sea on which to navigate and everything is a struggle for life, it seems a little incongruous. Through the Plaza Venezuela, a torrent of water pours as if down a mountain stream. It is the rainy season, and there is practically never a day without some rain. Everything seems to move at slow time; because of the altitude the cars supposedly lose 40 per cent of their potency, and so does even the barrel-chested *indígena* of La Paz. Walking – and it is all uphill – is a major effort. The police direct the slow-moving traffic from little turrets covered over with sun- and rain-shades. Their faces, dyed purple by the winds and ultraviolet rays burning through the thin air, are hard to distinguish from the navy blue of their uniforms: cheekbones so wide as to protrude on either side of the Potsdam-style peaked caps. The faces everywhere are fascinating, incredible; one might be in Mongolia, Tibet, or the north-west territories of Canada.

Up at the Plaza Murillo, goose-stepping troopers dressed in the ceremonial uniforms of the War of Independence are changing the guard outside President Torres's presidential palace. They then go to mount vigil over the catafalque of Santa Cruz in the cathedral next door. But the real presidential guard, dressed in American steel helmets and battle-dress, peer out over their heads through the doorway of the palace. The façade of the unpretentious building is pitted with bullet holes, relics of some past revolution. Just across the corner of the square stands a dispirited building with broken windows and an air of long disuse; Bolivia's parliament.[1] In front of the presidential palace stands a lamp-post with a tiny patch of carefully tended garden at its base. From it a previous president, Villaroel, was hanged in 1946. The various inscriptions state: 'The captain does not abandon his ship in a storm' (again, a curious sentiment for a non-maritime country!) and the claim that Villaroel was 'sacrificed by the oligarchy . . . but not in vain.' There seem to be various versions of the lynching of Villaroel. One says that he had become an oppressive tyrant, brutalizing political prisoners and making them swallow lubricating oil; that it was the university students (as so often) and not the wicked oligarchs who had sparked off the lynching – by way of protest against the government's interference in the university. In the middle of the Plaza Murillo is a small statue dedicated to *'Paz – Unión – Gloria – Fuerza'* – poignant reveries of a country that has known so little of all four. An elderly gardener is ineffectively flicking random grass cuttings away with a small whisk broom. Each day I pass through the Plaza there are congregated around the statue dreadfully poor-looking Indians and their families, who stand there patiently all day. They are unemployed ex-miners on a hunger-strike, holding before them pathetic hand-scrawled placards – '100 families without food', etc. One wonders how many miles they have trekked from the altiplano to present their petitions. Inside the ministry of information are hung warning notices – 'There are no vacant posts'; the ministry of the interior protects itself against the long queues of discontented by troops permanently equipped with anti-riot visors. The signs of unemployment and under-employment are everywhere. 'This happens each time we nationalize *Yanqui* companies,' says an anti-American Bolivian, hopelessly. By comparison, Chile is like California in a boom. On every street corner sit the patient, unsmiling Cholo women in their bright skirts and bowler hats, a few pyramids of nuts,

---

[1] Shortly after I left La Paz, the untenanted parliament building was put back into service again when it was seized by various elements of the far Left, who set up a 'People's Assembly' inside it and began to operate as an alternative government right alongside the president, without let or hindrance.

chewing-gum or chocolate carefully arranged on a handkerchief. They sit there all day, sweet faces full of patient dignity, never begging and seldom seeming to sell anything. On their pitch from dawn until late at night, they then slowly gather together their unsold wares to trudge to some shack miles away up on the rim of the canyon, and are back at their dispiriting task again at dawn. How can they possibly make a living? A few of the Cholo traders are apparently, however, quite prosperous. There is Señora Flora, a vastly fat and jolly lady who sells me a silver brooch; she is also supposedly a close confidante of President Torres, keeping him informed of the mood of the market-place. But the Floras of La Paz must be very few indeed.

Near Señora Flora's shop there is a whole street full of *brujas*, or witch-doctors. Apart from violently-coloured sweets lovingly counted one by one by grubby hands at regular intervals, their stalls are filled with strange herbs, starfish, seeds, coca leaves – that essential, ancient, numbing panacea for all the miseries of life on the altiplano – and a hundred and one unmentionable and unrecognizable medicaments; most of them, evidently, being in the line of anti-aphrodisiacs, harking back to the old, simple methods of birth control of the Incas. Also dangling revoltingly from each stall are dried llama foetuses. These are burnt by the purchaser and the ashes planted under the foundations of a new home, or at the corners of fields about to be brought under cultivation for the first time, by way of a propitiatory offering to Pachamama, the Goddess of the Earth. These ancient rites can hardly be helpful to stock productivity, but they suggest how deeply rooted beneath the veneer of Catholicism are the atavistic traditions of the Incas in Bolivia.

Visiting La Paz over twenty years ago, Christopher Isherwood noted his disappointment at the lack of any 'sophisticated luxury'. He assumed that the Indians had been robbed and exploited; but

Where are the fruits and flowers of crime? In Paris, perhaps, or Buenos Aires, or New York? Certainly not here, La Paz has no palaces . . . it hasn't even a Casino or a decent nightclub.

Things have not changed since then. The only nightclub I visited was totally empty, except for a shrunken head over the bar with the meaningful caption '*Deudo Moroso*', or 'Bad Debt'. Down in the upper-class suburb of Obraje, the nearest thing to a palace is a house belonging to the last of the wealthy mine-owners, who lives behind high barbed-wire with a pack of wildly barking, fierce Alsatians roaming incessantly across the flat roof. Along the Calle Inavi that runs into the Plaza Murillo, once the Rue Royale of La Paz, joists with carved lions' heads jut aimlessly out into the air, the balconies they used to support long since fallen away. Fake pilasters are peeling away from once semi-grand colonial houses. There is no opulence any longer in La Paz, even if it ever existed. Everywhere the cripples, the blind, the sour smell of urine in the market places. It is sad, it is lowering; and yet there is a soft sweetness about the Bolivians that engages and warms. (And, incidentally, they have one of the most civilized systems of public transport I have ever come across; taxis, or *colectivos*, that rattle up and down the main thoroughfares, filling up with passengers and dropping them off one by one at their destinations. Wherever you go, it seems to cost an invariable two pesos.)

Every day is overcast, and from the Crillon, risen from its ashes, I can see little beyond the opposite wall of the canyon. Then suddenly one morning the sun comes out and there looming above La Paz is Illimani, the Holy Mountain; a great molar with four pinnacles, 21,000 feet, and snow all the way down to where it is cut off from sight by the La Paz ravine. It has, they say, never been climbed; and the superstitious Indians say it never will be. Somewhere behind Illimani is Mount Chacaltaya with the highest ski run in the world: 17,860 feet. I yearn to try it. With the coming out of the sun, the reds, whites and purples of the weirdly eroded rocks of the La Paz canyon strike the eye with unimaginable force, so amazingly clear and luminous is the light in La Paz's impoverished air. The multitudinous colours of the *Cholo* ladies in the market places dazzle like iridescent paint.

My first interview is with the British ambassador, Ronald Bailey. He is one of those rather rare British diplomats who can project themselves with total enthusiasm into the country to which they are accredited. He has been four and a half years in La Paz, and is about to be transferred – but, apart from complaining that he is beginning to suffer from altitude amnesia ('couldn't remember the name of my daughter yesterday'), his passion for Bolivia and the Bolivians seems not a bit diminished; and La Paz cannot always have been the most rewarding of posts. His knowledge is formidable. The ambassador tells me, with a laugh, that he regards himself principally as a 'debt collector'. Recently a 'moralization' enquiry discovered that something like 90 per cent of all debts in Bolivia were bad ones: *Deudos Morosos*. The bad debts to British companies are endless. Corruption and graft reach imposing figures: The ambassador who was previously in the Yemen (where he was shot up by terrorists) notes that there 'the mark-up was only 1 per cent – here they want 10 per cent!' It is now very difficult to follow the political alignments in Bolivia, since Barrientos smashed up the M.N.R., he says. There are twenty-six identified political parties; the M.N.R. itself has split amoeba-like into five parts, and it is hard to get any public figure to define his adherence to any party. The prudent thing to be is an 'Independent Nationalist'. Today anybody who is what we would call a true democrat, or slightly right of centre, is automatically categorised as a 'Nazi', or 'Fascist'; while 'anyone to the Left of you is a "Communist".' There are at least four separate, recognizable Communist Parties. The Maoist-orientated are known locally as the 'Pekinese' while predominant influence is wielded by the Trotskyist POR; it is almost as if news of Trotsky's death had not yet reached the altiplano. In this political vacuum, President Torres's own position is weaker than that of any of his predecessors. He is not, says the ambassador, 'an extreme left-winger, but very nationalistic'. Few people in La Paz give him very long.

The planes out of La Paz are busy ferrying 'political extremists', who might rock Torres's precarious vote, into exile at a rate of several a day – mostly to Chile.

One of them exiled only the previous day is the brother of a secretary in the British embassy – Miss Ivanovic. She is distraught. The brother, aged twenty-four, was studying law at the university, and was a right-wing student leader.

The government claimed that he was mixed up in the January coup, and he was summoned at two in the morning, given no money, and packed on to a plane to Arica (Chile) together with a group of 'Pekinese' guerrillas. The press shows photographs of these political enemies shaking hands on the plane. Miss Ivanovic says the allegations against her brother are totally untrue: 'They call him a Nazi, but it is ridiculous.' Their father was a Serb, supporter of Mijailovic in Yugoslavia during the Second World War, who had to get out when Tito took over. He married a Bolivian, and all his family was born in Bolivia. 'What can we do? Where can we go now? Bolivia has become impossible, and it is getting worse all the time. All South America is going Communist – and where is there to go? This continent is becoming impossible.'

The ambassador kindly puts at my disposal the Bolivian political tipster of the embassy, Gonzalo Montes. Gonzalo is the Hollywood producer's ideal of a Latin-American conspirator. Each morning he relays to me the latest political *canard*, his eyes darting to the left corner, then to the right corner, followed by a warning finger on the lip. The ever-moving kaleidoscope of La Paz political currents and crosscurrents is like some daily T.V. serial that goes on without end. Gonzalo is a stimulating companion; his passion, strangely, is European military history, and he is extremely well read. He has a pleasant sense of humour; at one point in our conversation he assures me, with an engaging smile: 'We Bolivians are really very human people, basically – even though we string up a president occasionally!' Together we make a round, first of all, of the La Paz editors. *El Diario* used to have the largest circulation in Bolivia (35,000), but was one of the two newspapers seized by the La Paz students during the 'October Revolution' of four months previously. They then handed it over to its workers to be run as a 'co-operative'. The present editor, Señor Arieta, has a tired old *mestizo* face, with long jowls and bad teeth. Unsmilingly and with no false modesty, he describes how his fellow-workers elected him to the post: 'I have been forty years in journalism, and was the most serious and most estimated journalist on the paper.' Under its previous owner, Señor

Carrasco, *El Diario* had shown a 'fascist' bias; now, since it had been taken over 'by request of the students and the workers' it liked to describe itself as 'independent to the Left.' Arieta has no sympathy for the Communists, however: 'The day Communism comes to this paper, I go home.' He is convinced that the ELN guerrillas have failed in Bolivia: 'The Indians are so very conservative.' Arieta says that he would, of course, hand the paper back to Carrasco 'if the situation should change; one has to be very flexible, as a journalist in Bolivia.' He seems a simple, rather perplexed man. The offices of *El Diario* are seedy beyond belief, but Arieta insists that its finances are 'magnificent' and that the paper is receiving no subsidy whatever from outside. (Gonzalo whispers to me that *El Diario* is in fact nearly broke, and that it is generally believed that only money from the government keeps it going.) Arieta expresses puzzlement at the current state of investments in Bolivia. There is a basic contradiction; the Torres government tries openly to reduce U.S. investments to a minimum, but beneath the surface it continues to accept them. He does not think there is much hope of substantial investments coming from Eastern Europe; the most important is a zinc smelter the Yugoslavs are financing. Like General Richter of Peru, as well as many other Bolivians of the Left, Arieta expresses strong political sympathy for Yugoslavia: 'Perhaps it would be the best copy for any Bolivian government.' He thinks that President Torres would 'be delighted to pass his job on to somebody else'. But who?

In La Paz, the television is under government control; so is one radio channel, but there are sixty privately controlled stations. There is only one government newspaper, *El Nacional*, and all the other leading newspapers parade as 'independent' – even the official Catholic organ, *La Presencia*, describes itself as 'independent Catholic'. Its editor, Señor Estenssoro, in common with all the other journalists I spoke to, assured me that – unlike Peru – there was no direct government control over the media in Bolivia. Nor was the press subjected to the kind of indirect pressures experienced by *El Mercurio* in Chile. But Bolivian journalists have been known to suffer other, more brutal forms of compulsion. Less than a year previously, the independent-minded owners of *Hoy*, Alfredo Alexander and his wife, had been blown to pieces by a bomb placed under their bed. The paper is now run by their daughter, a plumpish lady in her fifties, with quite an imposing presence. Still dressed all in black, and wearing dark glasses, Señorita Alexander runs Bolivia's second most important newspaper from a very simple, austere office, decorated only by photographs of Lincoln and Churchill. Her father, ambassador to Spain in 1966, and a historian who had written a number of books about the War of the Pacific, had founded *Hoy* twelve years previously. No suspects had ever been picked up for the bomb outrage; though Señorita Alexander left little room for doubt that she held ex-President Ovando responsible. Like *El Diario*, during the revolt of 7 October *Hoy* had been attacked by students armed with sub-machine guns; occupied and 'co-operativized'. But the printers – not the journalists – handed the newspaper back to its rightful owners twelve days later, saying that they had no complaints about the management. Though outspoken in almost every other respect, Señorita Alexander cannot tell me what government she would like to see running Bolivia, or which personality at its head – because there are 'no organized parties in Bolivia any longer'. She just knows that she longs for a government that will 'bring work and tranquillity'. Though not of the Left, she is a staunch nationalist when it comes to the takeover of Gulf Oil; because she feels that the terms of the concession granted by Barrientos were too unfavourable to Bolivia.

But nothing provokes more vehemently nationalist sentiments from the courageous Señorita Alexander than the talks currently under way between Chile and Bolivia about a resumption of relations. Never outstandingly cordial, relations were ruptured by Bolivia eight years previously; the *casus belli*, a seemingly minor friction when Chile under Alessandri diverted water from a river on the North Chile – Bolivia boundary. On coming to power, Allende, eager to cement amity with a new left-wing neighbour, promptly sent a Communist senator, Volodia Teitelboim, off to President Torres with plenipotentiary powers. From Santiago it seemed, as it always has done, that all that was needed was a firm hand-shake and a slap on the back. But Bolivians – from Señorita Alexander to President Torres – did not see it quite that way. To them the basic issue with Chile goes back further, in fact nearly a whole century, to the War of the Pacific. When I met her, Señorita Alexander was particularly outraged by a contemporary article in *Reader's Digest* which seemed to imply that Bolivia had never legally possessed a Pacific littoral. To indicate what this imputation meant to the Bolivian mind, Torres had even gone so far as to make an official protest to Washington. The accompanying Bolivian communiqué referred to 'the unjust war . . . unleashed by Chile against Bolivia and Peru'. Señorita Alexander remarks that this is one of the very rare occasions when *Hoy* has found itself supporting the government; it is perhaps the only issue on which almost all Bolivians are united. 'This is our Alsace-Lorraine,' she says. 'The war is not yet finished.' A leader by her, commenting eloquently on plenipotentiary Teitelboim's visit, speaks of the 'old wound' separating the two countries, and the 'aggression suffered by Bolivia'; as a result of which Bolivia has remained ever since 'captive amid her mountains, isolated from civilization, asphyxiated in the Andes'.

On the face of it, Bolivia has a case; certainly few countries in this world would seem more deserving of generosity from their neighbours to offset the unkindness of geography. But, up to now, the Chileans have not shown themselves sympathetic. On a supposed 'goodwill' visit to Bolivia, President Ibañez once remarked with extreme acidity: 'Why do you need a port, when you have no sea?' a comment that only rubbed more brine into the old wound.

Bolivian reactions to Allende's initiative are instructive for two reasons. First, they emphasize how very different is the view as observed from Santiago windows, compared with how it seems at La Paz's rarefied altitude; perhaps yet another instance of the remarkable degree of separateness and lack of communication between the various Spanish-speaking countries of South America. Secondly, they must throw caution on any hopes Allende might have of smoothly creating a cohesive left-wing bloc of Andean nations.

The permanent secretary in the foreign office, Laredo, is

257

more sanguine about the prospects of Andean co-operation. With blue eyes and a small beard like Claudio Veliz, he is an intelligent leftist who has travelled widely, worked with UNESCO in Paris, and is still in his thirties. Warmly enthusiastic about Bolivian participation in the Andean Pact, he assures me that 'We will have to have *real political integration* here in the Andes before the end of the century.' I feel however that this may be representing his own idealism, rather than the line of the present government; especially when he adds that President Torres and the Peruvian generals should be looked on purely as a 'transition to Andean Socialism – and a Marxist Socialism'. (I wonder whether a similar remark could have been coaxed out of Sir Alexander Cadogan about either Churchill or Attlee.) Laredo admits that Bolivian feelings about those Pacific ports are passionate, but claims that, in fact 'Bolivia won't need the ports; because in twenty years we shall be all one unit'. He expects relations with Chile to be renewed within a month,[1] and reckons the Chileans are prepared to give Bolivia a port of her own, with a kind of 'Polish corridor' linking it to the hinterland. And what about Peru? He did not seem to have taken into consideration the fact that, under the peace terms following the War of the Pacific, Peru also has to give her blessing to any move granting Bolivia access to the sea. Meanwhile, poor Bolivia continues to exist, or subsist, as she has done for the past century – locked away behind her impoverished hills.

[1] This has not yet happened, and Bolivia has since acquired a new, more nationalist – anti-Left and anti-Allende – regime.

13

In Lyricism
of Che?

In Bolivia, perhaps even more so than elsewhere in South America, it is traditionally the armed forces that hold the balance of power, and are the king-makers. This has certainly been the case since the Barrientos era began in 1964. But now – over the past four turbulent years that have embraced Che, the Arguedas revelations, the death of Barrientos, the coming first of Ovando then Torres – the army has shown itself split and wavering as never before. It is not easy to discover exactly where the divisions lie; is it even clear, one wonders, within the army itself? Some observers reckon that the junior officers, captains and majors, are more strongly inclined to the Right, tacitly favouring Colonel Banzer,[1] the former Commandant of the Military Academy, who launched the abortive *Putsch* the previous month – and therefore anti-Torres. Others tell one that the rank-and-file for the first time is becoming seriously infected by Communist indoctrination; while the last two *golpes* show that at the top the armed forces are divided horizontally too. Confusion is absolute.

Accompanied by the faithful Gonzalo, I set off for G.H.Q., just across the ravine from the British Embassy. Inside the perimeter, the usual contrasts one grows accustomed to in Bolivia: women squatting in terrible mud, or hanging up laundry; scruffy, completely Indian troops wandering about with transistors glued to their ears; enormously smart,

[1] In August 1971, Banzer mounted from exile a new, and successful, *golpe* and is now President of Bolivia.

259

purposeful officers dressed in immaculate, rather Germanic uniforms of *Feldgrau*. Like the President's Palace, the High Command building bears numerous bullet scars from one or other of the past 186 *golpes*. The Commander-in-Chief, General Luís Reque Terán, aged forty-eight, was appointed by left-wing President Torres with the manifest aim of appeasing the army. He commanded the operations against Che in 1967, and he is generally regarded by the Left as a 'typical gorilla'.[1] They say he used to take particular delight in being beastly to his prisoner, Régis Debray. On my way to see the general, I am received by Colonel Cardenas, head of the 'Second Department'. His features suggesting predominantly Indian blood, Colonel Cardenas at first is rather distant: 'How long do you want with the general? Five minutes?' Then in the course of a brief conversation, I happen to drop the name of Liddell Hart, and when I mention that that great military intellect had been a close personal friend, Cardenas warms completely. He has read most of Liddell Hart's works, obviously understood them, and there follows a stimulating professional conversation. We then have forty-five– not five – minutes together with the Commander-in-Chief, in a room decorated with naive paintings of the Chaco War. After an enthusiastic introduction by Colonel Cardenas, General Reque is as open and friendly as he could be. He begins by giving me a brief run down on the work of the Bolivian army. When there is no guerrilla activity (which is, presumably, not often) the whole army is involved in *acción cívica*. Out of the army total of 15,000 men, some six battalions of engineers are constantly working on roads – mostly up in the jungle area of the Beni. At the same time they are occupied in building schools and 'developing' the *campesinos*, in the more remote areas. Soldiers are conscripted for a compulsory two years' service – but in fact only one year of it is now being paid. (I am left unclear as to how the troops live during their second year's service.) Many of the recruits are illiterate on joining the army, and their officers are made responsible for giving them

[1] The standard term of opprobrium for any right-wing military leader in South America.

primary school education. According to General Reque, they are 'punished' if their men do not come up to scratch on literacy.

The élite troops of the Bolivian army are the American trained 'Rangers', who rounded up Che, but now – under the prevailing wave of anti-*Yanquismo* – renamed 'assault regiments'. The term is – says General Reque – 'more traditional' (i.e. back to the nomenclature imposed by those military advisers of the *Reichswehr*). There are now three such 'assault regiments'. Where do the best soldiers come from in Bolivia? 'Why, of course, from Cochabamba!' replies the General unhesitatingly. (It is his home town.) 'Partly because men from its halfway altitude can more readily adjust themselves to either the jungle or the altiplano.' What about the guerrilla situation? General Reque explains that there are two kinds at work in Bolivia; the 'Pekinese' (Maoist) and the Castroists (ELN). The Pekinese work at getting their message over to the country people by indoctrinating the peasant masses; then – having achieved this – they try to bring it to the city. The army had recently captured the Pekinese leader, Oscar Zamora; under President Torres's benevolent policy (which the army obviously do not care for), all captured guerrillas are simply being exiled abroad, and Zamora was one of those to be shipped out to Chile the previous week with the right-wing Ivanovic. Cardenas and Reque talk of the most recent ELN resuscitation, the 'Teoponte guerrillas', referring to them (rather scathingly) as 'seventy students who got lost in the jungle'. Those few that survived were mopped up by the army, and also pushed over the frontier into Chile. 'What's the state of the game now?' Smilingly, but with reflection, General Reque states 'It's officially stopped, but it never ends.'[1] With Allende in

---

[1] The very next day there is a report in *El Diario* which quotes General Reque as admitting that two new columns of guerrillas had been detected north of Santa Cruz; one of them operating, symbolically, under the standard of 'Teoponte'. Telephoning Colonel Cardenas, at my behest, to enquire why Reque had not informed us of this new *foco*, Gonzalo is told rather apologetically: 'It is nothing serious, but – well, you know, sometimes we have to justify the existence of the army to the press!'

power, and the *miristas* roaming at will in Chile, was the any concern about the possible 'export of revolution' to Bolivia? 'No,' says General Reque, smiling and echoing the line taken by other Bolivian officials when I ask the same question, 'I think perhaps Bolivia should export her revolution to Chile!'

General Reque gives me a vivid account of the abortive Banzer *golpe* of the previous month. He claims that a week before it broke out, he had 'detected the movement'. He knew that the *golpe* would start at 4 o'clock on the morning of 11 January. At 10 o'clock the night before, the general ordered a staff meeting; then went to the President, to organize a counter-plan. He stayed in the Palace with Torres for two hours, returning to his office around midnight. 'All was in order.' But as he entered G.H.Q. alone in his car, 'An officer stuck a gun in my back and announced "General, you are a prisoner." I was a prisoner only for three hours. I explained to the insurgents that they were crazy.' Earlier that night Reque had agreed with President Torres that the Mustangs would attack, in any case, in the event of trouble, whether or not the Commander-in-Chief was held hostage. 'So they did – but only shooting into the air as they pulled out from their dive in the ravine.' The insurgents received none of the reinforcements they were expecting: 'We took away their guns, and it was all over by dawn.' Since that day, it had been agreed in principle that the loyal forces would 'attack' in future, regardless of whether General Reque or any other senior officer were held hostage.[1]

Bolivia, however, is 'the country of *disconformidad*,' admits General Reque. 'There is always discontent, always problems. Perhaps now the danger is greater than ever before, because Torres has given *complete* liberty to the country, and' – says he, paraphrasing de Tocqueville – 'the period in which most freedom exists is the one which brings the most problems.' At that moment, there is a commotion outside, and a flustered officer comes in to announce the arrival of *El Presidente.* General Reque and his entourage are obviously

[1] Following Banzer's successful *golpe* of August 1971, General Reque Terán swopped places with him in exile.

262

taken entirely by surprise; with that characteristic Bolivian courtesy, he says, regretfully, that the interview must end. Outside is President Torres, getting out of a large car, all smiles on his dark face; a small figure with a pot belly and the typically broad chest of the Bolivian Indian. The fact that he should be coming, unannounced, to call on his Commander-in-Chief, instead of summoning him to the Palace, seems to indicate as clearly as the sharply delineated pinnacles of distant Illimani just how much the precariously placed president has to rely on the buttressing of the army. (As it turns out, Torres was in fact checking with Reque to ensure the army's support over his recent manoeuvres to clip the wings of the COB – Confederation of Bolivian Workers – and his MNR adversaries). For all its schisms, it seems clear that it is still ultimately the Army on which President Torres – or any other Bolivian President today – must lean for his source of power.

We drive down the ravine to visit the Military Academy at Calacoto. On the way, the bright sunlight on the improbably eroded rocks of the canyon makes the red, green and ochre lacework stand out with almost aggressive sharpness in the clear, rarefied air – although they are several miles away. The entrance to the Academy is flanked by elderly Vickers field-guns from the Chaco War. Everything is very clean and tidy. The Commandant – who has succeeded the disgraced and exiled Colonel Banzer – is Colonel Victor Gonzales – an engineer with a quiet and pleasant voice, also from Cochabamba. As we talk on the roof of the school, down below the cadets are dashing about in grey uniforms, forming up on the square; elsewhere they are hard at work at fencing practice. The Commandant has four hundred cadets under his wing, from all three armed forces (that land-locked Bolivia should have a navy sounds like pure nostalgia for that 'lost' littoral; but in fact the Bolivian navy is busily occupied in tracking down smugglers and gun-runners on the bleak surface of Lake Titicaca). Trained in a confusing mixture of U.S. and European weapons, the cadets do a four-year course, of which one and a half months is spent on jungle training. During the 1952 revolution, like the cadets of the Toledo Alcazar or the St Cyriens of 1940, the cadets found themselves bloodily in

263

the front line when the Academy was besieged by armed miners' militia. Both the cadets and young officers are set to studying Mao and Castro for 'objective purposes'; but Colonel Gonzales does not believe that there are any Communist influences at work among the cadets. There are no longer any American instructors; nor do paratroopers still go to the U.S. school in Panama, but now receive their training instead in Cochabamba.

The U.S. Military Mission (or what remains of it) also has its headquarters inside the *Estado Mayor* compound. Its chief, Colonel Soler, is a steely-faced Texan who looks at me as a Regimental Lieutenant-Colonel in the Brigade of Guards would look at a newly joined recruit, when I deposit mud from the morass outside on his sparkling carpets. He tells me that his Mission is reduced to only twenty-four, and carries out training on weapons, equipment and logistics. U.S. personnel are strictly forbidden to participate in any Bolivian anti-guerrilla operations now, and his Mission has to rely entirely on Bolivian intelligence reports for news of counter-guerrilla activity. The operation against the Teoponte guerrillas was, he says, the first one to be entirely run by the Bolivians. Colonel Soler claims that the big cut-backs in the U.S. Mission were largely a response to domestic U.S. problems rather than Bolivian politics, but one cannot help feeling that he is putting a brave face on things. Since the Torres 'October Revolution' the *Yanqui* community in Bolivia has been living in a state of semi-siege. The anti-American outbreaks then were of quite extraordinary violence. Embassy offices were broken into and smashed up. One of the principal targets was the U.S.I.S.-run Centro Boliviano-Americano, operated by thirty U.S.I.S. employees, where some thousand Bolivian students study English. The doors were dynamited (a favourite and easily obtainable weapon among the Bolivian miners), and all the furniture and books pillaged. The seized Center continues to be used as a 'workers' meeting place' – despite three separate representations made to the Foreign Ministry by the U.S. ambassador. The Center in Oruro was also dynamited, and every single object inside it pillaged. The sack of the U.S. Centers was largely carried out by the students; as the rather lugubrious

U.S.I.S. chief in La Paz remarks to me: 'It used to be deliberate policy to place the Centers as near the universities as possible in South America – now we are making a hundred-and-eighty-degree turn, and removing them as far away as we can!' His own office, on an upper floor out of range of stones, was protected behind sliding steel doors, with an armed guard and wire-netting over the windows. In the prevailing mood, U.S. diplomats have abandoned carrying C.D. plates on their cars, and the *Clínica Americana* has changed its name to *Clínica Metodista*; in fact, anything to avoid blazoning the pejorative word 'American'.

Rather nervously, I enter *the* storm centre of Bolivia, La Paz's San Andrés University. It was from San Andrés that the left-wing students had launched the recent Teoponte operations; it was they who had been in the vanguard of the savage riots which brought Torres to power in October.[1] Outside a ochre-coloured, rectilinear building – that must have looked the acme of modernity when it was built in the 1940s, but now looks down-at-heel and tawdry – groups of students (appearing to be even more middle-aged than their constantly revolting Chilean counterparts) are clustered in earnest discussion; about physics, or the next guerrilla campaign? I talk to the Dean of the Philosophy Faculty, Doctor Arturo Osias, who has spent sixteen years at Tübingen University, and a fellow professor, Criespo. They tell me that there are very few pure Indian students at the University, most coming from the poorer middle-classes. There are 15,000 students altogether, of which only 200 belong to the Philosophy Faculty; 3,500 read Economics (the largest faculty of all), and 1,333 are would-be lawyers. (Alas, a plague for the country!) There are relatively few scientists and technicians and practically no history students: 'This is a luxury for Bolivia.' Courses last for five years, and students

---

[1] The University was also the last focal point of left-wing resistance during the successful Banzer *golpe* of August 1971, in which over 120 deaths were reported. For the third time in a year, the El Alto Mustangs were brought into action; but, instead of firing into the air and dropping dummy bombs, they apparently blasted the University façade with rocket and machine-gun fire, killing a dozen students before the fighting was over.

cannot be thrown out of the University for educational reasons. (In fact it is difficult to discover any grounds on which they can be sent down; lobbing hand-grenades at Bolivian soldiers is evidently not one!) In April 1970, the professors tell me, a 'student revolution' – led by Trotskyists – took over the University. As a result, the students obtained useful rights in the government of the University; on the *Consejo Supremo* seventeen students now sit opposite seventeen professors. (Only Guatemala, says Professor Osias a little proudly, has a similar system.) The students were also permitted to set up a *Comité Central* which has a veto right over the nomination of professors, and can also sack any incurring its displeasure. It has already done so with some vigour. In August, the students took over the University buildings for sixteen days before the government could drive them out. In the 'October Revolution', they took over the whole city – and almost the whole country. The professors say – again with pride – that San Andrés University is not as 'authoritarian' as European universities. They admit that the University is definitely 'left-inclined', with a preponderance of Marxists. But they add, with neither enthusiasm nor conviction, that most of the professors are 'independent' – that ubiquitous, superb Bolivian funk-hole.

Talking to the two professors is rather like wrestling with a jellyfish. They will not talk about the student guerrillas; are manifestly terrified of the students, and less forthcoming than any Bolivian I have yet interviewed. As I wander back down the drab corridors, I feel vaguely frustrated. Suddenly I am hailed in English (or rather American) by a passing student: 'Hi! What are you looking for?' He turns out to be one of the 3,500 economics students, called 'Julio', aged twenty-four and with two years still to go. He was schooled in Wisconsin, under an American Field Service scholarship. Immediately Julio says in English: 'Things are terrible here in the University; no one does any work, they only talk politics.' He seems a more interesting specimen than either of the professors, so we go off for a drink together. Julio's father, now dead, was a lawyer down in Tarija by the Argentinean frontier, which has no road or rail communication at all with La Paz. Julio is teaching French and mathematics to help

266

pay his way through college. He is in a quandary; he has applied for a fellowship to the U.S., but was told by the Rector of the University, 'You can't, because we don't have any kind of relations with the U.S.A.' He regards the Rector as 'Communist-orientated'. But, 'If I were to get my fellowship in the U.S., lamentably I would have to leave my country – because here they say I cannot get a job as an economist.' His conversation is heavily adverbed with 'lamentably'. He regards the U.S.A. as an 'imperialist power', but he says that he absolutely sees the difference between it, the U.S.S.R. and China – lamentably; 'That is one small word – freedom.'

We talk a little about the Teoponte students. Julio says that only eight survived out of seventy who went into the jungle last July. 'Many were friends of mine. They were mad. They were completely led by idealism and by lyricism in the memory of Che – lamentably.' The more I hear about the Teoponte guerrillas, the more they excite my curiosity. I am fortunate enough to get my hands on a set of the diaries kept by some of the principals – which have never yet appeared in English – and I spend my evenings in La Paz translating and studying them. They are, in my mind, among the most revealing, original and eloquent documents to come out of contemporary South America, and I take the risk of reprinting them here, in a severely edited form.[1]

Because of the special relevance of their contemporary setting – a turbulent Bolivia where anything could happen, Allende in Chile, Velasco in Peru, mounting chaos in Argentina, Tupamaros elsewhere, all of which is new since Che's *débâcle* of just three years previously – the Teoponte diaries demand attention. But they also offer some important clues on the motivations of the young, bourgeois Latin-American revolutionary in general; of the Pepes and Valentinas in Chile, the Raoul Sendics in Uruguay, the Camilo Torreses in Colombia. Parts of them, the 'Francisco' papers, are particularly illuminating about that new and most disquieting phenomenon, and apparent contradiction, the Christian–Marxist guerrilla. It has been recently suggested that perhaps half of all young priests throughout Latin

---

[1] By special courtesy of *Encounter*.

America, supported by a number of bishops, are today preaching the doctrine that Christianity and capitalism are now incompatible. In strife-torn Guatemala, for instance, a significant body calling itself COSDEGUA (Confederation of Diocesan Priests of Guatemala) has declared the struggle against capitalist materialism to be 'the Church's most important mission since the evangelization of the pagans of Europe'. More and more young priests, like the martyr Camilo Torres, and deeply religious lay churchmen, like 'Francisco' of Teoponte, are becoming prepared to do more than just protest. The Church in Latin America must take with desperate earnestness this 'least expected and least resistible of all revolutions' within its ranks.

During the Che episode, San Andrés students declared the University a 'free area', and in their revolt of April 1970 they surprised the government (then Ovando) by the quantity of automatic arms in their possession. At about this time clandestine discussions began there with a view to reactivating Che's ELN. The ringleader was twenty-nine-year-old Osvaldo ('Chato') Peredo, whose two brothers had both died for the cause ('Coco' at the side of Che, and 'Inti' the previous year, when a hundred soldiers and police had trapped and shot him down in a La Paz house) The Peredos came of a political family from Trinidad, the capital of the Beni, the vast Amazonian jungle area comprising the northern half of Bolivia. In common with the notable majority of Latin-American revolutionaries today, they were of *petit-bourgeois* stock. The group of seventy that Peredo collected out of the University represented many political factions; but most were affiliated not to any Marxist party but to the left-wing Christian Democrats.

One of this faction was a devout young medical student, Nestor Paz Zamora ('Francisco'), who later died with the Teoponte guerrillas, and whose own campaign diary is interspersed with intimate 'letters' to God. On joining the group he wrote:

I know that my decision . . . will produce a flood of accusations, from the paternalistic 'poor misguided person', to the open charge of 'demagogic criminal'. . . . [But] we cannot sit down to spend a long time reading the Gospel with cardinals, bishops, and pastors, all of whom are doing all right where they are, while the situation of the flock is one of hunger and solitude. . . . These persons, sad to say, are the Pharisees of today. . . . That is why we take up arms; to defend the illiterate and undernourished majority from exploitation by a minority, and to give back his dignity to the dehumanized person. . . . I think that the only efficacious way . . . is by taking up arms. . . . We don't want patches. New cloth can't be used to mend old garments, neither can new wine be put into old wineskins. . . . The sin of omission is the fault of our Church, just as it was of the 'lukewarm' members (Rev. 3: 14–22).

The planning and administration of the Teoponte operation seem to have been considerably more haphazard even than Che's. Although there were sinister rumours of Peredo being 'pushed' into it by shadowy *aparatchiks* of the La Paz extreme Left, the evidence seems to suggest that he had no central organization behind him whatever; no lines of communication and only the most primitive of equipment. In the words of one British diplomat, 'They went into the worst country in the world with little more than ham sandwiches'. The area selected by Peredo – apparently influenced by his own origins and contacts – was Teoponte in the wild foothills of the Alto Beni, some two hundred miles north of La Paz. It was an area that was urged upon Che – but rejected – for establishment of his own *foco* in 1967. From time immemorial, the Beni has been exploited by central governments, and used as a kind of private Siberia for political exiles. Its forests are distinctly more inhospitable to man than even the Ñancahuazú where nature so nearly finished off Che before the army did. Innumerable species of incredibly poisonous snakes abound (such as the *coralito* whose victims' blood is said, literally, to turn to water and burst out through the eyeballs). There are trees exuding moisture that burns like an acid; minute *borrachudo* flies that get through any mosquito net and bring the body out in a mass of tropical ulcers; beetles that cause blindness if they fly into the eye; torrential rivers inhabited by piranhas; and even the indigenous Indians have a struggle to sustain life from the food the hostile forest grudgingly provides.

What motivated Peredo and his troop to enter this hell so ill-prepared? As Julio remarked to me, 'they went out in sheer lyricism of Che.' To the alienated youth of South America, now in an intenser state of revolutionary ferment than ever before, the continued influence of Che is not to be underestimated. He may have failed – all the way along the line – but at least, unlike the continent's traditional leaders who (at best) produce reforms that are too little and too late, or (at worst) skip off to a numbered account in Madrid when the going gets rough, Che was *consequente*. He set out for nothing less than *victoria o muerte*, and when it became obvious that death would win, he never turned aside.

In many ways the Teoponte diaries seem to me more interesting – and certainly more moving – than Che's. In fact, were it not for the importance of Che, the martyr, his would be of little value. The Teoponte diaries give a far clearer and more graphic picture of the nature of the operation, the terrible problems of survival in the wilderness, and of the moral stresses and strains within the *guerrilla* itself. Above all, there is much more empathy with the human beings involved in the struggle. Che seems to have been a curiously cold and remote personality. Even his devotee Debray describes him as surrounded by 'a certain human vacuum'. Allowing for the fact that he was suffering miserably most of the time from his chronic asthma, Che's diaries reveal a complete lack of any poet's eye that could have shown insight into the tragedies of Bolivian history, expressed compassion for the suffering of the people or even some kind of response to the awesome majesty of the landscape. The Che diaries are basically a dead recital about machine-guns, grenades and revolutionary dialectic – 'correctly' interpreted by Che. To gauge just how far he falls down as a human chronicler, one needs to re-read such documents from the Yugoslav partisan campaign as that great and tear-producing classic, Vladimir Dedijer's *With Tito Through the War, 1941–1944*. Alas, because of the unforgivable heresy, it is obviously proscribed literature for Latin-American Marxists; which is a pity, because Che (who sometimes seems unaware that anything ever happened outside the Sierra Maestra) would have achieved greater stature had he studied the Yugoslav experience, in its infinitely more tragic proportions. Unlike those fallen angels of the Yugoslav guerrilla movement, Dedijer and Djilas, Che – however *romanticized* – was never a romantic. He was, I suspect, essentially a Valentina. Here, at least to some extent, the Teoponte papers seem to redress the balance, if only a literary one. Chato Peredo's chronicle begins on 18 July 1970:

Saturday 18 *July.* We are a 'motorized guerrilla' in three vehicles; two trucks and a pick-up belonging to the University. At 8.30 a.m. we left La Paz towards Caranavi, as a group of 'instructors in literacy'. We kept up the subterfuge as far as Alcoche, where we stopped for five hours waiting for nightfall. We continued motorized as far as Teoponte. Three or four kilometres from the town we blocked the road, taking hostages from among the lorry-drivers who suspected nothing.

At two the next morning, Peredo moved in on a U.S.-owned gold mine at Teoponte:

blowing up the dredger, installations of the offices and other properties of South American Placers, expropriating the money of the company (50,000 Bolivian pesos [or about £1,778]). We took as hostages two German employees (unfortunately there were no *Yanquis*). The operation lasted four hours. We had to wait for two hours more in order to cross the river. The task was great. We withdrew the ambush of the rear guard, and hid ourselves in the jungle after crossing the river.

The guerrillas then communicated with La Paz, demanding the release of ten political prisoners in exchange for the two German engineers. The most noteworthy of these prisoners was Loyola Guzmán, arrested in August 1967 as leader of Che's urban guerrilla organization; a fanatically brave girl, she threw herself out of a third-floor window when being interrogated, so as to give warning to her associates, but survived. This first operation was Peredo's one outstanding success. The mine was put out of operation for six months and the news of this unexpected resurgence of the ELN shook La Paz, taking the Ovando government completely by surprise. In the ensuing alarm, U.S. Peace

Corpsmen were swiftly withdrawn from the Alto Beni area. But, as Peredo's diary goes on to note, the Bolivian Air Force was on their tracks within twenty-four hours with the group already beginning to show the lack of discipline that was to dog it throughout.

20 July. After marching for two hours in the darkness, we realized Sebastian was lost. In the confusion and disorganization of the march, nobody noticed his absence. Possibly he was left sleeping . . .
21 July. Sebastian has not appeared; I think this is our first casualty. . . . The ants invaded our encampment and it was impossible to sleep. . . . The two *gringo* hostages are comporting themselves well, but with much fear . . .
22 July. . . . We were told by radio of the liberation of the comrades that we demanded in exchange for the German hostages. . . . The news has made its mark . . .
23 July. Before leaving at dawn, we liberated the prisoners. . . . In the afternoon, Marcos and Freddy[1] came to inform me that they were abandoning the *guerrilla*, on the pretext of being in poor physical state, which appears very absurd in Marcos who is robust and strong. Freddy says that he is suffering from acute gastritis. His two brothers talked to him . . .
24 July. I transferred Freddy to the centre. We camped in a good place; however at six in the afternoon there was heavy bombing, but some five kilometres distant. Everybody withstood it serenely, except for Freddy. Morale is high, and organization improves. Palm shoots (*cœurs de palmier*) abound here, and are an exquisite delicacy. We heard news of the capture of Sebastian.
25 July. One week of this great adventure. A day of worries; Freddy disappeared, together with his brother, the fat one . . .

The two defectors were picked up by the group the next day.

That night I spoke to all the people recalling the twenty-sixth of July,[2] and the significance of our struggle. I spoke to them about

---

[1] Their guerrilla pseudonyms. 'Freddy', alias Eduardo Quiroga Bonadona, was the son of a prominent retired general.
[2] The day in 1953 when Fidel Castro attacked the Moncada barracks, which marks the beginning of the Cuban revolution.

the privilege which is implicit in our activity and the continuation of this war initiated by Che . . .
Marcos insists on abandoning the struggle.
Marcos and Freddy have turned themselves into human trash.
Marcos wept and threw himself on the ground like a child . . .

Two days later, Peredo notes cheering news from La Paz. The school-teachers had gone out on strike, the University was boiling over, and the minister of information had resigned. At the same time, Ovando was coming under increasing pressure from the Right, headed by General Miranda. But yet another student, 'Chana', disappeared 'mysteriously' that day.

I took the opportunity to let go the stragglers, who are a nuisance and diminish the mobility of the column. This was brought home to these five once again when I insisted that those who do not feel themselves capable of continuing the struggle should abandon it. They left the column, dressed in civilian clothes and without arms. Their arguments were most absurd [There follows a list of eight names; including two of the Quiroga brothers.] . . . The shake-up was necessary to purge us, and I also believe to improve our combat effectiveness. We remain fifty-eight, but in good political condition . . .

On 30 July, the *guerrilla* made its first random contact with the Bolivian army.

Aníbal surprised them, but his weapon misfired twice; he saved himself miraculously, abandoning his pack . . . I gave the order to enter the forest towards the east, but those who were directing the march missed this, making a U-turn, and went out on the same footpath where I had ordered an ambush to be located. Before the order arrived, we ran into the enemy (13.15) and caused them three casualties. (At least one dead). . . . Rejoicing all round. We did not suffer one casualty.

There was more inaccurate bombing and machine-gunning from the Air Force. For the first time Peredo notes the problems of collecting food, complaining that 'the villages are occupied by the army.' Then:

273

The radio announces eight corpses belonging to us. These criminals treacherously assassinated the students.[1] It's a crime without name, worthy of Fascists. It's war to the death. This is what the enemy imposes upon us. The most painful thing is to know of the death of people who gave themselves, and who could have employed their energies with greater usefulness. Despite their defection it does not cease to cause pain. I am concerned about Napo[2] who has two brothers among the students; but his reaction apparently is satisfactory, and each day he emerges more as an efficient combatant and of great human quality. The group has toughened itself and displays better moral conditions. No one doubts any longer the felony of Ovando and his government when they promised guarantees to those who abandoned the *guerrilla*. We move very little. The Air Force, as is its wont, continues its nasty tricks. Today they dropped napalm . . .

4 August. . . . Food continues to be the main concern. We laid hands on the last fragment of dried beef. The radio announces that 'Operation Fan' has begun, the rumour being to allow us to escape towards Peru. Ovando does not want any 'shedding of blood'. Nothing is said about the napalm, or the daily bombings. He does not want to disclose the identity of the eight corpses. There is preparation of a *coup d'état* by Rogelio Miranda . . .

8 August. Rain lashes down all night. . . . Rogelio and Chuma were sick. The radio reports the capture of Raúl Sendic [3] in Uruguay. If it is correct, the news is a hard blow to the Latin-American Liberation Movement. . . . Today we killed a small monkey.

9 August. . . . There is Surazo[4] and much humidity. The loss of tins of milk and sardines is becoming chronic. What is most probable is that there are no such losses, but that the people themselves are eating them, which says much about the lack of indoctrination. . . .

---

[1] The eight who defected on 29 July. This was an episode that was to have widest repercussions, still resounding today.

[2] Presumably the third Quiroga brother.

[3] The Tupamaro leader. That week Peredo had a letter published in the Montevideo press, thanking the Tupamaros for their 'invaluable co-operation', but declaring that the Bolivian ELN still favoured rural guerrilla activity over the urban operations of the Tupamaros.

[4] A bitter cold wind blowing from Patagonia, that can cause an unpleasantly abrupt temperature drop in the Bolivian tropical jungle.

On the twelfth, the guerrillas found an isolated village not occupied by troops. Here they rested, replenishing their food supplies and propagandizing the peasants, who were 'at first suspicious'. They then broadcast 'Communiqué No. 1', revealing the 'crime' committed against the eight defectors, and declaring their political aims: 'Formation of a government of workers and peasants which will assure the development of a socialist revolution within the country; dissolution of the army and the formation of militias which will guarantee popular power; nationalization of all foreign businesses which exploit the riches of our people . . .'

On leaving the village, the guerrilla rearguard was caught by accurate strafing.

There is no doubt that we are pinpointed. It could have been a *campesino* who took out the communiqué . . . Alfonso abandoned the march, and headed for the interior of the forest. Already one was beginning to note something funny about him, and he is not going to be the last. . . . They found his pack without food. In his haste he left his mess tin and blanket . . .

16 August. Four weeks of life in the wilds. . . . Majority of the people are now more or less acclimatized. There are a few who tend towards demoralization and do not see the perspectives of our struggle . . .

17 August. . . . One still detects inexperience and a little fear which continues to diminish as we come up increasingly against the army. We have decided not to withdraw from the enemy and if possible to search for them. The news is good; the miners declare their support for the ELN, the University students also, and the government sees itself reduced to midgets . . .

18 August. We have had three collisions with the army with three casualties for them and one unconfirmed in the ambush of yesterday. On our side, we have ten casualties, but none in combat with the enemy . . .

19 August. . . . We killed a *vibora pucarara*[1] and ate it tonight . . .

Over the next days, Peredo notes more 'encouraging' news from La Paz. The students in the University were

[1] An extremely poisonous snake.

pressing the government to reveal the identity of the dead
guerrilleros, while General Quiroga was demanding the
corpses of his sons – 'and expressing solidarity with us. The
affair is heating up in our favour.' His position already
shaky, Ovando was now thoroughly put on the spot by the
army's apparently unnecessary act of brutality. He tem-
porized, declaring that – 'for security reasons' – the bodies
could not be handed over for ninety days; by which time
they would have decomposed to the point where it would be
impossible to ascertain the manner of death. Ovando's
evasiveness only added fuel to the flames, and passions continued to mount in La Paz.

23 August. We arrived at Mapiri. We decided to sacrifice the mule
because it delays the march very much . . .
25 August. As foreseen, the column goes on diminishing. Today the
'breakaway' is Juanito . . .
27 August. Felipe can no longer march. He has a broken bone in
his heel. The march is extremely slow, because he has to be
carried in a hammock at night in order to cross the open clearings.
There is no doubt that the army has detected us, through the
campesinos . . .

The next day, while trying to find a hiding-place in a settlement in which to leave Felipe, Peredo's detachment was
overtaken and nearly surrounded by an army patrol. A
disastrous shoot-up ensued.

We left early, in a mist, carrying Felipe, whom today we shall
leave in some concealed place, together with Nelson and Ringo,
the doctor of the vanguard who shows signs of deserting. Today is
his opportunity. . . . At 10 o'clock we perceived a movement on
the slope in front of us. When I asked for the binoculars, the
shooting began. . . . I organized a defence with the few people
who were there . . . Some twenty soldiers were shooting towards
the banana plantation. The weapons of Perucho and Chuma
which were at my side did not function. I shot off one solitary
round, and don't know if I hit the target, because at that moment
they opened fire on us with a 30-calibre. There was much confusion among us and many were throwing away their packs.

While we headed into the forest, Casiano [Benjo Cruz][1] was wounded in the arm and right foot. . . . A day of defeat. Sergio possibly fell into the stream with the first shots. Pablito, Gregorio, and César fell in the fa myard. . . . It makes a total of eleven casualties in a fight, the initiative of which was completely the enemy's. . . . We remain forty-five men with the bitter taste of defeat. Now we are experiencing in our own flesh that which we had repeated so often in order to prepare ourselves psychologically. War is cruel and hard and our sentimentality resists accepting that cruelty. Here was a factor in our sluggishness; not to have taken a decision over Felipe earlier, and allowing the moment of leaving him to fill with dramatics, we gave the enemy time to catch us still peacefully on the farm. . . .

Recalling one of the more disastrous days in Che's campaign, Peredo concluded:

All war is spattered with moments such as these, and for that reason it is strange to write the same as the most experienced and capable fighters wrote before us.

On Tuesday 1 September, the guerrillas were again surprised by the army – this time inside a river canyon, and they were split into two groups as one section took flight across the river.

3 September. The sense of defeat among the people is very marked, and becomes more acute with the defection this morning of the three *macheteros* [machete men] who used to form the head of the vanguard (they took a radio with them). We have only two bad machetes, and the forest is the worst possible and dense with *chumizales* [a kind of thick elephant grass]. . . .

At about this time, Francisco writes in his (undated) journal:

[1] A well-known young Bolivian poet, renowned particularly for his fiery invective against the Church and the mining *patrones* in a poem called *La Preguntita* ('The Little Question'), typified by the line: 'There is one thing in life that is more important than God; and that is that no one should spit blood in order that someone else should live better.' He died later in the operation.

I want my capacity to love to increase along with my ability as a guerrilla . . . that is the only way of qualitatively and quantitatively improving the revolutionary impulse. . . . In a vital way I am passing beyond the meaning of death, as a diminution of reality, to that of a fullness and a step towards a new dimension. . . . I don't know; I have the presentiment that I will not die. But if I am to die, I want it to be a death filled with meaning, which will have repercussions, and will recruit others to fight for the well-being of man. . . . We are passing through intense days, highly charged with meaning. These may be our last days, or they may be the first ones of our victory.

In Chile Allende has won. This opens enormous perspectives to us. I believe that in our America, people on a massive scale are capable of choosing socialism . . .

Francisco's entry ends with this rather striking juxtaposition:

Yesterday I was named 'Political Commissar' of our column, replacing Felipe. . . . I had the good fortune to find a New Testament which a companion had; it is like gold to me.

Chato goes on to remark of the Chilean elections:

6 September. . . . Allende's victory is a great stimulant for our revolution and we toast this triumph. . . .

The mixture of good and bad news continues in Peredo's diary.

Carlos and Mongol deserted.[1] The symptoms were evident . . .

9 September. First anniversary of the death of Inti.[2] The whole day absorbed in memories of him, thinking of the loss which he represented to us, and the problems that would have been avoided if I had been him. I have never felt more of an orphan than this day . . .

11 September. . . . Gaston and David counted 100 Ranger soldiers in the direction of Mapiri, who were certainly going to reinforce

---

[1] They too were apparently picked up and executed by the army, together with two other defectors.

[2] Brother of Chato, who was trapped in a La Paz house and shot by the police.

the troops now in all the settlements on the way. We were twenty men. . . . I spoke to them of the peril which was closing in on us, and that the only prospect of breaking the circle was by moving as much as possible by night. . . . I insisted that those who did not want to go on should abandon the struggle, but all are disposed to continue. . . . Sergio and Jaime deserted out of incapacity. Marcos has also disappeared; it is possible that he fell asleep in the obscurity and we did not notice. . . .

At dawn, Peredo realized that his diminishing group had encamped very close to a clearing occupied by the army.

12 September. The whole day we were a few yards from the troops, without either moving or making any noise, stuck in a small forest bordering the road. We heard their voices and saw them passing without paying any attention. They were not aware of our presence. . . . Yesterday's ration was one quarter of a teaspoon of lard with salt. . . .

That same day Francisco writes in his journal:

A Letter to God, 12 September 1971. Dear Lord, it has been a long time since I wrote to you. Today I feel a real need for you and your presence, perhaps because of the nearness of death or the relative failure of the struggle. . . . Perhaps today is my [Maundy] Thursday and tonight my [Good] Friday. Because I love you I surrender everything I am into your hands, without limit. . . . We are a group full of true 'Christian' humanity, and I think we will change the course of history. . . . No one's death is meaningless if his life has been charged with significance; and I believe this has been true of us, here.

Despair and starvation were approaching, and the army appeared to be rapidly tightening its net. On the thirteenth there was another collision with army Rangers, and Peredo came close to being cornered – like Che – inside a small canyon. There were three casualties on each side, and another of Peredo's men (Kolla) 'fled into the forest at the first shooting'. He, too, was reportedly later 'liquidated' by the army. Peredo now had only thirteen men with him, cut off from the other remnants of the *guerrilla*, partially lost and increasingly demoralized.

279

The army is showing itself to be aggressive and for the first time entered the forest in pursuit of us . . .
26 September. Until today the situation has been desperate on account of hunger. We fed ourselves on palm shoots, fungus, and a fruit resembling an acorn which was eked out among all of us. . . . At 2 p.m. Forte and Perucho turned up. They had deserted from the camp out of hunger, taking with them two tins of sardines from my pack [the strategic reserve for the fourteen survivors], money, and a small amount of lard which remained to me in my plastic bag. They were executed on the spot, despite the enormous esteem which bound me to Perucho. . . .[1] Today is the third anniversary of the death of Coco.[2] September seems to be a fatal month.
27 September. We reconnoitre very little in the area. Debility does not permit us to move much. We split up in pursuit of game, but without luck.
28 September. The days are slow and offer little.

At this point, Peredo's own diary comes to an end. He later added the following lines, after his capture by the army:

After 28 September, we resumed the march in search of a *chaco*[3] in order to solve the problem of food. We move with much difficulty on account of our advanced state of inanition. We are Mamerto, Cristián, David, and myself. After two or three days of this exhausting progress and without coming upon any *chaco*, Mamerto remained where he lay, dead of inanition. The three of us continue, with few hopes, and with an immense pain at such an absurd loss of this comrade who kept on growing both spiritually and as a human being throughout the course of the war . . .

In the course of the following week, the starving trio had another miraculous escape from the army, during which Cristián was slightly wounded. At last they spotted a village ahead of them:

---

[1] This appears to be the first, and only, mention of any disciplinary 'executions' carried out by the guerrillas themselves. It was a measure of the desperation of their plight.
[2] The oldest Peredo brother, killed with Che in 1967.
[3] A cultivated clearing in the forest.

that afternoon we camped on a rise of ground where we made, or more accurately where we dreamed, plans of what we could do when we arrived at the village. These were the last dreams of Cristián who that night sank into the definitive and eternal dream. Once again hunger (that invisible enemy) robbed us of another comrade. . . .

On gaining the village and being fed, Peredo says: 'Our stomach upheavals were indescribable.' They then 'made contact with the miners and *campesinos* of Tipuani who organized themselves into relief groups, to contact and take food to the comrades who remained behind under command of Omar.'[1] On 13 October, Chato and David were captured in Tipuani by the Rangers, apparently tipped off by a *campesino*.

In the meantime, much had happened in the outside world. Opposition to Ovando from the labour unions, students and the Church had reached a crescendo. Six people were killed in riots that broke out in most of the principal Bolivian cities, and a climax came when one Canadian and three Spanish priests were expelled after they had started a hunger strike in support of the students' demands for the return of the guerrilla corpses. The government declared hunger strikes to be a crime 'subject to the same penalties as attempted suicide'. On 9 October, General Miranda launched his right-wing revolt against Ovando which ended with the accession of Torres. The new left-wing president then promptly set about organizing an amnesty commission to bring the surviving ELN guerrillas out of the jungle.

From the Alto Beni, Omar continues the story at the point where he and Chato lost contact. With him is Francisco, his cousin.

23 September. . . . Alberto fainted in the afternoon. The symptoms of debility are increasingly evident. Slow and hesitating steps, sickness, clouding of vision, infection of wounds, etc.

---

[1] Alias Gustavo Ruiz Paz, Havana-trained, in charge of a group that became separated from the main column.

24 September. . . . I tried to shoot a toucan, but missed. . . . Without food for eight days; palm shoots and fungus are finished. . . .
26 September. Still nobody arrives. It's strange. . . .[1]
27 September. I was thinking of my daughter with nostalgia, about the sons of America who will have to defer their hopes of happiness if we definitively lose this battle. The lard-soup did not agree with me. If nobody arrives tomorrow, we shall go down in any event . . .
28 September. . . . Quirito, Alberto and Francisco are very weak . . .
30 September. From 10 o'clock to 5 o'clock, the march. We talked about the future with Francisco; it is necessary to organize ourselves, and to wait for reinforcements in order to rest ourselves, and to continue the struggle. It is painful to see how the best sections of our small army go on falling by the wayside . . .
1 October. . . . I slept with Francisco and we talked beforehand. We made numerous promises to each other, and I am invited to eat the marvels which Cecy[2] prepares. He loves Cecilia very much and misses her; as for the struggle, he feels himself physically feeble, but optimistic . . .
5 October. To cross the river took four hours, above all because of the tremendous weakness of Quirito and Francisco. My cousin wants to spend his birthday eating by the side of Cecy . . .

At this point Omar and Francisco become separated. In a last letter to his wife, Francisco writes:

My dearest Queen, It has been a long time since I wrote to you; I have had no strength to do so. . . . We are going through extremely hard and difficult times. My body is exhausted, but my spirit strives to remain intact. . . . We probably won't be able to be together on the ninth [his birthday]. . . . It is difficult at this stage not to despair. Confidence in the Lord Jesus gives me strength to go forward. We have definitely lost the battle, at least this one. [Francisco then expresses optimism about seeing Cecy again.] We'll bring a little Paz boy or girl into the world who will make us happy. We'll go forward. . . .

Omar continues:

[1] Omar's group was then waiting for help sent by Chato from Tipuani.
[2] Wife of Francisco.

9 October. It is my cousin's birthday, and we can't do anything about it. Next year we shall celebrate doubly, and in more comfortable circumstances . . .

Some days later he learns

the most painful news that I have received in my life; Francisco has died. The best combatant of our *guerrilla* has fallen; and not as he would have desired. . . . I spent the day reading his diary. I hope that one day the world will know of Francisco's love for humanity, so necessary from men such as him. Alberto told me . . . 'Francisco never got up again after we left him, and had to be helped to eat and to perform other necessities. He thought and spoke constantly of his comrades. He died in absolute tranquillity, as if he were sleeping. Quirito shot himself accidentally in the mouth with a Mauser, smashing his jaw bone, while trying to shoot a small bird . . .'

Francisco had died the day before his birthday; exactly three years to the day after the death of Che.[1]

Somehow, though now 'absolutely feeble', the remainder of Omar's group kept going. Then, on 12 October (the day before the capture of Chato) Omar hears voices which he presumes to belong to the army. In despair, he prepares to fight it out.

Perhaps this will end tomorrow; nevertheless our ideas will always live, and those who take part in the struggle are proud of having given everything for the revolution.
15 October. Salvation! The voices of yesterday belonged to four people who followed us to give help. . . .

The relief party brought remarkable news.

In forty days we shall taste rice and sweet coffee. The radio has said that Torres will arrange an amnesty. I don't believe it. . . .
21 October. Our situation is chaotic. The army is moving round us. We are alone in a forest which we don't know well. Food is growing scarce . . .

---

[1] In March 1972 Cecilia was killed, in a shoot-up with the Bolivian police, having herself joined the ELN guerrillas.

At this juncture, the wounded Quirito was evidently betrayed by a *campesino*:

the army returned and found Quirito alone, wounded, and assassinated him without pity . . .
30 October. While having breakfast the scout of the Amnesty Commission took us by surprise. On behalf of the president they are offering to respect the life of each one, hospitalization in the military hospital, and safe conduct. The miners don't trust anyone, and suggest we continue on to Chima, where we would be safe. From a place where our security is guaranteed, we could negotiate . . .

At the poor mining village of Chima, Omar and the survivors of the Teoponte *guerrilla,* now reduced to a handful, were taken under the wing of Torres's Amnesty Commission.

2 November. . . . Throughout the day we received an innumerable number of people who express to us their admiration and solicitude. All arrive with presents which range from caramels to beer, including exquisite dishes, special bread made with the motif of 'All Saints', fruit – and some made presents to us of grains of pure gold. It's impossible to find words to thank our people, for whom we threw ourselves into the struggle, for so much affection and receptiveness . . .

According to Omar, such moving signs of 'solidarity' continued until the moment of their departure. That day there was a last sharp dispute when the army proposed putting all the guerrillas in one plane and the Commission in another. Distrustful, Omar refused. The army climbed down. In the aeroplane, the student-guerrillas found themselves accompanied by none less than the Rector of their University, Dr Roell.

On arrival in La Paz:

a cloud of journalists pursued us. In the middle of all the agitation, I saw the mother of Quiroga Bonadona. A strong and valiant woman. There were other friends. In the aeroplane I met my brother, comrade, and chief – Chato. In a strong embrace we expressed our anguish and pain at having lost the battle started three months ago. Nevertheless, we have an infinite faith that, in the end, our ideas will triumph and the days of sacrifice we have lived will be of no importance if the recompense is the longed-for happiness of the people.

Later, before the assembled students of San Andrés and in the presence of the Rector, the University's Vice-Rector, an avowed Marxist called Rolando Costa Arduz, delivered an emotion-charged speech in memory of the fallen Francisco:

The Students of San Andrés de la Paz University, aware of the benefits of the Marxist–Christian dialogue, have decided to render homage to a revolutionary. . . . A sorrowful and grieving nation has received word of the disappearance of some of its noblest sons. . . . There is a truth which hammers at our conscience; a certain Christian refused to ignore Marxists . . .

The address ended with the exhortation:

Marxist students: Liberation has a long gestation period. Christians: the national liberation carries implicit in itself the fate of your Christian faith. Let us agree on this. This is not the time to discuss eternal truths and principles. . . . Neither Marxists nor Christians want violence for violence's sake. We want power for the people. Let us remember the Christian precept, that we will be judged by our deeds, not by our intentions. . . .

The pact implicit in this oration carried a message that Churchmen and non-Marxist political leaders throughout Latin America should disregard at their peril.

On 16 November 1970, Chato and Omar together with six other survivors of the seventy students were flown into exile in Dr Allende's Chile. They have, reportedly, now gone on to Cuba. Thus ended the Teoponte 'war'. But is it ever truly ended? As General Reque Terán had remarked, with the smashing of the Teoponte group the guerrillas were 'stopped but not terminated'. The reverberations continue. The massacre of the eight student deserters was to become one of the issues progressively making President Torres's tenure of office impossible. In August 1971, he was swept away by a new right-wing uprising. Momentarily, the Bolivian Left appears crushed. The students' defeat, following so closely that of Che, may well signify the final eclipse of the isolated, rural, Castroist guerrilla in South America. But what next? 'The reverses suffered by the Latin American revolutionary movement are truly minor,' writes Régis Debray, 'if one measures them in terms of the short period of time which is the prologue to the great struggles of tomorrow.'

When interviewed by Chilean journalists, Chato Peredo declared that the Bolivian guerrillas would henceforth switch to urban warfare. Is it probable that the 'great struggles of tomorrow' will now gradually translate themselves to the cities? In Latin America, where half the inhabitants – compared with 14 per cent in Southern Asia and about 13 per cent in black Africa – live in towns, many of them in the dreadful *callampas* or *villas miseria*, as the Argentinians so appropriately call them, the slum-dwellers must constitute a vast untapped reservoir for the revolutionary. Hitherto the men of the *callampas* have proved disappointing revolutionary material. A large proportion of peasants who have drifted in from the country, enticed by the glamorous image of city life created by radio and newspapers, they have brought with them the conservative instincts of the *campesino*, his individualism and fear of radical change, and they are not easily organized. But will it always be so? 'We have no impregnable strongholds in our country where we can set up a guerrilla base,' the Tupamaros declare. 'On the other hand, we have an enormous city that contains more than three hundred kilometres of streets and buildings, ideal for the growth of an urban struggle.' The Tupamaros have demonstrated just how vulnerable a modern city is, and – as the continent's consistently most successful guerrillas – in concentrating on the cities they seem likely to become the envy and model of many a revolutionary outside Uruguay; and perhaps even outside Latin America.

'There will always be other Peredos,' their non-Marxist comrade, Julio, assures me, and he observes that Bolívar was thrown out of South America five times, before returning to final triumph. What, then if the new Peredos do indeed take, not to the jungles where starvation and the army can pick them off with such pathetic ease, but to the fat towns instead?

14

The Carnival at Oruro

One evening the ambassador gets together at his house some of the leading La Paz economists for me to meet. They include René Ballevian, director of the Mortgage Bank, and Dr Tomás Guillermo Elío. Dr Elío went to the London School of Economics, and was foreign minister under Barrientos in 1968; his father signed the treaty ending the disastrous Chaco War, and he himself was Bolivian signatory of the Andean Pact of Cartagena in May 1969. He is a considerable expert and enthusiast about the Pact. Dr Ballevian is doubtful, with the conventional scepticism of the South American businessman I had encountered elsewhere. Colombia, he fears, may pull out – and then there will be no Pact. 'If I were a foreign investor, I would look elsewhere – for more attractive terms.' Dr Elío disagrees. 'Look at the Japanese. They are willing to come to Andean America; will go anywhere, take any risks. Or look at Bayer of Germany. There *are* the firms who want to get a foot in the market, who want to *be* there, rather than not — and regardless of how much they might lose on the *short* term.' He thinks that Bolivia, particularly, stands to benefit from the Pact, which contains special trade preferences for the two most 'under-privileged' countries of the group: Bolivia and Ecuador. The Pact is to finance the construction of special industries in these two countries, to help boost their development. Ecuador is to get a fish-processing and a petro-chemical industry, while Bolivia is allocated a ball-bearing plant – the first in South America. The choice of Bolivia seems to be founded on its sparkling clear alpine atmosphere; ball-bearings don't like dust. But they are also among the most technically complex and sophisticated of products to fabricate – so the ambassador, who was once consul in Göteborg, tells me – and it takes a precision-minded Swede to understand them. For backward Bolivia, the project seems about as ambitious as if Albania were to announce its intention of putting a man on the moon in 1975. But Dr Elío is convinced that, '*If* the Andean Pact can only exist for five years, it will become a great success.' The really important thing, in his mind, is to '*have a market*'.

Both the economists are derisive of the prospects of Torres's left-orientated government getting any sensible aid from Eastern Europe. Since Ovando opened the door just the previous year, the Soviet Embassy has grown to a staff of fifty, comparable in size already to that of the U.S.; the same old story. The credits, however, are not pouring in. The Hungarians have promised U.S. $10 million, but nothing has materialized yet; the Czechs are offering a loan for an antimony smelter, but they want 7 per cent interest; and the economists are sceptical that the financing of the Yugoslav zinc smelter may be 'just talk', too. There seems little hope of an improvement in world tin prices – so, as before, Bolivia looks like having to fall back on U.S. aid in some form or other. Most U.S. loans to Bolivia are serviced at low interest rates; but the Bolivian development banks through which they pass have such heavy operating costs, largely on account of the massive scale of the *deudos morosos* (plus what mark-up of corruption, one wonders?), that they are obliged to re-credit them at up to 12–15 per cent. So says the banker, Dr Ballevian. Thus the Bolivian consumer howls that the wicked *Yanqui* capitalists are lending him money at extortionate rates, when in fact these are imposed by the internal exigencies of his own banks. In any event, U.S. aid for the current year was down to $21 million, a substantial reduction on the past, and Washington has made it plain to Torres that there will be no more until the U.S. Centers seized by the students and miners have been handed back again.

It looks as though it may be Bolivia's endemic financial problems that will provide the last nail in President Torres's coffin. His régime grows feebler every day that I am in La Paz, the pressures on him mounting from both Left and Right. The powerful C.O.B. trades union federation has vigorously taken up the refrain of insisting that the army hand over the remains of the slaughtered Teoponte students; and its veteran leader, Juan Lechín Oquendo, now threatens Torres with *la lucha armada* (armed struggle) if the government does not meet wage demands made by the miners. There are widespread rumours that they are receiving guns being run through the new Soviet and Czech Embassies. Meanwhile, off in the wings in Brazil or Argentina the banished Colonel Banzer is planning a third right-wing putsch. Unable to depend upon a divided army, Torres seems groping at one moment for support from factions within the armed forces, then from some combination or other of students, miners and members of the splintered M.N.R.; He makes a nervous speech, hitting hard against the M.N.R., which retaliates by calling on all its ministers serving Torres to resign their posts. Some do, some don't. Even Gonzalo Montes, as he greets me each morning with his knowing conspirator's smile, has to admit that he too is thoroughly bewildered by the situation: 'My God, I usually know what's going on – but even I am confused. One thing is plain, though – Torres's days are numbered.' Tensions are rising. There is a general belief in La Paz that 'something' will happen during the Carnival, which is about to start. It seems as good a time as any – because then the army will be widely preoccupied in controlling the crowds and the traffic.

After one or two side trips to Lake Titicaca and up on to the altiplano, plus an abortive attempt to penetrate down into the Yungas – frustrated because the inevitable *derrumbe* had obliterated the road – I decided to get to Oruro for the Carnival. Oruro is a mining town, 150 miles south-east across the altiplano, half-way to Potosí and at the same altitude as La Paz. In its very different way, its Carnival comes second only to Rio's as one of the great spectacles of Latin America. I am told to report at 6 a.m., *hora inglesa*, but the bus doesn't start until an hour later. The round fare of U.S. $12 for the five-hour trip, plus tickets for the Carnival, etc., strikes me as being suspiciously cheap, and I soon discover why. The advertised 'modern omnibus of tourist type' (inspiring fanciful visions of bounding along in a superbly sprung Greyhound bus, with all mod. cons in the back) turns out in fact to be an ordinary La Paz town bus, pressed into service for the day. It appears to have no springs; the seats are unpadded narrow ledges, and for me, some eighteen inches taller than the average Bolivian, it is like being in the medieval torture cage where one cannot lie, sit or stand. I wonder seriously whether I can survive the five-hour trip, let alone reach Oruro in a proper Carnival mood. The La Paz professor next to me complains repeatedly: '*Es un barbaridad*; I am going to complain!' But to whom? To President Torres? Noting my particular distress, he amiably and selflessly promises that he will see I get 'transferred' at the first stop.

Climbing out of the La Paz ravine, we enter into a world of fog and bitter, searing cold. We are halted for an hour and a half in a seemingly endless queue at a police *tránsito* at the top of the ravine. A check on would-be revolutionaries? The whole of La Paz seems to be on the way to the Carnival, and an endless traffic jam piles up; it is the only one I have ever seen that has breadth as well as depth, because, with characteristic Latin-American individualism, drivers take off the road on to the hard altiplano to get around it, but are stopped by harassed armed officials. It is easy to see why this would be such a good day for a *golpe*. I spot the British commercial attaché, slicing through it all, in a Land-Rover with Union Jacks and C.D. plates flying. Beseechingly, I rush towards him, but the Land-Rover is loaded to its roof with children, and his face is hardly welcoming. Retreating in defeat, I discover that the amiable professor, as good as his word, has got me transferred to a marginally less inquisitional bus. Here my companions are Americans: a young professor of botany from Ohio, an expert on peppers, travelling for the *National Geographic Magazine*; his charming wife, and two well-behaved and astonishingly stoical small children. We are joined by two Peace Corps men. They are the best kind of young Americans, and fill one with respect. The cross-conversation helps provide distraction from the endless desolation of the altiplano and the bruising battering of the bus. George Curtmann, with glasses and long fair Dickensian sideburns, comes from Colorado and tells me he has been stationed for a year-and-a-half down in the Alto Beni jungle. He works with 'Operation Heifer', an internationally financed scheme to provide every *campesino* with one cow, a Holstein. The *campesino* undertakes to return the progeny each year to 'Operation Heifer', which then passes it on to another *campesino*, and so on. George arrived to take up his post in the Alto Beni on a bicycle, to the total astonishment of the *indígenas*. He built his own house, lives by himself, and says that often he doesn't see another *gringo* for two or three months.

The *diablada*, or 'devil dance' that we are going to see is deeply rooted in pre-Columbian superstition, and the Peace Corps boys swop fascinating reminiscences of *pistaco*, or witchcraft, in the backwoods of Bolivia and Peru. There persists, they say, an obsession among the Indians about blue-eyed, blond 'witches', dating back to the arrival of the con-quistadors. From time to time there are outbreaks of ritual executions and beheadings. Recently a British girl agrono-mist, stationed at Ayacucho, has been threatened and has had to leave in a hurry. They confirm what I had heard previously about the anti-aphrodisiac potions in which the family planning witch-doctors of La Paz and elsewhere specialize. On the other side of the coin, George tells me how one of his Peace Corps colleagues had been engaged in setting up a peanut butter plant at Santa Cruz; but the Indians had refused to eat the end-product – not just because they have highly evolved taste-buds, but because they consider peanuts to be an aphrodisiac, and therefore hostile to family plan-ning. Here seems to be at least one vital respect in which the Incas and their descendants may be more *évolués* than their Catholic conquerors in modern South America.

Once out of the La Paz crater, immediately one has a sense of frightening exposure up on the altiplano. In the extra-ordinary atmospheric clarity black dots of cattle and people are visible miles away in the distance. There are no trees to impede the view. The Bolivians say that, once upon a time, they did grow on the Altiplano, before the Spaniards re-moved them all to burn in the mines. Now, the murderous wind cuts down anything that raises its head more than a few feet. The nearest thing to a tree is a kind of stunted buddleia, the *quisuara*. The predominant colour of the flat, landscape is a kind of greyish-ochre, as if a painter had pulverized and mixed together all the browns, then burnt them and pulverized them all over again. Apart from an intermittent flocculence of poor grass, the bleak backdrop is briefly enlivened by tiny flashes of colour in the form of the bright, woven bags in which the itinerant *campesino* women carry their children slung over their backs; and, in cultivated pockets between stones and eroded wadis, by the red spikes of *quinoa*, a rice-like cereal that is a staff of life on the altiplano, or by the mixed yellow, mauve and white patches of potato blossom. (There are apparently a thousand and one different varieties of the potato up here, the home of them all, and recently an eminent British professor has spent months trying to categorize them all. The Incas anticipated science by discovering how to dehydrate potatoes as a provision against the vagaries and famines of the altiplano climate, and today this *chuno* is still a mainstay of existence.) We pass ruined *haciendas*, left by the once semi-prosperous feudal landowners. Little barrel-chested peasants stagger along the road, bowed double by piled-up sheaves of *quinoa* on their backs; they are the principal beasts of burden, as they always have been since the time of the Incas. Up here the agriculture (if you can call it that) is still very much what the experts dub the 'scratch-and-tickle technique', and the Indians scratching and tickling among the ruins of the old Inca terraces remind one of lean Australian sheep nuzzling for one subterranean clover plant in an acre of desert during an Australian drought.

> Pity my tears
> Pity my anguish
> The most distressed
> Of my children,
> The most distressed
> Of thy servants
> Implores thee with tears.

runs a sad little Quechuan prayer. How do they live up here? Why? Christopher Isherwood thought that 'outside of a madhouse or a prison, I suppose no place of existence could be worse'. Frequently other travellers have noted how impossible

it is, when the keen winds blow, to keep warm on the altiplano – however many blankets you huddle around yourself.
And, apart from llamas' droppings, there is nothing to burn
for heat. 'One is surprised,' puzzled Lord Bryce, 'that man
should have continued to dwell in a land so ungenial when
not far off to the east, on the other side of the eastern Cordillera, hot valleys and an abundant rainfall promise easier
conditions of life.' Under the Incas, as we know, things were
better organized, and it is often surmised that the climate
too was once upon a time more benign; nevertheless what
keeps the descendants of the Incas rooted to their upland
purgatory seems to be more tradition and strong bonds of
sentiment than practicality. They won't move; and even if
they do, as was discovered tragically during the Chaco War,
the altiplano *indígenas* removed to the moist hot lowlands
swiftly expire of tuberculosis and other lung diseases.

We pass a decaying adobe church with 'CRISTO LA UNICA
ESPERANZA' daubed in white paint on the front. What else
is there? The bus takes a wrong turning and plunges on for
some distance towards Cochabamba. We stop at a deserted
hotel, inscribed with the same signs – 'CRISTO ES LA UNICA
ESPERANZA'. A Land-Rover pulls up, filled – improbably –
with Jamaican university students *coiffés* with Black Panther
frizzes (are they on their way to set up a new Che-type *foco*?),
who set us right. As we approach Oruro, some Bolivian girls
on the bus produce confetti and streamers and sing cheerfully in a vain attempt to get us all in that Carnival spirit.
We arrive, bones and nerves jangling, teeth a-chatter. Among
enormous throngs we walk through filthy, mean streets with
fetid gutters reeking of urine, and showing every sign of most
acute poverty. Just two months previously there had been a
nasty massacre when the army had repulsed mineworkers
attempting to capture a barracks, and killed twenty. On the
way to the main square we pass various side-shows; including
a man on stilts, with a boa-constrictor round his neck. The
plaza is an oasis of elegance, a small memorial to the former
prosperity of the tin mines. Opposite the stand into which
we are packed with the same degree of discomfort as in the
bus, is the really rather splendid Ayuntamiento – a long low
grey building of graceful arcades, perhaps inspired by

Madrid's Plaza Mayor. At one end of it, there is a small office entitled 'Departmental Federation of ex-Combatants of the Chaco'. On the adjacent side of the square stands an imposing small opera building, the 'Palais Concert', with a façade of green pilasters and heavy silver caryatids; now a cinema house. One wonders what opera first nights could have been like in the days of Oruro's heyday. The source of that wealth, and misery, is clearly visible through a gap in the buildings, a bare fawn-coloured hill with mine galleries thrusting into it.

There is a long delay as the procession forms up. The thin wind swirls dust and confetti round the square. Bossy policemen harry the crowds back and forth, trying to clear the thoroughfare; one of them, with a quite exceptionally brutal face, looks as though he longs to lay about him with his billy-stick and is manifestly disappointed when no target presents itself. Underneath the arcades opposite us the huddled Bolivians betray anything but the Carnival spirit. One begins to wonder whether the painful trip has really been worth it. Then, in the distance, mounting the steep hill to the square, there is the sound of music; an exotic, unfamiliar rhythm. A cavalcade of cars moves slowly by, bearing the dignitaries of Oruro and with simple silver platters and bowls – products of the mines – armadillo shells and curiously inappropriate plastic dolls lashed across the bonnets. Next comes a sprinkling of individual dancers, in most extravagant costumes; a giant condor, Andean bears, diminutive children dressed as Cholo women with bowler hats and bright flared bolero skirts; a first sprinkling of 'devils' with curly moufflon horns, striped in rainbow colours, and wearing cobalt and crimson cloaks, every inch of them lovingly embroidered. Visually the brilliant costumes are impressive, but not overwhelmingly so. But suddenly there is a more powerful blast of the same bizarre music, and the whole square fills with a tourbillon of fantastic colour, magnified many times by that stratospheric luminosity, of a hundred – a thousand – dancers all whirling and leaping at the same time. Out of the mass of condors, bears, *negritos*, tiny mites carrying miners' lanterns or dressed as bulls, the multitude of devils wearing ever more extravagant masks, it becomes quite impossible to distinguish any individual figure from the vibrating, seething maelstrom of colour. The bands follow ever quicker on each other's footsteps. One squat, green-clad drummer spins and jigs with a huge drum balanced on his head. There is something captivating and magical about the Bolivian music, the counterpointing of the soft, sad melodies played on the *quena* – a reedy bamboo flute – against the throaty, virile and rapid strumming produced from the *charango* – a kind of balalaika, made from a scooped-out armadillo shell. Hour after hour the carnival music throbs on; but none of the Bolivians sway, or twitch, or tap their feet, or show any sign of being moved by the pounding rhythm. It seems to penetrate deeper than that. I could myself hear it in my inner ear weeks later, even long after returning to England; and still hear it sometimes now, like the roar of distant waves in a conch shell.

The tradition of the *diablada* at Oruro (which, as recently as the eighteenth century, was selected as the centre of a movement to restore the Inca regime) has become so overlaid with different strains over the years that it is quite difficult to decipher. Supposedly, it is a ritual depicting the triumph of Good over the Devil; but it is far from clear whether, in the atavistic Indian mind, the Devil is in fact all bad. Down in the mines, for instance, there are effigies both to the Virgin Mary and to the Devil; it being reckoned that the subterranean world belongs specifically to the Devil, and therefore those who enter it would be prudent to propitiate him. Similarly, the syncretization of religions has led to the Virgin Mary becoming identified with Pachamama, Mother Earth, the fertility goddess. In the course of the Carnival procession, the Archangel appears and makes a show of killing the devils with a serpentine sword. Apparently it is the duty of each angel to kill seven devils, representing the seven deadly sins; an eighth figure, a lady provocatively dressed in scarlet swinging skirts and silver kinky boots, who is the personification of Carnality, is however pardoned at the moment of execution. And how are the angels portrayed? They are faintly comic figures, with vestigial wings, shining German *Pickelhaube* spiked helmets, pink complexions and bright blue Osbert Lancaster pop-eyes. The spectators love them, and roar with laughter. Is it not possible to interpret a certain duality here? It is the wicked, fair-complexioned *gringo* invading and ransacking the Devil's own kingdom, and slaughtering wilfully the native deities and Reverend Vices.

Behind each separate section of dancers comes a sombre, serious-faced little group of men and women in everyday clothes, bearing with them religious banners and little effigies of the Virgin in glass cases. These, evidently, are the supporters and financiers of each group. They come from the various outlying communities in the neighbourhood, and annually vie to win the prizes given for the most spectacular costumes. The contrast between the incredible, exorbitant fantasy of the dancers and the threadbare poverty of their 'supporters', their cheap clothes and rough shoes, the children accompanying them gnawing hungrily at crusts of bread, tells a sad story that – like the music – provides its counterpoint to the delight of the Carnival. Despite the desperate, grinding poverty of these miners and their families, they save up every spare penny throughout the year to provide the costumes for this one moment.

Over four solid hours the dancers keep on coming. They never smile, and one is reminded of the grim-featured clowns beating a drum in Rouault's famous painting, *La Parade*. When they pause for a moment or two their faces look bleak with joylessness. Then I realize that it is sheer exhaustion; they have danced their way uphill for two-and-a-half miles, at an altitude where fifty yards of this kind of exertion would paralyse a European. A kind of semi-religious frenzy, no doubt supported by coca-chewing, seems to drive them on. It is not just the excitement of the rhythm, the splendour of the costumes and masks that etches itself on the memory, but – in the midst of such stark poverty – the human spirit behind it; the rather perverse spirit that built Machu Picchu. One wonders in awe at such tremendous application of energy. It seems symbolic, somehow, of a facet of all South America. It is not *mis*-directed energy – for how could dedication to so much colour, so much emotion, be misdirected? But it is energy that seems in an odd way tangentially, obliquely applied. (And to what extent, indeed, does it represent the Indians' traditional method of retreat from the white man's world?)

As we leave Oruro, a long week of assiduous drunkenness begins, a harking back to the old Inca principle that, at its proper time such as a *fiesta*, intoxication is a ritual necessity. For us, there is a two-hour wait at the *tránsito* leaving Oruro. When the bus creeps up within sight of the checkpoint, it is discovered that this time it has been taken over by students. The police have 'disappeared'. Is this the prophesied *golpe*? A heated argument ensues between the driver of the bus and the students. It appears that they are demanding a toll of one peso per head. Why? 'Because it is a new law passed today.' 'Whose law?' 'Why, the University's.' The driver refuses to submit to this blackmail. One or two passengers leave the bus and harangue the students outside. A struggle breaks out. Suddenly the driver charges the bus at the barrier, snapping off the pole. We make a successful break for freedom; fortunately, the students – rather unusually for Bolivia these days – appear to be unarmed. We drive on joyously for about a quarter of a mile, until a girl bursts out weeping inside the bus. It transpires that one of the courageous passengers distracting the students at the critical moment of the charge was her husband, and he has been left behind. There is a lively discussion as to whether we should return to save him, thereby plunging the rest of the busload in unpredictable jeopardy, or drive on and leave the brave one to his fate. The passengers are moved by the pleas of the distraught wife, and a consensus decides we should turn back. The American professor and family, understandably, are distinctly nervous in view of the anti-American violence that has swept Bolivia in recent months. I suggest they lie down and keep very quiet at the back. Fortunately, just before the moment of truth, another bus arrives with the missing hero abroad. We escape the students, and a Bolivian girl murmurs to me, 'You see, *anything* can happen here!'

It rains all the way back to La Paz, and the route is scattered with cars overturned off the road; but after our experience at the *tránsito* nothing will stop our driver now. The threatened revolution has not, however, taken place. We reach La Paz at 2.30 a.m. Dead. After four hours of sleep, with the first serious signs yet of *sufocación*, I leave La Paz for Lima. The plane is full and it takes an agonizing forty-five seconds, right to the end of the runway, to lift off. We are cheerfully informed that there is still absolutely no trace of a Bolivian air force C46, missing since Wednesday. Coming out of the clouds over Lima, I can see the circling guano birds below and Sunday crowds thronging the Pacific surf beaches. How incredibly fertile the Peruvian fields seem after the altiplano! It is like returning from the moon.

15

High Tension in Colombia

After a week of de-Bolivianization in Lima, I am back in
Bogotá. It almost comes as a surprise once again to see the
afternoon sun shining from the south over sumptuous green
fields filled with fat Holsteins. Dino telephones, as excitable
and volubly Neapolitan as ever. He has just returned from
an 'anti-Tupamaro course' in Florida, which most senior
U.S. diplomats in Latin America are now being put through.
Subsequently they receive vast American limousines with,
apart from the conventional bullet-proof glass, half a ton of
steel concealed in front of the motor and a specially strengthened chassis. The technique is that if you see a Tupamaro
road block of cars forming up in front of you, you simply put
your foot on the accelerator and slice through them. Dino
is like a child with a new toy as he outlines to me the joys of
the course. 'Boy! you just don't know how wonderful it was
to smash up four cars a day in that course; it really lets out
all your frustrations!' His own anti-Tupamaro chariot has
yet to arrive in Bogotá. When it does, I dread to think of the
fate of obstructive Bogotano taxi-drivers; the temptation will
be too great.

But Dino may well need his tank. Even over the few weeks
that I have been away, the temperature in Colombia has
unmistakably risen. It is not just the climate of that curious
midway altitude of Bogotá, which immediately makes one
feel irritable and full of *Angst*. There is an atmosphere of
tension, of expecting unknown bad things to happen, such as
I have experienced nowhere else in the Andes – not even in
Bolivia. Something is boiling up, nobody quite knows what.
Outside the University, I note newly painted red signs:
'*Camilo vive – ELN*'. The fifth anniversary of Father Camilo

Torres's death has just been celebrated. There is a protracted and heat-generating strike of teachers throughout the country, which the Pastrana government seems incapable of settling, and a one-day token general strike in Bogotá has been called for 8 March – which could spark off serious troubles. Perhaps the most disturbing, new feature of the past weeks has been the mass *'invasiones'* of *fundos* out in the country.

About 9.30 that night a squadron of old American 'Honey' tanks and half-tracks rumble at high speed past the Tequendama, heading for the University. Dino says it's probably just a routine exercise, but the next morning the papers report arrests of 'suspects'. They say that, over the past week, the number of *invasiones* has risen to over fifty; there are photographs of a tiny boy mascot of the squatters with the inspiring revolutionary name of Harold Wilson Gutiérrez. The government announces, nervously, that it has uncovered a 'subversive plan' to confront the government with the first major crisis of its six months' administration, by co-ordinating the strikes and the *invasiones*. Among the left-wing groups involved in this 'subversion' is said to be the Golconda group of revolutionary priests who operate in the name of Camilo Torres.

I go to see Enrique Santos, editor of *El Tiempo*, whom I had met with Bill on our earlier visit to Bogotá. *Tiempo* is the biggest newspaper, with a circulation of over 200,000, a vigorous and high quality product written in mandarin prose as one would expect in Colombia, and working out of offices that – by comparison with down-at-heel newspapers in La Paz – seem as prosperous as anything in North America. *El Tiempo* is nominally Liberal; Enrique Santos himself is a staunchly establishment figure, but his nephew, who is also an editor of the paper, is fairly far to the left. They are typical of the generation-gap in present-day Colombia. Both the Santoses quiz me anxiously about Chile. Like many Colombians, they see almost everything that is happening in Colombia at the moment as echoes of events in Chile. The *invasiones*, the mass strike planned for 8 March, both have their 'central motives' borrowed from Chile. Since my last visit, the Maoists, the official Communist party, and the Socialist party are trying to form a new United Front, together with the *anapistas* of Rojas Pinilla, and are in search of an Allende. It is the first time that this has happened in Colombia, and Enrique Santos considers that it is a direct copy of the successful Chilean model, with the critical elections of 1974 in mind. He is deeply shocked when I tell him that the Nationals and the Christian Democrats in Chile were refusing to co-operate with one another in their opposition to Allende; 'The fools . . . how could they!' But is this not exactly what is happening in Colombia, increasingly, between the Liberals and the Conservatives? He seems not to see it.

That afternoon (26 February) I am invited, very secretly, by a right-wing Colombian, 'Carlos', to the offices of a sinister-sounding underground organization called *Mano Negra* – or 'Black Hand'. It operates from an unpretentious office building in down-town Bogotá under cover of a firm publishing art books. As a young man Carlos was a wealthy international playboy; now he is a deeply earnest, *engagé* figure. His tenseness mirrors the uncertainties prevailing in Colombia. He tells me that, for the first time, there are signs of serious depression and demoralization in Bogotá. The papers are full of advertisements of houses for sale. *Mano Negra* appears to be largely financed by the bankers of Colombia, and also by Carlos himself, who is one of its key figures. Despite the unpleasant connotations of its name, *Mano Negra* (I am assured by neutral observers) does not indulge in the kind of shady rough stuff that is such an integral part of Colombia's lurid past; it works largely by means of the 'media'. In the days of President Lleras, it used to specialize in organizing counter-demonstrations against the students when they started breaking windows, by getting 'simple people' out into the streets to protest. It once had considerable support within the university; but now, Carlos tells me, it has little influence there.

When I arrive, there is a tense political meeting going on in the next room. It is interrupted by a telephone call with news of serious trouble in Cali. Some two hundred air-miles south-west of Bogotá, Cali is the home of *criollo* aristocrats contemptuous of the Bogotá *nouveaux-riches* who arrived 'as late as the eighteenth century'. But, surrounding it, poverty-stricken mountain Indians and coastal Negroes, plus a shanty town population of migrants larger than in any other Colombian city, provide it with a particularly explosive instability. The clash in Cali appears to have taken place between striking students and police, but at first there are no specific details. The telephone rings again, reporting that the police have opened fire and killed four students; a curfew has been imposed and the Army called in. Carlos, dreadfully agitated, strides up and down the *Mano Negra* office, cracking his knuckles and exclaiming: 'The fools! What fools! There has been nothing like this since the 1950s. If there really has been shooting, it's disastrous. It will immediately put people on the side of the students and against the Government.' The news gets worse; the casualties rise to seven dead and over fifty injured. That night President Pastrana broadcasts announcing a 'state of siege' throughout the country, and pleading for calm. His sonorous Colombian Spanish sounds more like the incantation of a priest, or Pablo Neruda reading one of his poems, than that of a strong leader announcing stern measures. The army turns out in force in Bogotá, equipped with plastic shields and anti-stone visors. Dino expresses concern that its 40,000 men may be spread too thin should there be simultaneous troubles in all the city, together with a recrudescence of guerrilla activity in the country. The next day Bogotá is nervously quiet. The government suggests that 'foreign hands' have been at work in the Cali riots (it sounds as though the hints might be directed at Allende); while the conservative *El Espectador* declares: 'We are on the edge of the abyss.' It is all indicative of the latent nervousness in Colombia.

That morning I leave for a four-day visit to a tropical cattle station down in the Magdalena valley. Recalling the *Bogotazo* of 1948, it seems possibly a good moment to be out of town. My host at La Dorada is an old friend, Luís Robledo; educated at Downside and formerly Colombian commercial attaché in London, Luís is a square-framed, powerful figure who started his own soccer team on returning to Bogotá. To leave Bogotá in the '*Estado de Sitio*' we have to get a special permit from the army. It is a gruelling trip of a hundred miles, crossing three massive mountain ranges. We climb up to 10,000 feet, out of the ancient lake bed of Bogotá, through temperate and prosperous farms. On the summit, the common sight of an upside-down bus. Then the steady descent. The rich pasture gives way to coarse Kikuyu grass. That begins to thin out, and we pass into a zone of oranges and bananas and palm trees. Past the week-end villas of rich Bogotanos. Next, large and vigorous poinsettia trees, and giant bamboos thirty feet high. Bright red blossoms of flame-of-the-forest trees. Sugar-cane growing on steep hillsides. Papayas. Suddenly it is very hot; just an hour and a half earlier we had left Bogotá wearing overcoats. Then the zig-zag road goes up into cool air once more; then down again into coffee terraces. Forests of strangely beautiful trees with bright vermilion trunks as smooth as a woman's thighs. A house half demolished by a landslide. The mountains seem to go on for ever, leading one back and forth through every imaginable climatic zone. At last we come out over a vast range, with a spectacular view over the Magdalena valley. A haze hides the white-capped Andes beyond; apparently it comes from the burning of weed and scrub in the typical 'burn-and-slash' agriculture of the Central American states, wafted down all the way by the prevailing north winds. More landslides and a pungent smell of molasses grass.

We climb down to Honda on the Magdalena River; 3,000 feet, and sizzling hot. There is a regatta under way, and hundreds of people are watching canoeists shoot rapids in the river below. In colonial days the Spanish viceroys used to come up by boat from Barranquilla, some six hundred miles downstream on the coast, disembark at Honda and then make their way slowly and painfully by mule over the mountains to Bogotá. As recently as the 1930s, La Dorada, just a few miles further down the Magdalena, was – according to Luís – 'nothing more than a whorehouse' for sailors making the three weeks' trip up to Honda. The hinterland was a jungle infested with yellow fever and malaria. Nobody, not even indigenous Indians, ever lived there. Then Colombian pioneers – among whom Luís's father was one of the most prominent – opened up the area and cleared the jungles. La Dorada is now a frontier town of some 50,000 people; but the hopeful, dowdy whores still hang around everywhere in the open-fronted billiard saloons. In a shanty town on the edge of La Dorada, we pick up some children struggling to drag home for firewood the root of a large tree. 'They are really poor here; the parents probably unemployed,' says Luís. 'Kids, kids, kids – that's the killing problem of Colombia. But what can you do about it? Most of the poor families have no electric light. Therefore no T.V. Therefore what the hell can they do in the evenings – except make children!'

The ranch is in a flat, wide valley; to the west, weird sculpted hills like the eroded desert buttes of Arizona, but covered with viridian vegetation. The sun burns down, and with an eighty-inch rainfall the grass grows faster than the cattle can eat it. So on his 4,000 acres of cleared jungle, Luís grazes 4,000 head of pedigree zebu (*bos indicus*), a prize-winning herd, built up over the years. To the unaccustomed European eye, they are uncouthly exotic-looking beasts. The fully-grown bulls weigh up to a ton; ungainly, waddling monsters, all humps and bumps, like U.S. Phantom bombers, with wattles and great papaya-shaped scrotums dangling almost to the ground. No paddock will keep them in, says Luís. On the approaches to the *hacienda*, Luís has planted avenues of fast-growing teak trees which he hopes will make his fortune in no less than ten years' time. Unfortunately the bulls have already pushed some of them over.

The breeding of the prize stock at El Palmar is a carefully computerized operation, as scientific as anything in the United States or Britain. The ranch is managed by Luís's young cousin, Alvaro, a wiry, dark-skinned Colombian trained in Florida Tropical Agricultural College. He has seventy men on his payroll. Some of the cowboys receive an average of seven pounds a week, plus bonuses for each successful birth, which is considered high pay by Colombian stanpards. They also have their own cattle, which run with the general herd. Some of the El Palmar bulls are valued at £5,000 apiece, and Luís says he *used* to believe that Colombia had a tremendous future as a meat and livestock exporter.

'Used to?' Because Luís has come down this week with the express purpose of selling up at least a third of his herd – before it can be taken away from him. Luís is deeply pessimistic as to where land reform will lead. Colombia's was one of the first serious Land Reform Acts to be passed in South America (1961) and it provoked such furious conservative opposition that there was actually gunplay inside the chamber. Nevertheless, its provisions were so mild that – combined with Colombia's impossible birth-rate – they were to make far less of an impact on social needs than Frei's reforms in Chile. According to a writer in *Le Monde* of 5 March 1971, over the past nine years only 5,300 peasant families were resettled: 'At this rate it would take a thousand years to redistribute property in Colombia.' Under pressure ex-President Lleras gave birth to an *Asociación Nacional de Usuarios*, the peasants' own trade union. Now, says Luís, the number of votes chalked up in the 1970 elections by the populist Rojas and his allies, coupled with Allende's success in Chile, has so alarmed Pastrana that he has accelerated land reform regardless of the consequences: 'In the last few weeks we have gone back twenty years.' The *usuarios* are egging on the peasants to enact *invasiones* in emulation of the Chilean MIR; while the system of *reforma agraria* currently being adopted in Colombia is basically similar to what Allende and Chonchol were pressing at top speed in Chile – with predictably disastrous effects. But Colombia, as Luís points out, is just that much more vulnerable, because nearly half of the total population derives its livelihood from the land – which produces approximately 30 per cent of the country's gross domestic product. Luís considers that redistribution of the most highly developed land in Colombia – however pressing the needs of social justice – makes even less sense when two-thirds of the country (equal to several times the area of England) is still undeveloped, crying out to be cleared and opened up for land-hungry farmers.

He brings out a map; huge tracts less than a hundred air-miles south-east of Bogotá are white. 'Look, in thirty years time the population will have grown from twenty-one to forty million, and INCORA policy is to cram this population into one-third of the country – not to encourage people to go out to develop the great blank spaces of the Amazon basin. Look at Brazil. There they are creating a criss-cross of roads into Amazonia, with the Government offering two hundred yards of road frontage and as much behind as a man can develop, together with all sorts of free aid. Logically we should be opening up the new lands of the south-east, as my father did here, but this requires huge sums of capital; and who will now risk it when expropriation is the inevitable end to all one's labour and risk?' Like so many of the managerial class elsewhere in South America, Luís has unbounded admiration for Brazil: 'It is the only country which has faith in itself, which is pushing back the frontier and planning ahead.' But it is Chile, not Brazil, that he sees Colombia emulating; he expects INCORA in Colombia to pass a new law – such as Chonchol expressly desires in Chile – which will enable the Government to expropriate stock and movable assets as well as the farms themselves. 'Otherwise it is crazy; everybody will kill their cattle and ruin the economy as they are doing in Chile.' That is why he has come to El Palmar to start selling up his superb herd: 'Because I can see which way things are going.' He is deeply depressed at the prospect at having to give notice to faithful cowboys who have been with him many years – when there are already so many unemployed around La Dorada. He thinks he himself may be allowed to keep no more than one or two hundred acres. Other owners in the neighbourhood, however, will not go so easily, he says: 'Some of them are toughs who built up the *haciendas* themselves; and some of them are bandits from the times of the *violencia*. They are heavily armed, they won't go without a fight, and there will be killing again.'

We talk about the *violencia*. During those bad times La Dorada was a liberal area, but the Robledos – though Conservatives – were left alone. Everybody had machine-guns, and nobody lived at night on the *haciendas*. Coming back from Europe, Luís said that he was simply unable to understand what it was all about, and it still mystifies and shocks him. Like many Colombians he is haunted and – in so far as such a physically robust personality can experience fear – fearful of that spectre of violence lurking beneath the surface. This must be an ever-present factor in Colombia's prevailing nervousness. Will the *violencia* burst out again when that Wimbledon-style truce ends in 1974? In what form? Will the army intervene to replace the weak Pastrana even earlier?

There is this added cause which Luís puts his finger on: each of the other Andean nations – Peru, Bolivia, even Ecuador and now Chile – has had its 'revolution'. They at least know the worst – which provides a kind of vicarious stability. Colombia, the odd man out, lives on in the uncertainty of *not knowing*, and torn by the uncertainty of the murderous forces existing within itself. That night the wind builds up suddenly; the crickets and chicharras cease their frantic songs, and the *violencia* bursts on us in the shape of a savagely potent tornado. The dogs bark and howl, and somewhere close outside a wild animal – perhaps a monkey – scrabbles for shelter in the dried leaves. The house, comfortable and airy but by no means luxurious, must be wonderfully built. It takes a tremendous buffeting; the wind blowing through the open insect screens whips the sheets off my bed, but the house itself emits no creaks or bangs.

With astonishing abruptness the tempest subsides, and the early morning skies are swept fragrantly clear and cool, yet loaded with the overpoweringly sensual aromas of the tropics drenched by rain. But there is another storm brewing between Luís and Alvaro, his cousin-manager. Alvaro flies into a tropical rage when he hears of Luís's intention to sell up part of the ranch. He accuses Luís of being panicky. Luís in his turn is furious when he discovers that two of his prize zebu bulls have been allowed to get into a fight, with the result that one has broken the femur of its hind-leg. Alvaro, impatient and with the pragmatism of the technocrat, wants to shoot the bull at once. Luís says, 'No.' It is worth £5,000 and they must try to repair the leg; at least the bull will be good for artificial insemination. The drama develops. We mount horses and ride out to the paddock at the far end of the ranch which contains the injured bull. The horses are tiny *caballos de paso* with an enormously fast, silky trot that they can keep up indefinitely. They also have mouths like satin – which I discover almost too late. After my mount has reared alarmingly several times, Alvaro laughs – 'We nearly killed a *Yanqui* a short time ago – he didn't know about these horses and their delicate mouths – he pulled it back too hard, it stood up on its hind-legs, then fell over backwards on top of him!' The cowboys look like centaurs as they ride by long-

307

stirruped, at a fast trot without ever moving in the saddle. We trot out over the flat plain, towards the exotically-moulded foothills that themselves resemble the contours of a zebu. Graceful white egrets, attendant tick-birds – contrasting absurdly with their lumpy, sepia-tinted companions – flap lazily into the air as we pass. A red-shirted cowboy races round, firing a shotgun from the saddle at buzzards that have an unattractive habit of attacking the young calves, tearing at their tender sphincters.

We find the injured bull close to the swamp, grazing unconcernedly but with its hind-leg trailing at a disturbingly unnatural angle. Luís is immediately convinced that the bull can be saved: 'Being a zebu his chances of recovery are good: now, if this were a Charollais or a Santa Gertrudis, he would already be lying down waiting for the buzzards to peck out his eyes!' Alvaro is clearly sceptical. Swiftly and decisively Luís gives orders. We clear the other cattle from the field, so as to leave the bull unworried. The cowboys will come out and build a shelter and paddock round him. Hernán, with the red shirt and gun, will mount guard – because, says Luís, 'There is always the danger that somebody will come out, find him helpless, then cut him up for meat.' Meanwhile the vet will be summoned and instructed to splint the broken leg. Looking at the injured leg with an unpractised eye, it is difficult not to share Alvaro's doubts.

That night the vet arrives after a ten hours' trip from Medellín. He has a face like Francisco Pizarro: long nose, dark-skinned and pointed black beard – topped by a jaunty black-and-white sombrero. He shows great partiality to Luís's superb rum concoctions. His one sentence of English as he reaches for the jug is 'a bird must fly on two wings', and before the evening is over he has sprouted as many as a squadron of dragonflies. That night there is no wind or storm; nothing but the deafening, intoxicating rhythm of countless varieties of *cicadas, hylas* and unidentified tropical night creatures, all orchestrated together like an unceasing samba band. The news seems momentarily more peaceful too. The radio reports total calm over all Colombia. But the *estado de sitio* continues. The next morning we ride out again to the bull, horses laden with medical kit. A hot thundery day. A grey-spotted cur cringes as the surgical cavalcade rattles across the river bridge; fishermen on a bamboo raft wave. On seeing the bull, the vet immediately shakes his head. The bones are too far apart to mend by themselves. But Luís, sitting in the saddle with arms akimbo and chin thrust out, as *macho* as any ton weight of zebu bull, is unmovable. The leg will be splinted. Cowboys ride back to the ranch for reinforcements and plaster of Paris. It is already five o'clock, and the sun is getting lower. Inside the swamp frogs begin their *cuoic-cuoic* chanting; black and bright yellow chested small birds with a cry like *chi-chi-bu* flit back and forth. An old cowboy skilfully lassoes the bull with a rawhide. The others, in absolute silence so as not to frighten the bull, criss-cross thongs around its body, through the hindquarters. In a matter of minutes it is trussed like a turkey and completely immobilized. Then all start tugging. Red-shirt pulls hard on the tail; the bull very slowly topples over on to its side. Perfect. The thongs are removed and the three good legs bound together. The operation begins.

The tension is unbearable. One feels that the whole fate of South America is in the balance. The doctor manipulates. The bones can be heard crackling; 'It's worse than I thought, there are six bones broken near the knee.' Five cowboys pull on the rope, trying to get the leg back into position – unsuccessfully. Finally Hernán of the red shirt ties a traction rope to the saddle of his horse and spurs it. Apart from a thunderous fart the bull lies there unprotesting. In ten minutes the doctor gets the leg back into position. Then roll upon roll of plaster of Paris is applied. The moment of truth arrives. The ropes are untied, and the 950-kilogram bull, groaning and emuncting, rises to its feet, and makes a desperate attempt to shake off the plaster. The leg still looks very crooked indeed. The night sounds are multiplying. Black long-tailed birds and a yellow-breasted kingfisher with a deep blue crest fly into the swamp to roost for the night. Fireflies begin to appear. We set off for the *hacienda*. From a long distance in the dusk one can still make out the white blob of the plaster on the bull's hindquarters.

The vet is obviously delighted by his handiwork, and that night he and Alvaro set off for La Dorada – 'to make some telephone calls'. 'Nonsense!' snorts Luís after they have gone.

'They are off to the whorehouse. Alvaro spends his life there. I don't know anybody who has had clap more often – and each time it is harder to cure. I can't bear the smell of those places.' The next morning, the vet, still wearing his jaunty sombrero but with a face like a boiled dog, takes off on his ten-hour trek home. An uneasy calm continues over the country, but the papers (1 March) now report that the Cali students were planning to kidnap a senior army officer, as a hostage for student urban guerrillas arrested the night the tanks were out in Bogotá. There are horrid stories that police officers captured by students in an earlier riot were roasted and tortured. We ride out to the bull again; a wonderful sunny day with a light cool breeze. The fawn-coloured calves with their floppy ears and eyes like a Siamese dancer begin to grow on one; there is almost an oriental beauty about them. The bull still has his cast on, but the leg looks even more horribly bent. Black tick-birds with parrot-like beaks watch attentively from the swamp, while two buzzards circle ominously above. With extraordinary skill, the cowboys are already at work building a shelter, all from raw materials out of the swamp; giant bamboos, four inches in diameter, for the uprights and crosspieces, palm fronds slit down the centre for the roofing, impenetrable to rain as well as sun. When finished in just a matter of hours, it looks as though it will last for ten years. Luís sits there in the saddle, supervising and studying the bull. There is a world of contrast between his own taurine figure, dogged and explosive, but prepared to go to any lengths to save the bull, and the hot-blooded, impatient, lithe Alvaro, visibly bridling under Luís's criticism; the college-trained, intellectual farmer anxious to cut short-term losses, but declining to face the wider, strategic threats of expropriation.

For a moment I thought I saw the whole turbulent drama of South America passing before my eyes. So much passion and effort expended in the struggle to mend the leg of the prize bull – which, judging from the distorted shape underneath the plaster, probably would survive to be nothing more than a cripple; an operation so out of phase with the real facts of life when a revolution as fundamental as *la reforma agraria* was poised to sweep away the whole existing order of life. A memory floats back of the Carnival at Oruro, of the distorted dream-world of García Márquez's own, Colombian, 'Macondo'.

Back at the *hacienda*, there is a large gaudy toucan sitting in a rubber tree near the house, intently watching the coming and going. In the nearby cattle-yard, the calves are being culled from the cows. 'We won't get any sleep tonight,' warns Luís, and all night long the zebus low in their deprivation. It is more like the bellowing of lions than the high-pitched moo of European cattle. In the small hours, the fugue is joined by a tremendous barking from the dogs in pursuit of a giant iguana, and Luís roaring angrily at them. The next morning the creek near the house, a tributary of the Magdalena, is filled with brown swirling waters from the storm of two nights previously. Luís tells me that, about three years ago, the creek nearly removed the kitchen. Now he is trying to persuade it to change its course, by placing huge boulders that will attract silt on to the *hacienda* side while distracting the treacherous river to eat away at the opposing bank. Which of the three potent, opposing forces will have triumphed at El Palmar in a few years time; Luís, INCORA or the river?

We set off for Bogotá. There are reports of more troubles. A curfew in Medellín. Fighting in Bogotá. There are heavy, menacing clouds forming over the tops of the mountain ranges. Back in Bogotá, several companies of troops fully equipped with anti-riot paraphernalia are formed up in the Independencia Park opposite the Tequendama. Yesterday, apparently, there had been a serious student beat-up there. They tried to stone the U.S. Embassy; a hundred were arrested and then impounded in the Santa Maria bullring. Twenty were wounded, police as well. Worse is expected for tomorrow, 4 March. But the biggest news is that President Pastrana has summarily sacked the director of INCORA, Carlos Villamil Chaux, an appointee of President Lleras who had held the post for the past three years. Villamil is said to have criticized the slow rate of agrarian reform and to have expressed sympathy with the *invasiones*. Pastrana now appears to be thoroughly alarmed by the tempo events have begun to assume, whipped up by the example of the *mirista tomas* in

Chile. It seems that – setting his rudder against the tide running in the other Andean countries – he will now veer away from agrarian reform – but such vacillation can only provide more fuel for the extremists. A few days later the bishops of this most conservative Church in South America joined together to issue a fourteen-point statement calling for – among other things – an *acceleration* of land reform. The weather is oppressively heavy, and one's temper is like a mass of plutonium suddenly become critical. There is an electric storm of extraordinary violence that night; balls of lightning explode deafeningly, close to the ground inside the bowl of the city.

The next morning I have an interview with Monsignor José Joaquin Salcedo, a really conservative priest and the antithesis of the *golcondas* of Camilo Torres and Father García. John Gunther describes him as 'one of the most powerful – and somewhat frightening – personalities I met in South America'. A man in his early fifties with veiled eyes and close-cropped grey hair, the Monsignor has something of the fervent, overgrown schoolboy look of Richard Crossman. His distinction is that he has, for the past twenty years, been running *Acción Cultural Popular*, the most outspokenly anti-Communist Catholic organization in South America. It describes itself as 'an institution specializing in service for the culture of the peasant peoples'; has at its disposal, apparently, the biggest radio network in the continent, and is enormously influential. The funds behind ACPO come partly from the Government, partly from foreign support (Protestant as well as Catholic) and partly from *campesinos* who subscribe to the educational services which ACPO provides them. Monsignor Salcedo is intensely media-conscious. He stresses how suddenly the advent of T.V. and the transistor has revolutionized the outlook of the *campesino*; 'Everyone now has a desire to live just the way they see the Queen of England lives – on television, in the newspapers.' Fidel Castro managed to get over to people that it was the injustices of the oligarchy and of Yanqui imperialism that were the only obstacles, in fact, to having a life like the Queen of England. Now television especially teaches the peasants to 'take away from them that have' so as to reach the Queen-of-England level. (I begin to wonder whether the Monsignor's special message for me to take back to the Queen is that Her Majesty should appear less on television?) He explains that ACPO's function is to teach the *campesinos* that the most important thing is development of *themselves*. 'Suppose, now,' he says, 'you swapped fifty-five millions of Britons with Latin Americans? Why, within six months the Latin Americans transported to Britain would have destroyed 400 years of progress, the whole civilization structure of Great Britain.' I protest mildly that the British are now doing it themselves, though perhaps not quite so quickly, that he is too pessimistic about his own people; he pays no attention however, and continues. 'The necessity for the acquisition of land is purely emotive. . . . What is required is the development of *men, not of things*,' the Monsignor insists. For instance, education in itself is not the problem – but its *quality*, 'Education is a question of how to live – not to learn about *things*. Why, for instance, do we teach simple Colombian farmers the history of Egypt? It's much more important to teach them, first, how to look after their cows, and what makes the cows die.'

From education we move on to the delicate subject of birth-control. Yes, Monsignor Salcedo agrees that some system of 'decelerating' the rate of *la explosión demográfica* will have to be adopted. But first must come education, the number one issue: 'It doesn't matter what the system of birth-control is, if the *campesinos* don't understand it.' He believes all that can be done is to make them *aware* of 'the immense economic folly of having another son'. He does not regard his views as being contrary to the Papal Encyclical; nor do the technical aspects of contraception impress him. He points out that over the past five years the V.D. rate in Bogotá among the young has increased 75 per cent.

Repeatedly, Monsignor Salcedo comes back to explaining how he is opposed to the principle of material aid. President Kennedy was fundamentally mistaken in trying to give South American *campesinos* dollars to buy houses when they were incapable of running a house. 'That money should have been spent in increasing the responsibility of individuals – *not* in offering economic miracles. It's like pouring water on to infertile soil.' It is impossible not to be moved by the Mon-

313

signor's dedicated sincerity; ten, fifteen years ago one might have been even more impressed by the practicality of his arguments. But now? With the Allendes, the Pepes and the Christian-Marixsts of Teoponte fermenting impatiently, always silhouetted against the luminous spectre of *la explosión demográfica* – is there still time for the simple people of South America to save themselves by developing self-reliance within a Catholic framework? Although he claims to be 'a realist, not a pessimist', Monsignor Salcedo says he fears that all countries in South America are bound now to follow the 'anarchic path' of Chile; 'Latin America has perhaps fifteen years ahead of it before the total *terremoto.*' As far as the present troubles in Colombia are concerned, the Monsignor – borrowing medical imagery strangely similar to that which I had once heard in the mouth of Colonel Papadopoulos of Greece – says: 'When a body is sick, it erupts in spots all over – the police and the army are only an ointment, they cannot cure the body.'

At that moment an aide enters and whispers to the Monsignor that rioting students are blocking the area: 'Monsignor can only get home for lunch if he leaves at once by the back exit.' Abruptly, the Monsignor takes his leave, disappearing like a Dumas cardinal, and I find myself out in the street by the front door. Almost immediately cars begin reversing rapidly down the street, and a mass of students chanting '*Camilo vive! Camilo vive!*' appear advancing along it. They are moving very fast, like a column of African army ants. A nasty feeling. Recalling the bloody Bogotazo of 1948, I let cowardice take precedent over curiosity and beat a rapid retreat on the Tequendama. Outside in the Independencia Park, where the troubles of two days ago took place, the students are beginning to congregate round the squadded army concentrations – at a respectable distance. From my window I can see a young girl in a gaily-coloured poncho baiting the troops. Closer and closer, until she plays Ring-a-Ring-o'-Roses with one of the platoons, flicking her poncho in the soldiers' faces. All at once she is seized by a sergeant and a couple of men, and marched off, hands above her head, into the bullring. The students follow, angrily jeering. Once again the atmosphere is heavy and oppressive and one feels that

314

any moment the human storm will burst and the shooting begin. That afternoon I run the gauntlet nervously into downtown Bogotá, to buy a *ruana* for my wife at a shop renowned throughout Colombia. But on arriving I find that it has been smashed up by the students and is deserted. The police are busily and brutally engaged in heaving students into trucks. Then, mercifully, the hail storm breaks. I have never seen anything like it. Hailstones half the size of golf balls strike almost with the same painful impact as a rubber bullet; and even greater effectiveness. Within minutes the streets are flooded, gutters filled with an icy mush four or five inches deep. The roads are cleared. The students detained in the bullring are broken, flattened by the hail just as a field of wheat by an English summer hailstorm. The riots are over. It evokes the divine intervention of the deluge which dissipated the Chartists marching on Parliament in 1848; I wonder whether Monsignor Salcedo had uttered a special invocation that afternoon.

The next morning the road to the airport is covered with stones. A police car is parked, with a rock through its windscreen. I leave South America to the accompaniment of broken glass and with another atmospheric storm on its way.

16

Ploughing the Sea

'Thunder and avalanches in the mountains, huge floods and storms on the plains. Volcanoes exploding. The earth shaking and splitting. . . .' Latin America remains, as Christopher Isherwood wrote a quarter of a century ago, 'a land of violence'. Certainly it is a land of change, and of increasingly violent change. In the short time since I flew homewards out of Bogotá, Bolivia has had its expected 187th *golpe*; Ecuador, a generals' *putsch*; Uruguay, a new president and more Tupamaro violence. In Argentina, a heightening of guerrilla activities concomitant with increasing economic and political anarchy, and even in Mexico – for long the widely envied symbol of relative political stability – a serious new threat from rural guerrillas. And in Chile, Villarica, unexpectedly and insidiously, has blown up, and earthquakes have scourged Valparaiso as a kind of natural counterpointing to the artificial *terremoto* orchestrated by Dr Allende.

What else may not have happened by the time this book appears in print? What next? Bolivia's 188th revolution? A change of generals in Argentina? Border warfare between Colombia and Venezuela? Civil war in Chile? Whatever a crystal-gazer may prophesy, events are likely to outflank him – if not to prove him fundamentally wrong.

In Colombia high tension and uncertainty remain the keynote. After the troubles of March 1971, the universities kept their doors closed for another six months, rendering a whole class of students free to pursue more hair-raising extracurricular activities than simple street rioting. In October there was a sudden reappearance of 'Tiro Fijo' (or his namesake), who by killing fourteen soldiers in a week inflicted one of the worst defeats in years on the crack Colombian army.

316

General Valencia Tovar was shot through the buttock in an assassination attempt by the Castroist ELN. The ELN, the 'Pekinese' EPL and the pro-Soviet FARC announced they had agreed to swallow their ideological differences and resume the armed struggle under a *Frente Unido de Acción Guerillera*; an ominous development if it were true and the United Front were to prove durable. Later there were also reports of General Rojas's ANAPO co-operating with the guerrillas at local levels. Meanwhile, after vacillating back and forth over agrarian reform, President Pastrana finally called a temporary halt to the programme. In the light of Chilean experience, his motive – an imminent food shortage – was perfectly reasonable, but it left the half million *usuarios* feeling deprived of something promised. Fears that the *campesinos* would take the law into their own hands in a new wave of *invasiones* were realized when Pastrana's new minister of agriculture, Señor Jaramillo, was among the first to have his *fundo* invaded. In despair for the future, and in company with many other realistic Colombian land-owners, Luís sold off three-quarters of El Palmar. The bull survived, but encased in an iron brace.

Colombia's economic prospects in general hardly look rosy. During 1971 the cost of living increased 16 per cent, the sharpest rise for three years, and unemployment also rose. The external payments position, so shackled to coffee prices was bad. Following her disenchantment with gone-Marxist Chile, the U.S. had inflated her AID programme to Colombia to $77 million a year, the third largest in the world – but the returns hardly look like being commensurate. Then, half-expectedly, Colombia struck a hard blow at the Andean Pact when its Supreme Court ruled that the accord on treatment of foreign capital reached by the other signatories was 'unconstitutional'.

At several times it seemed as though, politically, the Pastrana National Front government was about to collapse, following a threat of abandonment by the Liberals. In November 1971 ex-President Lleras Restrepo returned from Europe bringing with him new propositions of 'constructive left-wing policies'. At important municipal elections five months later, Lleras surprised the psephologists by trouncing the Pastrana Conservatives and routing ANAPO – which had come so astonishingly close to victory in the 1970 presidential race. For its two remaining years in office, the Pastrana government henceforth looks like being little more than a lame-duck, minority regime. Colombians still gaze towards the milestone year of 1974, when the 'Wimbledon truce' of the National Front ends, with dread apprehension, but the chances are that Colombia will find herself ruled by a left-wing Liberal constellation, with extremists still further to the left pushing hard – like the MIR in Chile. So Colombia seems bound to move leftwards. Unless the Army takes exception. . . .

From Lima, Peru's generals maintain their heavy-handed, centralized rule. The guerrillas remain passive; possibly waiting for the political breakdown that pessimistic Peruvians, such as Bedoya Reyes, regard as predictable if not inevitable. Like soldiers-in-politics from time immemorial, General Velasco and his disciples came in on an anti-corruption ticket, but their opponents say that they too have now become corrupted by absolute power. The accusations are not easy to nail. There are jobs for the boys, of course. Huge sums of money (about $250 million since 1968) have been spent on that inalienable passion of generaldom – extravagant weaponry. Mirage fighters and a hundred new French AMX tanks seem hardly more likely to influence internal order than Colombia's German mini-submarines impress Tiro Fijo, but they have certainly had a baneful impact on Peru's strained budget, already aggravated by a 10 per cent fall in revenue over the first six months of 1971. On the other side of the coin, however, our friend General Pedro Richter, Velasco's then Intelligence chief, has proved an energetic Minister of the Interior, relentless in his attack upon the more obvious forms of corruption. He has arrested Lima's leading brothel-owner in the act of paying a 4 million sol bribe to a police officer, and broken up one of the country's most important drug-exporting rings.

The most offensive act of heavy-handedness by Junta was the ousting, in January 1972, of seventy-five-year-old Pedro Beltrán as owner and director of *La Prensa*. The Junta had passed a law enabling the expropriation of assets belonging to any Peruvian who was abroad for more than six months out of a year. Don Pedro returned after six months, eleven days as visiting professor at the University of Virginia to find the law invoked against him. The sequestration of *La Prensa*, the most outspoken and influential of the Junta's critics, caused an uproar in the liberal press across the world (except, of course, in Britain where it passed largely unnoticed) 'purely and simply a savage vendetta against one of the most respected journalists in the Americas', declared the *New York Times*. If they wished to crush a hostile press, the generals might have learnt a thing or two from the subtler techniques of Dr Allende.

Like Allende – and Pastrana – the Peruvians have run into difficulties on their agrarian reform programme, which, on face value, once seemed the most hopeful of the three. The trouble has come, curiously, not from resistant land-owners but from disgruntled workers on the co-operativized Tumán and Cayaltí sugar estates. Once one of the most efficiently run in the country, the huge Tumán estate seems to have lapsed into administrative chaos. Thirty to forty *campesinos* protesting at the rigid discipline on the co-operatives were arrested, with the government chiding them for 'not understanding the co-operative idea'.

On the long term, the overall economy *should* be set fair with the discovery of massive oil reserves in the Amazon basin. Will the generals with their top-heavy bureaucracy be able to make the most of it? Their offer of fifteen-year contracts and a fifty-fifty share-out seems likely to be acceptable to the international oil companies, and may well form a model for other Latin-American producer countries. There are further indications that realism is coaxing the Junta into being more conciliatory with foreign capitalist investors, notably *Yanqui*. For the first time President Velasco has described the revolution as being 'socialist', and he has gone through the motions of renewing relations with Castro, but in real terms the trend looks marginally rightwards, doubtless articulated by the deterrent economic lessons of Allende's Chile. Meanwhile the generals continue evincing no anxiety to return to their regiments. And, if they did, would their successors be capable of creating a happier Peru?

319

In August 1971, Bolivia's 187th revolt dethroned President Torres, replacing him with (third time lucky) Colonel Banzer. After eighteen months of grim economic recession largely provoked by the withdrawal of U.S. investment that had followed the post-Barrientos expropriations, the last straw had come that spring with the creation in La Paz of a 'People's Assembly'. Comprised of all factions of the Left – the COB trades union, the orthodox Communist Party, the 'Pekinese', the Trotskyist POR and the Christian Democrat Revolutionaries – it set up house in the vacant Congress Building right next to the Presidential Palace. Under the chairmanship of the veteran trades unionist, Juan Lechín Oquendo, it began to act – with complete impunity – as a kind of alternative government, a first Bolivian 'Soviet', and the enfeebled Torres regime proved powerless to dislodge it. Though (typically) it was soon squabbling among itself with the Muscovites accusing the *Pekinistas* of being 'petit bourgeois dedicated to leading the working class on a new adventure', the Assembly panicked Bolivia's remaining bourgeoisie and its conservative easterners, and finally united the army by threatening its very existence.

With Brazilian (and probably C.I.A.) support, Banzer struck. For sixteen hours there was savage fighting in the streets of La Paz. Miners made desperate attempts to dynamite access roads. Torres fled as tanks closed in on the Palace. The last stronghold was San Andrés University where armed students held out until the Mustangs – this time not using dummy bombs – blasted the building, backed up by bazooka-firing infantry. Twelve students were killed out of a total of over a hundred dead and five hundred wounded. In Oruro students were also reported to have been machine-gunned. ELN guerrilla *focos* re-emerged in various parts of the country but were swiftly crushed. Among those killed were Cecilia Paz, wife of 'Francisco', and Loyola Guzmán, Che's female lieutenant whose release the Teoponte guerrillas had effected. Major Ruben Sanchez, one of Bolivia's ablest young officers who had commanded Torres's presidential guard, went underground and is said to be running the Bolivian 'resistance' from Chile – under the benevolent eye of Dr Allende (*pace* C. Casanova) – while 'Chato' Peredo was spotted back in La Paz, hotly pursued by security forces. After the discovery of large quantities of arms arriving from the U.S.S.R. and Czechoslovakia, Banzer summarily expelled 119 Soviet diplomats from an embassy that had expanded so swiftly under Torres. He showed the same ruthlessness in dealing with opposition journalists, a hundred of whom were reported to be in prison, hiding or exile, as of October 1971.

One of Barrientos's better ministers, Banzer now finds himself operating from a power base only slightly more stable than his predecessor's. His cabinet embraces such irreconcilables as the indispensable MNR (which also served Torres) and the extreme right-wing Falange. These could easily fall out, as has already strong-man Colonel Selich, commander of the élite Rangers and Banzer's first minister of the interior. Banzer promptly made brave attempts to regain the confidence of foreign investors, and has hitched his wagon closely to his benefactor, Brazil, for development aid. But the grim spectre of Bolivia's inherently unviable predicament must haunt him as it has his predecessors. Meanwhile, as Brazil gains an ally, so Allende loses one. Prospects now of re-cementing relations between Bolivia and Chile seem approximately as remote as Allende presenting Banzer with that long-coveted port.

In Chile the relentless power struggle, turning on the question of whether the world's first freely-elected Marxist government can remain in office constitutionally, abiding by the (bourgeois) rules, continues to fill more space consistently in the serious world press than any Latin-American nation has done for many, many a year. The struggle goes on developing – fascinating to outside observers, tragic for Chile – but all its developments are as projections of the hypotenuse traced by Allende and the U.P. in those first ninety days.

April 1971 brought an important milestone in the fortunes of Allende's U.P. in the shape of nation-wide municipal elections. Chileans were granted their first opportunity, since the presidential polls of the previous September, to express themselves on the government's popularity. For the first time, also, eighteen-year-olds were permitted to vote, bringing a new and unknown quantity into the political arena. Well beforehand it had been widely reckoned that the U.P. parties would gain a clear overall majority, which Allende would take as a vote of confidence and would then rush ahead with a referendum to create his unicameral 'People's Assembly' in place of the 'obstructive', Christian-Democrat-dominated Congress. In the event, Allende's socialists impressively increased their share of the votes to 22.3 per cent, leap-frogging the Communist Party. It was an imposing personal victory for *El Compañero Presidente*, but altogether the U.P. only totted up 49.7 per cent; a solid advance on the 36.3 per cent gained in September, but far from presenting a clear-cut mandate – especially considering that there was a 25 per cent absentee rate compared with the usual 19 per cent. Allende, with his highly-developed sensitivity to the electoral pulse, calculated that he could not risk a referendum and the possibility of humiliating defeat, but that he would wait for a more opportune moment.

In fact, however, April 1971 may well turn out to have been the high of Allende's pop rating. Since then a combination of circumstances – food shortages, economic problems, the effrontery of the MIR – has caused a marked falling away among the U.P.'s marginal supporters. So Allende decided to soldier on, pressing his radical reforms as far as he could without infringing the sacred constitution, in the teeth of a hostile congress: *la via chilena*, as it has come to be called.

The political fortunes of the opposed groupings, U.P. and opposition, oscillate back and forth. A splinter group, calling itself the Left Christian Movement (MIC) breaks away from the Christian Democrats to join hands with the U.P., and for a time it looks as if the party might split into a Left under Tomic and a Centre and Right under Frei, sitting on opposite sides of the house. On the extreme Left, the hotheads of the MIR repeatedly threaten to repudiate Allende's too 'moderate' line; then, eight months later (April 1972) the small Radical Left Party (PIR) abandons the U.P. coalition in distress at the excesses of Allende's fiscal policy. The two big opposition parties, the Nationals and the Christian Democrats, not speaking while I was in Chile and still described some time later as resembling 'battleships with their guns pointing the wrong way', began, *in extremis*, to co-operate.

322

In January 1972 they triumphed when joint candidates won two important by-elections against strong U.P. contenders. But this rather unnatural alliance between two bedfellows only acquainted in misery is a brittle one; the ITT revelations (March 1972) that American big business had attempted to upset the 1970 elections were sufficient to shake it severely. Then, under pressure from the Communist 'moderates', the U.P. has striven to reach a compromise with the Christian Democrats over the tempo of nationalisation. On the whole, however, the political scene in Chile has switched to that of a relatively united opposition facing a relatively disunited government. The most significant internal dissensions are those which have steadily developed between the Communists on the one hand, and the MIR and its supporters among the Altamirano faction (which probably now outweighs the moderates) of the Socialist Party on the other.

The MIR maintains its pressure in the countryside, while there are also indications of its having moved in on the towns, and the government seems to have done little more to discipline it. In April 1971 there was a serious shoot-up when one of Comandante Pepe's lieutenants attempted to seize a *fundo*; six were wounded, seventeen arrested and one young man died of a bullet in the abdomen. Pepe became a wanted man, but was never brought to book. Allende made a gesture of sacking the governor of Panguipulli Department for conniving at his escape, but Pepe soon surfaced again – running his empire around Liquiñe in the summer and busy with the work of *concientización* in Valdivia during the winter months, quite openly it seems. In June 1971, Chileans were deeply shocked when Pérez Zujovic, a right-wing Christian Democrat and Frei's former minister of the interior, was machine-gunned by VOP terrorists while driving his daughter to a yoga class. A week later two brothers involved in the killing were shot down by the police in a five-hour gun-battle. Allende made rather unconvincing comparisons with the Schneider assassination of the previous year; the extreme Right uttered thinly veiled calls to rebellion, while the Opposition closed ranks a few paces further. Later it impeached minister of the interior Toha for his permissiveness in dealing with the MIR, but

323

Allende adroitly dodged the issue by switching Toha to another post. The MIR next surfaced in Santiago itself as bosses of a slum stronghold, the 'Che Guevara' *población*, containing 1,200 families under a 'Compañera Natalia', with the declared objective of 'encircling' bourgeois Santiago from its slums.

There is little doubt, however, that the unbridled activities of the MIR were one of the principal factors in the U.P.'s reverse in the 1972 by-elections, and the wider dissatisfaction of which this was symptomatic. In February 1972 the Communists held an important reappraisal of the U.P.'s first fourteen months in power (details of which were leaked to the press), in which they blamed the extreme Left—censuring Altamirano, the Socialist Party secretary, as its accomplice – for weakening the government. It was essential, they said, to open a 'dialogue' with the Christian Democrats 'in order to forge links that will enable us to talk to their supporters,' (i.e. to woo and reassure the middle classes) and isolate the right wing. The tactics of this policy of 'moderation', so much in line with the Italian and French models, were quite clear and gradually seem to have gained the support of Allende; in contrast to the Altamiranist wing of his own party with its repeated emotional and abrasive demands to crush 'fascist sedition' and the 'class enemy'. Thus the rifts within the U.P. coalition spread, and there are three assumptions which can be stated with some safety:

1. However 'soft' it may appear through its tactics, the strategy of the Communist Party remains as it always has – in Czechoslovakia as in Poland, as in Hungary – the establishment of a monolithic authoritarian regime, purged of any bourgeois taints. A document published in 1972 by the Soviet Institute of Marxism-Leninism gave a revealing blueprint for the seizure of total power through the means of united fronts;

Having once acquired political power, the working class implements the liquidation of the private ownership of the means of production . . . [then] there remains no ground for the existence of any opposition parties counterbalancing the Communist Party. . . .

That the tactics of sweet reason as played by the Communists in Chile are paying off – as intended (page 157) – may be seen in the remarkable closing of ranks in the French Left. In 1972, for the first time in history, the French Socialists were seduced into agreeing upon a joint programme of government with the Communists, à la *Unidad Popular*.

2. Over the long run it is the Communist Party which, with its superior organization, is likely to emerge the dominant power on the left in Chile. It is the *Communists'* policies that by and large have prevailed within the U.P. to date; *their* counsels of prudence and 'consolidation' that seem most likely to attract supporters both among moderates of the Socialists and left-wing Christian Democrats.

3. The U.S.S.R., not eager to have the economic burden of another Cuba on its hands, will continue to oppose any Chilean policy so radical as to bring the economy to its knees, or the country into a collision with the U.S.A.

The zeal of the U.P. planners has indeed already come close to fulfilling the Russian nightmare, with Chile's economic straits seeming most likely to bring down the government electorally – that is, *if* truly free elections are to be held in either 1973 (congressional) or 1976 (presidential), which is still very much an open question. Under Chonchol's ruthlessly accelerated land reform, greatly stepped up even since I was in Cautín and now embracing one-third of all agriculture, the expected food shortages have occurred. Chile currently has to import over $250 million of food a year, thereby greatly increasing her trade deficits, and in this rich agricultural country there are now twelve meatless days a month when it is prohibited to sell beef in shops or restaurants. During Castro's visit at the end of 1971, thousands of middle-class women demonstrated angrily in Santiago, beating empty saucepans as a protest against the food shortages (plate 40). Allendistas claim that these result directly from the massive redistribution of income, which has led to far more Chileans being able to buy meat. But this is only part of the truth. Meanwhile productivity on the farms continues to sink. Goodness knows how Chile will solve her land reform problems now. In Guatemala a new government tried to put the clock back by returning to its original owners properties that had been redistributed to a hundred thousand peasants in an over-zealous land reform. They succeeded only

325

in sparking off the hatreds and killings that have poisoned Guatemalan society ever since. The same could happen in Chile if a future non-Marxist government sought to reverse the present order.

To a noteworthy extent the U.P. has achieved its aim of redistributing incomes. Some new building has been launched. Unemployment is down from its high of 1971. Consumer spending increased enormously; but has it, as the since replaced Señor Vuskovic intended, genuinely succeeded in priming the pump of Chilean industry or simply created new shortages and added to inflation? There is now evidently a one-year waiting list for T.V. sets; two years for automobiles, which have risen in price an average of 56 per cent over the past year. (In 1971 a Peugeot cost 90,000 escudos but an official of the Chilean Central Bank told me that before leaving he was offered 120,000 for his 1968 model). Because of the acute and growing currency crisis, all sorts of simple imported goods have begun to disappear from the shops; from cigarettes to needles to Tampax – a further cause for the women of Chile to find dissatisfaction with the regime. In 1971, wages increased by 50 per cent while money in circulation went up 118 per cent. With the new year even the government was forced to admit inflationary pressures by permitting a rise in basic food prices, as well as another 30 per cent on wages – a conspicuous departure from its price-fixing policy. But this almost certainly did not reveal the full extent of invisible inflation, which was largely a product of massive government spending, devoted, not to investment in any new capital equipment or new technology in industry, but to the wholesale purchase of private companies. For the first five months of 1972 alone, the rate of inflation was put at 25 per cent.

Nationalization plans have now already far exceeded targets first announced by Allende, with the government revealing (in February 1972) its intentions to take over a further 120 companies, representing 55 per cent of Chilean industry. The allied opposition reacted violently with a constitutional amendment that would remove the blanket right of nationalization from the Executive, bringing each individual case before Congress. If pursued it could yet bring a blunt end to Allende's *via Chilena*, the road to radical economic reform by means of constitutional processes; and possibly even force the confrontation dreaded by the moderates.

Pari passu Allende pursued his goal of expropriating the U.S. copper companies with the minimum of compensation. When it looked as if the U.P. calculations of tax arrears, excess profits, etc., would leave some of the companies with a debit rather than a credit, Washington growled that it might invoke the Hickenlooper Amendment, and credits for the purchase of three Boeing airliners were refused. But the U.S. was in a cleft stick; if she did invoke Hickenlooper, Chile could allege unfair discrimination on the grounds that such action had not been taken against Peru when the generals grabbed I.P.C., and gain wide support in Latin America; on the other hand if she did *not* take any economic reprisals, the Chilean action would set a seductive example for every other have-not country. Except for an occasional crack in the smile, the U.S. continued throughout to maintain its dignified 'low profile' attitude. Yet the outcome may well be that Chile will encounter difficulties in getting aid or refinancing credits in years to come. Meanwhile, Chile's copper nationalization has not been the hoped-for panacea. Many technicians emigrated and mines found themselves dependent on U.S. spare parts for machinery; the Chuquicamata miners struck for many weeks for higher wages, and overall production fell. Worst of all, world copper prices slumped from £620 a ton in 1969 to £412 a ton today. The acute fall in revenue that this represented slashed foreign currency reserves from the U.S. $380 million inherited by Allende to somewhere around $60 million, and plunged Chile, already owing $3.7 billion in foreign debts, into a most acute crisis, still unresolved at the time of writing. Ambassador Korry seems to have been wrong.

Non-Marxists in Chile continue to fear that the essential liberties are being eroded away. Nothing so obscenely crude as the dispossession of Pedro Beltrán has happened in Chile; which still possesses – *for the time being* – one of the most outspoken presses in Latin America. When Allende attempted to nationalize the leading paper manufacturer – which could have provided an efficient way of imposing censorship by

327

refusing paper to critical newspapers – 15,000 of the shareholders refused to sell their shares to the government, although
it was offering several times their actual value. But the opposition press may not always be in a position to fight back.
Coupled with union pressure, the U.P.'s nationalization of
private industry has, as intended, gnawed harshly at its
economic roots. Then, over a brief period of time, Allende
showed his teeth when he ordered the closing down of the
United Press offices in Chile; refused to allow the Christian
Democrat T.V. Channel 13 in Santiago to operate on a
national basis; and formed an 'Assembly of Journalists of
the Left' which would grant special privileges to the chosen
few, while discriminating against the non-Marxist 'hyenas'.
In the face of protest, Allende characteristically withdrew a
pace or two; but opposition journalists had a nasty premoni-
tion of what a U.P. government *might* do once it felt suffi-
ciently secure.

The struggle for the press in Chile is of far more than
parochial significance. Institutions and union pressures in
this 'England of South America' do bear such similarities to
those in Britain that Fleet Street – where some of the most
powerful organs are already tottering on the brink of economic
doom without application of either direct or indirect political
leverage – could do well to study the Chilean blueprint, and
prepare itself.

In the universities, the microcosm of the great debate outside, the battle goes on. Claudio Veliz has lost; Chile's
Chatham House has ceased to exist, and he has left for
Australia, a loss to Chilean intellectual life and a nasty
warning that the Chileans could one day soon share the fate
of Czech academics. That will be the day when, tactically,
the Communists feel they can afford to efface their present
ingratiating smile. Meanwhile another threat, all too familiar in Eastern Europe, the threat against the freedom to
emigrate or leave the country at all, may be developing.
Under the ready pretext of the foreign exchange crisis, a
plethora of bureaucratic controls have been imposed on
travel abroad; and now all tickets can only be purchased
through the Central Bank. A Chilean wrote to me in
July 1971:

I feel in gaol. Income tax department says I don't pay enough taxes to justify the buying of a 540 dollar quota, the official quota as of three weeks ago. At the same time if you leave without buying any dollars you are liable to be stopped at the airport for questioning, it being taken for granted that you have dealt in the black market.

The doors are still open; but the instruments are there if ever it were decided to shroud Chile in an Iron Curtain, or a Berlin Wall.

With admirable aptness, Allende has been described in Chile recently as resembling a bra, that 'oppresses the opulent, uplifts the fallen and deceives the unwary'. Chileans like the sex-orientated imagery, and indisputably the *Compañero Presidente* remains the U.P.'s strongest card. His extraordinary political astuteness has brought the U.P. through fresh crisis after crisis. Shortly after his accession with a 1.4 per cent margin, Allende declared (possibly with a double meaning): 'I am president of the U.P. – I am not president of all the Chileans. I would be a hypocrite if I said the contrary.' But to the rest of Latin America Allende is definitely the *President of Chile*. His first foreign visits, to Argentina to make friends with a cool Lanusse, to Peru, Ecuador and Colombia, were unqualified successes and accorded Allende – at home as well as abroad – the status of more than just a national figure. Castro's visit in November 1971, his first to Latin America since 1959, gave an additional fillip to Allende's already well-developed *machismo*. The Caribbean *caudillo* had evidently not heard the adage 'fish and visitors stink after three days', and after three weeks of his verbose bombast even some of his staunchest Chilean fans were finding Allende's style more palatable. To the left-orientated Latin-American youth, Allende may be replacing Castro as *the* inspirational figure of the 1970s. But how does it seem, now, that history will rate him? As a Harold Wilson or a Kerensky? The one carrying out radical reforms and then submitting to parliamentary democracy, if necessary accepting political defeat; the other unleashing forces that will sweep himself away and lead to a far more catastrophic *terremoto*? One thing seems

329

certain: Chile will never now return to oligarchic rule, or even to a Frei-style Christian Democracy. The very mildest prospect is that a British Labour Party brand of socialism is there to stay. The crucial question remains, as Debray put it: 'Is the proletariat going to assert itself over the bourgeoisie, or will the bourgeoisie gradually remould the proletariat and reabsorb it into its world?'

By far the most depressing recent trend, much more menacing than her economic plight, has been the steady polarization of forces in Chile. Political divisions have hardened and, with the erosion of the middle ground, the country is rapidly splitting into two camps – Marxist and non-Marxist. The camps, it seems, are becoming armed. *Mirista* groups, like Pepe's, have long been training with weapons up in the hills, and now even the professedly pacific Communists are reported to be building up their own armed cadres to face a possible *enfrentamiento*, even though it may not be of their seeking. 'Pedro' and 'Juan', the two young men who so alarmed us with their lunch-time talk in Santiago, have now emerged as important leaders on the extreme Right, and bodies associated with them are also believed to be developing along para-military lines. In March 1972 an article of the *Economist* entitled creepily 'Birth of a Civil War', described the emergence down in Cautín of a well-disciplined right-wing vigilante movement, called the *Guardia Blanca*, which was reoccupying, by force of arms, *fundos* seized by the MIR. Sticking rigidly to the orders received at the time of the original *tomas*, the *carabineros* also declined to intervene now; a kind of silent rebuff to the government. The armed forces, flushed with massive pay rises, still support Allende but apparently with increasing reserve, as the proliferation of illegal para-military bodies is permitted to grow apace.

A left-wing Chilean living in Paris writes:

I went back to Chile seduced by the 'new experience' because my tendencies lean to the Left. I thought I ought to see with my own eyes whether I should live the historical moment in Chile myself. When I got there I couldn't believe my eyes.

He returned to Paris, quite disenchanted. What had most shaken him was the mounting passion of internecine hatreds,

between Mapuches and European Chileans, between political factions, between *tuvos* and the new *tienes*. something so alien to Chile in the past.
> Hate is like a swordfish,
> Working through water invisibly . . .

writes Neruda in *Estravagario*. And a swordfish is a lethal creature, difficult to reason with once enraged. There may be, alas, much truth in Debray's prophecy that, in the 'game' being played in Chile, 'the path from polite hatred to open hostilities is shorter than either side had thought', and that the precarious existing state of 'truce' could be broken any day. When Pepe insisted to me that civil war was 'inevitable' at the time it seemed unthinkably remote; but as more and more Chileans ardently pursue the course towards an *enfrentamiento* so the possibility becomes a dreadfully real one.

One general conclusion is fairly incontrovertible: as she has been since Allende came to power, Chile will continue to be the seismic epicentre for all Latin America. Developments there send their shock-waves coursing across the continent and up into the stalk of Central America. With the exception of Brazil – which, despite its repressive police system and the misery of the underprivileged areas, stands out as *the* economic success story of Latin America today – and a perhaps transient aberration in Bolivia, the general trend is everywhere leftwards. There will be more revolutions, even though, as Bolívar pessimistically noted, often in Latin America 'he who serves a revolution ploughs the sea'. The ideological struggle between the different factions of the Left will continue to bubble and boil still more furiously, but it is from the steady penetration of the orthodox Soviet-line Communists that the long-term danger comes; Maoism is lunatic fringe, Trotskyism ditto, the Castroist ELNs 'infantile disorders' – perhaps until such a time as they turn to the cities, as co-ordinated terrorist wings of the official Communist Parties. Within the Church the leftward trend will, if anything, become accelerated. The Church needs to study carefully such phenomena as the 'Franciscos' of Teoponte. For in the words of that controversial priest from Cuernavaca, Ivan Illich, 'angelic aloofness has placed the Church on the side

331

of the oppressors' in the eyes of many young Latin Americans today.

U.S. influence will continue to wane, with the deepening humiliation in Vietnam, and there will be more expropriations of foreign investments – notably U.S. The U.S. will face its essential dilemma of whether to lie still, or to take reprisals by withdrawing still further. There will be more economic chaos, and a greater need for European – and Japanese – investors to fill the responsibilities vacated by the U.S.; if they can face the risks. Above all, alas, *la explosión demográfica* will, in almost all certainty, continue its horrifying course, making it more and more difficult ever to close the economic gap between the rich and the poor nations, and rendering the wretched at the base of the pyramid constantly more susceptible to the demagoguery of the left-wing revolutionary.

Shortly after returning from Chile, my travelling *compañero* told me he had received a guarded telephone call from the White House. It was from an aide to Dr Kissinger, who said with transparent obliquity: "My principal's principal would like to have a forty-five minute briefing from you on South America.' Bill, with his highly-developed instinct for self-preservation, managed somehow to duck this command performance. But how, I wondered, how could you possibly explain all South America to the President of the United States inside of forty-five minutes? What would one tell him about? About Pepe and the violent young *Yanqui*-hating revolutionaries up at Liquiñe? About 'Pedro' and 'Juan' prepared to go to the wall for their concepts of *La Patria*? About 'Francisco' dying for Christian-Marxism in Bolivia? About Luís and the bull and the conundrums of land reform? About the Oruro Carnival; the hopelessness and the courage, the passion for colour at any price, the lovable irrationalism of the South Americans, the poverty and the gaiety?

Select Bibliography

Angell, Alan. 'Chile; from Christian Democracy to Marxism?' *The World Today*, vol. 26 (London, 1970).
————. *Labour and Politics in Chile*, St Antony's Papers, No. 22 (Oxford, 1970).
Bailey, N. A. *'La Violencia* in Colombia,' *Journal of Inter-American Studies*, Gainesville, Florida, October 1967.
Bryce, James. *South America, Observations and Impressions* (London, 1912).
Burr, R. N. *By Reason or Force; Chile and the Balancing of Power in South America, 1830–1905* (Berkeley, California, 1965).
Conrad, Joseph. *Nostromo* (London, 1905).
Debray, Régis, *Conversations with Allende, Socialism in Chile* (London, 1971); *Revolution in Chile* (New York, 1971).
————. *Revolution in the Revolution* (London and New York, 1967).
Elío, Tomás Guillermo. *Objetivos y Proyecciones del Acuerdo Sub Regional Andino* (La Paz, 1970).
Encina, Francisco A. *Historia de Chile* (Santiago, 1964).
Fluharty, Vernon Lee. *Dance of the Millions, Military Rule and Social Revolution in Colombia, 1939–1956* (Pittsburgh, 1957).
Galdames, Luís. *A History of Chile*, tr. by I. J. Cox (Chapel Hill, North Carolina, 1941).
Gerassi, John (ed.). *Revolutionary Priest, the Complete Writings and Messages of Camilo Torres* (London and New York, 1971).
Gheerbrant, Alain. *L'Eglise rébelle d'Amérique Latine* (Paris, 1969).
Gott, Richard. *Guerrilla Movements in Latin America* (London, 1970; New York, 1971).
Gross, Leonard. *The Last, Best Hope; Eduardo Frei and Chilean Democracy* (New York, 1967).

Guevara, Che. *The Diary of Che Guevara,* ed. Robert Scheer (New York, 1968).

————. *Guerrilla Warfare* (New York, 1961).

Gunther, John. *Inside South America* (London and New York, 1967)

————. *Inside Latin America* (New York, 1941; London, 1942).

Hemming, John. *The Conquest of the Incas* (London and New York, 1970).

Hobsbawm, Eric. 'The Revolutionary Situation in Colombia,' *The World Today,* vol. 19 (London, 1963).

Isherwood, Christopher. *The Condor and the Cows* (London and New York, 1949).

Madariaga, Salvador de. *Bolívar* (New York, 1952).

Mander, John. *Static Society, The Paradox of Latin America* (London, 1969).

Márquez, Gabriel García. *Cien Años de Soledad* (Buenos Aires, 1967).

Mercier Vega, Luis. *Guerrillas in Latin America; The Technique of the Counter-State* (London and New York, 1969).

Moss, Robert. *Urban Guerrillas* (London, 1971).

————. *Revolution in Latin America,* Economist Brief 24 (London, 1971).

Neruda, Pablo. *Selected Poems* (London and New York, 1970).

Osborne, Harold. *Bolivia, A Land Divided* (London and New York, 1954).

————. *Indians of the Andes: Aymaras and Quechuas* (London and New York, 1952).

Pendle, George. *A History of Latin America* (London and New York, 1965).

Pike, F. B. *Chile and the United States, 1880–1962* (Notre Dame, Indiana, 1963).

Pinto, Anibal. *Chile—una Economía Difícil* (Santiago, 1964).

Rodman, Selden. *South America of the Poets* (New York, 1970).

————. *The Colombia Traveler* (New York, 1971).
Sitwell, Sacheverell. *Golden Wall and Mirador* (London and New York, 1961).
Valenzuela, Germán. *Los Partidos Políticos Chilenos* (Santiago, 1968).
Veliz, Claudio (ed.). *Obstacles to Change in Latin America* (London and New York, 1965).
————. *The Politics of Conformity in Latin America* (London and New York, 1967).
————. *Latin America and the Caribbean, a Handbook* (London and New York, 1968).

NEWSPAPERS AND PERIODICALS PARTICULARLY CONSULTED OR QUOTED

The Economist
Latin America
The Guardian
The Times
The New York Times
Le Monde
Frankfurter Allgemeine Zeitung
Neue Zürcher Zeitung
El Espectador (Bogotá)
El Tiempo (Bogotá)
La Prensa (Lima)
El Comercio (Lima)
El Mercurio (Santiago)
El Clarín (Santiago)
La Nación (Santiago)
El Siglo (Santiago)
Punto Final (Santiago)
La Prensa (Santiago)
PEC (Santiago)
La Firme (Santiago)
El Diario Austral (Temuco, Chile)
Hoy (La Paz)
El Diario (La Paz)
La Presencia (La Paz)

Index

50, 243, 247, 255; War of the
Pacific, 97, 100, 239, 257, 258;
and Yugoslavia, 255, 288. *See
also* Ovando Candía, Alfredo;
Torres, Juan José
Borges, Jorge Luis, 36*n*
Bornemann, 201*n*
Bornemann, Helga, 180–81
Bowers, Claude G., 102
Brandt, Willy, 158
Braniff, 54
Brazil, 27; and Bolivia, 320, 321;
economy, 331; land reform,
305–306; police repression, 13,
331; press, 144; Roman
Catholic Church, 230;
"Squadron of Death," 13; and
U.S., 24
Bryce, James Bryce, Viscount:
on South America, 13–14, 60,
231, 248, 293
Buckley, William F., Jr., 12, 16,
28–30, 332; and Chile, 28, 92,
93, 97, 98, 119, 121, 136,
159–60, 235; and Colombia,
45–49 *passim,* 300; and
Peru, 56, 57, 60, 69, 71, 75,
81, 82

Cabieses, Manuel, 143
Calvo Sotelo, Señor, 139
Cardenas, Col., 260, 261*n*
Caretas (Peru), 87–88
Carrasco, Señor, 254–55
Casanova, Cristian, 117–18, 166
Castro, Fidel, 17, 20, 24–25, 26,
38, 312; and Allende, 49, 130;
Chile, visit to, 138*n*, 158, 325,
329; in Colombia, 35; on Frei,
109; on Guevara's death, 246;
influence of, *see* Bolivia,
ELN; Chile, MIR; Colombia,
ELN; on O.A.S., 158

Catholic Church. *See* Roman
Catholic Church
Chaco War, 239, 242, 293
"Charro Negro," 38
Chibchas, 51–53
Chile, 90–236, 321–31;
agriculture, 18, 167, 175–76,
208, 216, 222, 223, 325 (*see
also* land reform *below*) ;
alcoholism, 229; Andean Pact,
49–50; and Argentina, 15, 164,
226, 229, 329; army, 28,
103–104, 105, 110, 136, 140–41,
142, 198, 330; banks
nationalized, 123, 147, 149; and
Bolivia, 100, 256–57, 258, 321;
and China, Communist, 117,
158; Christian Democrats, 27,
88, 99, 105, 106, 107, 110–14
passim, 125, 136, 137, 143, 144,
149, 150, 179, 188, 221, 231,
301, 322–23, 324, 325; civil
war, 101; and Colombia, 329;
Communist Party (P.C. Ch.) ,
91, 94*n*, 104, 105, 107–12
passim, 117, 120, 127–28, 135,
137, 143, 151, 153, 155,
156–57, 187, 249, 322, 323,
324–25, 330 (*see also* Unidad
Popular *below*) ; constitution,
102–103, 109, 114, 127, 156;
copper, *see* mining *below;* and
Cuba, 49, 118, 138*n*, 142, 158,
325, 329; CUT (*Central Unica
de Trabajadores*) , 128, 156;
DIRINCO, 121; divorce rate,
229, 230; earthquakes, 97, 98*n*,
178, 181, 188; economy, 104,
105, 107, 110; economy under
Allende, 103, 119–20, 121, 171,
233–34, 322, 325, 327, 328; and
Ecuador, 329; education, 27,
104, 108, 152–53, 201, 328;

Colombia (cont'd.)
43, 229, 230, 231, 300, 312, 313;
Socialist Party, 300; and Spain,
33, 34, 51, 52; Thousand Days
War (1899), 34; and U.S.S.R.,
42; United Front, 39–40; and
U.S., 48, 49, 50, 51, 317; and
Venezuela, 44; violence, 33–34,
306; *La Violencia*, 33, 34–36,
38

Communist Party, 17, 187, 331;
Bolivia, 40, 244–45, 253, 320;
Chile, 91, 94n, 104, 105, 107-12
passim, 117, 120, 127–28, 135,
137, 143, 151, 153, 155, 156–57,
187, 249, 322, 323, 324–25, 330;
Colombia, 38, 40, 41, 82, 300;
Czechoslovakia, 324; France,
156, 157, 324, 325; Hungary,
324; Institute of
Marxism-Leninism, 324; Italy,
156, 157, 324; Peru, 69, 77, 82,
83, 187; Poland, 324. *See also*
China, Communist; Cuba;
revolutionary and guerrilla
movements; U.S.S.R.

Concepción University, 131,
153n, 185, 200

Conrad, Joseph: *Nostromo*, 34,
242

Corvalán, Luis, 128

Costa Arduz, Rolando, 285

Costa-Gavras, 88, 151–52

Cruz, Benjo, 277

Cuba: agriculture, 222; and
Chile, 49, 118, 138n, 142, 158,
325, 329; and Colombia, 44,
49; and O.A.S., 49, 158; and
Peru, 319; and U.S., 24–25, 49,
158. *See also* Castro, Fidel

Curtmann, George, 290–91

Cuzco, 51, 60–65 *passim*, 70

Czechoslovakia: and Bolivia, 288,

289, 321; Communist Party,
324

Debray, Régis: on agrarian
reform, 187; and Allende,
dialogues, 113, 122, 123,
125–31 *passim*, 139–40, 143,
144, 158, 186-87, 224; in
Bolivia, 125–26, 245, 260; on
the bourgeoisie and
proletariat, 186, 330; on
Chilean constitution, 100; on
confrontation and provocation,
126, 139–40, 221, 331; and
Guevara, 245, 270; on legal
and extra-legal means, 122,
123, 128; on revolutionary
movements and reverses, 113,
286

Dedijer, Vladimir, 270, 271

de Gaulle, Charles: on Chile, 27,
141

de la Puente, 72, 82n

Diario, El (Bolivia), 247, 254–55,
256

Diario Austral, El (Chile), 175

Disney, Walt: *Three Caballeros*,
24

Dominican Republic: and U.S.,
17, 27

Donne, John, 17

Drake, Sir Francis, 99

Dulles, John Foster, 24

Durán, Julio, 106

Ecuador, 68, 316; Andean Pact,
49–50, 287; and Chile, 329

Edwards, Agustín (Doonie),
21–22, 118, 140, 147, 148

Edwards, Chavela, 21, 22–23

Edwards, Sonia, 148

Edwards family, 21, 143, 146;
Banco Edwards, 147, 149, 150.
See also El Mercurio